ESCAPE FROM B

ESCAPE FROM BATAAN

*Memoir of a U.S. Navy Ensign
in the Philippines,
October 1941 to May 1942*

Ross E. Hofmann

Edited by David L. Snead *and*
Anne B. Craddock

McFarland & Company, Inc., Publishers
Jefferson, North Carolina

LIBRARY OF CONGRESS CATALOGUING-IN-PUBLICATION DATA

Names: Hofmann, Ross E., 1917–1996, author. | Snead, David L.
(David Lindsey), editor. | Craddock, Anne B., 1948– editor.
Title: Escape from Bataan : memoir of a U.S. Navy ensign in the
Philippines, October 1941 to May 1942 / Ross E. Hofmann ;
edited by David L. Snead and Anne B. Craddock.
Description: Jefferson, North Carolina : McFarland & Company, Inc.,
Publishers, 2016. | Includes bibliographical references and index.
Identifiers: LCCN 2016022321 | ISBN 9781476665689 (softcover : acid free paper) ∞
Subjects: LCSH: Hofmann, Ross E., 1917–1996. | World War, 1939–1945—
Personal narratives, American. | Bataan, Battle of, Philippines, 1942. | World
War, 1939–1945—Campaigns—Philippines. | United States. Navy—Biography.
Classification: LCC D767.4 .H64 2016 | DDC 940.54/25991092 [B]—dc23
LC record available at https://lccn.loc.gov/2016022321

BRITISH LIBRARY CATALOGUING DATA ARE AVAILABLE

ISBN (print) 978-0-4766-6568-9
ISBN (ebook) 978-1-4766-2562-1

Printed in the United States of America

*McFarland & Company, Inc., Publishers
Box 611, Jefferson, North Carolina 28640
www.mcfarlandpub.com*

Table of Contents

Acknowledgments

In many ways, Ross E. Hofmann's memoir has been a collaborative effort from the beginning. Without his friendships with Jack McClure and Bud Snow, he probably never would have been stationed in the Philippines and endured the trials of the first six months of the war in the Pacific. Without the help of his family, his experience would probably still be unknown. We owe a debt of gratitude to many people.

First and foremost, we need to thank Ross Hofmann for having the foresight to make meticulous notes soon after his escape from the Philippines and arrival in Australia in 1942 and having the bravery and creative ability more than 40 years later to relive these difficult experiences and find the courage to write about them with vivid detail, color, serious thought, and a touch of humor. Throughout, he showed the intelligence of mind and lightness of spirit that marked his personality throughout his life.

Many years later after his death, Anne made a commitment to see her father's memoir published. She is an artist and a flower-child at heart, so the study of war was new for her. She was aided in her understanding of the tremendous suffering of America's fighting men and nurses in the Philippines by reading Michael and Elizabeth Norman's *Tears in the Darkness* and Elizabeth Norman's *We Band of Angels*. They took courage to write and inspired Anne's further commitment to the task of getting her father's book published.

As every historian will attest, having colleagues to turn to for advice and guidance is critical. We need to thank Ron Chrisman who recognized the value of Hofmann's manuscript and introduced the two of us. John Gordon, Rich Meixsel, Elizabeth Norman, and James Zobel read the memoir and editorial additions critically. The final product is much stronger because of their input. Dwight Messier and Robert Underbrink provided invaluable insight concerning PBY operations and blockade-running in the Philippines, respectively. Robert Hopkins assessed the memoir and offered critical comments and encouragement.

We owe special gratitude to Alexander Mendoza and Alyce Guthrie from the PT Boats, Inc. Alex produced the excellent maps that make Hofmann's adventures through the Philippines much easier to follow. Alyce provided a document that verified a key part of Hofmann's experience that previously we could not corroborate.

David's colleagues and students at Liberty University assisted him in many ways. Dean of the College of Arts and Sciences at Liberty University Roger Schultz and History Department Chair Carey Roberts generously provided funding for numerous research trips. Kris Burdeaux and Ruth Ronk were always available to make copies, scan documents, and make travel arrangements. Many students helped with the project at one time or another, but particularly Nathan Curtis, Alison Fishburne, and Katie Hoffmeyer offered valuable help in its early stages.

Numerous archivists and librarians provided invaluable assistance through the course of our research. The aforementioned James Zobel offered excellent guidance going through the records at the Douglas MacArthur Memorial Library and Archives. Bob Cressman, John Hodges, Barbara Posner, and Laura Waayers at the Naval History and Heritage Command Archives patiently answered numerous inquiries. Mark Mollan and Nate Patch at the National Archives helped our search for information on U.S. operations in the Philippines. Tim Mahoney, Melissa Murphy, and Kelly Sparks at the Baker Library at Harvard University provided invaluable documents on the U.S. Navy Supply Corps Training School located there during World War II.

Last, but definitely not least, we need to thank our families. Several of Anne's family members were critical in moving Hofmann's manuscript towards publication. Hofmann's youngest stepdaughter, Victoria Strauss Nunez, helped complete the first copy editing. His grandson, Alexander von Hofmann, found the manuscript so interesting and valuable that he made extra copies for family members and later transcribed it, in its entirety, from the printed to the electronic form. Finally, Dr. Susan Cotton, Hofmann's youngest daughter, supplied notes concerning his history that he dictated to her, family photos, valuable correspondence between him and his father, and other important documents. All of this information was essential to the research process.

David's children, Reagan, Delaney, and Darel, had to share their dad with this project for several years. Through research trips, and nights and weekends working, they never complained. Instead, they supported him at each step with encouragement and the desire to learn more about a naval ensign in World War II. David's wife, Lori, remains a wonderful wife and mother, and a treasured friend. She understands him like no other and is always there when he needs that extra encouragement. As the editor of the editors, we cannot express our appreciation to her enough.

Last, but definitely not least, we need to thank our families and friends. Several of Anne's family members were critical in moving Hofmann's manuscript towards publication. Hofmann's youngest stepdaughter, Victoria Strauss Nunez, worked tirelessly with her grandfather to complete the first copyediting. His grandson, Alex von Hofmann, found the manuscript so interesting and valuable that he made extra copies for family members and later transcribed it, in its entirety, from the printed to the electronic form. He and Louise Therry produced a beautiful edition of Ross's memoir under the title, "The Road from Cavite," for his son, Curt Hofmann, as a present for his 60th birthday. They were aided in the project by a number of family and friends, including Edith Osei-Tutu, Daniel Brumley, Courtney Therry, Belinda Lonsdale, Charlene Wilson, and Kathryn Sprigg. Without this initial labor of love, none of this would have been possible. Finally, Dr. Susan Cotton, Hofmann's youngest daughter, supplied notes concerning his history that he dictated to her, family photos, valuable correspondence between him and his father, and other important documents. All of this information was essential to the research process.

Preface
(by David L. Snead)

Ross Elwood Hofmann was no different from most recent college graduates in the late 1930s. He wanted to move past the Great Depression and make his mark in the business world. After graduating from the University of Toronto in 1939, he quickly landed a job at McGraw-Hill in New York City and began a publishing career. He advanced quickly at McGraw-Hill, and after a year and a half on the job, he left the business to form his own publishing company. However, within a week of turning 24 years old, one telephone call on June 13, 1941, changed his life forever.

It is unclear when and why Hofmann joined the U.S. Navy Supply Corps Reserves, but sometime prior to June 13 he had done so. He left no records explaining why he did or what he expected. Since he was always adventurous and a risk-taker, perhaps he saw the reserves as just another adventure. He was possibly influenced by the stories of his grandfather, Major Charles Joseph Ross, who had acted as an Indian scout on the Great Plains, fought in the Boer War, and served in East Africa in World War I.[1] Hofmann would later mention him on several occasions.[2] Regardless, he received a surprise call from a navy reserve office on June 13 requiring him to report to the Supply Corps Training School located at the Harvard University Business School on the following Monday, June 16. Little did he know that he was about to begin a series of adventures that would rival those of his grandfather.

The U.S. Navy Supply Corps initiated planning for expansion after Germany attacked Poland in September 1939. After announcing U.S. neutrality, President Franklin D. Roosevelt declared "that a national emergency exists in connection with and to the extent necessary for the proper observance, safeguarding, and enforcing of the neutrality of the United States and the strengthening of our national defense within the limits of peacetime authorizations."[3] While not placing the United States on a war footing, it did set the stage for the eventual expansion of the military as well as increased aid to the country's allies.

The Supply Corps in World War II has received relatively little historical attention from scholars.[4] American soldiers, sailors, and airmen who served in combat have rightfully received well-deserved attention. Without their efforts, the United States would not have been on the winning side in World War II and other wars. However, the percentage of U.S. military personnel who actually served in combat units during World War II was relatively small. For instance, Gerald Linderman found that less than one million out of the over 16 million Americans who served in the military during the war actually participated in combat.[5] The majority of military personnel toiled in relative obscurity behind the front lines providing the necessary support for the combat units. While this role is critical to any military effort, few scholars have examined it in any detail. Furthermore, in periods of limited defense spending, the military will often make cuts to its support units. The result is a scarcity of funding for organizations like the Supply Corps.

The period between World War I and the late 1930s was no exception. The U.S. Congress limited spending in many areas, and the navy's Supply Corps struggled to meet its mission.[6] It is not that military strategists and leaders failed to understand the importance of supply and logistics. Antoine Henri Jomini explained, "Logistics comprises the means and arrangements which work out the plans of strategy and tactics. Strategy decides where to act; logistics brings the troops to this point." Other renowned strategists ranging from Sun Tzu to Carl Von Clausewitz taught the importance of logistics. Sun Tzu warned, "The line between disorder and order lies in logistics," while Clausewitz argued, "There is nothing more common than to find consideration of supply affecting the strategic lines of a campaign and a war." These lessons were not lost on U.S. military leaders. Dwight Eisenhower wrote, "You will not find it difficult to prove that battles, campaigns, and even wars have been won or lost primarily because of logistics." Reflecting his reputation, George S. Patton was even blunter: "Gentlemen, the officer who doesn't know his communications and supply as well as his tactics is totally useless." Finally, Admiral Ernest King argued in 1946 that World War II was "a war of logistics."[7] The difficulty was finding the resources to meet a military's logistical needs.

As part of the navy's general growth and move to greater preparedness after the outbreak of World War II, its Supply Corps began to increase the number of its officers in the late 1930s, but especially in 1940 and 1941.[8] The navy operated a Supply Corps Training School at the Philadelphia Naval Yard from 1934 to 1941 to train active duty officers. Over the course of its existence, it graduated 344 students. The navy also started Supply Corps Naval Reserve Training Schools at Georgetown University, the Washington, D.C. Naval Medical Center, and National University in Washington, D.C. It ran courses at these schools at different times between July 1940 and October 1941. However, it decided in the fall of 1940 that it needed to increase the number of its available officers beyond what these schools could provide and began making efforts to find an alternative location where a larger pool of officers could be trained.[9]

Ross Elwood Hofmann, early in his naval career (courtesy Hofmann family).

The navy reached an agreement with Harvard University to provide facilities for training and housing new Supply Corps officers beginning in June 1941. To fill the new officer positions, the Supply Corps decided to recruit 400 men as ensigns in the U.S. Navy Reserves primarily from recent college grad-uates. In its recruitment, it wanted "only outstanding young men of recognized officer-like qualifications and [who] had received their college degrees."[10] Since Hofmann had graduated with Honors from the University of Toronto in 1939 with a B.A. in economics and had shown important skills in his brief career to that point, he fit the description of the men the Supply Corps wanted.[11] While how exactly he learned about the Supply Corps' need and why he made his decision to join is unclear, he became one of the initial 400 ensigns to train as Supply Corps Officers in the inaugural training class at the Harvard University Graduate Business School.[12]

Soon before Hofmann began his training, America's position in the world had grown increasingly precarious as Germany's expansion in Europe and use of submarine attacks in the Atlantic threatened to embroil the United States in the war. Furthermore, Japanese expansion in China and Southeast Asia offered challenges to America's allies as well as its territories like the Philippines. Recognizing the growing threat, Roosevelt worked to prepare the country for possible participation in the war. On May 27, 1941, he issued a proclamation asserting that "an unlimited national emergency confronts this country, which requires that its military, naval, air, and civilian defenses be put on the basis of readiness to repel any and all acts or threats of aggression directed toward any part of the Western Hemisphere."[13] He followed this proclamation with an announcement defend-ing America's right to protect its interest, announcing that "the Nation will expect all individuals and all groups to play their full parts ... and without doubt that our democracy will triumphantly survive."[14] More fully than at any time previously, the president laid out America's case for preparing for war while pursuing peace.[15]

The United States had begun to rearm after Roosevelt came into office but did not begin to truly accelerate until 1940. Annual U.S. Navy expenditures increased from just under $300 million in 1934 to more than $891 million in 1940. Army expenditures increased at similar rates from roughly $408 million to $907 million during the same period. Spend-ing accelerated in 1941 as army expenditures reached more than $3.9 billion and naval spending $2.3 billion.[16] Growth in military personnel showed similar increases. Naval personnel, including the Marine Corps, increased from almost 109,000 to around 339,000 between 1934 and 1941. Army personnel increased from 138,000 to almost 1.5 million during the same time.[17] Yet, the military build-up was uneven at best.

Roosevelt had to balance many, often competing, factors as he tried to prepare the country for the war. Because he desperately wanted Great Britain and, once it entered the war in June 1941, the Soviet Union to survive Germany's onslaught, he gave priority to supplying these countries. This included sending ammunition, weapons, airplanes, and ships to these countries even when the U.S. military needed many of them to prepare for war.[18] By December 1941, the United States was better prepared for a war than it had ever been in American history, but that speaks more to its lack of preparedness in the past than true readiness for a new world war.

One of the areas that the United States had to protect from possible Japanese aggres-sion was the Philippines. It had occupied the islands during the Spanish-American War. In 1934, Congress passed the Tydings-McDuffie Act which promised the Philippines their independence in 1946.[19] During the interim, the United States was supposed to prepare the Philippines government and military for their new responsibilities. Filipinos elected a government under Manuel Quezon in 1935 and began developing a local defense force as a step toward the eventual creation of a national army. Quezon turned to General Douglas MacArthur to become the military adviser to the commonwealth government. Working with the U.S. military, MacArthur and Quezon began the slow process of creating a Filipino Army. With the exception of some patrol boats, the Philippines still depended on the U.S. Navy to defend against a landing from a determined enemy.[20]

In terms of Japan's plan of expansion, the Philippines were critical. The islands did not possess great intrinsic value in terms of resources, but their geographic position near British and French possessions in Southeast Asia and the Dutch East Indies in the southwest Pacific made them a potential threat to Japan's plans. The Japanese Navy viewed the Dutch East Indies as crucial because of their many natural resources, particularly oil. While Japan hoped to acquire the resources peacefully, there was a clear recognition that any conflict with the Dutch or the British would more than likely lead to a war with the United States. Admiral Yamamoto Isoroku, the commander-in-chief of the Japanese Navy, counseled against war with the United States, but recommended that if Japan decided to go to war, it should strike devastating blows initially. The blows would be against U.S. forces in the Philippines, Pearl Harbor and other bases in the Hawaiian Islands, and a few other smaller U.S. possessions.[21]

Ross Hofmann had no clue what he was headed into after he finished his training and boarded a ship in San Francisco for Shanghai, China, in the fall of 1941. He recognized the potential dangers because of the ongoing Sino-Japanese War but had not even considered being stationed in the Philippines. His temporary stop in Manila in October 1941 while in transit to Shanghai turned into a permanent assignment once ashore. Admiral Thomas Hart, the commander of the U.S. Asiatic Fleet in Manila, was in the process of withdrawing all remaining forces from Shanghai because of Japanese pressures and believed it unwise to send additional naval personnel there. His office changed Hofmann's orders and sent him to Cavite Naval Base near Manila for a new assignment.

Hofmann served as a supply officer there from October until the outbreak of the war. On December 7, Japanese naval planes launched a surprise attack against American forces in Hawaii. Hours later, Japanese planes struck U.S. airfields in the Philippines.[22] Caught by surprise in both locations, U.S. forces suffered crushing losses. While the Japanese had no intentions to seize the Hawaiian Islands, they did want the Philippines. In the weeks that followed, the Japanese launched a series of air and amphibious attacks against the Philippines. In the process, they destroyed almost all U.S. air power and forced U.S. and Filipino forces to retreat on Luzon. Ultimately, these forces retreated to the Bataan peninsula.

Because of these losses, Admiral Hart ordered most of the Asiatic Fleet to sail southward to more protected areas, creating an uncertain future for naval shore personnel stationed at bases like Cavite. Japanese air attacks on December 10 destroyed most of Cavite and led the navy to transfer its shore personnel to Mariveles on the southern tip of Bataan. During this transition, Hofmann participated in numerous salvage missions to Cavite and Manila before ultimately settling into a variety of roles in Mariveles. His principal duty was to serve as a supply officer for several anti-aircraft batteries manned by members of the 4th Marine regiment and other personnel in the area. He also served for a short time as part of a hodgepodge infantry unit composed of Army Air Corps ground personnel, Marines, and ground-based navy sailors after a Japanese military force made a surprise landing near Mariveles.

In March 1942, he and several other Supply Corps officers received orders to leave Mariveles and proceed to Cebu in the central Philippines to help facilitate the efforts to move supplies through the Japanese blockade of Bataan and Corregidor. While often involving extreme gallantry, the blockade running program never produced more than a trickle of supplies for the American and Filipino forces. Further, within a week of Hofmann's arrival in Cebu, Japanese forces landed on the island, forcing him and other Americans to retreat further to the south. This was extremely difficult and dangerous as the Japanese controlled both the air and seas around the Philippines, and there was no organized American military effort to facilitate the evacuation. In essence, the Americans were on their own to find their own means of escape.

Hofmann and a PT-boat officer he knew from Cavite and then Mariveles worked together to make their way across several islands and over dangerous waters to reach an American base on Mindanao. It was during this time that they received word that American forces on Bataan had surrendered. Their adventure involved working with smugglers and others to avoid being captured by the Japanese.

Once in Mindanao, Hofmann received orders to help set up a small seaplane base on Lake Lanao that would facilitate the delivery of supplies to and the rescue of military personnel from Corregidor. As Japanese landings began on Mindanao near the lake, two seaplanes from Australia landed at Hofmann's base to refuel, flew to Corregidor to deliver some supplies, picked up roughly fifty passengers, mainly army nurses, and returned to Lake Lanao. In a truly harrowing experience, one of the planes hit a rock while trying to take off from the lake for the final leg of its flight to Australia, made an emergency return to the little base, and sank in the shallow water. The passengers on the plane were sent to a nearby army airfield in hopes of catching a flight on a land-based plane if possible. The seaplane's crew, Hofmann and a few other naval personnel, and some army airmen who were in the area serving as an improvised infantry worked feverously to refloat the plane and patch the hull. As Japanese forces converged on Lake Lanao, the seaplane, with Hofmann aboard, managed to take off and complete its flight to Australia.

Hofmann served the next two years in Australia before finally returning home in the fall of 1944.

Hofmann's fascinating memoir provides a much needed addition to the historiography of the U.S. military's experiences in the Philippines. Scholars have examined many aspects of the war in the Philippines. Louis Morton's *The Fall of the Philippines* remains the standard, especially for the army's experiences and studying the American defense of the Philippines in 1941 and 1942.[23] Clayton James's magisterial biography of Douglas MacArthur should be the first volume scholars examine in trying to understand the enigmatic general.[24] Accounts of the army defenders of Bataan and the infamous death march are many and varied. The best come from the pens of John Whitman and Michael and Elizabeth Norman.[25] William Bartsch has written several studies that thoroughly explore the experiences of American airmen in the Philippines.[26] Additionally, Elizabeth Norman captures the emotions of the army nurses trapped and ultimately captured on Bataan better than anyone to date.[27]

The historiography of the navy's experiences in the Philippines is not as extensive. While scholars have given due attention to the history of the U.S. Asiatic Fleet in the Philippines and the PT boat and seaplane squadrons, the experiences of the naval shore units and Marines who served there have not received the same treatment. W.G. Winslow and Edwin Hoyt admirably explore the unhappy account of the U.S. Asiatic Fleet in the early months of the war in their respective works.[28] James Leutze has a fascinating biography of Admiral Hart.[29] Dwight Messimer's account of the seaplane pilots and their crews remains the standard for understanding their contribution to the defense of the

Philippines.[30] Finally, William White's chronicle of the PT boats and their crews in the Philippines during the first six months of the war remains a classic.[31]

Until relatively recently, little scholarly work had been done on the navy's ground personnel and the marines who served in the Philippines in late 1941 and 1942. Michael Miller's short history commemorating the Marines who served in the Philippines is an important starting point for looking at their history.[32] However, it is John Gordon who advanced the historiography tremendously with his *Fighting for MacArthur: The Navy and Marine Corps' Desperate Defense of the Philippines*. He explores the navy and Marine Corps' previously little recognized role in the defense of Bataan and Corregidor and shows just how important they were despite the obstacles they faced in working with MacArthur and his staff.[33] Hofmann's memoir adds further to this historiography by giving a voice to the individual junior naval officer's role in the Philippines. While he obviously was not representative of all junior officers, particularly in that he was not captured, his experiences do reflect how many Americans lived and fought in those desperate times.

As with all memoirs, Hofmann's needs to be read with careful scrutiny. Without question, information in memoirs is invaluable as it provides the reader the history and views of someone who participated directly in significant events. The memoirist provides a unique perspective that can help explain an event. For understanding the American defense of the Philippines in 1941 and 1942, only a general can explain why he decided to send a division to this location or another. Only Army Air Corps personnel can describe their frustration at seeing the Japanese destruction of their planes on the ground at air bases on Luzon. Only an American nurse serving on Bataan can explain her experiences providing medical care in the desperate months of early 1942. However, these perspectives, by themselves, only offer one view. Taken together, they provide a much fuller understanding of what happened in 1941 and 1942, even if the history would still be incomplete.

The reader also has to take into consideration what motivated someone to write a memoir in the first place. Generally, the writers of memoirs have a distinct agenda—they want to tell their side of an experience. This is especially true of military and political leaders. While their works still contain valuable information, memoirs by leaders often attempt to enhance the writer's reputation. Seldom do they delve into issues where they made a wrong decision or could be questioned. This problem can be seen even in works by "less important" writers. There is a natural tendency to want to put one's experiences in the best possible light. For example, Hofmann clearly wanted to tell the story of junior naval officers who served ashore during the defense of the Philippines. While very descriptive, he definitely shows a bias in favor of the navy and its leadership.

Another potential problem with memoirs revolves around when they were written. Many memoirs are written years and even decades after the events being described occurred. This is especially true of the memoirs of lower-ranking military officers and enlisted personnel. These men and women often decide later in life that they should recount their histories for their families and maybe their friends. Most of the time, they have no aspirations to have them published in any official way. They record their histories to the best of their abilities, recounting events as they remember them. Each one of these memoirs is unique. Some are incredibly reliable as the writers have strong memories and strive for accuracy. Others suffer from failing memories with the passage of time. While the information in these memoirs can still be valuable, it has to be used more carefully and in conjunction with other reliable sources. Hofmann began writing his memoir soon after arriving in Australia in 1942, but he did not complete it for almost forty years. I have attempted to attest to its accuracy by providing as many corroborating sources as possible.

The question now is, How important is Ross Hofmann's memoir? He describes his experiences in 1941 and 1942 and offers the perspective of a junior naval supply corps officer in the Philippines. For that reason alone, it is valuable. While there are published memoirs of military leaders, army infantry, nurses, and others who served in the Philippines, Hofmann's is the first from a junior Supply Corps officer's perspective. As mention previously, Gordon's *Fighting for MacArthur* does a wonderful job of describing the relatively neglected experiences of the navy and marines in the defense of the Philippines. However, his account covers these forces broadly and does not focus on the experiences of an individual junior naval officer. Hofmann provides this perspective.

While potentially important, the significance of Hofmann's memoir can still only go as far as its reliability. He completed the memoir four decades after the war. Further, he includes a large amount of dialogue from his conversations with others. As I reviewed and edited the memoir, this was my biggest concern. I often asked myself how he could remember things in such detail, Other than learning from talking to his family that Hofmann had a nearly photographic memory and always recalled the littlest details, I cannot prove the conversations occurred as they did. However, they definitely fit the context of his memoir well and reflect the types of conversations I have seen in other memoirs.

What convinced me that his memoir was accurate is the fact that I have been able to confirm much of his account through other sources. Various official naval documents place him at the locations he identifies, and at the times he states. Accounts by other survivors from the Philippines mention his presence and involvement in the activities he describes. Additionally, there are at least two sources that he wrote fairly soon after leaving Mindanao that show consistencies in his recollection, and one indicates that he began recording it soon after his arrival in Australia. In the fall of 1942, he wrote a long letter to his parents describing his situation in Australia and spent about a page discussing his experiences in the Philippines. He mentioned his living conditions before the Japanese attack as well as his ultimate escape. He told his parents to read the article "They Were Expendable" from the September 1942 issue of *Reader's Digest*, explaining he was actually involved in the last part of that story, even though his name was not included. He also mentioned how he had started to write a book about his experiences but decided to put it on hold because he worried "about the boys" captured in the Philippines. He explained, "if ever anything happened [to the boys] as the result of my writing…. I would never get over it."[34]

Two years later, Hofmann, who had recently returned to the United States, was asked to speak to the Washington Board of Trade. Much of the speech concerned how Australia assisted the United States in the war effort, but roughly one-third of it addressed some of his experiences in the Philippines in 1941 and 1942 (see copy of speech in the appendix). He mentioned the Japanese attack on his base at Cavite, the navy's efforts to salvage any useful materials from the remains of the base, the role of the Supply Corps officers and the other naval personnel on Bataan, and ultimately his escape from Mindanao.[35] While he did not provide tremendous detail in his speech, he did outline most of the experiences that he addresses more fully in the memoir.

One other problem that happens in memoirs, probably including Hofmann's, is the insertion of information and detail that the writer learned after the fact. Besides the many conversations that Hofmann recounts, he often includes specific numbers of planes and troops that are generally accurate. He also provides comments on U.S. strategy and tactics in the Philippines even though he would not have been privy to the high command's discussions of these issues. While he identifies his sources, generally junior officers from the navy or another part of the military, it is unclear how much he could have actually learned as a junior naval officer. It is likely that as he wrote his memoir he consulted other sources.[36] He mentions one book in his Prologue, Winslow's *The Fleet the Gods Forgot*, and he surely consulted White's *They Were Expendable* and Morton's *The Fall of the Philippines*. White wrote the *Reader's Digest* article, "They Were Expendable," that Hofmann mentions in the letter to his parents in late 1942.[37] That article later became part of his book on the PT boats in the Philippines. Hofmann never identified Morton's work specifically. However, when he provides specific numbers for troops, they are similar to the ones found there. The reader has to decide whether this is a problem or not. I have concluded that it is not as I have been able to verify significant parts of his memoir through other sources.

I also know that a great deal of "secret" information did circulate openly, including in the press at that time, and it is very possible that Hofmann learned the information he presents from the sources he identifies, such as other officers with whom he spoke. Prior to the war, officers from the different military branches frequently gathered at the Army and Navy Club in Manila for a round of drinks and to share their experiences. Hofmann includes several of these in his memoir. Further, various newspapers published articles that discussed the situation in the Philippines, sometimes with significant detail. The *Washington Post* ran an article under the heading "Air Force Large in Philippines" soon after Hofmann arrived in Manila and quoted General George Marshall as saying that the Philippines were the "No. 1 Priority" for rearmament.[38] The *New York Times* noted in mid–November 1941 that the United States had shifted its defense strategy in the Philippines. It reported that United States now planned to defend the Philippines and announced that any Japanese attacking force "against the Philippines would be the target of a large and powerful group of some of the best fighting planes in the world, with a range extending well beyond the coasts of the archipelago."[39] By the end of December, the *New York Times* was announcing that Japan "rules the air over the Philippines."[40] While these articles did not contain specific numbers, they do provide an indication that a tremendous amount of information was circulating in the months before and after the war started.

Once Hofmann and the other naval personnel retreated to Mariveles on southern Bataan, he worked even more closely with officers from the PT boat squadrons and other naval units, airmen who had evacuated air bases from other parts of Luzon, and Marines sent to defend the area. In an environment where there was little contact with anyone outside the Philippines, I have little doubt that they shared information often and freely.

To corroborate his account, I examined as many primary and secondary sources as possible. I utilized records from the National Archives of the United States, the Harvard University Archives, the Harvard Business School Archives, the MacArthur Memorial Archives and Library, and the United States Army Heritage and Education Center. I supplemented these records with published sources, including diaries of military personnel who served in the Philippines, after-action reports from battles in which Hofmann participated, and numerous secondary sources that addressed events in the Philippines in

1941 and 1942. While many American records were lost when Japan captured Bataan and Corregidor, the official records that survived along with sources that have been published provide tremendous support for Hofmann's account. There is no question about his service in the Philippines, and the records corroborate most of his experiences there. While some may question the detail he provides in some of the conversations he describes, there is nothing in the historical record that refutes them or even raises any serious questions.

All things considered, I have come to believe that Hofmann wrote an accurate account to the best of his ability. While he may have used other sources as he wrote the memoir, it contains tremendous amounts of information that is not available in other sources. The letter he wrote to his parents as well as the speech he gave later in 1944 indicate that he at least began to write his experiences during the war. When taken into consideration with the other sources identified in the notes, his memoir rings true and provides a very unique look at the experiences of a junior naval officer who survived the harrowing defense of the Philippines.

Prologue (by Ross E. Hofmann)

Forty-five years is long enough to let this story lie sleeping. When the Pacific War was over, there were few of us left alive who had survived the events that I describe, and as each year passes, our little group shrinks further. I was fortunate to be one of those survivors. In this memoir, prepared from notes I jotted down immediately after Corregidor surrendered and I had escaped to Australia, I have attempted to give a personal description of the debacle that took place in the defense of the Philippines, as seen through the eyes of a young naval officer who was there.

Captain Walter S. Winslow's *The Fleet the Gods Forgot* is an excellent narrative of what happened to the ships of our tiny Asiatic Fleet as they engaged in attacks against the vastly superior Japanese forces, and one by one were sunk. This is an account of what happened to the rest of the fleet, the shore people who were left behind when the ships sailed off to Java to fight the enemy. These were the "dry land" sailors, most of them survivors of the Japanese obliteration of the Cavite Navy Yard, the men who were forced to retreat to Bataan with the army and Marines.

To engage in a war of aggression is repugnant to most Americans. Vietnam clearly proved that. On the opposite side of the coin, Americans do not permit their military leaders to lose a defensive war. Sometimes it takes years for the verdict of history to come forth, for public relations to be replaced by the cold truth. For several years that verdict has been in on the war in the Philippines. When MacArthur retreated to Bataan and then abandoned his army to flee to Australia, we suffered the worst defeat in a defensive campaign in our history. Of the almost 28,000 American army, navy and Marine Corps officers and men in the islands at the beginning, many did not survive.

History has revealed that the defense of the Philippines was a disaster, not because of a lack of courage on the part of the small force of Americans, but rather because of errors in judgment and bad tactical decisions made by American leaders. Sadly, when the survivors returned to the United States in 1945, they were pretty well ignored. Rather than being given a friendly "welcome back" by the public, they were painted with the stigma of the errors of their leader. They did not deserve that.

So I am dedicating this rather personal account to the thousands of Americans who were killed during the fighting or who died later while in the hands of the Japanese. May they rest in peace with the knowledge that, unsupported and finally abandoned, they did their best to uphold America's honor. I also leave them with the hope that their descendants will never be left in the same state of unpreparedness and poor leadership that they faced in 1941.

Introduction (by Ross E. Hofmann)

A beam of sunlight streamed through the window, targeting me like a searchlight and forcing my eyes open no matter how hard I tried to keep them closed. I gave up the struggle and realized I had forgotten to close the night curtains when Louisa and I retired.[1] I pushed the covers aside and walked to the window. My watch read exactly 7 a.m., and I looked out at a typical spring day in the Philippines. The sky over Manila Bay was a light turquoise, broken by a few pure-white, puffy clouds to the west. Saturday was market day in Manila, and within an hour, the scene below would change to one of bustling activity.

As I showered, I thought about my sudden impulse to fly to Manila after an absence of thirty-seven years.[2] Three days before, in Singapore, I decided I had to come. It was not on our travel schedule, and normally, I stay strictly on schedule. I also usually do not give way to sudden whims and changes in direction, but this time an inner voice insisted that I go back to Luzon.

I think talking with Mickey Hsu, my regular taxi driver in Singapore, had started the feeling. He always picked me up each morning at the hotel and drove me the roughly one hour to my job site. We filled the time by talking about the island, the people, Mickey's family, and my family. Mickey was a loquacious driver and could talk for hours on a variety of subjects. I asked Mickey how old he had been when the Japanese took over Singapore.[3] He looked at me in the rearview mirror and said, "I was ten." Then he added, "The bastards. I do not forget, even now. They are no good, none of them." I had never heard an outburst like that from Mickey. "Was it pretty rough?" "Sir, you cannot imagine what it was like. I lost my whole family. We Chinese, we could not fight; we could not resist. The British soldiers were supposed to defend the island; it did not last long. My family did not know much about the Japanese, but we heard rumors; we had heard that they hated all Chinese; that they had killed hundreds of thousands of Chinese on the mainland, innocent civilians. My father was working on the docks one day, slipped, and let a crate fall. He was an old man, and two Japanese soldiers came up and beat him to death. He was the first. By the time the occupation was over, my whole family—my mother, my older brothers, and my two sisters—were all dead. I was the only one left. I guess I was too young for them to kill me."[4]

I thought about this conversation the rest of the day and felt some of the old feelings returning. After forty years, I thought I was over these emotions, but obviously, I was not. That evening, Louisa and I talked about our upcoming travel schedule as we headed to the hotel elevator. We were planning to spend a week in Bangkok and then come back to Singapore so that I could check the progress at the work site. When the elevator opened, there was only one person in it, and he was obviously Japanese. He wore a dark blue suit, dark silk tie, white shirt, highly polished black shoes, and steel frame glasses, and he had slicked backed, black hair. The man rushed for the opening, pushing Louisa heavily into the railing that ran against the wall without an apology. After that incident, I felt a flood of emotions that I had not experienced since the end of the war. My anger at what the Japanese did to our men and women in the Philippines and my frustration at the failure of American leadership there remained stronger than I realized.

The next morning I told Louisa I wanted to change our travel schedule. I arranged to delay our trip to Bangkok for a week and then booked a flight to Manila and a hotel there. As we were flying, I leafed through the pocket guide to the Philippines that I had picked up at the airport. As I read, I recalled most of the history and the geography. However, the statistics on the growth of the islands since I had last visited them in 1946 were impressive.

The guidebook stated that Malays and Polynesians settled the islands originally; that Magellan was the first European to land on them; and that he claimed the lands for Spain, naming them in 1521 after King Philip. The book reviewed the period of Spanish colonization that lasted until the end of the 19th century and described the easy-going existence of the Spanish settlers, utilizing cheap Filipino labor. It explained how the English and Americans brought the ideas of democracy to the islands and how they fueled the fires of independence and revolution among the Filipinos. The Spanish-American War of 1898 drove the Spanish out of the Philippines, but the Americans soon followed.[5] The guidebook went on to describe how World War II affected the Philippines; that General Douglas MacArthur had returned; and that, on July 4, 1946, the United States had granted them their independence. I had attended the ceremony while working for the Truman administration and remembered it well.

When I reviewed the geography of the islands, I scanned the statistics that had impressed me years before; that there were over 7,000 islands in the Philippine chain, with less than ten percent of them inhabited. As I relaxed, I visualized the vast size of the Philippines. Spread out over a lot of ocean, the island chain stretches for twelve hundred miles from north to south and almost seven hundred miles east to west. Big neighbors lie nearby as it is only six hundred miles to the Chinese mainland and a two-hour flight by jet to Darwin, Australia. On the other hand, the United States, the traditional guardian of the Philippines during the first half of this century, is a long way off. In fact, it is 13,773 air miles from Washington, D.C., to Manila.

I thought about the different times I stayed in Manila and had travelled through Luzon during and after the war. The first time was in 1941 and 1942 when I was getting used to the idea that I was a navy officer and that there was a war going on. The second time was in August 1945, after too many invasions of atolls and islands, war having become a way of life that seemed to go on forever, and we decided to drop the big bomb on Hiroshima and Nagasaki. The third time was between May and August 1946 when the U.S. government wanted my little group to salvage supplies the army and navy had abandoned throughout the Pacific during the war. I had not been back to the Philippines since that last trip.

After we arrived in the Philippines, we stayed at the refurbished Manila Hotel, and I had to admit it did not look like I remembered it before the war.[6] The face-lift had been complete. We sat in one of the small lounges off the lobby as the early evening shadows lengthened. We strolled along a walkway at the rear of the lobby that led to an outdoor pool and the high-rise tower of rooms I had noticed in the morning. We saw the piers behind the hotel, with inter-island ships tied alongside and the larger freighters anchored in the bay. This much did seem familiar, though much tidier than I remembered it from the last time I had been there.

The next day we drove to my destination of the day, the Libingan Ng Mga Bayani (Graveyard of Heroes) and the Tomb of the Unknown Soldier. Nearby, set out in huge circles, were row upon row of unnamed, stark, white crosses, marking the remains of over 17,000 Filipinos and Americans who died fighting the Japanese invaders over forty years earlier. This was the Manila-American Cemetery.[7] As we stood there with a slight breeze blowing in our faces and the sun beating down on the well-kept grass and illuminating the whiteness of each cross, I wondered how many people back in the United States realized the number of troops who had died attempting to defend Bataan. We had once estimated that in all of Bataan there were only 12,000 Americans and perhaps as many as 80,000 Filipino soldiers. Did that mean that as many as nineteen percent of the total force were now resting here? What about the hundreds and maybe thousands who were blown to bits by shells and bombs or buried in unmarked fox holes in the jungles and never identified? What was the total percentage of the troops that went into those jungles and never returned to their homes?[8]

The next morning our driver met us to drive to the Bataan Peninsula. To the west as we drove past San Fernando, I could see the ridges and further down, the mountains of the peninsula. On a tall mountain, part way down the peninsula, an enormous cross had been erected, no doubt in memory of all the Filipinos and their American helpers who fought and died in their attempt to prevent the Japanese from seizing this small piece of real estate in 1941 and 1942. The high mountains and the jagged ridges in the center of the peninsula looked as forbidding as they always had. The trees still rose to great heights, and the tangled vines, bamboo thickets, and dense foliage still seemed as oppressive as they did forty years before.

The drive to Mariveles proceeded without any problems, and the road finally rose onto a flat plateau of brown, dry grass. From its appearance, it could have been anywhere in the American southwest except that it overlooked the water of Manila Bay. Overhung by haze and heat waves about two miles off the coast, I saw the long grey-blue outline of Corregidor. The road curved to the right at this point and twisted down it like a snake. We were about to descend into the flat basin that formed Mariveles Bay.

Our driver took the hairpin bends and steep descent very carefully. I craned my neck to see what I could of the basin below us. I remembered the white sand beach where we used to swim, the crystal clear waters of the bay that were always an azure blue, the three streams that came down from Mariveles Mountain, and how peaceful a place Mariveles had been. Thinking back forty years, Mariveles seemed to have been a pleasant place from which to fight a war.

The road followed the wharf and the harbor front and on the landward side we passed a collection of three story, white buildings, one after another, covering all the land for at least two blocks from the bay front, spaced tightly together, with concrete roadways in between. A man was walking on the road ahead of us and I had our driver stop the car as we drew abreast of him. He was a tall, blond European and when I asked what went on in Mariveles, he replied in an English accent, "We are very big in running shoes and tennis balls."

Forty years before, the navy base, with its little pier, Quarantine Station, and little wooden green buildings, occupied the western part, with a low ridge separating it from the eastern section that now contained all these factory buildings. The ridge was still there and the road had been cut around it right at the water's edge to permit driving to the western part. We rounded and looked straight ahead, expecting to see the base I had left so many years before. In its place, the Filipinos had constructed a village, no doubt the dot that the road map identified as Mariveles.

The village of Mariveles was tightly spaced on each side of the road. The few hundred feet on the bay side consisted of a cluster of houses covering the area between the main street and the waterfront. Projecting out into the bay was a small pier and a crane. On the landward side of the main street were a few more houses and small warehouses. The buildings that fronted the main street itself consisted of small shops, bars and eateries, all with open fronts and loud radios blaring out music.

After we had re-crossed the bridge over the Mariveles River, I recalled another memory from forty years before. I told Louisa, "See that dirt road that follows the ridge away from the one we are on. That road was there when we were here. We used to have our cots and mosquito nets set up on it during the war, and we could look down on Mariveles paddy and out onto the bay. About half way up that ridge road is a small, flat plateau and that is where we slept at night. There was always a breeze up there, and it was cool at night. The trees on the ridge used to be full of monkeys that were so tame they would come right down to us and try to steal things."

We returned to the port and drove up the rising ground behind it to a hotel. After lunch in the hotel's small restaurant, we walked out onto a terrace that overlooked the port and from which we could see almost the entire shoreline of the bay. As I stood there taking photographs, I started feeling a little foolish and wondering why I thought all progress would stop for forty years just because this little part of Bataan had been the scene of some memorable occurrences in our war with Japan.

The next morning our driver took us around the bay to Cavite. As we drove south along Roxas Boulevard circling Manila Bay, I remembered the old road and the rattling taxis that used to drive us back to Sangley Point after an evening of rum and conversation at the Army and Navy Club, the Manila Hotel, or some less respectable establishment. The Navy Yard and Sangley Point were located at the end of a long narrow peninsula that curved out into Manila Bay. Cavite peninsula was of a peculiar shape. It had two prongs that looked like a lobster's claw on the map and formed a small, protected bay between them, while the entire curved peninsula formed a larger bay with the mainland. On the two pincers of the claw were situated Sangley Point and the Cavite Navy Yard. Crowding the entrance to the Yard was the old Spanish walled city of Cavite. It got its name from the fact that the peninsula actually was hook-shaped. A hook is called "kawit" in Tagalog and the Spanish had translated that into "Cavite."[9]

From east to west, Cavite was only ten blocks long, narrow, and hemmed in by the old masonry battlements along the water. Four streets traversed its length, ending at the Navy Yard. At the west end as you entered, were the remnants of Spanish bastions and a gate. Behind these were a church and a theater. I remembered driving past concrete and stucco walled buildings, houses and shops with roofs of wood or corrugated iron, stores with small signs and open fronts, and old Spanish churches with their towers rising above all the other buildings. I remembered large trees and brilliant tropical foliage, and over all, the pungent smell of wood smoke. I remembered the light brown faces of the people and the constant smiling, the easy-going pace, the friendliness, and politeness of everyone.

I remembered the wide west gate of the Yard, the Marine guards, and the high wire fence. When you passed through those gates you entered into a different world. I remembered wharves with destroyers and submarines; sailors in denims, officers in white shirts and shorts, and Filipino Yard workers in a variety of dress. I remembered trucks and barges moving supplies, the sparking of welding torches, coils of rope and of wire, and the slow swinging of a crane's boom. I remembered the clacking of typewriters coming through the open windows of white buildings and the slow turning of ceiling fans inside the rooms. I remembered the little bay that was enclosed between the two prongs, and looking from the Yard across the bay at Sangley Point and Canacao, with its golf course and hospital, the radio station, and the officers' housing. I remembered the sound of a patrol plane starting its engines; and the distinct sound of a torpedo boat engine being tested.

I also remembered the ear shattering blast and wave of concussion from an exploding bomb, followed by silence and then the noise and concussion repeated, over and over again, while the ground heaved beneath me. I remembered the fires, black smoke, and stench from burning oil and wood. I remembered the bodies lying on the road and on the grass, some still, some moaning, and some screaming. When we returned to the hotel, I was emotionally drained but glad that I had returned to the area that had haunted my dreams for four decades.

As we flew back to Bangkok, I thought about how MacArthur had mishandled things during the Philippine campaign of 1941 and 1942.[10] I thought about all the mistakes he had made and the fact that he had not been replaced by Washington, but instead had been made a hero.[11] In those first months of the war, we had no heroes. We had generals and admirals who were too timid or unprepared to fight a war. We had people like MacArthur who did not understand modern warfare, despite all the tactics the Germans had been teaching the world for over two years. We had men who lost entire squadrons of warplanes sitting on the ground; men who did not know how to use naval vessels under 1942 wartime conditions; and men who forgot what Billy Mitchell had taught them years before about what bombers could do to ships.[12]

I thought of how MacArthur continued to act like a hero during the years that he spent in Australia and how the hero bit wore off quickly down there. He was not able to get back into the newspaper headlines that he so dearly loved until his carefully rehearsed "I shall return" movement onto the beach at Leyte in October 1944. I remembered standing in an office in Brisbane when MacArthur tried to tell Admiral Bull Halsey how to fight a naval war and how Halsey had told him at the top of his lungs that he was full of it.[13] I was two offices away and still made out every word.

When I looked back at the whole story of the Pacific War, I knew that time and again it was having the necessary supplies when and where they were needed that usually spelled the difference between success and failure. So many times during attacks or landings on islands, while the guts of the ranks played a large part, having the right supplies usually tipped the balance. The knowledge that we had, and would be able to use, the weapons and ammunition, the planes and ships, the landing craft and bulldozers, the food, clothing and medical items, allowed all those thousands of military decisions to spell success in each campaign.

Most Americans read the headlines about the generals and admirals who led the forces, shouting, "Follow me" or hear stories about the courageous airman, sailor, and soldier. They seldom read stories about the people who made it possible for those officers and combat forces to fight. These people managed to put together and deliver all those thousands of items without which there would have been no following of the leader. Someday, somewhere, I know I am going to enter a quiet town in America, with white church steeples and a local drug store, and I will drive through to the town square, where there will be a couple of fountains spraying clear water and beds of bright flowers. In the center of the square, between the fountains, I will examine a block of brownish granite, on top of which, beautifully sculptured and cast in bronze, will be a life-sized statue of a U.S. Navy lieutenant. He will be seated at a desk and on it will be a thick pile of papers. In front of him will be a smaller pile, and he will be signing these with the pen in his hand. At his feet will be a steel helmet, a .45 caliber automatic, and a pair of combat boots. I know that someday I will see that statue.

1

Training and Movement Overseas

The voice on the telephone on Friday, June 13, 1941, was crisp. The navy officer told me to report to the Harvard University Graduate School of Business Administration in Cambridge, Massachusetts, on the following Monday by 1400 hours. I was being called to active duty as a reserve officer in the United States Navy.[1] The fact that I might feel I was holding down an important job, and that other people might be depending upon me for their livelihood, and that I had numerous pressing commitments for the following week and into the future, did not seem to be of interest to the navy. I held a reserve commission, which meant I served at the navy's pleasure. Those instructions gave me one short weekend to get rid of an apartment, store everything that was storable, make arrangements for someone else to handle all the business details I had been managing, give final instructions to half a dozen of my co-workers, and drive to Boston early Monday morning. It seemed that it would be impossible to accomplish all of that over a weekend. I had become a settled, twenty-three-year-old executive for a publishing house, and things did not normally happen that fast in that atmosphere.[2]

Yet, at six a.m. Monday, I left Long Island for Boston. It was turning into a beautiful spring day, bright sunshine and a cool breeze blowing in from the Sound. I found I was actually looking forward to this drastic change in my life. My income would be cut at least seventy percent, but money was not everything.[3] The navy meant ships, faraway places, mysterious ports of call, deep blue oceans, and tropical sunsets. I became more excited about the whole idea as I climbed the hills of northern Connecticut and swung east into Massachusetts.

By midafternoon, with four hundred and twenty others, I officially enrolled as an Ensign[4] in the Supply Corps of the U.S. Navy.[5] During the next few days of orientation, I found that most of us had graduated from college in 1939 or 1940 with majors in Economics, Accounting, or Business Administration, and that we came from just about every state. The navy had recruited us from the junior executive ranks of major American companies, and we represented a cross-section of American business. I also found out that, like myself, the majority of the recruits had no idea what a supply officer actually did, or what our training would cover.

As we assembled in the classroom for our lectures on how the Supply Corps operated and what we would be doing, all of us figured that we would be taught what there was to know about the navy. Since ships were the business of the navy, we assumed we would be educated on the various aspects of ships: what they looked like, how they operated, and what their roles were. We figured we would also learn how the supplies were obtained, stored, issued, and used. However, this was not quite the way things worked in the Supply Corps of 1941.[6] During the entire twelve weeks that we spent at Harvard, being trained in the intricacies of carrying out the duties of a supply officer, we never even saw a photograph of a ship, much less have the opportunity to actually climb aboard one.[7]

It seemed that everything a supply officer should know was covered by rules and regulations written in a thick, loose-leaf book, with a heavy, almost indestructible cover, entitled *The Supply Corps Manual*. We each received one of these manuals and a thick pile of pages that represented all the changes that we would have to make to bring our manuals up to the status of June 1941. We estimated that the changed pages covered corrections that went back at least to 1925. Some of the pages had been changed fourteen times since then, and we had to go through the exercise of chronologically replacing the replacements as we worked our way through them to the current month. No one ever read the obsolete pages that we discarded; we were too eager to get to the present and complete the damn operation.

Once we had our manuals completed, we settled down to the business of learning how the Supply Corps operated. It did not take long to find out that its unofficial motto was "Paper Work Was God." It was up to the Supply Corps to see that everything that was issued to ships was properly requisitioned, delivered, and recorded. The trainers drummed into our heads that times had been tough for the navy, supplies were costly and scarce, and God help you if you could not account for every bolt, nut, and can of beans.

Since the end of the First World War, it had been a navy that had to scrimp, save, and hoard the supplies and equipment it had been able to acquire. It had to pinch every penny that had been doled out to it by a reluctant Congress. In fact, many of those congressmen had felt that a land mass like the United States had little use for a military presence, now that most of the Indians were on reservations.[8] Years of having appropriations cut and being told about all the things that they could not have sank in deeply among the admirals, and they in turn made the rank-and-file know just how tough times were.

As the Supply Corps was up to its neck in purchasing, storing, and issuing these supplies, it was on the front line in seeing that there was no waste. We learned that you were an excellent Supply Officer if you were a *NO* man—*NO*, we do not have it; *NO*, you cannot have it; *NO*, it is not on your allotment. We were left with the impression that the *CAN DO* man whom industry loved would end up being the supply mentor for a single rowboat in some remote and unpleasant corner of the globe.

Most of us had entered our new profession with rather misguided ideas of what we would be handling and how we would be operating. We had visions of sitting behind a desk in some busy office, large flow charts on the wall behind us, while the phone rang constantly, expediters bounced in and out, and mountains of new materials rolled out of factories and warehouses across the country. We realized that for the first year, we might not control all the major movements, but we sure would be the expediters that broke any log jam that threatened progress. Again, *The Supply Corps Manual* brought us down to earth. It offered no statement that we were to be experts in technical procurement and distribution. Nowhere did it describe us as movers and shakers. However, it did let us know that we were to be more than mere clerks who dealt only in paperwork.[9]

The first thing that we learned was that every Supply Corps officer must know how to be a Disbursing Officer, which meant that each of us had to be capable of paying the wages of the entire crew of a large battleship. We had to be able to do this in cash, and we had to know how to deduct from each man's pay his allotments to his family. As a seaman second class earned $21 a month and the pay went up to over $140 for junior officers, and there were over a thousand in the crew of a large ship, we figured we would be doling out a lot of bills and silver.[10] We also learned that if we made any mistakes in handling all this cash, we would be in big trouble. If the cash did not balance to the penny after the mad rush of sailors, we would spend the rest of our lives breaking rocks at the navy's grim, fortress like prison, in Portsmouth, New Hampshire. There was not one ex-bank teller among us, and the reaction to this news about the potential duties of a supply officer was not heartwarming.

We were then told that a supply officer may be given duty as a Commissary Officer. The navy had its own cookbook and insisted that the meals be prepared and balanced in certain ways. The navy even purchased and roasted its own coffee beans. Food was a top priority, and ships preferred it to be fresh when possible; therefore, we were expected to know how to purchase such provisions. The total knowledge of food buying and serving in the entire class seemed to be limited to one man whose father owned a restaurant. We also discovered that the navy was proud of its clothing purchases and these too came under the jurisdiction of the Supply Corps. The navy ran a clothing factory in 1941.[11] This was not foreign to the men who had come from department store management, so we felt we were getting a little closer to home in the intricacies of supply.

All of this, when we summed it up, was still on the periphery of a fleet of ships, and far removed from the functions we had envisioned performing for the navy. As the weeks dragged by we kept wondering when we would get to the part of the course that would provide details on the end-product we would be serving, namely, ships: battleships, cruisers, aircraft carriers, submarines, destroyers, and support vessels like minesweepers and tenders. The only water we saw during our twelve weeks of training was the peaceful Charles River flowing past our buildings, and the only vessels were the rowing sculls and sailboats that floated past on the river. We decided we would look foolish the first time we had to board a naval vessel, without knowing port from starboard, or bow from stern. We might be wearing the uniform of a U.S. naval officer, and we might be carrying our Supply Corps manual with all thousands of changes made right up to date, but God help us if we were told to find our way unaccompanied to any location on the vessel we had just boarded.

It was almost at the end of the course before we all were willing to admit that the navy was training us to be "dry land" sailors or members of the shore establishment, who would spend their careers in an office or a depot, maybe no closer than a thousand miles from the nearest ocean. Only the largest ships had their own supply officer, and there were not too many of these vessels. The navy assigned the few with real seawater in their veins to these ships, and the rest of us to naval yards, depots, and warehouse complexes. For us the sounds of battle would be far away if war ever came. Not only that, the office in which we would be shuffling those papers would probably be in the United States, not in some far-off country. If we had wanted to see deep blue seas and distant lands, we had chosen the wrong part of the navy.

The lectures on *The Supply Corps Manual* did not take up our entire time. The navy had formed all the members of the school into a naval battalion of seven companies.[12] Some afternoons we marched around the grounds, dressed in our khakis and wearing black ties under the assumption that at some time during our naval career we might have to enter a parade and should know the left foot from the right. Other times, we performed calisthenics whose sole purpose seemed to be to wake us up. The most vigorous exercise we experienced were the games of touch football.[13]

When not training, I was lucky. In New York, I had shared an apartment with a native Bostonian, and he had returned to his hometown a year before I started training at Harvard. Three days after my enrollment in the navy, I met up with him. He had many friends and introduced me to them. They seemed to form a close-knit group that did things together. My ex-roommate had become engaged, and his fiancée knew a lot of the girls in the area. One of the girls in particular attracted me, and it was not too long before we became a couple in the pairing off that usually takes place in such groups. Fortunately for me, she had no current boyfriend to spoil the arrangement. She was about my height,[14] with dark blond hair and the most beautiful, grey-blue eyes I had ever seen. She was slender, neat, and self-possessed. She enjoyed life and had a wonderful smile. I had never known a New England girl before and after the brittle career-girl types I had known in New York, she was refreshing. Her name was Dorothy, and we often would talk for hours in my free time.

We toured the streets of Boston from Beacon Hill to the outer reaches of Common-wealth Avenue. We looked at historic buildings, country lanes, beaches, and wooded hills. I drove the Buick, while Dorothy acted as guide. We drove along curving Cape Cod, with its white beaches, and visited old Provincetown with its weather-beaten houses and narrow streets. We explored the Massachusetts coast as far north as the historic waterfront in Newburyport.

When we were not out in the fresh air and sunshine, we were investigating the pleasures of central Boston, anchored by the Common, or at the Statler.[15] In fact, the Statler seemed to be the favorite hangout for the members of my Harvard class. Many of my classmates became quite knowledgeable about the byways around the Common and seemed to discover an unending succession of attractive girls. Some even discovered the delights of Scollay Square, a territory where the real sailors from the fleet were inclined to roam.[16] As the summer progressed, our "Don Juans" made fresh conquests and the tales got wilder and wilder. Dry land or not, a lot of them were turning into navy men, and a few were threatened with jail for a couple of escapades.

Finally, it was early September, and our twelve weeks of instruction were near an end.[17] By September 7, we would have our orders and would know where our immediate future lay. The week before receiving our orders was one of intense speculation. We were more knowledgeable in the ways of the Supply Corps, and our innocence had evaporated. We knew that our immediate future could be interesting or boring, and that there would be little choice in the matter. When the navy told you where to go, you went.[18]

Some of us, however, still followed the old adage that "where there is a will, there is a way." Following this line of thinking, there seemed no harm in asking for a more interesting assignment. The question was how to go about it. Three of us had become close friends during our twelve weeks of training. Looking back, I now realize that all three of us were inclined to be restless types. We looked upon ourselves as "The Three Musketeers" who could accomplish spectacular results once we were positioned in the right place.

Our idea man was Jack McClure. Jack came from Harvard, where he had graduated with a degree in psychology and taken advanced courses in English and philosophy. He had joined a large medicine company and had worked his way up to being their sales promotion and advertising manager. Jack had a way with words, and rather romantic ideas of what we should be doing as naval officers. The other member of the trio was more like me. He had helped his father run a manufacturing plant and had assumed a lot of responsibility at an early age. He was a pragmatist and felt that he had more to offer than spending his next few years stamping his signature on requisition forms. His name was Bud Snow. Jack was tall and dark and had been raised in central Pennsylvania, while Bud came from northern New Jersey and was tall with sandy hair and a lighter complexion.

We directed our first attempt to arrange our futures to our instructors. They were not much older than we were, and it soon became obvious that they always went along with the system. The navy made the decisions concerning your future and that was it. When we cross-examined them as to where we might be sent, we found that the most likely choices were the Navy Department in Washington or in a major supply facility such as Mare Island in California. After all, we were of the new breed and the places needed men of our background and training.

At first glance, an assignment such as that was appealing. We would be with the movers and shakers and have the opportunity to show the Annapolis boys what reserve officers had to offer. We decided that we should discuss this among ourselves and examine it from all angles. We climbed into my Buick and drove to the Statler where we sat in the deep, dark chairs in the lounge off the bar and started our analysis. Being up and coming executives in a navy that would be going through a massive reorganization, at first seemed like a great opportunity. Within a couple of years, we might be able to influence its actions and get things happening fast.

Jack said rather casually, "You know, this idea of being in a place like Washington or the West Coast has a lot to offer, but is that really why we came into the navy?" "What do you mean?" I asked. "Well, we will be stuck in the continental U.S. and maybe never go on board a ship or see the world. Is that really why we are here? It probably would not be much different from our civilian lives, except then we were doing what we liked to do and this will possibly be a little boring. If we have to spend our time juggling requisitions, wouldn't it be better to be doing it in an interesting place, say overseas like in England, where there is more action?" Neither Bud nor I had thought of that. Jack continued, "We have all taken a hell of a cut in pay and set back our civilian careers by a good two years to help our country. It seems that we should have some say in how and where we are going to be doing this." He paused and then said with emphasis, "I came into the navy to see the world and I am damn well going to do it."

Bud had been quiet and doing a lot of thinking about the turn the conversation was taking. He looked at Jack and said, "What is wrong with Washington, or California, for that matter?" Jack replied, "I hate California. I set up a program out there for the company and I never met so many phonies in my life. Of course, that was in Los Angeles, not the Bay area, but it's still California. And Washington. Have you two ever spent any time going through one of those government offices? I have. No one does any work. They shuffle papers and try to look busy. Three guys like us are not going to change things down there. It has been that way ever since the start of the New Deal. It would be boring as hell. After two years of that, no one in the civilian world would hire you."

"What does that leave?" I asked. "We have been told that we have no chance of being assigned to the fleet on board a battleship. And Washington or California beats the hell out of being stuck in some puny depot where they couldn't even find you, like in Colorado or Utah. I'll take Washington any day, or California, over that." Jack responded, "What is left for people like us, who want to help the navy and see the world at the same time, is foreign duty. Do you realize that no one at school has even talked about a foreign assignment? I mentioned England. There is a war on there and the Brits are in the front line defending democracy. I have never been to England," he added with a faraway look in his eyes. "What we should do is see if we can get assigned to England. That is the only foreign duty I can think of where they could send us, so it is simple. We ask for a foreign duty assignment, and we will be the only people in the whole class doing so. And the place that they will send us will be England." We thought about Jack's reasoning as we sipped more martinis and had to admit that it made a lot of sense. If we were going to be stuck for two years, England would be ideal. The British possessed a real fleet and were fighting a real war. Jack then added the clincher—the English were very friendly toward Americans, particularly the English girls.

We were now determined to request overseas duty and went to the school commander's apartment. I know he took the job of running the school very seriously, and none of us had ever seen him smile. He was stocky, red cheeked, and appeared to have a liberal amount of seawater in his veins. We knocked authoritatively on his door and waited. After a delay of a minute or so, we knocked again. Finally, the door opened and the commander stood there. "What is it?" was all he said with no warmth of greeting. McClure drew himself up to his full six feet and acted as the spokesman for our trio. "Sir, may I respectfully suggest that we came into the navy to see the world … and we would prefer not to see it from an aircraft plant in California, sir. The three of us would like to volunteer for foreign duty, sir." The commander stared at the three of us for a long time and did not say one word. I began to feel a little nervous. Finally he said dryly, "I think that can be arranged," and closed his door after we had given him our names.

We were walking on air as we headed for our quarters. We were convinced the statement McClure had made that we were "volunteering" for foreign duty had done the trick. We doubted that any other member of the class had volunteered for anything, much less to leave the United States and head for a war zone. We figured that within a month we would be in England seeing the sights.

Two days later the commander posted the duty assignments for the class on the bulletin board. The three of us ran our eyes down the alphabetical list of names. As we had asked, all three of us had foreign duty assignments and were going to the same place. There it was in black and white. We were the only members of the class who would be leaving the continental limits of the United States.[19] We read our names in neatly typed letters with the same location after each: U.S. Naval Facility, Shanghai, China.

I broke the news to Dorothy immediately and arranged to meet her for dinner. I told her, "Don't worry about it. Foreign duty like this is always just a short stint. I'll be back in the States before we know it and put in for duty in the Boston area." Dorothy was dry-eyed and was very serious. "I hope so. You know how far Shanghai is from Boston; and the news people are saying that the Japanese are throwing their weight around again. You know they are being pushed by their military to start something." I spoke as only a navy man could. "That is one thing that will never happen. Between the British and us, we have the greatest naval power the world has ever seen. We stretch across the Pacific from the West coast through Hawaii and the Philippines to the coast of China and the British come up from Singapore and Hong Kong. The Japanese might be fighting some Chinese warlords, but they would never dare tangle with the American and British navies. They would be wiped out in a couple of weeks."

"But Shanghai is in China and from what I have read the Japanese have a lot of troops all around it," Dorothy said as we ate our dessert and lingered over our coffee. "I realize that, but we are on friendly relations with the Japanese. If that ever changed, we would know well in advance and the Americans in China would be well protected. Don't forget, I will be like a diplomat out there, with special status, like all diplomats have. The Japanese would never touch us. They may push the Chinese around, but they will leave the Europeans and us alone. They need us; they are not about to rock the boat." The discussion continued until late in the evening and Dorothy remained unconvinced but resigned to the way things stood. I promised to phone regularly until I left the United States and then write frequently from Shanghai during the few months that I would be there until I returned.[20]

After I left Boston, I spent the next ten days in Toronto visiting my family. The Canadians, along with the British, had been at war for a full two years, and uniforms were common on the streets. Every friend from college days that I phoned seemed to be in some branch of the service and all were out of town. Many were with the Canadian Army in England, or in some far corner of the world. Others were in the Canadian Navy, either on North Sea patrol or on convoy duty in the Atlantic. Some had already become casualties. Those telephone calls brought home to me the reality of a war that during the summer had seemed remote and limited to news stories.

Jack and Bud met me in Buffalo, and we traveled together. The miles clicked off with regularity through Cleveland, past Detroit, around Chicago, then through Omaha and another night, then through Cheyenne, where we saw our first real Western cowboys, then Salt Lake City and into Reno, where we ate dinner, filled the tank with gas, paid our hotel bill for the night, and counted our money. We figured that we each had about twenty dollars left and that would get us to San Francisco the next day, so we decided to see the town. Jack pointed out a saloon called the Silver Dollar. He stated that all such establishments in Nevada housed a casino and suggested that we try our luck.

The building was large and crowded. Most of the customers were dressed in jeans, open shirts, and boots. We also learned that the house liked to live up to its name and pay off winners in silver dollars. As we wandered among the crap tables and slot machines, I realized that none of us knew a thing about casino gambling. Our total experience in gambling was limited to friendly crap and poker games with the boys. Jack and Bud sidled up to the crap tables where the betting for and against the dice thrower was furious and loud. Swept away by this frenzy, they were both broke in about ten minutes.

I decided that I would take a more sophisticated approach. For years, I had heard my father talk about the skills required to beat a roulette wheel. He considered himself an expert and much to my mother's disgust he always claimed that he had a system that could beat any honest wheel. I stood in an empty space at the side of the roulette table and watched all the westerners with their individual systems spread chips in every possible combination. I kept staring at the red and black compartments on the highly polished wheel. It seemed to me that the conservative approach would be to bet on one of these two colors. I picked red and laid down five dollars' worth of chips. The croupier picked up the little white ball, spun the wheel, and expertly threw the ball on the wheel's outer rim. The little ball tore madly around the rim as the wheel spun. As we watched with bated breath, the wheel finally slowed down, and the ball nestled in a red compartment. The croupier called out, "Twenty-seven, Red," and proceeded to sweep all the chips from the table except mine, which he doubled. After a slight delay, the croupier said, "Place your bets."

I had been considering my next move and had left my doubled chips on the red. A man standing next to me said, "Let it ride." I was five dollars ahead and decided why not. I kept saying, "Let it ride." After all my total investment was only five dollars. Red came up eleven times in a row, while I kept repeating, "Let it ride." At that point, the manager of the floor came over. He looked at the croupier, then me, then the crowd, and finally announced, "This wheel is closed." Dazed, I realized that I had won around $10,000 in a matter of minutes.

The following day we were up early and rolling down the pass through the mountains and onto the flat land bordering San Francisco. By noon, we were checking into the hotel. As I was the instant millionaire, I volunteered to foot the hotel bill, and we booked a suite. The next four days are a little hazy in my memory. During the day, we completed our travel arrangements to the Far East. I sold my Buick for more than it had cost me originally. I bought traveler's checks with my winnings. We ate in restaurants from Fisherman's Wharf to Nob Hill. Each evening we attempted to drink the Bay dry, figuring that this would be our last fling in the States for several months.

~

The ship that carried us to the Far East was gleaming white, with lounges, and stewards who waited on us. It was a typical cruise ship that took passengers from San Francisco to Honolulu at a speed of 22 knots.[21] Recently, it had been running the whole way across the Pacific, carrying material and military personnel to the Orient and bringing back civilians to the States who were becoming nervous about Japanese intentions.[22]

The passengers on our trip were representative of the American presence in the Orient. Our trio was part of a small group of U.S. Navy officers. A lieutenant commander, three lieutenants, and all the rest were lieutenant junior grades or ensigns like me. Our senior man was a good twenty years older than the rest of us. There were also a few junior officers from the Army and the Air Corps. The majority of the civilians were missionaries on their way to China. They gave us military types a wide berth, no doubt due to the fact that we spent a lot of time drinking in the lounges. Surprisingly, there was also a group of Japanese naval officers aboard who were returning to their homeland. How they got on the same ship with us and what they had been doing in the States, I never learned. They kept entirely to themselves with rigid discipline and spoke only to one another in Japanese.

Our cruise was a continuation of the easygoing days and nights we had experienced at Harvard. The weather was perfect, with bright sunny days spent lounging in deck chairs, swimming in the ship's pool, getting tanned, eating the cruise ship food, drinking at the bar, and watching dolphins race alongside the ship. The nights were equally brilliant, the sky glistening with stars. We spent most evenings drinking and playing poker. The ship stopped for a day in Honolulu to unload some of the passengers and cargo and to load on more of the same. The cruise soon continued its relaxed style, and I had the impression that everyone would have been quite content to let this trip continue forever. After Honolulu, the main excitement came when we crossed the equator and held a Neptune Party that involved half drowning the neophytes among us in the pool.[23] We kept heading west and south, and one night one of the lieutenants pointed out the Southern Cross constellation.

Shortly after, it was announced that there would be a Ping-Pong tournament for the passengers. For years, I had played Ping-Pong and considered myself pretty good. I breezed through my matches and won the semifinal without thinking too much about it. The night before the final, the lieutenant commander summoned me to a meeting in his cabin. When I arrived, I found the eight most senior of the naval officers assembled there. They were all Annapolis graduates and examined me with great care.

The lieutenant commander puffed on a cigar, turned to me, and asked, "Do you know who you will be playing tomorrow?" "Sure," I replied. "One of those Jap Navy guys." "Do you think you can beat him?" asked one of the others. "We have been watching him come along and he seems pretty good." "I don't know if I can," I said. "He is good; serves like a pro. He may beat the hell out of me." There was an uncomfortable silence. My ship-mates looked at one another and then they all looked at me. Our leader frowned. "Mister," he said. "You had better change your attitude and take this match seriously. And you had better damn well win tomorrow. Because if you don't, you sure as hell don't belong in this man's navy." I thought that was funny and said with a laugh, "You sound as if I'm going out there to fight a war." Our leader did not smile. He bellowed, "You're damned right you will be fighting a war; and you'd better win it." The leader looked me over again and said, "Go to your bunk and get your shut eye. And no drinking."

The match took place in the early afternoon in the lounge. All the Japanese lined up on one side of the room, and all the American forces were on the other side. None of the spectators spoke, not even in whispers. The points and the games seesawed back and forth. My opponent would win a point or two, then I would catch up and pull ahead. Finally, we were tied at twenty each, and after eight attempts, neither of us could win two points in a row to win the match. On the ninth attempt, my opponent went off the table and once more, it was my advantage. The Japanese took a deep breath and then let go with a terrific serve that seemed to shoot from his paddle like a bullet. It caught my end of the table with an inch to spare. In a reflex action, I swung my paddle, caught the ball, and whistled an equally hard shot back at him. It too caught the end of the table and flew at the Japanese officer. He took a wild stab at the ball, and it went sailing past my chest and into the wall behind me. The match was over.

My opponent looked straight ahead, his face frozen. He turned to the Japanese spectators, and they turned as one man and filed out of the room. He followed them. War whoops from the U.S. side of the room soon broke the silence. That night there was another session in our leader's cabin. It seemed that the entire navy contingent was pushing into the small space and each one was offering me a drink. "Mister," said our leader, "you did good, and you learned something today. We are better than those little yellow freaks.[24] We can beat them anytime, every time if we keep our guard up and stay prepared. None of you forget that." "What do you think his buddies are saying to him now?" I asked. "Oh, hell," the commander snorted. "They have probably handed him a hara-kiri knife and told him to use it."

We kept heading west and south. One afternoon the ship's captain announced that from then on we would travel at night with a blackened ship. Blackout curtains would be placed over every window and porthole; no lights of any kind, not even a cigarette on deck, would be permitted. The junior officers descended on the commanders asking if we were at war, and he calmly reassured us that we were not. He added, however, "They're sneaky bastards. If they thought sinking this ship would give them some advantage, they would do it." Then he smiled as he looked at the ocean. "Maybe the word will get back to Tokyo that this is Asiatic Fleet territory and we are waiting for them. We're not sitting on our asses out here like those people in California."[25] That night the sea breeze blew a little cooler. I remembered Dorothy's words, "There are a lot of Japanese around Shanghai," and we were headed straight for them.

~

Five of us stood at the bow of the ship, anxious for our first view of Manila Bay. It was not yet dawn. The only lights came from the sparkling phosphorescence on the ocean, the pinpoints made by thousands of stars above us, and a few tiny yellow lights from villages along the shore. As we stood in the darkness, I saw a red line emerging at sea level, straight ahead of us in the east, the first glimmer of the coming dawn. Slowly an enormous dark red disk rose from the sea, turning to orange as it rose higher, sending a glow into the sky, and then suddenly bursting into a bright fire that changed the eastern sky into brilliant yellow shot with streaks of orange and red.

A lieutenant standing beside me said we had entered the South Channel and were on our way into Manila Bay. To starboard, I saw a coastline with hills behind it. Then ahead off the port bow rose a long, low island, a grey blue against the brightening blue of the water. Our lieutenant pointed out that it was Corregidor. "Can it really cover the entire entrance of the bay with its artillery?" I asked. "The entrance to the bay is only twelve miles wide," he said. "The guns on Corregidor can cover both shorelines and out to sea a good ways. The bay is the entrance to central Luzon and Manila. That is why the guns of Corregidor are so important. Whoever controls that island controls the bay and the capital. Of course, in addition to Corregidor, the bay entrance has been mined since August to prevent any sneak entry by submarines."

"How far is it from the entrance to the port of Manila?" Jack asked. "It's approximately thirty miles. Manila Bay is shaped like a chemist's flask with the narrow twelve mile-wide neck, and then widening out to a good thirty miles at the eastern end." The lieutenant looked ahead and added, "There should be a fair amount of shipping in the bay as we get further in. A lot of military cargoes have been coming in over the past two or three months." After about an hour of travel in the bay, I noticed a point of land off the starboard bow and several vessels anchored near it. "What is that?" I asked. "You are looking at Sangley Point and the Cavite Navy Yard," he replied. "And straight ahead of us you can see Manila."[26]

We could see the buildings getting larger, and as we approached, we began to make out piers and a mixture of structures along the waterfront. At least a dozen freighters were lying at anchor. The ship slowly eased its way toward the longest pier that I could see and our guide announced, "We are berthing at Pier 7. That tall building at the end is the Marsman Building, where Admiral Hart now has his Flag."[27]

After being confined to the ship for three weeks, we were looking forward to stretching our legs on shore and exploring the exotic places in Manila. We had learned that Manila was a city that had been started by the Spanish but had been in American hands since the end of the nineteenth century. Our shipmates had told us that it was filled with friendly people, and entertainment was cheap. The Asiatic experts told us that the local beer, San Miguel, was the best in the world and that rum flowed like water. We also heard that the nightclubs and hotels were filled with beautiful and willing women.

Suddenly the ship's loudspeakers crackled with static, "Now hear this. Now hear this. Upon docking, all U.S. Naval personnel are to proceed ashore immediately and report to the personnel office in the Marsman Building. All U.S. Naval personnel report immediately to the personnel office in the Marsman Building." Bud and Jack looked at me, and we wondered what was so urgent. Maybe we would have a delay before going to Shanghai and get to visit Manila, or maybe they were going to transfer us to another ship for the last leg of our journey.

The entire group headed into the personnel office. Our trio presented our orders to a yeoman. He looked at them and then got up from his desk and disappeared into another office. After about ten minutes, he came back and told us to wait for instructions. We waited for another thirty minutes and then a lieutenant came through another door, called out our names, and asked us to follow him. He sat behind a desk, and I saw the assignment orders for each of us in front of him. "We cannot believe your orders," he said frowning. "No one is being sent to China. We are going to haul everyone out of China in the coming weeks—marines, navy, and civilians. We are certainly not sending in replacements right now. New orders are being typed for you on Admiral Hart's instructions." He then told us to report to the Cavite Navy Yard Supply Office to begin a new assignment.[28] "Well," Jack said as we walked out of the building, "I guess we had better learn to talk Filipino. It seems it might be awhile before we have to brush up on our Chinese." "Amen," said Bud.

2

The Philippines,
October–November 1941

At the Cavite Navy Yard, a sailor directed Jack, Bud, and me to the Supply Office. When we got there, different people examined our orders, starting with a yeoman and ending with a lieutenant. We got the impression that no one knew what to do with us. The lieutenant told us to find quarters and to contact the Supply Office each morning over the next few days.

As I stood there wondering what to do next, an ensign came up to me. He wore an open, short-sleeved, white shirt, with his rank and corps insignia on the collar, white shorts, white socks, and white shoes. "Hi," he said, "I'm Doug Carson, but people call me 'Red.' Welcome aboard."[1] I introduced myself, and we shook hands. "I hear that you need a place to bunk," he added. "We have a spare room at our house and you're welcome to it. Grab your gear, and we'll get you settled." I put my bag in his van, and we started walking. "Where was your last duty?" Red asked. "This is really my first. I just got out of Supply Corps School last month." I decided he had better know how I got to Cavite and explained how we had orders to Shanghai that were changed when we got here.

Red looked at me a little dumbfounded, and then he said, "You're telling me that those damn fools are sending people to China at a time like this. Who in hell is running things at the Bureau? Don't they know there could be a war any time? Even those people in Washington must know that Tommy Hart isn't kidding. They sure raised enough hell when he sent the dependents home last January.[2] Even MacArthur sent the wives home in May."[3] Red continued as we walked to explain how the Asiatic Fleet was the only thing between the China coast and Pearl Harbor. He stressed, "This is the front line, mister. The admiral has had the fleet on a war footing for weeks now. Most of the time the ships are at sea in full battle drill and they come back only for supplies and what repairs they need."[4]

Red suddenly stopped and looked at me. "Why were they sending you to Shanghai? What in hell were you supposed to be doing there?" "I have not the foggiest," I replied. "We asked for foreign duty, and that is what they gave us." He exclaimed, "You are damn lucky they pulled you off the ship in Manila." Red reminded me again of Dorothy's words about the number of Japanese around Shanghai. Maybe those stateside people really did not know what was going on in the Far East.

The yard seemed to be bustling with activity. There were many Filipino civilians

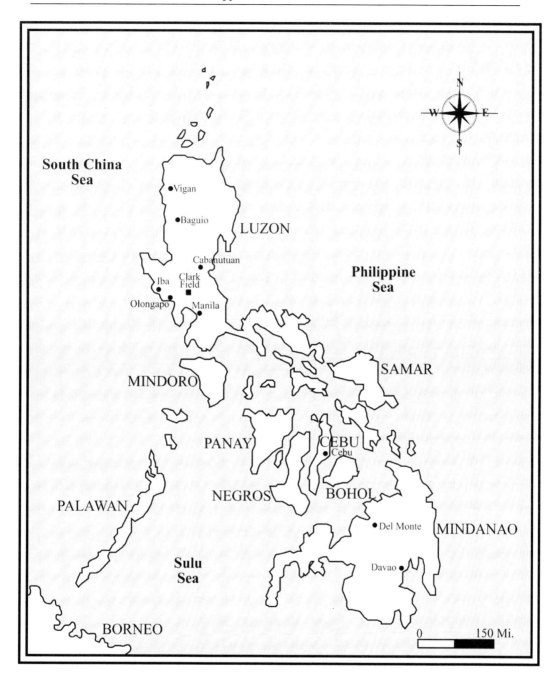

Philippine Islands, 1941–42.

walking the roadway, going in and out of buildings and working on equipment of different types on the wharves. Every now and then, I spotted a sailor in work dungarees and occasionally an officer. Red noticed my stares and said, "Cavite is the largest naval base west of Pearl Harbor.[5] We handle all the repairs, and store and issue all the supplies for the Asiatic Fleet. We can't berth too many vessels at one time. That is why you see those ships laying off out there." He pointed to the destroyers I had seen in the bay when we arrived. "We use the wharves mainly for repairs; most of the loading is done by lighters." I asked, "What are lighters?" "There is one," replied Red pointing to a squat black wooden vessel tied up alongside the wharf. It looked like a floating bathtub on a large scale.

"How many ships are in the Fleet?" I asked. "The flagship is a heavy cruiser, the *Houston*.[6] Until the admiral moved into the Marsman Building last June, she was his flagship.[7] She is fast and not too old—built back in the late 1920s. She carries 8-inch guns that can knock out anything up to fifteen miles away. She has 5-inch guns to take care of smaller stuff. She has 3-inch guns for anti-aircraft fire and a bunch of pom-poms for low flying planes. All the ships are brushing up on their air defenses because they figure that there will be attacks by planes, just like in Europe. The *Houston* is some ship," Red added proudly.

"Our other cruiser is the *Marblehead*.[8] She is a good ship, even if she is a little old. She carries 6-inch guns. The bulk of the fleet is made up of destroyers. They are all four pipers from the last war—that is they have four smokestacks.[9] I guess they are a little old too, but I bet they can out fight anything the Nips have out there." I interrupted with "One of the men on the ship coming out said that there is a big submarine fleet here." "There is," said Red. "We have seventeen now, and I hear that there are more on the way. All but a few will be the big, new Fleet type. See, over there. That is one of the fleet types." He pointed to a long black hull tied up to a wharf across the water from where we were standing. "Look," he pointed, "they are loading torpedoes for her now. Those fish carry a large warhead and can knock a big hole in anything the Nips have at sea."

"Of course we have a lot of support stuff, like tenders," he added. "What are they?" I asked and from Red's expression, I could see that he felt my education had not been too complete. "They are fairly large ships that look after the other ships. They hold supplies and have repair shops and even ice cream plants on some. They go along with the fleet and keep it self-sufficient when it is away from the yard. We have three for the submarines, one for the destroyers, and four for the seaplanes. We also have a submarine rescue ship, a fleet tug, and six minesweepers. We even have an aircraft carrier; at least she used to be an aircraft carrier before they cut her flight deck. She is the *Langley*, the first carrier the navy built.[10]

"The navy uses her now as a seaplane tender for the PBYs that make up Patrol Wing 10.[11] The admiral keeps them flying out over the China Sea watching for the Japanese. They have a hell of a range; I guess they can do a good job at bombing, but they are pretty slow." As we walked back to Red's van I said, "With that much firepower I would think the Japs would stay clear of these islands." "If they do get any ideas, we're ready for them," answered Red as he turned on the ignition. "As I said, Tommy Hart keeps the fleet out at sea, patrolling as much as possible. If things do start as an air war, the bay is in bombing range of Formosa and whether the Japs are any good at dropping bombs or not, the admiral isn't going to take chances."[12]

After I thought about that I asked, "If they think that the Japs might use bombers against Luzon, why don't they station carriers and fighters out here?" "Personally, I don't take this talk about air attacks from the Japs very seriously," said Red. "Everyone knows they have a lousy air force.[13] The only thing they hit in China was a gunboat and that was sheer luck. Anyway, the army has the job of defending the islands with fighter planes. They must have brought in over a hundred new fighters in the past couple of months, just into the fields on Luzon.[14] If any kind of an air war does start, we have a hell of an edge on the Nips out here. You should see Clark Field.[15] They have been bringing the big Flying Fortresses from the States, you know the B-17s, the most powerful bombers in the world.[16]

"If there is going to be any kind of an air war, it will be a damn short one. With the army and the navy both flying patrols over the China Sea, no troop transports would have a chance. The Japs would have to travel hundreds of miles to get down here. If they ever tried it, we would finish them off in two or three days. With the Air Corps and the navy here, these islands are impregnable."

~

That afternoon I decided to explore the officers' housing area, seeing that no one had given me anything else to do. I strolled along a curved street where all the houses were painted white and raised a full story from the ground on foundations of wooden timbers. I learned that this was to keep the monsoon rains from flooding the living quarters. Most of the houses had screened porches, and at our place, as well as at several others, under the overhang of the porch, the household staff was hard at work.[17] I saw two of them beating away at laundry. Another woman was ironing. Two more women were talking and laughing while they were cutting up some chickens; another woman was slicing a pile of vegetables. A couple of little children were squealing and chasing each other. The staff looked large enough to care for a hotel.[18] All the houses were screened, with open windows to catch the breeze blowing in from the water. The whole area was quiet and tranquil, and the only sounds seemed to be the low murmurs of the household staffs and the odd squeak of a child. There was the background whisper of palm trees as the wind stirred the fronds and an occasional tweet of a bird.

My footlocker arrived in the late afternoon. When I unpacked, I spread out my wrinkled dress blues. Tucked inside the footlocker was the officer's sword that each of us had to purchase in Boston. I hung up the dress blues, thinking it would be some time before I would be using a heavy uniform. I looked at my shiny sword with its engraved blade and fancy handle. The more I examined it, the more it struck me as being a ceremonial antique from those times long ago when sailors boarded enemy vessels waving cutlasses.

As I stared at it, I recalled my grandfather's two swords in Toronto. There was an engraved dress sword and a shorter working sword. They had steel scabbards of a dull grey color and strong hilts. My grandfather had been a pretty wild frontiersman, a scout for the Canadian Mounties, an Indian fighter in Alberta, and finally a scout for the Canadian force in the Boer War.[19] He had spent much of his life on a horse. As a child, I used to picture him in cavalry charges against the enemy, and I would unsheathe one of the swords to see if I could find any bloodstains on the blade. With all the present talk of 8-inch guns, heavy cruisers, torpedo warheads, and concentrated firepower, that dress sword of mine was definitely out of place.

Late that afternoon I met two more of my housemates. Both were regular navy and both were Supply Corps. Swede Jensen was the elder of the two. His appearance matched his name exactly; pale blond hair and light blue eyes, with the typical pinkish tanned skin that would peg him as a true Swede anywhere. His accent was neutral Californian. He was about six foot one, slender, and his walk spelled out his navy drilling. Swede was the only member of the household who was a lieutenant junior grade, or JG; and he was the only one who was married. His wife had gone back to the States when the dependents went home. The other member of our household that I met that day was another ensign, William "Mac" McGibony. He was almost as tall as Swede, sandy haired, and a native Georgian. Mac had a very dry sense of humor.[20] I learned that there were two more ensigns quartered in the house. Both were with the PBYs stationed at Sangley Point.[21] With the admiral insisting on constant air patrols of the coast, the PBY crews were spending all their daylight hours flying over the China Sea.

At dinner, I also met the man that ran the establishment. His name was Ah Tong. He had come to the Philippines from north China as a young boy. When I studied him, I figured he was about twenty-five years old but was surprised to learn that he was over forty. I asked Swede how many people worked there. Swede said, "I couldn't swear how many there are on a full-time basis, but when I counted I came up with fourteen, including the kids that were running errands." "That must cost a fortune." I said, wondering how far my navy pay would go to support my share of such an elaborate enterprise. Red laughed at my reaction. "You have to understand how things work out here," he said. "We each give Ah Tong twenty-five dollars a month. From this, he hires all the help and pays them. He then buys the food and anything else that is needed to keep the house running.[22] He keeps what is left. Ah Tong is a good manager. I figure by now he has a tidy sum tucked away in a sock for the day he will return to China."

As we talked, they asked me for the latest news from the States. I was not much help in bringing them up to date. The local radio in Manila, plus the U.S. coverage by a few short wave sets that were scattered around the area, seemed to keep everyone as well informed as if they had been living stateside. I found that a favorite pastime was to talk to friends all over the United States. By using one of the ham operators nearby and making hook-ups through hams in the States, Swede had talked to his wife in California the week before.

I did want to make one point to them, and I said, "The people back in the States do not feel the way you do out here. No one back there seems to think we are going to get into a war with Japan." "That figures," said Swede. "They figure the Japs are our bosom buddies, who spend all their time bowing, drinking tea, growing rice, fishing, and selling us junk toys. You get fed up with that crap after a while." I said, "I think some people feel that the Japs will continue to push in China. Many of the newspapers are saying that, but they do not seem to feel that they will move against the United States. We were told that they have been dealing with the State Department for some time now, to work out some sort of nonaggression pact. Why would they want to take on the United States in any kind of a fight?"

Swede continued, "The Japs have had a grand plan for years. They want to strengthen and increase their empire. They have no raw materials in Japan. That is why they bought scrap steel from us and got upset when we decided to cut them off.[23] Down in Malaya and the Dutch East Indies are the oil, tin, and rubber they must have to survive. Admiral Hart seems to feel that they will try to take them by force. That means they will have to protect their flank. It means that they will have to finally leave the mainland and go out into the China Sea and the Pacific. East of here, the Japs have a lot of islands they have held under mandate since 1920—the Marianas, the Carolines, and the Marshalls.[24] That is the real border of their territory. We are sitting between them and those islands, so we are definitely in their way." Mac added his opinion. "Hart has been trying to tell them back in the States how the Japs are going to leave the mainland of China and strike both south and east. No one in Washington seems to give a damn for his ideas. According to the stateside people, the Asiatic Fleet is full of warmongers. Even the people on MacArthur's staff seem to think so. A major was mouthing off at the Club the other night about how the Asiatic Fleet was looking for a fight with the Japs."[25]

Red spoke up. "I think the Nips are dumb enough to try attacking us. They have that guy Tojo up there, and he has the military in control of everything.[26] I don't think they realize what we have to clobber them with if they start anything. Between us and Hawaii, we have put together one of the strongest air and naval forces in the world. Look how the B-17s have been able to fly out here from the States. Look at the air power we have here and the back up in Hawaii.[27] We may not have a big fleet here, but we have enough to hold things until the big boys come steaming in from Pearl. If the Nips do try to start something against us, it will be over pretty quick. However, I think they may be stupid enough to try it."

Swede continued, "When the Japs are running around in China, they have things their own way.[28] The only troops they are facing are a bunch of bandits. To leave the mainland and come here is another story. If the Japs tried to invade these islands with a fleet of slow moving transports, the slaughter would be horrendous. With our bombers and fighters, our fleet of attack submarines, and the confined area in the China Sea between Luzon and Formosa, I am not sure any of the transports would make it."[29]

I felt sort of foolish asking a rhetorical question, but seeing we were discussing grand strategies I went ahead with it. "What would happen if by some way the Japs were able to make a landing on Luzon and actually start pushing toward Manila?" Swede replied with a laugh, "Our strategists have developed a plan for every contingency this past year. It is called Plan Orange; supposed to be secret, but everyone knows about it.[30] If by some freak chance the Japs were able to land on Luzon and were able to get in enough reinforcements so that they were able to move on Manila Bay, we would retreat to the Bataan Peninsula and hold off the Japs until the reinforcements came in from the States. By holding Bataan and Corregidor, the Japs could not use Manila Bay, and Manila would not be much use to them. I guess if it ever happened, the Air Corps would move to fields south of here, and we would still control the air." Mac added, "While the Army was holding a strong line across the top of Bataan, Pearl's Fleet would come in to help our fleet here and any Japs on the Islands would be caught in a pincer movement. There would be no way they could bring in reinforcements with our fleet and the Pacific Fleet out here, plus the Air Corps in a position to bomb anything that moved. We all figure that six weeks would be more than enough to kick the Japs out if they ever did make a landing."

I asked them, "What is on Bataan; is it fortified?" Swede replied, "I don't know what the army has down there. Of course, there is Corregidor at the end of Bataan, guarding the entrance to the bay. The navy is building a base at the bottom of Bataan at Mariveles, and we already have a base north of there at Olongapo." Red added, "The main thing that we have at Mariveles so far is food. I have been handling the storage. We are putting in balanced rations for at least fifteen hundred men for six months on a full calorie intake. The base will be self-sufficient when we are finished. I guess the army has done the same in Bataan under the Orange Plan."[31]

I had not considered a plan such as this when I asked another question. "You mean the navy would pull up stakes and go down into Bataan with the army; what navy people do you mean?" Mac replied, "People like us that are attached to the Yard and not to a

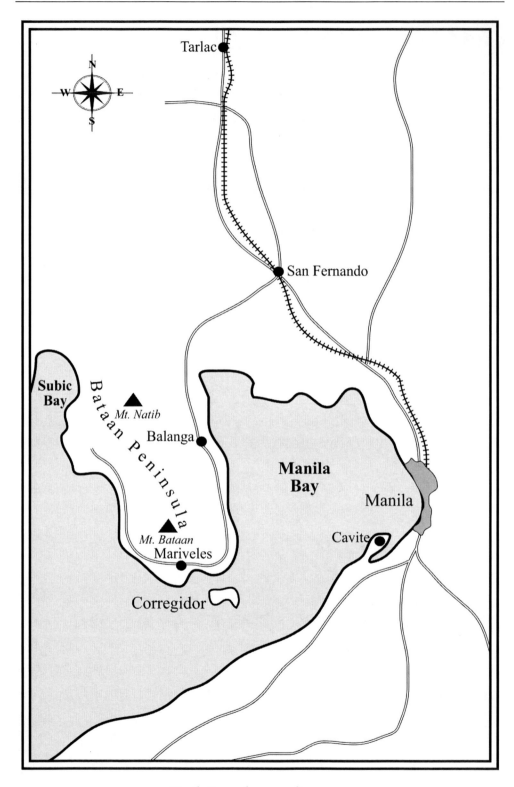

Manila Bay and surrounding areas.

ship. Of course, the top brass would go over to the Rock.[32] With the fleet out of here, there would not be too many of us left."

~

A few days later, with Red at the wheel of his van, and Mac and I as passengers, we were on the road from Manila to the town of San Fernando. Swede had told us that we would be unloading two more lighters filled with provisions at Mariveles. He asked me to go along to help, and I was glad to be useful.

This was my first view of the Philippine countryside. Between Manila and San Fernando, the road swung to the northwest, away from the bay, passing over a flat plain that was lush green, with rice growing as far as the eye could see. Every now and then, there was a lone house with a palm roof, and occasionally a row of trees. Two or three times, I saw Filipinos with wide straw hats leading water buffalo through the fields. The road was almost deserted, and I saw no barrios for miles, just fields of rice that stirred slightly in the breeze.

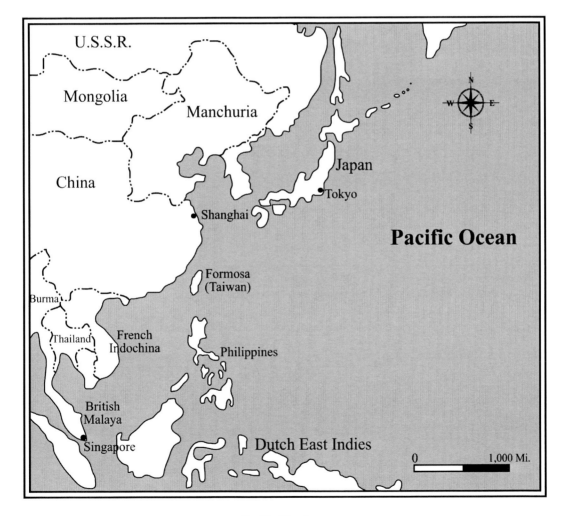

Pacific Theater

About thirty miles past Manila we came to a wide river, spanned by two modern steel bridges. Mac said, "This is the Calumpit River. It starts way up north, and dumps into Manila Bay about twenty-five miles south of this bridge." I looked at the movement of the water as we rattled over the bridge. "Why don't we follow the shoreline of the bay on our way west?" I asked. Mac replied, "The road has to swing north because between here and the bay the land is one big, impassable swamp. The east side of the river is also swamp country. Except for that swamp area, all of central Luzon is a flat, fertile plain;

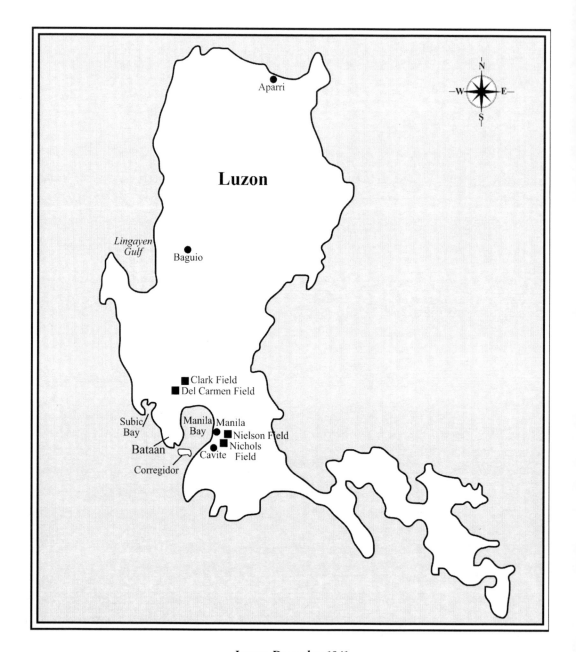

Luzon, December 1941.

you might call it the food basket of the island." Red added, "Both the west and east coasts of Luzon are protected by mountain ranges, and this plain is the only flat land from Manila north. The whole of northern Luzon to the very top is all mountainous country. I hear some is so remote and rugged it has not been properly explored."

In less than fifteen minutes, we were entering the town of San Fernando. It was the largest barrio I had seen since we left Manila. Small shops lined the main street. As we slowed through the center of town, I could hear radios blaring out songs in English and what I assumed was Tagalog. Behind the buildings on the street, I saw the steeple of a church. Despite the size of the town, dogs, chickens, and even some goats were intermingled with the people. Several of the adults, particularly the women, waved to us as we drove by, as did all the children.

At the center of town, we made an abrupt left turn and headed south. Mac said, "Now we are on Route 7. It goes southwest for twenty miles to a barrio called Layac. At that point, you can head west towards Subic Bay, Olongapo, and Lingayen Gulf, or you can turn left and go east to a little barrio called Hermosa. That is really the entrance to Bataan. The road from Layac through Hermosa is called Route 101. We call it the East Road and it follows the east coast of Bataan all the way to the tip at Mariveles. The Filipinos call it an improved highway, which means in the rainy season you have a fifty-fifty chance to get through without bogging down." I had imagined that Bataan, which I had only seen from the ship as we went up the bay, would have rugged mountains and heavy forest right up to the bay side. As we proceeded down Route 101, I was surprised to see that we were still in rice land; the ridges and heavy forest seemed to be at least five miles to the west. I asked Mac about this.

"Bataan is divided in the middle, all the way from the north to the southern tip, by a series of extinct volcanoes, with ridges cutting across it from east to west, and deep valleys and heavy jungle in between them. The heavy growth and rugged country extends all the way to the west coast of the peninsula and ends at the sea, with high cliffs and a coastline of wooded points with tidal bays in between them. The east coast that borders on the bay is completely different as the rugged high ground and the spine of the mountains stops about five miles to the west of this road, and leaves a plain of flat land, swamps, and rolling country between the jungle and the bay. It is rice country in most areas, not as flat as what we drove through from Manila to San Fernando, but still fertile."

As we sped down the so-called improved road, with the springs of the van bottoming out every now and then, I looked at the jungle and the dark mountains that rose up to the west all along our route. On our way, we passed through a few small barrios that always seemed to be located where a river flowed down from the western ridges into the bay. Each time we crossed one of these streams we did so on a rickety, wooden bridge and each time I wondered if it would collapse. I asked Mac if the road circled Bataan completely. He said, "When you get to the bottom, at Mariveles, this road stops. Then going north from there, up the west coast, is what they call the West Road. It goes about three quarters of the way to Subic Bay and then just quits. It isn't even good gravel; not much more than a dirt track."

I next asked, "What roads are there going east and west across Bataan?" "The mountains and the jungle valleys make road building across the peninsula a rough deal," he replied. "There is one coming up in a mile or so. It crosses the peninsula all the way to a barrio. They were able to construct it because between the Mariveles Mountains in the south and higher mountains in the north central section, there is a saddle across the

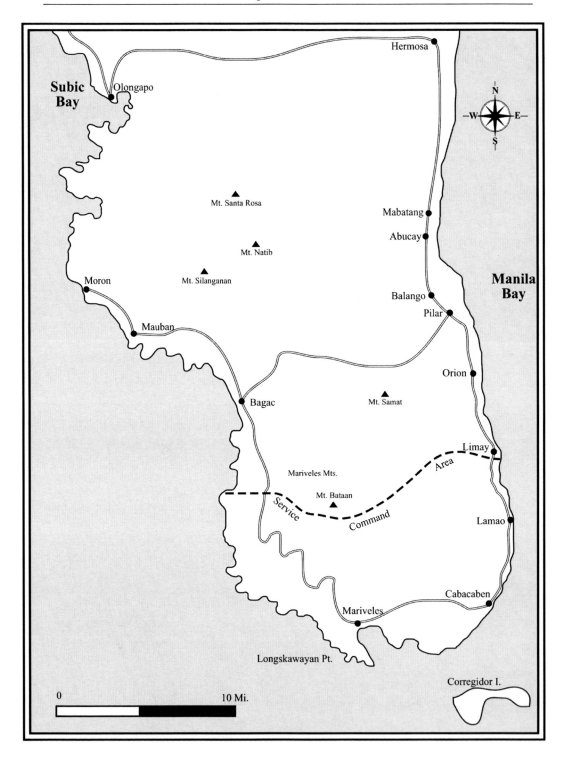

Bataan Peninsula.

peninsula that is fairly open to the west. The only other road that I know of across Bataan is the one we were on at the very top that goes to Subic Bay. There are supposed to be trails across the peninsula, but I have never talked to anyone who has travelled them."

After passing through the little barrio of Orion, Red pointed out three more villages: Limay, Lamao, and Cabcaben. I had to admit that Bataan was not an overpopulated area. Cabcaben was located on a high rolling plateau, and past it, we entered into a long curve toward the west. Red stopped the van in the middle of the curve and pointed Corregidor to the southeast. He said. "It lays off the coast only about two miles at this point." Mac added, "It's bigger than it looks from here; its three and a half miles long and the western end is a mile and a half wide."

I got out of the van and looked around. I was standing on the shoreline of a bay, shaped like a half moon. To the west, I saw a long line of low ridges, densely covered with tall trees and thick undergrowth. They extended out toward where I assumed Corregidor lay and formed the western anchor of the bay with a jagged point at the south end. Looking to the north, I saw a high mountain, dark, heavily forested and looking impenetrable. The palisades that we had come down formed the eastern end of the Mariveles basin, and I could make out the twists and bends of the road we had driven around as they appeared in open spots through the trees.

We got back in the van, and Red drove around a sharp curve and yelled out, "Here we go; down the chutes; hang on." I grabbed the door as the van swayed down a steep drop and looked out on a canyon of trees, dense scrub and rock, with the road appearing and disappearing below us in a series of hairpin bends. As we accelerated around the last sharp curve, we tore into a straight stretch like a slalom racer heading for the finish line. We swung around a low ridge right at the water's edge and as we passed the tip, I saw that it divided the Mariveles basin into two parts, east and west. Immediately after clearing this ridge, we rattled onto another rickety bridge with a fast flowing stream below it. Past this river, a cluster of wooden buildings stretched along the shoreline, and at the far end of these, two little piers jutted out into the bay. Red stopped the van about halfway between the stream and the buildings.

Red explained, "This area, west of that ridge we just went around, is the settled area of Mariveles. It all used to be a rice paddy. Two rivers coming down from Mount Mariveles border it, the Mariveles and the Pucot. Those buildings furthest to the west and the piers in front of them, are the Quarantine Station that the Filipinos used for ships coming into Manila Bay. The navy uses the rest of the buildings comprising our base for storage, offices, and a mess hall." As Red said this, he pointed out these various features. I looked over the flat ground behind the waterfront buildings and noticed that several trenches had been dug. Red said, "The navy has been working on the base for months."

Besides the buildings along the waterfront, I saw there were several other wooden huts scattered through the paddy between the West Road and the stream they called the Mariveles River. They were all spaced evenly on the field. It reminded me of an army camp I had seen in the States with barracks and mess halls. Everything was painted forest green. Red explained, "The smaller buildings are our storage warehouses. Some hold hardware and spare parts, but the bulk of them hold provisions. The whole area is supposed to be healthy and free of malaria, and the water in the rivers is supposed to be all right to drink, but I would not try it if I were you. It comes down from the mountain, and God knows what has been tramping and crapping in it before it gets here."

Red drove the van to the entrance of one of the small piers. Moored alongside were two lighters. Lounging around the dock entrance were about twenty Filipinos, some shirtless, some in ragged shirts and pants, most without shoes. A sailor in denims, puffing on a cigarette, was sitting behind the wheel of a truck, its tailgate down, parked next to the pier entrance. "I see our stevedores are here," said Mac to the sailor. "Yes sir, Mr. McGibony; they have been here for an hour," he replied. Red pointed to the green buildings spread across the paddy. "Those sheds are getting pretty full, especially with all the dry stores that have come out here lately. From now on, we are going to do things a little differently. I want dunnage put down around the edges of the paddy and under the trees making squares ten feet by ten, fifty feet from the next.[33] Then, we will take these cartons of canned goods and make a block on each square about six feet high. When we have finished a cube of provisions, we'll cover it with a tarp, just in case it rains. Keep the dunnage high enough so that the bottom cartons are well off the ground. There is plenty of room under the trees on the west side, so start there." Red walked on to the pier and called out, "O.K. let's start unloading these lighters."

When they cleared the tarpaulin off the first lighter, I saw that it was loaded with cartons of canned meats, fish, vegetables, and fruits. I started reading the stenciled lettering on the sides of each: navy stock number, manufacture number, contents—corned beef, stew, Vienna sausage, tomatoes, corn, spinach, green beans, wax beans, lima beans, potatoes, salmon, tuna, apples, peaches, pears, and fruit cocktail. Mac and I supervised the building of the wooden platforms in neat squares. The Filipinos formed a line along the dock from the open lighter to the bed of the truck. Cartons started filling the truck as the human conveyor slowly carried them along the dock. Red kept checking a list and arranging the cartons on the truck in a certain order. When he was satisfied with the load, the sailor drove it to one of our wooden squares where another group of Filipinos unloaded and placed the cartons as we directed them. Mac told me, "Each one of these squares will hold a balanced ration for one hundred men for a month. In addition, we have the dry stores, like coffee, sugar, and flour, and a lot of canned milk. No one in the navy is ever going to starve if we have to move to Mariveles. It just takes a little forward planning. I hope to God the army has done the same thing."

After about three hours, the assembly line started to slow down, and Red called for a break. Mac pointed to the Filipinos who were squatting around the pier. "See what I mean about calorie intake and a balanced diet? These fellows start out strong and work steady, but they tire a lot faster than Americans do. Their diet is mainly rice, so it is just about all starch. It fills their bellies, but it lacks the vitamins and minerals they should have. They augment it with some fish and chicken, and maybe some caribou, goat, or pig now and then, but mostly they eat rice. They just can't keep handling heavy loads the way an American can."

When the two lighters were empty, Red said, "Come with me. I want to show you something." He led me to one of the little green buildings and opened the padlock on the door. We walked inside. It was dark, with the only light coming from screened openings near the rafters that supported the roof. "This building has only dry stores in it; flour, sugar, coffee," he said pointing to the burlap sacks that were piled almost to the rafters, with narrow aisles to permit access. "I keep it well guarded." I figured this was another Asiatic Fleet wild tale as no guard was visible. "Look up at that rafter," said Red, pointing. I looked but did not see anything. Then when I looked closer I saw the rafter begin to change shape and develop a bulge. The bulge moved and slowly crept into the faint light. Then the rafter began to uncoil and wind and turned into spots of dark green and yellow, emerging as a snake about fifteen feet long, that slowly lowered itself onto the sacks below. "Meet Gladys, our pet python. She is tame as hell and eats all the rats that come in here. She has been here since we built this place."

~

By the final weekend of October, I finally considered myself an officer in the U.S. Navy. For almost a week, I had been learning the ropes and had discussed grand strategy in the Pacific with my professional peers. I had visited Mariveles and spent a day assisting in the carrying out of this strategy. In the Yard, I had supplied materials to real fighting ships and had met people who knew a lot about these ships. I had learned a little bit about the organization and layout of the Cavite Navy Yard and its relation to the town of Cavite and to Canacao, the twin of Cavite at the end of the Cavite peninsula. These two points formed the claw of a lobster when seen from the air. The entire peninsula was in the shape of a hook, jutting out into Manila Bay, curving back toward the shore to form a protective bay with the mainland. The two points at the end held another, smaller, quiet bay between them. The lower and smaller pincer of the lobster's claw held the town and the Yard. The larger and upper pincer held the cleaner and quieter facilities used by the navy, including the hospital, the radio station, the officers' housing, and a golf course.

To get into the Yard, we had to drive through the crowded, old, Spanish-walled town of Cavite itself. At the town's west entrance, the Spanish had erected bastions and a gate.

Cavite Peninsula, October 1941 (National Archives, photograph #80-G-178320).

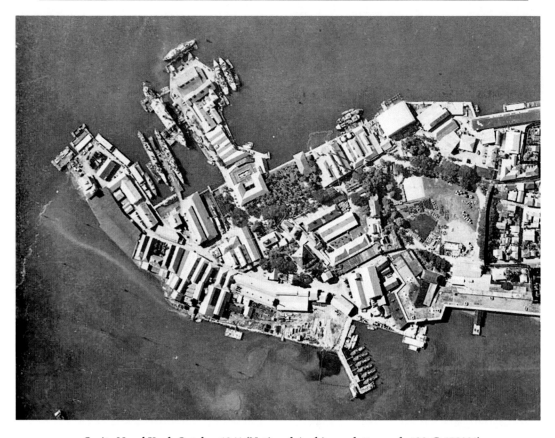

Cavite Naval Yard, October 1941 (National Archives, photograph #80-G-178321).

Once we crossed this barrier, we had a choice of four streets to travel the ten-block length of the town until we reached the fence and main gate of the Yard itself. Every small lot contained a structure, usually made of concrete with a stucco finish and a wooden or corrugated iron roof.

Some of the most imposing buildings were the churches. I counted five of them as I drove through the town. One of the most imposing, architecturally, was the San Pedro, located three short blocks from the Yard main gate. The widest street in the town was Calle de Isabel, halfway along the east to west length, dividing the settlement into two almost equal parts. It held some of the shops and eating establishments.

Residences made up the bulk of the town, many owned or rented by the Yard workers. Blended in between these were a variety of stores, bars, small workshops, and cottage industries. A lumberyard and an enlisted men's hotel were near the main gate of the Yard, and the navy still used an old Spanish iron foundry. The navy rented other buildings for the quartering of enlisted personnel. Once you emerged from the town and passed through the gate of the Yard, the architecture, the spaciousness, and the landscape changed. The buildings were larger and the streets appeared cleaner and better kept, though many retained the old Spanish style architecture. Immediately north of the main gate of the Yard was an open field, bordered by trees on three sides. Facing this on the east was the Fort San Felipe, with its masonry walls, that centuries before the Spanish engineers had designed to protect the entire installation from marauding invaders that might sail down Manila Bay.[34] Inside these walls, the Marine detachment had their barracks. The open field and the fort occupied the center portion of the Yard and wrapped around this large area were the warehouses, shops, offices and support facilities the navy required.

At the southeastern corner of the Cavite point, projecting into the bay, were the main wharves for the ships of the Asiatic Fleet. The two largest were built on solid ground and spaced about four hundred feet apart. The longest of these, the Machinist Wharf, was over six hundred feet in length. The outboard one, with the waters of the Manila Bay washing its side, was about two hundred feet shorter and much wider. In between these two was another wharf, known as the Central Wharf, and on each side of this, on the shore, were the ways for hauling vessels onto the land for dry dock work.

Along the waterfront facing the main bay, north and east of this wharf area, were shops and warehouses that held the bulk of the Yard supplies. Tied up in a line on the western, protected, side of this pier, I often saw the six PT boats that had come out to Cavite three weeks before I had arrived.[35] The center area of the Yard, between the wharves and the warehouses along the bay side, held the various offices of the Yard. Located here was the Commandacia, the nerve center of the operation. Along these streets were the Yard support facilities, such as the Dispensary, the Receiving Station, the powerhouse, and the Ammunition Depot. Near the West Gate and the Ship's Service Store was the Yard's swimming pool.

In addition to learning my way about the Yard during my indoctrination period, I had straightened out some personal affairs, so that I could be an established member of my new community. I converted my winnings from that night in Reno, combined with the dollars from the sale of the Buick, into a bank account with the National City Bank in Manila. When I looked at the deposit amount, I realized with some shock that this was the largest sum I had ever had in my life. I had equipped myself with an Asiatic Fleet uniform: white shorts, short-sleeved white shirt, and white buckskin shoes.

The bar and the lounges of the Army and Navy Club were crowded with late afternoon drinkers that last weekend in October.[36] Swede had told me that after seven p.m., the club went formal, and we had to wear ties. Mine was in my pocket. Conversation and laughter were loud, indicating that many of the members had arrived some time before and were ahead of us in the liquid refreshments. A man about my height with short-cropped hair joined our group. "What are the marines up to?" Red asked him. The Marine replied, "I hear they are pulling all the marines out of China next month. They should all be down here by the beginning of December." "All of them?" asked Mac. "Yeah, they will be sending two ships up to Shanghai to pull them out lock, stock, and barrel. Then another ship will follow to get the fellows from other areas. Looks like these islands are going to be defended by some real fighting men. A lot of those guys have almost twenty years in."[37] "Where are they going to be stationed?" I asked. "Olongapo from what I hear. The brass figures that if the Japs try anything it might be a landing around Subic, so they want some professionals there to take care of things."[38]

"Let's go over to the hotel," said Swede. I had learned that the hotel in those parts meant only one—the Manila Hotel. As we walked, Swede pointed to a long brown wall ahead to our right. "That's the Walled City," he said. "And beyond it, which you can't see, is Fort Santiago by the Pasig River. The river cuts Manila into two parts. The city itself is north of the river." We entered the Manila Hotel and headed for the bar. Swede said, "MacArthur lives in the penthouse and plans his grand strategies for handling the Japs from there. Probably spends more time here with his house boys than he does at headquarters." I wondered whether I would see the famous leader at the bar discussing those strategies. I did not.

At exactly seven, we put on our ties. For the first time, I had the opportunity to see what the Manila upper crust looked like when they dressed to go out on the town. Following the Spanish custom of eating dinner very late, there were not many around the lobby as of yet. I was staring at the women. They certainly did not look like the women I had seen around Cavite. Many were beautiful and looked Spanish. Their hair was glossy black, and most had it piled high on their head, often tied in a bun at the rear. Their dresses were long and made of light or lacy materials with large puffed shoulders. At least half of them were carrying lace shawls. Swede noticed my appreciative stares at the group. He said, "The Spanish have controlled the Philippines for centuries. A lot of those girls you are ogling are Mestizas. That means they have European blood in their family tree, mostly Spanish. Many of those mixtures are damn good looking."

Whether these girls were Spanish, Filipino, or a mixture that Swede called Mestizas, as a group they were about as good looking as I had seen in a long time. I was convinced that this had nothing to do with prolonged absence from female companionship. I determined to find out more about these girls. They all seemed to be happy. They were smiling and laughing, obviously enjoying themselves. I remembered reading a book once about the Tahitians. The writer had said they had a child-like innocence that was so appealing to Europeans. These girls seemed to have that same quality. There was nothing phony about how they looked and talked to one another. There was none of that attempt at sophistication that I had seen when a group of American career and ex-debutante types were hen pecking at a typical cocktail party. The more I looked at them the more I was intrigued by what they might offer an American so far from home.

My romantic notions quickly faded when Red nudged me. A tall, brown haired man had joined our group, and he was introduced to me as the gunnery officer from one of the four piper destroyers. Red told him that I was trying to get educated on the Asiatic Fleet units. He gave me a five-minute course on the destroyers. He said, "As you know we have thirteen of the four pipers in the fleet. They make up Destroyer Squadron 29, with a flagship and three divisions of four ships each. Red has probably told you they have been around out here for quite a while and have some age on them. The admiral says they are all old enough to vote. But they can do all the things that destroyers are supposed to do. They have a top speed of thirty-two knots and have four 4-inch deck guns, a 3-inch anti-aircraft gun, twelve torpedo tubes, submarine detection gear, and depth charges." He continued, "Compared to modern ships that is not much speed or firepower, but their main problems have to do with the amount of service they have had. It takes a lot of parts and maintenance to keep them battle ready."[39]

I still did not know exactly what destroyers did in a war, aside from pitching and rolling in rough seas and needing to be fixed a lot. So I asked, "What exactly do the destroyers do out here? I mean, what is their role in the fleet?" "Oh hell, our mission is real simple," he smiled. "All we have to do is protect convoys, stay out ahead of the cruisers, screen and hunt for them, and sink any enemy submarines that threaten our ships. If the Nips try any landings, all we have to do is tear in and get past their destroyers, cruisers, and maybe battle wagons, dodge their air cover, and then sink all their transports before they can land the men. Once we finish an attack, we then get the hell out of there before someone bigger takes a crack at us."

The conversation drifted into other matters, such as the latest scuttlebutt on the Japanese and Admiral Hart's plans for the fleet. Our destroyer man said that he had heard that there was a good chance the fleet would be sent south, maybe as far as Java, to join the British and Dutch.[40] This rumor was being discussed in every war room in the squadron, and he felt that it might be true. I had a couple more rum punches while I thought about the destroyers and the guts it took to stay on one. Mixed in with this military analysis, my mind kept flitting to the Filipino girls. I realized I was getting hungry and had a slight headache. Red said, "We can eat here, go back to the Club, or go into town." Mac spoke up. "Let's go to that place across the river that has those big prawns. We can hit Jai Alai later when the action is better."[41]

The taxi dropped us off near a restaurant that served prawns. The only thing I knew about prawns was that they were a sort of freshwater shrimp that were eaten in the bayous of Louisiana. The waiter brought us a huge platter and set it down in the middle of the table. On it, with steam rising from a sauce, were a pile of what looked like peeled lobster tails. Each was about seven inches long. "Now these are prawns," said Red. Steaming platters of vegetables and rice filled the empty spaces on the table. When a platter was empty, another of something different was put in its place. We ate for almost two hours, and I was stuffed. The spices and all the different tastes killed the sickly sweetness of the rum punches I had swallowed. Pots of tea washed down the food. Finally, the waiter brought bright purple ice cream for dessert. "That is made from the taro root," said Red. "The Filipinos love it, and I guess use it to color everything from ice cream to God knows what. And they eat it as a root. It is starchy."

With a full stomach, I decided it was time to attack Manila at night. We went to the Jai Alai Building. Mac asked if I had ever seen Jai Alai played, which I had not. In fact, I had never heard of it before. "It's sort of like squash." he said. "The ball is made of ivory. See how it works. They catch it in that wicker basket that is tied on to their arm. It's called a cesta. It gives them a longer arm and allows them to whip out the ball at a hell of a speed. The rules are like those in squash. They can hit the ball off the front wall, above and below the designated lines, rebound it off the back wall, or carom it off the sidewall onto the front wall. The idea is to make your opponent miss, or carom the ball into the net that you can see runs the whole way along the front side of the court. That net stops the ball from going out into the spectators and probably killing someone."

While I was watching my fourth game, someone poked my shoulder. I turned around and saw Bart Caulfield, a line officer I had gotten to know on the cruise ship coming out. He was handsome and apparently quite a success with the girls. He had become friendly with a good-looking passenger on our cruise from the States. We compared notes on what we each had been doing since arriving in Manila. "Remember that girl on the ship that was going to join her friend out here?" he asked casually. "How could I forget her; she was the only good looking girl on the ship." He continued, "She has a girlfriend here; another American; good looking. If you're interested I can get something going there for you. She is an interesting girl, if you know what I mean." We talked about this and decided that we would be able to make a foursome for one of the coming weekends.

Bart left to keep a date with his girlfriend, and I joined Swede, Mac, and Red at the bar. Red was talking seriously to a short, red-faced man. Red said to the rest of us. "He is with the P-40s." We asked him where he was based, and he told us up north, at Clark

Field. "They say the P-40 is a hot airplane," I said. "The best there is," said the pilot. "The Japs don't have anything that can touch it. We can outgun them and outfly them."[42] Red added, "He is with a pursuit squadron and their job is to protect the bombers and knock out the Nip fighters." I asked, "Are we building up the fighter squadrons?" "You can bet your ass we are," he replied. "We got a batch of P-40s in September, more early this month, and expect another group to arrive soon.[43] By December," he lowered his voice, "we will have almost 200 fighters, many equipped with P-40s."[44]

Swede said, "I hear some of the big bombers flew in from the States last month, the Flying Fortress B-17s." "That's what we will be nursing," said the pilot. "They are based at Clark too. Those that flew in from the States joined the 19th Heavy Bombardment Group. More B-17s are due to arrive in a couple of days.[45] That will give us thirty-five of the best heavies. In addition, we have some B-18s, B-10s, and A-27 bombers.[46] They are going to fly in more Flying Fortresses over the coming months. They will be protecting the hell out of these islands."

"Do they have enough long runways to handle planes that big?" I asked. "Not now," he said. "Only Clark can handle them now. But they are going to improve Nichols and I understand that they are going like hell on Del Monte down in Mindanao so it will be able to handle the B-17s before long." He paused. "I think it would be smart to base all the heavy bombers down at Del Monte and let us P-40 guys take care of anything the Japs might try to send in from the north of here. I guarantee they would never make it past the edges of Luzon."[47]

We left Jai Alai and went back to the Army and Navy Club. Swede started talking to a tall blonde man who had one of those Hollywood-looks about him. When he talked, he never stopped smiling, but it came across as arrogant. For some reason, I took an instant dislike to him. Mac whispered to me, "That two striper is with the Office Naval Intelligence and claims to be the Fleet's leading expert on Japan.[48] He also claims to speak fluent Japanese after spending eighteen months there."

The Japanese expert turned his smile on us. "How are the Supply Corps troops tonight?" We responded that we were doing all right, and asked, "What's the latest dope on the slant eyes?" He replied, "We are up on every move they make. I was briefing the staff again yesterday." He said this with all the pontification of a senator telling reporters how he had just advised President Roosevelt. "We all know that they may head south one of these days. The French have given them Indochina as a base. We have made life miserable for the Japanese by stopping shipments of scrap and petroleum. They are hurting, so they will want the rubber and tin and other things from Malaya. They also want oil from Java and Sumatra. However, to get these materials, they will have to make deals with the British. There is no way they can get into the Dutch islands with Singapore in the way.

"Admiral Hart keeps saying they are going to hit the Philippines, no sir. Their top team is in Washington right now setting up a peace treaty with us. We do not want a war with the Japanese. The Russians are the real enemy they face. After they have consolidated their position in China and put all those warlord bandits where they belong, they may force the Russians to be sensible. Before that though, they have to do a lot of consolidating in China. They are spread from Manchuria and Korea to Indochina. They have supposedly equipped fifty-one divisions and are trying to build a military of six million. With all those Chinese, they will need them. As I say, they may go south to Malaya to get the things they need. They may do it by invasion through Indochina if the Brits will not play ball. This talk of them wanting to invade the Philippines and head out into the Pacific just does not make sense. They need our friendship. Washington will give it to them. The United States is a peace-loving nation. The Japanese are good people when you really get to know them."

I was getting fed up with this Japanese expert who claimed to have all the answers. My headache seemed to have returned while he talked. I said, probably too aggressively, "And what if it doesn't work that way? What if they hit us and hit the British as well and consolidate a little further out into the Pacific than you're talking about?" The smile stayed, but he gave me a rather pitying look. "My young Supply Corps friend, you just do not know how the Japanese mind works. The Japanese do everything very carefully. They plan for months, even years before they do something. They are extremely thorough. This means for us in the intelligence services that there are always leaks of information that we can rely on. We in ONI do not even have a whisper to indicate that the Japanese are planning any unfriendly action toward the United States. Despite all our admiral's preparations, I am certain that he must feel the same way, and, my young friend, we must warn all of you recent arrivals to the Asiatic Station against being warmongers. We are at peace with the Japanese. We intend to stay that way."[49]

I did not say anything more. I was convinced he was a jerk.

3

On the Eve of War

The first two weeks of November were hectic. I decided early in the month that I needed to get in shape. I had been smoking too much and probably not doing one thing to improve my physical condition. I got into the habit of taking an early morning swim in the pool. I had a companion in a tall lieutenant, who apparently did this every day of his life. He would do laps in the pool with a slow and easy crawl for as long as an hour at a stretch. I figured he must do a mile or better every day. I found out his name was Carl Faires, and he was from Atlanta. He was a graduate of Annapolis and the Disbursing Officer for the Yard. He paid all the troops and all the Yard workers.

Getting in better shape helped as the pace of work accelerated as the month progressed. Admiral Hart wanted his surface ships to take on the Japanese Navy, not defend themselves against attacks by high-level bombers that their guns could not reach. Since the Japanese could only reach Luzon and the Manila Bay area from their bases on Formosa, Admiral Hart shifted many of his heavier surface ships to the Viscayan group of islands in the Central Philippines which were out of the range of the Japanese bombers.[1] As a first step in his rearranging of the fleet, the heavier surface vessels sailed for the Viscayas during the first week of November. This meant that we had to move material quickly to get them loaded with everything that they needed. The old *Marblehead* and most of the destroyers left about the same time.[2]

It soon became obvious that we would be relying on our submarines as our principal weapon around the shores of Luzon. Our fleet of seventeen increased rapidly as around a dozen new ones arrived.[3] This meant a lot more supply movement and torpedo loading. An ensign submariner had lunch with me toward the end of the month. He said we now had a real wolf pack, equal to what the Nazis were using in the Atlantic.[4] This many submarines patrolling off Luzon could make a coordinated attack that would demolish any slow convoys of transports. The German record of sinking convoys over the vast distances of the North Atlantic would be small potatoes in the relatively narrow waters between Formosa and Luzon. He felt it would be like shooting fish in a barrel with half the transports sunk in a matter of hours. When that happens, any sensible invading commander would call off the whole idea and try his best to get back to where he started.

As we talked I asked him why it looked like we had two different sizes of submarines. He explained that we had over twenty modern fleet submarines that were almost three hundred feet long. He added that the submarines could travel at twenty knots on the surface and over ten knots submerged, and could dive to over two hundred and fifty feet.

He further described how they each had eight torpedo tubes and used the new Mark-14 torpedoes. I was impressed when he added that they had a cruising range of over twelve thousand miles.[5]

The other six boats in the fleet were not in the same league. They were much smaller and very cramped for space. They were hot, had poor ventilation, and stank all the time. When they were on patrol and surfaced at night, the men would stand under an open hatch or the tower and take turns breathing fresh air. My friend called these smaller vessels "S" Boats. He said the navy called them "Pig" Boats. They were all old by submarine standards. If everything were working right, they could do fourteen knots on the surface and way under ten knots when they were submerged. He told me that they were armed differently from the big Fleet boats with only four torpedo tubes.[6]

We then discussed the amount of maintenance the submarines required and I learned they were in the same fix as the destroyers. It was obvious that no fighting ship was able to keep going without something needing to be repaired, and maintenance was a continual requirement. However, the ensign continued, "the submarine fleet is pretty self-sufficient out here. They have three tenders.[7] These support ships have just about anything we need to keep going, including machine shops and a bunch of master machinists that can make anything. They carry all our spare parts, our torpedoes, food, clothing, and whatever else we might need. That is why the tenders follow us from base to base. It makes us mobile as hell in all these islands out here. If we can continue to get torpedoes and diesel oil, we could set up base just about anywhere in the Western Pacific."

That raised a thought. Torpedoes did not work like shells fired by guns. I knew that they had their own propulsion system, were propeller driven, could be set to run at different depths, and had some sort of fuse setting so that they would not detonate until they hit a solid object or had gone a controlled distance. "The German U Boats have pretty effective torpedoes from the way they hit the North Atlantic convoys. Do we use the same sort as they do?" I asked. "I have never seen one of the German torpedoes," he replied, "but I am sure we have much better ones. I mean the torpedoes are the name of the game. It doesn't do any good to have great boats and the best crews unless you have the best there is in torpedoes. The torpedo is your basic attack weapon. It is what you sink ships with. If you don't have the best, you might as well not go hunting."

~

When Red had first told me about General MacArthur's grand strategy for defending the islands against Japanese attack, he had mentioned the general's ideas of using naval forces. The main weapon was apparently to be squadrons of motor torpedo boats that would sink the transports attempting to land troops. They would fire their torpedoes in droves and then the Air Corps would finish off what was left. The idea went back to the days when he was the military adviser to the islands.[8] To start things rolling in this direction, the Filipinos placed an order with the British for some of these boats. By the time September 1939 came around, only two had been delivered. From then on exports of anything by England to the Philippines had a low priority since it was at war with Germany.

When the Filipinos could no longer import whole boats to add to the two they had received, they tried building them locally and importing engines to drive them. In three years, they had managed to construct one hull. I asked Red how the general's naval strategy had developed. It sounded plain crazy. He told me that the general had very fixed ideas about a navy. It should be used only for defense and was not an attack weapon. As the Filipinos were not mad at anybody and did not want to embark on conquering other countries, a defensive navy made up of PT boats should do the trick. Besides, if you went for something bigger in the ship line, it would cost a hell of a lot more money than the Filipinos had available.

From what I had heard the past few weeks about submarines and cruisers, and the tactics of attacking and defending a coast line, the idea of defending the islands from a seaborne invasion with little speed boats seemed pretty far out to me. Those transports would have guns on them, and their escorts would have really big guns. Speedboats were one type of vessel with which I had some experience. Since I was fifteen years old, I had raced motor boats. I had learned that, at top speed, any boat I had driven kept you busy just staying afloat on a quiet lake or a big river while you were avoiding the other boats' wakes. To take a speed boat out on the open sea and try and aim a torpedo at a ship defended by machine guns, seemed to be suicidal.

The more I thought about it, the more I wanted to find out about our six PT boats. I figured that they must have something going for them I had not considered. The crew of the boats hung around off Sangley Point, and I started to hang around them in my spare time to see what I could learn about the boats, their crews, and the tactics they used. The six launches were part of Motor Torpedo Boat Squadron Three.[9] Each was seventy feet long, and their hulls were constructed of reinforced mahogany. They had three large Packard engines, and these ran on 100-octane aviation type gasoline. In addition, they carried four torpedoes and their launchers, two to a side, on the deck. Along with these, they had two twin .50 caliber machine guns, one twin to a side, and the ammunition to keep them firing. Added to all this metal was the weight of an average crew of nine men.

When you design a high speed racing boat, you normally try to keep the weight well down in the hull. The more that is topside, the more the boat rides unsteadily. All those guns and torpedoes on deck made a lot of weight up in the air. Speedboats are designed to get up out of the water and stay there. When you watch a race, you get the impression that the fast boats are merely skimming the water, in order to avoid hull drag. Apparently, these PT boats did not operate quite that way, because they were driven by men standing up on a bridge. No one in their right mind should be standing up when going forty to fifty knots an hour over choppy water. On a PT boat, everyone seemed to be standing up to fire torpedoes, man the machine guns, steer the boat, or give out orders.

Another point that bothered me about these PT boats as a war weapon was that those big Packard marines would require a lot of maintenance. Racing boat engines are torn down after a race of a few minutes. Their "down time" is horrendous. A PT boat would have to go for hours, maybe days, awaiting that sort of engine maintenance. With all these thoughts in my mind, I finally talked my way into a ride on one of these new weapons. The Executive Officer of MTB Squadron Three was Lieutenant Bob Kelly, and he was the one who took me for my ride.[10]

The trip was not very long as Kelly only had to deliver a package to Corregidor. Standing on the bridge, we took off from the little dock and headed out into Manila Bay. The pounding on my legs when he opened up the throttles was even heavier than I had anticipated, and I had to hang on tight. This was a smooth water day on the bay. I asked Kelly what the fuel capacity was and he told me the tanks held two thousand gallons. I did some mental arithmetic on how fast those three Packards would gulp down aviation gas at a speed of around forty knots, with a full weight load on the boat, and figured they would be lucky to do three hundred miles on a fuel load. When I wanted to know if my mathematics were correct, Kelly politely let me know that the top speed and range of the boats was classified information. Secondly, it would be hard for him to think of a cruise around Luzon extending to three hundred miles. Thirdly, the design of the hull and the engines was a little bit more efficient than this kid who raced civilian boats was giving them credit. All of which goes to show that it may be hard to translate civilian experience into a military setting.

~

When we had nothing better to do, the talk would often get around to an analysis of the Japanese and all their weak points. The general opinion was that the Japs had several physical weaknesses. We assumed they all wore eyeglasses, had poor eyesight, and could not see at night; therefore, this automatically made them poor pilots and inferior marksmen. We further believed that they lacked the stamina that was required of all fighting men. Mac figured they were like our stevedores in Mariveles. If you subsisted on a diet of rice and a few pieces of fish, you would tire out in a few hours under heavy exertion.[11]

We talked about the clothes that their troops wore. We had seen magazine pictures of them in China: baggy shirts and pants, and floppy helmets. The pictures showed them in cloth helmets with flaps coming down around their ears. We knew that they were short, bandy-legged people, with buckteeth. The anthropological experts among us stated categorically that this led to a lack of coordination. I thought about a Japanese gymnastic team I had seen once. They sure were coordinated. Though I did not understand our experts' reasoning, I went along with it. The exceptions who were gymnasts probably were too special to be in the military.

From this analysis of their physical weaknesses, the discussion usually turned to their lousy military equipment. The naval experts said their battleships and cruisers were top heavy, to the point of being dangerously unseaworthy. Their submarines were too small and lightly built. Their torpedoes would not run true. Their guns all lacked fire control, and the ammunition was usually defective. The air force jockeys at the Army and Navy Club tore apart their planes, from fighters to bombers. Their fighters would not maneuver like ours, and they were light, underpowered, had inadequate armament, and possessed poor firepower. I gathered that a P-40 could be flying in circles around a Japanese fighter. When it came to discussing their bombers, the flyboys really demolished them from wing to tail. The Japanese did not have the carrying capacity, the speed, or the defensive firepower that even our older types had. Compared to our B-17s they were back in the Dark Ages. Most important, they had nothing like our bombsight, and anyone knew that if you could not aim accurately you could not hit the target. If the Japs tried to bomb you from high altitudes, the safest place to sit would be the center of the target. No one knew much about their torpedo planes, or if they had any. In China, they had used dive-bombers, but the rumor was that the wings were so weak that a lot crashed after they broke off.[12]

Our confidence began to wane late in November as we heard more stories about the lack of preparedness of our army and Filipino forces. We were sitting around the bar of the Army and Navy Club in the late afternoon, and as usual, we were discussing the strategy of defensive and offensive war. Each time I went to the club in November the number of army officers in uniform seemed to increase. I knew very little about the U.S. Army in general, and this one out here in particular, but it seemed that it was approaching the Japanese threat quite differently from the way the navy was going.

Tommy Hart had his show on the road, organized, and was practically at war with the Japanese already. The army seemed to be fudging around, talking about training a defense force.[13] There seemed to be a lot of talk but little action. We felt that this was due to MacArthur and his staff. To us navy officers, the army leader was a name only, a shadowy figure. Further, we junior officers had fixed ideas about General MacArthur that we had inherited from the older members of the Asiatic Fleet. We thought that he was tied too closely with President Manuel Quezon and the local power structure in Manila.[14] None of us had ever seen MacArthur in person, but we knew positively that he walked around with a lot of gold braid and entertained the Filipino wheels in the luxury of his penthouse atop the Manila Hotel. We felt that generals should be closer to the troops, not hidden from our view like some oriental potentate.

There was another thing about the army setup out here that puzzled me personally. I did not understand how the American Army fit with the Filipino Army officers and men. I had learned a few things, but not much, in the past few weeks. I knew that the Filipinos had initiated the draft and had inducted people into a reserve force. I had seen a certain amount of ROTC-type drilling and marching on the university campus. I had also been told that the Filipinos had some professional soldiers, the Philippine Scouts, who were supposed to be pretty good men.

I could not figure out, however, where the Filipino officers who were leading these locals were. They were not flocking into the Army and Navy Club. Everyone I saw there seemed to be an American. I figured they must have their own club. Red had told me that when the U.S. Army Forces in the Far East were formed a few months back, the Filipino Army was put under the U.S. Army.[15] The U.S. Army now paid, fed, and equipped all their regulars and draftees.

However, this apparently presented a problem, as the Filipinos had only a handful of officers to train these troops. They were trying to build an officer group as quickly as possible. In the meantime, they were using American officers to handle this training and to lead units. I was positive that this was bum dope, and that up in the hills, in camps I had not seen, were thousands of white American soldiers, veterans from the States, with regular army training and experience. They were what we would use to clobber any Japanese troops if they ever succeeded in landing on the islands. The army was obviously keeping quiet about how many of these men there were, so the Japs would get the surprise they deserved. It had to be that way.

As we sat in the lounge of the Army and Navy Club, a rangy first lieutenant with infantry insignia on his collar slumped into a chair next to me. He looked beat. He finished the drink he was holding in four swallows. He turned to Red and said, "Hi Red, how goes the navy?" Red introduced him to our group as Joe Williams.[16] "Joe is training the Filipinos up north of here. How is it going?" After taking another drink, he exclaimed, "To put it in one word—lousy. It's frigging hell." He doubted that they could ever train the Filipinos. He finished with an ominous statement, "Sometimes I think Custer was better equipped when he headed out to the Little Big Horn and you know how he got his ass whipped."[17] It did not sound like we would get much help from the draftees for a while.[18]

On the way back to Sangley Point that night I said, "Thank God we have six months or longer to try and equip and train those draftees a bit. At least we have the Air Corps and the submarines to knock out any landings. The Japs have to get ashore before those army people have to do their thing." None of my navy peers said anything to that, but everyone was looking a bit pensive. It was not a festive taxi ride.

～

By Thanksgiving, the entire house was in a state of excitement and anticipation, not in expectation of turkey and cranberry sauce, but because the big event of the year was about to take place: the annual Army-Navy game in Philadelphia. We all were to go to the Army and Navy Club and listen to the game by short wave radio. Loudspeakers had been set up throughout the club and on the grounds, and the American armed forces would be there en masse. Jack, Bud and I, having come from universities and colleges other than Annapolis and West Point, did not have the enthusiasm for the rivalry that seems to stay with the military academy graduates for years. To us this was just another football game. To our professional peers, it was a duel to the death between the two services.

When I realized that we would hear the game in Manila between two and five in the morning, due to the time differential with the eastern United States, I was convinced that all these graduates of the two academies had to be crazy. No one, not even the most rabid fan, listens to a football game at such an ungodly hour. However, by midnight of game day, we were sitting in the mobbed bar of the club, ready for the big game. The whole place was decorated as if expecting a college homecoming: paper lanterns, mascots, and signs of GO ARMY and GO NAVY. A play-by-play scoreboard had been set up, with the yards of the field marked on it and a moveable disc representing the ball in order to keep track of the game. With coverage such as this, it was like we were all sitting on the fifty yard line.[19]

By three in the morning, the game was fully underway and everyone was shouting encouragement whenever their team made yardage. The spirit was as strong as if we had been at the actual game, instead of listening to an announcer who was thirteen thousand miles away. From the announcer's description, the field was wet with November rain. Players charging through the line would slip and be stopped for a loss; or the defense would leave a hole and the offense would streak through for an eight-yard gain. Passes would be either successfully completed or dropped from fumbling hands or a hard hit. Every move on the field brought shouts or groans from the rabid listeners.

Army was leading by halftime and its rooters were going wild, while the navy cheering section was looking a bit glum. As the fourth quarter approached, I realized I was having a hard time staying awake. I kept getting up from my chair on the lawn and walking around the crowd of listeners whose enthusiasm had not fallen off since the game started, all of them still cheering wildly when their team rushed or passed for a few yards, or groaning almost as loudly when their players were set back. It dawned on me that at previous games I had been able to sip bourbon sitting in a freezing stadium and stay wide-awake. However, to do this on a hot night in Manila was not the same.

I felt someone shaking my shoulder and then I heard a lot of people yelling excitedly. I had fallen asleep on the lawn. I opened my eyes and saw Jack standing over me. "What happened?" I asked. Jack replied, "Come on; get up. We're going home and hit the sack." "Who won?" "Navy," he replied. "Did you ever doubt it?"[20]

～

One morning I was surprised to see the *Houston* moored at the Machinist Wharf. I had figured she would be down with the other ships in the southern islands. She was every bit as impressive and formidable as Red had said. Her length exceeded anything I had imagined. The eight-inch guns protruding from her turrets looked enormous. The high bridge and the masts, bristling with radio gear and other wires and gadgets, towered above the Yard buildings. Some of the crew told me the masts would be even more impressive after they installed her new radar gear.

After she docked, the Filipino Yard workers and the sailors swarmed over her like bees around a hive. The work went on day and night. They placed big floodlights along the wharf to turn the night into day. After the first few hours, her decks were a confused clutter of snaking electric cables, hoists, parts, plates of heavy steel, people, and welding machines. Other long cables snaked their way up her mainmast. Scaffolding draped over her sides and held sailors who were welding bolts around all her portholes, while steel battle plates were cut to attach to these bolts. They were determined to prevent the slightest leak of light escaping from her innards while she patrolled dark waters looking for Japs.

Arc welding and cutting of steel plate seemed to go on continuously. The blue and white flame of the welding torches, the sputter of melting steel, and the showers of sparks heading toward the deck made the whole area look like a Fourth of July sparkler demonstration. Steel splinter shields surrounded her exposed five-inch anti-aircraft guns to protect the gunners from fighter planes. The workers took off her old three-inch anti-aircraft guns and replaced them with rapid firing 1.1 pom-poms to further ward off any low-level plane attacks.[21] They said her searchlights were old and not powerful enough, so they removed them and placed them on the wharf. New, modern ones were due in from the States any day. The machine shop seemed to be working around the clock, making or changing metal assemblies.

While all this repair work was occurring, I noticed that many of her crew were constantly drilling on battle station readiness. One fellow said they had the time down to one of the fastest in the entire navy. Their new skipper was tough, the sailor noted, and when an alert occurred, he wanted her to be the most efficient cruiser available. Everything seemed to be a race against time. She was the heavyweight of the Asiatic Fleet, and the admiral wanted her to be on the best war footing possible, as fast as possible, so she could get down south with the destroyers and show the Japs we were not fooling around.

Suddenly on December 1, I found that she had left the wharf. They said she had gotten underway in thirty minutes, which set some sort of a record. Apparently, the radar everyone had been waiting for had not arrived, so she left without it. Also, her new, fancy searchlights had not arrived, so they hauled the old ones off the wharf and reinstalled them. They said that in the final few hours there was a mad scramble to finish the work. By eleven that morning, she was heading for Corregidor.[22]

When the *Houston* left for the Viscayas, it seemed to me that we had a drastically changed fleet around Manila Bay. Two of the submarines and destroyers were undergoing repairs. Only three of the destroyers were left to patrol the Bay. Red pointed out to me that we still had five minesweepers on duty, but these did not strike me as the type of fighting ships we could throw against Japanese cruisers if they attacked our island.

We had our submarine fleet, and it looked as though that was our main defense for the bay and Luzon. As the ensign had said, this was a truly formidable force with their powerful warheads on all those torpedoes. The trouble with submarines is that they stay beneath the surface most of the time when they are patrolling. They are not visible, so you do not know if they are out there, fending off the invaders. We had our PT boats as our most visible attack vessels. They were constantly tuning their engines and making runs over to Corregidor or Manila. We also had our PBYs, so we did have our own air force. One of the squadrons was still at Sangley Point and the other was up at Olongapo.

~

One morning I looked at the calendar, and I realized that I had been in the Philippines seven weeks. It was already December 5 and in three more weeks, less one day, it would be Christmas. I wondered how they celebrated Christmas out here in the tropics. Did they decorate palm trees with coconuts, bananas, and painted mangoes? This would be the first Christmas that I would spend without snow on the ground.

We were joined by an ensign from the Yard and two JGs from the destroyers. Our group was now nine, and we were all hungry. Red gathered us together and said, "Let's hit the road for Chinatown and Wong's place. I don't know about you guys, but all week I have been tasting that mandarin dinner he is putting on for us." When the taxis dropped us off at the entrance to a street that was crowded with people, I felt that Chinatown looked like the other sections of the old part of Manila I had seen, but with the buildings squeezed more tightly together. Virtually every structure had dark green awnings stretched from the top of the first floor out to the road. The whole district was crowded with people walking, pushing carts, riding bicycles that had side carts fastened to them, and driving horses that were pulling little red carriages. I did not see any automobiles. The narrow streets were used for walking as much as were the sidewalks. In fact, as we moved well into the quarter, it seemed as though the street and sidewalk were one, with a slow moving river made up of hats, torsos, feet and wheels, moving past the banks made up from the buildings on each side.

Virtually every building had an open stall on the ground floor facing the street. In these, just about anything imaginable was being vended, displayed, hung, cooked, or offered to the passing crowd. Entire kitchens were in operation in spaces no more than six feet wide, with the dim interior glow from a single bulb highlighting steam from boiling foods, or smoke from roasting meats. Other stalls emitted a musty odor from tables piled with clothing and from racks that were tightly packed together with hanging garments. There were a few Chinese pharmacies with their shelves filled with jars and bottles of mysterious powders.

After walking three blocks, we came to a four story, green, stucco building, with a bright red door. It was more impressive than the other buildings. Red led the way, and we entered a large room filled with Chinese eating their evening meal. The smell of frying meats and fish, and of garlic and spices, permeated the atmosphere. The diners were hefting bowls of soup, or rice, or noodles in one hand, while deftly using their chopsticks with the other to snatch morsels of food from platters that filled the center of most tables. Chinese boys and a few girls were scurrying between the tables, carrying huge metal trays with platters of food or piles of soiled dishes.

As we threaded our way among the crowded tables, a short, Chinese man approached who was groomed impeccably in a grey silk suit. I assumed that he was Mr. Wong, our host. He held out his hand to Red and with a smile that revealed several gold teeth said, "Ah, Mr. Carson. It is so pleasant to see you again. If your party will please follow me, I have arranged your table in a private room upstairs." He led us up a narrow flight of stairs to a wood-paneled room with some large paintings of Chinese landscapes. At each end of the room were large, six panel screens of gold dragons on a scarlet background. The center of the room held an enormous round table, at least ten feet in diameter, with settings of porcelain dishes and bowls dividing the circumference into nine equal parts. By each setting were a pair of ivory chopsticks and a large spoon resting on a brass stand. I had been told that a mandarin dinner was the top of the line in Chinese food, from the variety of dishes that were served and the sheer quantity. This meal was on the house, repayment for some vague favors our host had obtained from his navy friends in the past.

One of the destroyer JGs had spent some time in China, and he started talking about Chinese customs and in particular about their food. It was obvious that the study of Chinese cooking was high on his list. After some reminiscing about his gastronomic experiences, he said, "Food is a total experience with the Chinese. Their recipes are designed to excite the palate, as well as be appealing in appearance and texture. They say food should please all the senses. Everything in a Chinese banquet is designed with contrasts in mind: cold versus hot, sweet versus sour, vegetables versus fish or meat, chewy or crisp versus soft. Foods are combined so that different fragrances blend to give a certain overall aroma. Colors are combined to give artistic effects. Crunchy items like water chestnuts, or hard foods like nuts, are combined with soft foods like bean curds to achieve a given texture."

After we sat down, three Chinese girls brought each of us a steaming hot scented towel. I thought that this was a great way to start a meal, by wiping the dust of the Manila streets from your face and hands. Our culinary expert told us that soup is usually last in a Chinese meal, as we would serve dessert. However, in a banquet like this one, it is served first and is usually unique or elaborate. That night they served Bird's Nest soup. From the name, I did not know what to expect. I anticipated cutting into a half sphere of twigs and grass, a real bird's nest that may have been hard-boiled and maybe still had a few eggs left in it. Instead, I was served a broth with a gelatinous substance floating on the surface. It had a faintly sweet taste to it.[23]

That was the start of our feast. We ate and talked for almost three hours. I lost track of the number and variety of dishes that were served. We would have as many as five different platters on the table at one time, each with a different recipe and as our expert would say, contrasting with one another. The waiters constantly refilled our bowls of rice, and I finally learned how to handle a rice bowl in one hand and chopsticks in the other, dipping the food into the rice to sop up drips and sauces. By the time the meal was half over, I decided that there was nothing that was grown or raised on land or that swam or crawled in the sea that we had not been offered.

About that point, when I was convinced that I could not eat another bite, Swede said the piece de resistance was about to be served. He called it Peking Duck. The waiters brought in two enormous covered platters and sat them down on side tables next to cutting boards. Two chefs with high hats appeared and removed the lids revealing four roasted ducks. A chef would hold one and deftly slice off thin sections of skin and meat, very thin sections. Then he would roll these in a thin grey pancake and served it in a crepe. It was delicious. As soon as I ate one, the serving girls would place another one on my plate.

It was almost midnight when the girls brought the final courses, fruits and rice cakes. Notwithstanding some memorable Christmases and Thanksgivings, this was the largest feast I had ever eaten.

⌒

While eating was a favorite pastime, I had not lost interest in female companionship. My friend, Bart, had arranged to meet me in the lobby of the Manila Hotel at 3:00 p.m. on December 7.[24] He said that he would bring his girlfriend and a friend of hers, and we would have cocktails and then dinner. Then we would see what developed and let the evening follow its natural course. I recognized the good-looking girl from the ship sitting next to Bart at a small table in the lounge. On his other side was a girl in a pale blue dress. She was beautiful. She had blond hair, a peaches and cream complexion, enormous blue eyes under long lashes, full lips, and dimples. From what I could see, her figure was excellent, her waist small, and her legs long and slender. My immediate reaction was how could I have been missing this for seven weeks, while I was spending time ogling demure Filipino girls.

Bart made introductions, and his girlfriend's friend said, "It's real nice to meet you. Bart has told me so much about you and how you came over on the same ship with Mary." The accent was pure Georgian. Bart had come up with a Southern belle right out of *Gone with the Wind*. Her name was Betty Lou. Mary drank a daiquiri, while Betty Lou drank rum and Coca-Cola. Bart and I stuck to scotch. The afternoon passed pleasantly and quickly. I learned that Betty Lou worked for a large sugar-exporting firm and had been in the islands a little less than a year. She seemed to know her way around the Philippines. Finally, we asked the girls if they were hungry. "Oh my, I'm just starved," said Betty Lou. "I had brunch at the Polo Club, but everyone just wanted to drink and we hardly ate a thing."

Bart asked the group if we would like to eat at the Manila Hotel. "Oh Bart honey, not there." Betty Lou said this while looking at a group of Filipinos that had just walked in. "I know the cutest little restaurant in town. Well, actually it is out a ways. It is so continental. It has a French chef, and you boys will just love it. I know you will." It was news to me that there was a French restaurant in Manila. But then, I had not covered the town the way Betty Lou had. We got a taxi and drove for what seemed like miles through traffic to the north end of the city. It was obvious that the taxi driver had never heard of the place to which we were going, and Betty Lou directed him for the last part of the trip. We finally pulled up in front of her continental restaurant. It was an old house, set on a large lawn among huge, spreading trees. A wide veranda ran around the sides and across the front. As we walked up a gravel path to the veranda, I saw a sign proclaiming that we were going to eat at "Le Manoir."

The maître d' greeted Betty Lou enthusiastically, making quite a fuss and kissing her hand. She gave him a slight curtsy and said, "Merci, Monsieur Jacques." The maître d' did appear to be French, at least he had a heavy French accent. Everyone else that I saw was definitely Filipino. The menu was large, with all the items written in French in a flowing script. The prices were closer to Manhattan than Manila. Betty Lou asked the Frenchman whether he still had some bottles of that wonderful Chablis. He admitted that he had a few in his special cellar, and after a few minutes he brought one back to the table, making quite a production of showing Bart the label and stating that it was one of the best years still available. When it was properly chilled in the ice bucket, Bart had the privilege of being the taster. Then, the waiter filled all four glasses. I took a tentative sip; it was so dry it curled my tongue. I also would not award the meal my four star stamp as most of it seemed to have been cooked the day before.

I can best describe it as fancy New York franchise at its worst. In the tradition of all such establishments, a small candle illuminated each table. There was no other lighting and the effect was not far from total darkness. Betty Lou kept squeezing my hand and asking me how I liked the food, the wine, and the romantic surroundings. She kept reminding all of us how difficult it was to find such a civilized, such a romantic place, like "Le Manoir" in a town like Manila, where everything was so Spanish, so Filipino. I had to admit that the coffee at the end of the meal was pretty good. As for the rest of the meal, from soup, salad, bread, main course, to pastry dessert, I merely nodded agreement with Betty Lou and decided not to rock the boat.

At the end of the meal, Bart and I agreed to go our separate ways for the rest of the evening. After a long wait, the maître d' was able to obtain two taxis for us. Betty Lou directed our driver to her house. When we arrived there, she asked me if I would like to come in for a nightcap. It was the best offer I had had all week, and I accepted immediately. The house was small with a single story, a living room, a kitchen, two bedrooms, and a bathroom. All the furniture was white rattan and all the cushions and other fabrics were in pale colors. The furniture in the living room consisted of a long couch, with a coffee table in front of it, and two easy chairs. Along one wall was a white rattan cabinet with a radio on top. The door to one of the bedrooms was open and I saw a large bed with a rattan headboard, which seemed to fill most of the room.

I settled down on the couch and Betty Lou said, "You all will have to pardon the way things look. I've been so busy lately; what with everyone talking about those terrible Japanese people and wanting to get everything done so fast, a person just doesn't seem to have time to think anymore." I told her I thought her house looked great. "I'm afraid I only have rum and Coke. I know you all drink scotch, but I'm afraid I must have run out of it. Will rum and Coke be all right honey?" I hate rum and Coke, but when in Rome....

She opened the wine cabinet and removed a quart bottle of rum. From the little kitchen, she brought in four bottles of Coca-Cola, a bowl of ice, and two glasses. She poured at least four fingers of rum in each glass, and then added a dash of Coke and a lot of ice. I sipped my rum. I noticed that she was gulping her drink pretty fast. Her glass was empty, and she was refilling it when I was only half through mine.

For the next hour, we talked and drank Betty Lou's dark rum with dashes of Coke and ice. Actually, Betty Lou did most of the talking and I listened. Between sips of Coke and rum, she told me much of the story of her life. Her daddy raised fruit and other things in South Georgia. What he had was not a farm but a plantation, and it had been in the family for years, like way before the Civil War. She had gone to University of Georgia for a couple of years and had been in the nicest sorority. While at school, she had done some modeling and entered the Miss Georgia beauty contest.

Suddenly she stood up and said, "It gets so damnable hot in Manila. Honey, do you mind if I put on something cooler?" Without waiting for my answer, she walked into the bedroom. She was gone about five minutes and came back wearing a filmy, almost see-through negligee. Actually, it was quite see-through, and she wore nothing under it. I could not help wondering why she bothered with the negligee. She went over to the wine cabinet and refilled our glasses with the rum, Coke, and ice, and came over to the couch. "Honey, are you sure you're comfortable?" she asked and started to undo the buttons on my shirt. I told her that it was indeed hot and proceeded to remove my shirt. While I was doing this, I noticed that she was gulping down her drink and explaining once more how hot it gets in Manila and how thirsty it makes you. She turned back and slowly began to kiss me. I was trying to sit up when suddenly she arched her back, gave a loud moan, shuddered, and passed out. There was only one way to describe her condition—she was dead drunk.

Carefully I picked her up, carried her into her bedroom, gently laid her on her bed, and covered her with the sheet. Quietly, I shut her bedroom door, went back to the couch, put my shirt on, turned off all the lights, and let myself out her front door. I had to walk a good half mile before I found a place where I could get a taxi. As I made the ride to Sangley Point, I could not help but think that the gods had turned against me. The one gorgeous creature that I had found in all of the Philippines had turned out to be a lush. My big evening was finished.

4

Time of Destruction,
December 8–12, 1941

I was suddenly wide-awake. I was lying on my bed, naked, drenched in sweat, the sheet crushed into a pile at my feet. My head ached, and I felt sick. I heard feet pounding down the hall, and two people yelling. One voice screamed, "Get your ass moving. We have to be ready to take off in ten minutes." I heard another saying, "Those little yellow bastards. Hitting Pearl. Those bastards." I recognized it as Tom's voice, one of the PBY pilots, who had the room next to mine.[1]

Lights were on in the hall. Two figures dashed past my open door and raced down the stairs to the ground floor. I looked at my watch, and it read 3:45 a.m.[2] I forced myself to go to the window, and I saw lights coming on in every house. I put on a pair of shorts and went down the stairs to the living room, my head pounding with every step. Mac, Red, and Swede were standing there, looking out the windows. When I came in Swede said, without turning around, "The Japs bombed Pearl Harbor, about an hour ago." My mind refused to accept this. "How could they? It's too far away for them to bomb it."

Swede was still looking out the window and explained, "It's straight dope. The Marsman Building got the flash and passed it on to the Yard. The Yard has been put on full alert, and the PBYs have been ordered on war patrol." Mac added, "I checked the Yard just now. Our orders are to stand by. We might as well sit tight until dawn, because if we go over there in the dark some trigger happy Marine guard may shoot us." My mind still would not accept what was happening. "But Pearl Harbor, my God, it's thousands of miles from anything the Japs have for a base. It's impossible." "Impossible or not, they hit it with something," said Mac. "Did they do any damage?" "We don't know," replied Swede. "The only thing anyone knows is that we are on alert, and the PBYs have been told to keep patrolling until they run out of gas."

I was hungover, and I could smell the rum on my breath. My mind was not functioning, and the idea of the Japanese attacking Pearl Harbor made no sense. "The only thing I can figure is that they used a carrier," said Red. The fog in my head was beginning to clear. I said, "If that is the case, that carrier has not a hope in hell of getting away, not with all the patrol craft, and all the fighters and bombers that are based in Hawaii. How much damage could dive-bombers from a carrier do against a place as well fortified as Hawaii? The pursuit planes would knock them down like flies before they could ever reach the islands." "I hope you are right," said Swede. "It must have happened between seven and eight Sunday morning, and I hope they were awake and everyone was paying attention. They have plenty of radar.[3] No one should have been caught napping."

We talked about it some more and agreed that the possibility of any damage from a surprise attack was slim. A carrier could hold just so many planes, and they would have to use dive-bombers if they wanted to do any real damage. These would carry limited loads, and U.S. interceptors would have outnumbered them. Maybe some were knocked down off the coast and that was what this suicide attack was all about. However, all of us had a nagging worry, without saying it. Why did they say that Pearl Harbor had been bombed? Was it possible that a couple of Jap planes had made it through the fighter and anti-aircraft screen?

After we first heard the alert, Swede had turned on the radio in the living room. So far, all that had come through was static. A little after six, we heard an announcer's voice. "President Roosevelt has just announced in Washington that the Japanese have attacked Pearl Harbor from the air. The Japanese also attacked naval and military facilities on the island of Oahu. No further details were given at this time." That sounded as though more than a couple of isolated planes had come through the defensive screen.

When we arrived at the Yard, everything seemed calm. The main difference that I could see was that the marines at the gate were checking the passes of the Yard workers very thoroughly. None of us was certain whether we should be doing anything differently from what we had been doing the week before. We kept ourselves busy and decided that we might as well stay with our normal routine, maybe seeing if things could be done a little faster. Around 9 a.m., one of the JGs from the Marsman Building came into the office. He told us that they had heard that the attack on Pearl Harbor had been pretty heavy and that the Japs had used a lot of planes and hit some army installations as well as Pearl. He also said that they had a report that the Japanese had bombed Guam as well. We felt that all this was a little unreal. There were too many planes involved. In addition, there was no mention of our own efforts.

I started thinking back to our conversation with the P-40 jockey a few weeks ago at the Army and Navy Club. One thing was certain. After we had learned of the Japanese attack, our fighters and heavy bombers were up in the air going somewhere. While our own PBYs were patrolling off shore, the army was probably hitting the Japanese fields on Formosa. I tried to remember the figures the pilot had given us. We had 35 big Flying Fortresses and 40 other bombers; and by now we should have around 100 P-40s and 70 other fighters, all now flying above us, out protecting Luzon; or maybe some of them were on the way to Formosa, escorting the big bombers.[4]

I figured all hell would be breaking out soon, if it had not already started. About then, someone said that one of the ships had spotted a group of our fighters patrolling Manila Bay and heading toward Bataan. I silently patted myself on the back for the strategic planning I had been doing to hold up our end of this so far undeclared war. We ate lunch and digested rumors. We had nothing factual to go on. What we all wanted to know was where the Army Air Corps was flying and what they had accomplished in the nine hours since the attack on Hawaii.

An hour later a lieutenant told us that the yard had just received a flash that a large fleet of Japanese bombers was attacking Clark Field and that Japanese fighters were strafing it.[5] This sounded ridiculous to us. What were they bombing and strafing? In our imagined strategic plans, our planes had been gone for hours hitting Formosa and other

Jap bases. Our interceptors were knocking down anything that came near Luzon. We had been ready for nine hours for anything that might be in the air.

The afternoon dragged on with no confirmation of anything. It was as if our group was in a total news blackout. We subsisted on rumors on top of rumors. They flew through the Yard, good, bad, and in between, but they were just that: rumors. If someone in the Yard had hard news, it did not reach us. Finally, in the late afternoon, one of our chiefs showed up in the office. He had been sent to Clark Field to deliver a package. He was visibly shaken and gave us our first eyewitness account of what had happened at Clark. He was less than a half-mile from the field when the Japanese bombers arrived. The first planes came over the field at 12:30. All of the B-17s were lined up neatly on the field, close together.[6] When our chief saw the Japanese planes, he jumped out of the car and waited to see what was going to happen. Unfortunately, none of our fighters were in the air. The P-40s were sitting on the field, lined up as neatly as the bombers. The chief figured the pilots were all off eating lunch because a Filipino had told him that they had returned from patrol only a half hour before.

The chief heard the air raid siren go off at the same time that he saw the Japanese planes and the first bombs drop. After the first planes dropped their bombs, another group came in and circled the field for about fifteen minutes, dropping bombs. There was considerable anti-aircraft fire, but all bursts were below the circling planes. By the time the second formation of Jap bombers hit the field, at least eight P-40s were racing to take off but only a few got into the air. A couple of squadrons of Zeros followed in after the bombers. They strafed the planes on the ground, the buildings, and people who were on the field.[7] The chief said that the strafing attack was extremely effective and apparently killed or wounded a lot of personnel. He figured that the damage to the ground installations was as serious as the loss of the planes. There were fires and crumpled buildings all over the field.[8]

Later in the evening, we got the word that a large number of Japanese bombers and fighter planes attacked the fighter base at Iba. All but two of the P-40s were lost. The destruction at Iba was apparently as complete as it had been at Clark.[9] We also heard that the P-35s from Del Carmon had been able to take off untouched and had shot down three Zeros.[10] That night we were still hearing reports of the damage done at Clark as over 100 men had been killed or wounded. When we tallied the destruction of the planes, it appeared that our Air Corps had been cut in half.[11]

As the losses by the Air Corps finally sank in, our main reaction was one of anger, not against the Japanese but against the army staff, and particularly MacArthur. We all felt that someone had goofed badly. We heard a rumor that General Brereton, the head of the Air Corps in the Far East, had wanted to take off early in the morning and bomb Formosa. We were told that General MacArthur had at first ignored him and then had refused to give permission for the planes to take off.[12]

We felt that there was more to the story than just stupidity on the part of MacArthur and his staff. The Japanese attacked Hawaii a full nine hours before they hit Luzon. There was plenty of time to prepare our planes for defense of the fields. Our bombers and fighters did not have to be on the ground when the Japs came over. We had a complete aircraft warning system all around Luzon.[13] Who in the hell was running it? Those Japanese planes either had to come down the coast or over land from north to south. Our PBYs had not seen them come in from the sea to the west. That meant they had to have been over Luzon for at least a half an hour before reaching Clark Field and Iba. Why was there no warning of their approach? We wondered who allowed the bombers to be lined up neatly on the field as if they were in a peacetime parade. Again, the fields had nine hours of warning that something might happen. Why were the planes not dispersed? Was it just to make it nice and easy for the ground crews to service them?

If MacArthur was too timid to want to bomb Formosa as soon as he learned that Hawaii had been attacked, why had he not moved our bombers out of harm's way down to Mindanao?[14] Then, they could wait and see what was going to happen. This was what our P-40 jockey had suggested, and it made sense to us. Keep the big boys safe like we were doing with our ships, until you were ready to use them. If we had had a hundred or more interceptors in the air when the Japanese bombers arrived, the slaughter would have made the Battle of Britain look like a Sunday School picnic, if the fighter jockeys were even half as good as they claimed to be.

We went to bed that night feeling completely disgusted with our army.

The next day the bombing by the Japanese started early and was closer to us. A flight of Japanese bombers hit Nichols Field before dawn. We heard that they did a lot of damage to the shops there and knocked off a few more P-40s. The PBYs kept up their long, slow patrols over the China Sea all that day. They carried full bomb loads but did not see anything of the enemy. During the night, the *Langley* and the three destroyers that had been patrolling the bay left to join the rest of the fleet in the Viscayas.[15]

$\sim$

December 10 started like all the previous days, sunny with a slight breeze. During the morning, we discussed where the Japanese might bomb next. They had destroyed the airfields and most of the army's planes. Maybe, they would now try a run on Manila or the bay. So far, they had ignored the navy. At 11:45 a.m., there was an air raid alert, and Japanese planes again attacked nearby airfields.[16] Either the Japanese were getting excellent intelligence or our Interceptor Command was not learning by experience. We were running out of fighters by letting the Japanese eliminate them on the ground. Interceptions in the air by our people were few and far between. Our air attack plotting system seemed non-existent, and we had the impression that no one in our Air Corps was minding the store.

At about 12:45 p.m., Swede and I were crossing the ball field on our way to the north side of the Cavite Yard when we heard the sound of explosions, faint and to the north.[17] It seemed as if the Japanese were bombing Manila or possibly attacking ships in the bay. We paused in the middle of the field and as we stood there the air raid sirens screamed, and we heard the sound of engines. "That sounds like a plane over the bay to the south of us," said Swede. "Looks like the P-40s are fighting back." I glanced back over the trees and thought I saw a plane diving from the sky into the bay behind us. At that moment, we heard the sound of more engines to the north toward Sangley Point, and Swede said, "The PBYs are going up." Then, I heard a higher pitched sound, and Swede added, "Some Japs are chasing them. I hope they got off all right." This was followed by the sound of the AA guns on Sangley Point opening up and Swede yelling, "Get 'em. Get 'em." The air war had finally come to our area.

The air raid siren sounded again, and this time it seemed even shriller, if that was possible. Then I heard the heavy drone of many engines, getting louder. At that moment, Swede grabbed my arm, pointed to the sky, and yelled, "Look!" I saw a "V" formation of silver dots very clearly, against a blue sky. I did not take the time to count them, but I was told later there were 27 in the flight. They kept coming toward us and then I saw some puffs of black smoke as the Marine AA guns opened fire on them. The formation wheeled over us very slowly and headed out over the bay to the south. The black puffs of anti-aircraft smoke did not seem to disturb them. I heard no explosions of bombs as the planes disappeared from view.

I looked around the field and recalled our discussion on the Japanese ability to bomb accurately. We figured that the safest place to sit during one of their bombing attacks would be in the center of the target. Our field was not in the center of the Yard, but it was close enough. Further, from what we had learned of their ability during the past two days, they did not seem to waste their bombs on open fields. They could be very accurate when they set their minds to it. We hoped this ability was still holding, and they would not waste their bombs on this vacant field with only two people standing in it.

While these thoughts were surfacing, Swede yelled, "Hit the deck!" Another "V" formation of silver dots appeared, and this one seemed to be higher. Again, I heard the 3-inch AA guns and saw the puffs of exploding shell, way under the slowly moving formation of planes.[18] As the puffs of smoke blossomed, I saw what looked like glistening raindrops slowly coming toward me. Swede grabbed my arm and hurled me to the ground, yelling, "Damn it. Hit the deck! Those are bombs!" As I landed on the grass, burying my face into the dirt, a loud explosion and a wave of concussion swept over me. It sounded as though it was a few feet away, and we literally bounced on the grass. Then there was complete silence except for the fading drone of engines. I glanced at my watch. It read 1:18 p.m.

I rose on one knee with my ears still ringing and heard Swede yelling again, "Stay down! Stay put! They are coming back." I looked up and saw the formation of silver dots heading toward us once more from the north. My hearing seemed to have been affected as I could not hear the sound of engines. For the next hour, formation after formation crossed above us, lazily circling the Yard. Nothing interfered with them. The AA guns stopped firing after the second wing had gone over, as obviously their rounds could not reach the attackers.[19] Somewhere close by I heard what sounded like a .50 caliber machine gun firing. Then it too stopped.[20]

As the planes made their passes, there would be explosions close by, followed by a wave of concussion that would bounce us on the grass. Then there would be another short period of silence while our ears rang, and then another loud explosion, concussion, and bounce. During one of the pauses between explosions, Swede turned to me and yelled, "my wife is going to blow her top when she hears I got myself into a dangerous situation like this." I yelled back, "Count your blessings. Those Japs are not in the least interested in this ball field." We lay there and waited. I kept glancing toward the sky. I looked at my watch again and saw that it read 2:11 p.m. We slowly sat up.[21]

Swede said, "I think they have gone." My ears were ringing so badly I could not tell if the sound of motors had died away. We got up and looked around. As far as I could see, not one bomb had hit our ball field. For a moment, we just stood there, as there did not seem to be any reason to go anywhere at that point. I expected to see clouds of dust, smoke and fires raging, people and sirens screaming like I had seen in the newsreels of the bombing of London. None of this happened. There was just complete silence and the sun beating down from a cloudless sky. We walked toward the trees to the east and then I saw the first sign of smoke. It was coming from the direction of the wharves, a small black curtain rising above the buildings. My first reaction was that despite all the Japanese bombs, the Yard had suffered little damage. As we walked along the road toward Fort San Felipe, intending to head for the wharves from where we now could see heavier smoke rising, we noticed four Filipino Yard workers lying on the grass motionless. As we approached them, I saw Mac and Red running down the street toward us. Red was yelling something, but I could not understand him as my hearing was still not functioning. I saw the Filipino nearest to us begin to twitch and then open his mouth in what must have been a scream. By then, all four of us were running toward the Filipinos. As we got closer, I saw that the one who was screaming was lying in a pool of blood that was spreading from beneath him. One of his legs was almost severed from his hip and was lying at a peculiar angle. As we bent over him, we noticed that the other still bodies along the road were coming out of apparent shock and attempting to move. Swede said, "We have to get these people to the hospital before they bleed to death."

Red said, "The van is just down the street. We were driving toward the gate when the first planes came over. We hit the deck in a ditch. I'll get it. We have nothing to stop that kind of bleeding, so we had better work fast." Mac replied, "There were more of them down the street behind us." We ran to the van and headed back toward the Yard gate, collecting Filipinos as we drove. Swede kept saying, "Pile them in as fast as you can. If a man is dead, or you think he is, leave him. Let's try and help those that have a chance." By then shouts seemed to be coming from every section of the Yard, and looking back, I saw that the black smoke was now covering the sky above the whole wharf area. We raced to the Yard gate and when we got there, we found a scene of complete chaos. Torn and bleeding bodies were lying all around it. On the other side, in the town itself, just past the gate I saw some smashed buildings. We learned that when the raid started the Marines had closed the Yard gate. A lot of the Yard workers had panicked and were running toward the gate when the bombs dropped.[22]

At least seven bombs had landed in an area that extended from the buildings immediately outside the gate into the Yard itself and ripped into the swarm of terrified workers who were trying to escape. A Marine guard estimated that over fifty had been killed or wounded. He also told us that the Dispensary had been hit and all the wounded would have to be removed from the Yard. At that point, another Marine came running up. He said, "They are setting up a temporary station in the church yard, and another one here. Put your wounded down, and we'll take over. The doctors and nurses from the hospital are arriving right now."

We heard more sounds of sirens. Two ambulances pulled into the gate and a group of corpsmen from the hospital leapt out and started moving through the Filipinos. Swede said, "I think we can be put to better use elsewhere—let's head for the wharves. From the looks of the smoke, that area took the worst pasting and they are going to need everyone to fight those fires." As we attempted to drive down past the fort toward the wharves, we began to realize how much damage the bombing had caused. The planes had concentrated on the wharves, the shipways, the Commandancia, and nearby buildings. We decided that our vehicle was only going to add to the confusion, so we parked it clear of any buildings and ran the rest of the way.

We headed down the narrow street to the Central Wharf. That was where the *Perry* and the *Pillsbury* had been undergoing repairs the past several days.[23] As soon as we arrived at the wharf, we found that the *Pillsbury* had gone and the entire wharf seemed to be in flames. Some sailors were trying to fight the fires, and the smoke was rising so heavily we could not see the end of the wharf. One of the men told us that the *Pillsbury* had managed to get underway and out into the bay before the first bombs dropped. The *Perry* had not been so lucky. She had cold boilers and could not move. Bombs had gone off in the water next to her, had hit the wharf beside her, and one had gone right through her fire control platform and exploded below. A lot of her crew had been killed or wounded.

The Central Wharf was on fire from the oil soaked wood and other inflammables. Despite all the water that was being pumped, I was certain that the flames would spread to the destroyer. Then through the smoke and flames, I saw another vessel moving out past her toward the bay, and the four piper slowly started to pull away from the flaming wharf. A small group of enlisted men next to us started to yell and cheer at the top of their lungs as she gathered speed and headed into the open water and the safety of the bay.

We had a hard time seeing clearly through the smoke, and Mac asked one of the sailors what had happened. "That's the minesweeper, the *Whippoorwill*, that's pulling her out. The first two times she tried, the *Perry* would not move. I guess everyone was excited, and the sailors forgot to cut her lines to the wharf. This time they did it right, thank God. Those fires were getting mighty damn close."

Red yelled at us, "Look at the Machinist Wharf. The subs are in real trouble." I looked across the small expanse of water to the Machinist Wharf. Burning pieces of wood were floating in the water and a patch of oil was on fire. Spilled oil seemed to be every-where, and I was convinced that before long the entire waterfront would be in flames. The two big fleet submarines were berthed at the Machinist Wharf, one outboard of the other. I had seen them both there that morning. The outboard one was the *Sealion*. Now I could no longer see her, and I sensed rather than saw through the smoke her conning tower poking out of the water. She must have received direct hits and had sunk to the bottom of the harbor.[24] I could see the other big submarine, the *Seadragon*, still next to the wharf.[25] She appeared to be wedged there by the sunken boat. I also saw in the flaming water, between the two wharves, one of the minesweepers. Red said it was the *Bittern*.[26] She had apparently been tied up outboard of the two submarines, and she also had been hit and was on fire. As we ran across toward the wharf to join the firefighting group, she managed to get under way and pull out toward the bay. We could see the men on her deck fighting the flames that threatened to engulf her.

The fires on the Machinist Wharf were rapidly increasing. At any minute, the entire wharf and the buildings along it would go up in flames.[27] No amount of water being poured on the heavy, smoky, oil fires was containing the flames, and they were devouring everything on the wharf. The heat was becoming intense, even as far away as we were from the actual fire. Through a blur of flames and smoke, I saw another ship ease her way in from the bay and slide along the far end of the wharf. I recognized her as the sub-marine rescue vessel, the *Pigeon*.[28] Agonizingly slow, she inched forward until her bow almost touched the bow of the trapped *Seadragon*. Two men leapt on the bow of the sub-marine and tied a line to the submarine's deck. No sooner had they done this than a tongue of flame leapt from the wharf and engulfed the deck where they had been standing seconds before.

We heard the roar of the *Pigeon*'s engines as she started backing down at full throttle and simultaneously the revving of the fleet submarine's diesels as she thrust her bow against that of the *Pigeon*. She started to move. In slow motion, with scrapes and screeches as she slid along the wharf, the submarine moved away from her stricken sister. As she moved further, flames from the buildings covered the entire wharf. Just as the submarine's stern cleared the end of the wharf, the entire surface and the buildings on it exploded in a surge of fire and sparks, with flaming oil pouring into the water and tongues of flames licking out as far as the sunken *Sealion*.[29]

At that moment, a group of men ran past where we were standing. They saw us and yelled, "Come on. Lend a hand! The fire is spreading toward the Ammunition Depot." If the depot caught fire, it would be the end of all of us. We ran up the road following them. When a fire threatens, you cannot move a depot full of black powder, mines, and explosives. Since it cannot be pulled into the bay like a ship, you just have to pray that you can keep it from catching fire. You have to protect and shield it, because if it goes, everything around it will go with it. One of the lucky breaks during the bombing, and it may have been the only one, was that the Japanese bombers did not hit the Ammunition Depot. If they had, none of us would have survived.

As we pounded up the road, I saw Tommy Bowers, the Yard Ordnance Officer, directing the firefighting.[30] The wharves were important, but eventually the fires on them and the buildings around them would either be controlled or would burn themselves out. The Ammunition Depot represented a danger that was impossible to calculate. Every available pumper and hose in the Yard seemed to be spraying thousands of gallons of water on the wooden roof and sides of the building. Once flames did catch on the roof and another time they licked at one wall. Each time we extinguished them before they spread. At least twenty of us used buckets of water or sand to extinguish vicious little fires in the dry grass that tried to spread their way to the building.

Fighting that potential fire, near so much high explosive, was something I do not care to experience again. It was the first time in my life that I experienced sheer, black terror and my nerves reached the breaking point. I was sweating heavily, not just from the heat of the fires but also from my imagination. Within a few feet of me, inside this flimsy building, were thousands of pounds of some the most powerful explosives that man had ever invented. A single one could blow us all to bits. If the little shells started popping, they would drive us away and soon the big bang items would take over and destroy us. When the planes flew over as tiny specks in the sky, dropping their bombs and lazily circling away, I was dealing with something that was remote. Here, inside this building, instant death was right next to me.

About half way through the firefighting, I heard small arms fire coming from the waterfront. Now, added to everything else, we were either being attacked or were shooting at attackers. The people next to me paused in their firefighting efforts and listened. It sounded like strings of firecrackers going off. There would be short bursts, then a steady succession, a rapid *brrrumph* of sound. A lieutenant came running up the road, asking where he could find Bowers. "We have a problem, at the waterfront; a pile of small arms ammo has caught fire. There is nothing that we can do except let it blow itself out and keep away." A short time later, another messenger from the waterfront came running up the road. A barge load of torpedoes for the destroyers had caught fire. The messenger estimated that they were a total loss.

The fire protection operation lasted for hours. By midnight, we had what was probably the wettest building in the Yard, but it did not catch fire. By then, all of the fires in the nearby buildings had either burned themselves out or been extinguished.[31] The sweep of the fires across the dry Yard had stopped in one area by the swimming pool. This prevented the flames from completely engulfing the lumberyards and the Ship's Service Store.

The waterfront, in the area of the main wharves and the shipways, was another matter. All around the sunken fleet submarine, the destruction was total. Even the rubble seemed to have leveled itself out on the ground, leaving few skeletons pointing toward the sky by dawn. The adjacent warehouses were left with the walls standing, but the roofs and the bulk of the supplies had vanished. The Japanese knew exactly where the Commandancia was located and they concentrated their attack on it with great precision, leaving only some walls as a reminder of their visit. The Japanese had hit the power plant, but the stacks were still standing. Not only did they hit the dispensary, but also an air raid shelter adjacent to it, killing everyone in it. It was the only shelter that was hit in the entire Yard.[32]

We finally headed back to our house to snatch a few hours of sleep. We were tired to the point of exhaustion, covered with black, greasy stains on uniforms, hands, and faces from the oily smoke. On the way we saw floodlights, and as we approached we came upon a huge lighted area, as bright as day. The medics had established a complete operating suite under canvas in the open. There were too many seriously wounded men to be handled in the Canacao hospital.[33]

As we approached, I could hear a diesel generator running, and I saw that at least a dozen tables had been set up. Shattered people were lying everywhere, even this long after the bombing. Corpsmen and sailors were moving litters loaded with crumpled humans, most of them Filipinos. Nurses were handing the medics instruments, or checking the occupants of the litters. When we got close to this field hospital, I was surprised to see a dentist and at least two other doctors I knew, who were not surgeons, operating right along with the surgical specialists.

It was an assembly line of broken and ruptured bodies being moved from litter to table to litter to ambulance. There was no time for a detailed diagnosis of each case. The only goals were to fight shock, stop bleeding, put parts back together as well as possible, remove metal splinters, keep the heart beating, and the lungs breathing. The norm was cut, suture, bandage, and move to the next victim. The niceties of major surgery and fancy anesthesiology had to wait. The medical team had been at this task all afternoon and night. Their white surgical gowns were saturated with blood. The tables and litters were soaked. Sweat was dripping off the faces of the doctors, nurses, and corpsmen. The combination of heat, exhaustion, and the smell of opened bodies almost overpowered me after the exertions of the past seventeen hours.[34]

A corpsman told us that over four hundred Yard workers had been seriously wounded and possibly fifty killed. All afternoon and night, they had searched through the burning and bomb wrecked buildings. They had located close to one hundred sailors and officers who were wounded or burned, and at least twenty who had been killed. He figured that it would be the next day before the whole tally was in.

～

When they awakened me five hours later, I was still groggy. The sudden conversion from the routine of normal operations to the violence of actual warfare takes a little time for the mind to accept. All the next day I was a little punch drunk. We talked about the accuracy of the bombing. All but a few of the bombs had landed within the confines of the Yard or among the ships and launches moored adjacent to the wharves. The Japanese smashed the critical elements of the Yard completely: the major wharves and ship repair ways, the shops, a large percent of the supply warehouses, and the Commandancia. A lot of the offices were either damaged or gutted by the spreading fires. As a ship repair and supply facility, the Yard was a total loss.

Miraculously the Ammunition Depot was safe. Equally miraculous, a large stock of submarine torpedoes had escaped untouched. Due to the action of a lot of fast moving people and their ships, we had saved a fleet submarine and two destroyers. We had lost only one major vessel despite all the bombing of the wharves, though that loss was a serious one: large fleet submarines are not easy to replace. Our two destroyers and our other submarine had made the safety of the bay. The *Pillsbury* had not been damaged and would join the fleet in the south. The *Perry* had been damaged and had been towed to a small yard in Manila where they were working around the clock to get her running again. Our fleet submarine, that had escaped the flames, had some good slashes in her conning tower, but they said she would survive after a little welding.

All that day and the next, we rooted through the rubble of the Yard, checking inside buildings to see what was salvageable.[35] Despite the losses, in some areas we did find a few things, such as that pile of untouched torpedoes. We may have lost a lot of spare parts and useful ship's stores and all our repair facilities, but our ammunition and explosives escaped virtually untouched. If we had the guns and the ships to fire this lethal

Cavite Naval Yard on fire after Japanese bombing, December 10, 1941 (National Archives, #SC-130991).

Damage at Cavite Naval Yard after Japanese bombing (National Archives, #80-G-243717).

material, we could still cause the Japanese a lot of problems. The PT boats had taken off for the safety of the bay when the Japanese bombers came over and they spent their time dodging some bombs. When they returned to their pier after the bombers had left, they had to face up to the fact that most of their spare parts had been destroyed and that their future operation would mean a lot of improvisation.[36]

The Japanese left us alone as we tried to assemble and move what was salvageable from the Yard.[37] They must have figured there was nothing left worth hitting. At the end of the second day of scrounging, we were talking to one of the Marine sergeants in charge of a security detail. Suddenly he said, "Sure glad they got that Jap loving sonofabitch, Mr. Carson." "You mean one of the pilots had to bail out, and they caught him?" asked Red. "No, no. That guy in Cavite that led them in." "What do you mean? What guy in Cavite?" we all asked at once. "The one that had been giving the Nips the dope on the Yard. That American bastard with the Nip wife. Haven't you heard about them? Thought all the offi-cers knew about it." Swede said, "Back up. This is the first we have heard about any of this." The sergeant exclaimed, "Oh. I thought the dope was all over the Yard by now," and he proceeded to tell us the story.

"This scum ball was an American, had a photo shop in Cavite, and had a Nip wife. The two of them were spies, traitors. They had been telling the Nips a lot of things about the ships and the Yard. Yesterday, when the raid started they were spotting for the planes. Our guys caught them at it. They took them away and shot them I guess." There had been rumors of spies and Fifth Columnists around Luzon for weeks. With so many Japanese on the islands, along with Filipinos who were Japanese sympathizers, there was bound to be some fire where there was smoke, but up to now, none of us had heard anything about spies in the Yard area. This was a first.[38] The sergeant continued. "They had been suspicious of these people for a while and were watching them. One of the Filipinos told one of those FBI people that he thought these people were spies, so they started keeping tabs on them. Quiet like. Yesterday, before the raid, the FBI had a truck parked near the scum ball's home. They had gear in it that would pick up radio signals. When the Nip bombs started dropping, they picked up signals from the guy's house. Three of the FBI people went in through the front door, kind of forceful, you know what I mean, but there was no one downstairs. Then, they found a locked door toward the back and they got through and found a flight of stairs leading to the roof. They went up those and busted through another door at the top. There was this bastard and his Nip wife, in a little room with a lot of fancy radio equipment. The guy was looking out some slits in the wall and had a pair of real powerful field glasses. When you looked out like he was, you got a real pretty view of the Yard and the wharves and all the stuff out on the bay. They figured he was sending out coded messages to the bombers; telling them what to hit, what they had hit, what they had missed, and what they should hit next. The FBI guys clobbered him and his wife, smashed all the radio equipment that was installed there, and took them away. I guess they shot them when they got downtown."[39]

Maybe our wondering about the deadly accuracy of the Japanese bombing had a simple explanation after all.[40]

5

Retreat from Cavite, December 1941

Jack said to us when we returned to the skeletons in the Yard on the thirteenth, "Twelve days until Christmas. Back home they are mailing out cards, buying presents, and planning the big dinner." Looking around at the ruins and desolation, he added, "There is nothing very festive in what we see here. I wonder where we will be eating our turkey." Those twelve days turned out to be about as hectic as any twelve days I had ever experienced.

At the beginning of those twelve days, we were in a state of shock. We still regarded our base at Mariveles as merely transient quarters—a place to go for a while, because our regular abode was out of commission.[1] We thought of Mariveles as a sort of temporary stop along the road, until the navy would make its next move and tell us what to do and where to settle.[2] By Christmas, we were not sure of how long temporary would be, or when the navy would be making any move that would affect us.

Soon after the attack on Cavite, we went into Manila and dropped off our footlockers, filled with our navy blues and whites, our swords, and all our extra possessions, at the Army and Navy Club with the management instructed to hold them until we returned.[3] We joked about the fact that everything would need a good pressing when we got them back. As of Christmas, we were wondering when we would be picking them up again, if at all.[4]

By December 15, we had equipped ourselves for an expedition to the Bataan jungles: folding cots, mosquito nets, blankets, canteens, Marine style boots, and other clothing suitable for the bush. Initially, all this had a novelty about it. It was as if we were outfitting ourselves for a camping trip. By Christmas, the novelty had worn off, and we were regarding these items as standard issue for our new way of life.

For days after the bombing of the Yard, our thinking and our conversation was on naval matters. Before Christmas, the Japanese had landed in force on Luzon and were attempting to move swiftly on Manila. We were beginning to admit that we might be somewhat dependent on the army's ability to fight back. We started to talk in army terms, covering subjects like holding lines, flanking movements, and fallback positions. The twelve days before Christmas forced us to admit that we might be facing an uncertain future and that thought was disturbing. We began to feel our first loss of confidence and started to wonder whether the might of the U.S. Navy could let us down.

In addition, deep down in each of us, there was developing a small, but nagging respect for the Japanese. This was surfacing grudgingly, but it was there. They seemed

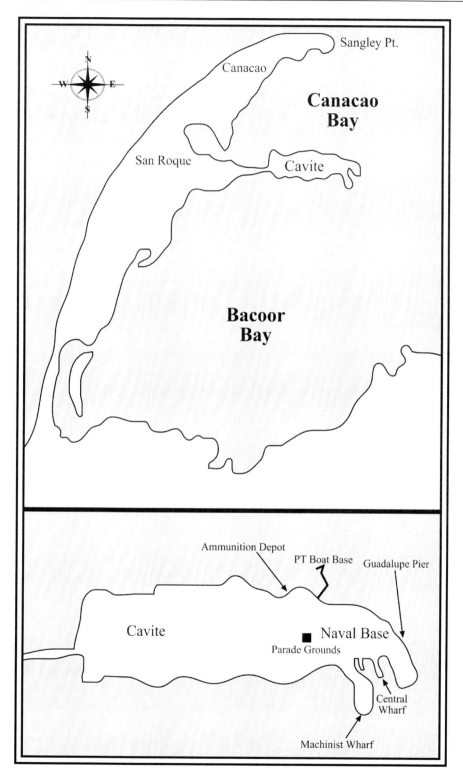

Cavite Naval Base.

to have the ability to outmaneuver us. They had destroyed most of our air arm. They had chased away our major surface ships. They seemed to be using their resources far better than we were using ours. We knew nothing of their army, but we felt that it might offer some additional surprises. We kept saying that we hoped MacArthur was better at using ground troops than he had been at using airplanes.

All the surface ships were leaving Manila Bay as quickly as they could. The night after the Yard was destroyed, the *Pillsbury*, the minesweepers, three of the China gunboats, and two of the tenders slipped past Corregidor and headed south to join the rest of the surface fleet. On the first day of war, there were forty merchant ships in the bay seeking refuge from the Japanese. After they had seen the results of the bombing of the Cavite Navy Yard, they apparently felt that their chances would be better in the open waters of the China Sea. By the 13th, the bulk of them had fled to southern waters.

Nothing in the Supply Corps Manual had covered procedures for cleaning up the debris from a bombed navy yard. Neatly printed requisitions and accountability went out the window. Personal judgment and speed replaced all that we had been so carefully taught. We either wrote off an item for later destruction by the demolition crews or painstakingly salvaged and sent it to what appeared to be the safest place for avoiding further destruction. We kept records in pocket notebooks so that someone could be advised later where these precious items could be found.

Scrounging for salvageable items among the almost free standing walls that were missing their roofs, stacks from boilers that were punctured by shrapnel, and a ground level rubble of charred wood, broken concrete, pieces of corrugated roofing and broken, twisted machinery, was both dangerous and nerve wracking. No one was certain when one of those walls might collapse as we picked our way over or around twisted metal and broken concrete. Further, we always had one ear cocked for the sound of Japanese planes that might be returning to finish us off.

While the planes did not bother to hit the Yard again, they did attack all the airfields in Luzon, doing their best to destroy the remaining fighter planes. We kept getting reports that they were using hundreds of high-altitude bombers, dive-bombers, and fighter planes to do this. On the morning of December 12, we heard the army had around thirty P-40s and other fighters. By the 14th, there were less than ten usable fighters in all of Luzon.[5]

Our own PBYs took a similar beating. During the raid on the Yard, despite some skirmishing, the Sangley Point squadron did not suffer any damage. All the next two days, our squadron and the one at Olongapo kept up their long patrols over the ocean. On the 12th, the Japanese fighters decided that these slow moving flying boats were too good a target to ignore. After the Olongapo squadron landed to refuel, Zeros sank seven of the PBYs. The next day they finished off the rest of the Olongapo PBYs.[6] The squadron at Sangley Point decided that there was no point in waiting for the same thing to happen to them. A PBY, with its limited firepower, lack of maneuverability, and slow speed, is virtually defenseless against a Zero in the air and completely helpless against attack when sitting in the water. On December 14, we said good-bye to Tom Pollock and the other pilots. They loaded the flying boats and three seaplane tenders with extra crewmen and all the spare parts they could carry. The planes took off, dipped their wings in a farewell salute, and then headed south. The tenders slowly steamed down Manila Bay, bound for Java where the planes would find a new base. Naval aviation was finished in Luzon.[7]

At times such as we were facing, you live on tension and ache for hard news. It was not until five days after the bombing of the Yard that we had confirmation that our surface fleet was undamaged, had reached its southern ports, and had not engaged in any battles with the Japanese. That same day one of the technicians from Manila came to Sangley Point to perform some task at the radio station. He told us the story of a sea battle that the British had just lost. It turned out that it was not a sea battle in the usual meaning of the term. Rather, it was a battle that showed how determined pilots, with the right types of planes and bombs, can sink the mightiest ships. The Japanese sank the British *Prince of Wales* and *Repulse*.[8]

The technician from Manila also told us that the day the Japanese bombed the Yard, they had landed some troops on the northeast and southeast coasts of Luzon. He said the forces were small, and should be regarded as "feints," virtually suicide missions that would be eliminated easily. He added some details that made us feel better about our Air Corps. He said that four B-17s had come up from the south to bomb ships off the north coast of Luzon. They clobbered the transports at Vigan, and one B-17 was supposed to have sunk a battleship.[9] Although only scuttlebutt, we were excited to hear any possible good news.

~

During the twelve days before Christmas, we did find salvageable items. The hospital at Canacao was undamaged, but the doctors and nurses had all moved to Manila with their patients, so the medical supplies had to follow them. There was radio and communication equipment that would be useful on Corregidor. Also, there were some spare parts and material that we put on board the *Canopus*. There was a tremendous amount of ammunition left in the Yard, and we attempted to move as much as possible to Corregidor. There was transport to move even the heaviest items such as the mines and torpedoes. It seemed that we spent twenty-hour days loading, moving, and unloading. We all felt that the salvage operation had to proceed quickly. No one knew if the Japanese might bomb the Yard again. We used every possible means of transport: truck, van, tug, lighter, and launch.[10] It meant moving in daylight and ignoring the Japanese. For the most part, they ignored us in return.[11]

During those days, Manila and its citizens changed quickly and drastically. It was no longer a happy-go-lucky city operating on an easygoing basis. After the bombing of the nearby airfields, the Yard, and the ships in the bay, confused and frightened people filled Manila. All the residents were convinced that the Japanese were going to bomb the city next. Everyone had visions of Manila becoming another London, with shells of blackened buildings and raging, uncontrolled fires.[12] When they saw the black smoke over Cavite, their terror increased.

On our frequent trips through the city, we saw its appearance change. Citizens striped windows with tape, and filled and placed sand bags outside the entrances of many buildings. Traffic clogged the streets making movement almost impossible. The flow was both into and out of the city. People in the city who had homes or relatives in the country were fleeing outward, figuring the enemy would not be interested in attacking a small town. People who lived in the country were fleeing inward, convinced Manila offered protection not found in their own barrio. Trucks, cars, buses, horse drawn carts, and bicycles filled the streets going in both directions, loaded to the sky with all of the family possessions they would hold. Chickens, pigs, goats, and dogs blended with the thousands of humans in this snarled stream of traffic. To add to the confusion, drivers became more reckless than ever before, and accidents rose astronomically. There was a run on every bank in the city. Everyone hoarded food, and everything suddenly became in short supply in every store; prices skyrocketed; and sales were made for hard cash only.[13]

As the terror and the confusion among the populace increased, so did the rumors. We were convinced that the Japanese had an excellent Fifth Column that was well organized and efficient.[14] We could not believe that their effective military actions during the first week of the war were the result of poor management on the part of our forces. There were too many reports filtering through both the town and the countryside of sabotage, of guiding enemy planes to targets, of subtle propaganda that stressed the invincibility of the Japanese, to dismiss as the sheer imagination of the Filipinos.

We heard our share of such rumors as they flew through the remnants of the smashed Yard. We would listen to these, digest them, and usually shrug them off as another fantasy and go on with our work. One story was different. One of our friends in the Ammunition Depot group passed it along to us. He was a very serious officer, who dealt only in facts. When he told you something, it was the straight dope. He had a younger brother and the two of them were very close. By coincidence, both brothers were attached to the Yard. One evening, at the end of that first week, our friend, the older brother, stopped us near the Yard gate and asked, "Did you hear about Peggy?" I assumed he meant Peggy Saito. Peggy was easily the most beautiful girl in the entire Cavite area. She had a Eurasian background that was hard to identify. She had glistening black hair, large almond shaped and luminous black eyes, a high forehead, a flawless complexion, and brilliant white teeth. She was petite, with a gorgeous figure. Everything was proportioned just like the figure of a Balinese dancer we had seen in a magazine photograph.

Peggy worked for the communications group in the Yard, a sensitive position since she constantly saw messages involving the Yard operations and Fleet movements. Despite the fact that everyone knew that Peggy was more Japanese than she was anything else, we trusted her completely. Peggy was family—a loyal member of our establishment. With her startling beauty, Peggy attracted the attention of the U.S. Navy officers. One ensign in particular had fallen head over heels in love with her. Peggy had a small house in Cavite City, and she and her ensign used to spend all of their spare time there. A lot of us knew about this and envied the lucky guy. We had to admit that they made quite a couple.

Swede asked, "What about her?" "She was killed," said our visitor. "Good God," I exclaimed, "don't tell me Peggy was killed in the bombing of the yard." None of us had heard this, and we were certain that we would have, as well known as Peggy was. "No," he replied. "She was killed the first night of the war." "How did it happen?" We all asked. "It was no accident. It was deliberate," he answered. "You mean she was murdered?" I could not believe it. The idea of someone as wonderful as Peggy meeting a violent death was difficult to grasp. "In a way," he replied. Then he told us the story.

For weeks before December 8, counterespionage forces had been set up composed of people from the Constabulary, the Philippine Secret Service, the Army G-2, and ONI, and kept the Japanese in Luzon under surveillance. They had taken an unusual additional step by bringing in some FBI men from Hawaii who were Nisei, American citizens of Japanese ancestry. These Japanese-American FBI agents circulated among the local Japanese residents, picking up information on espionage activities. One of these agents made contact with a Japanese importer in Manila and managed to convince him that he was a native of Tokyo. He told the importer that he could put together a network that could supply information on the U.S. Navy. The importer told him that his network was not needed since they already had one in operation and asked him to join them.

In less than a month, the agent found that the importer's network was efficient and effective. Some source at the Yard was passing extremely sensitive information to Tokyo. A courier would bring papers to the importer. He would send them by another courier. Then fishermen skippering fast boats would carry the papers to the Japanese who were north of Luzon. It took less than twenty-four hours from the time of the original pick-up at the Yard until the material arrived in Japan.

These people were smart. They did not use telephones or radios. The FBI's problem was to find out how all this information originated. Working backward from Manila to the source was not easy; but the Nisei agent was good at his job and got a lucky break. After the Cavite to Manila courier had a motorcycle accident and wound up in the hospital, the importer asked the agent to make his next trip. He drove to Cavite and met a man in a shop, who handed him a bulky envelope. When the Nisei left for Manila, another FBI agent shadowed the man from the shop. It took two days. The man was either careless or over-confident, or the FBI agent was good. The man never knew that he was being tailed. The third day, he came out of a house with a parcel in his hand. He met the Nisei agent again in the shop and turned the parcel over to him. Before he took it to Manila, the other agents opened and photographed the contents.

The counterintelligence agents checked the ownership of the house from which the man had brought the parcel, and it belonged to Peggy. The source had been located. The ONI people from Manila quietly picked up Peggy's ensign and grilled him for hours about Peggy and his relationship with her. Either the questioners let slip that they had caught her red-handed, or her ensign put two and two together. That evening after the airfields had been bombed, the ensign went to the little house to spend the evening with Peggy. No one knows what happened for sure. What is known is that sometime in the early hours of the morning, he blew her brains out with a navy-issue .45 caliber Colt. When our narrator finished his story, he began to sob, long dry heaves. He had been very fond of the beautiful girl who he expected would be his sister-in-law one day.[15]

∽

By the end of that week there did not seem much left for us to do in the Yard. It was apparent that the time had come for us to move on. It was also becoming clear that Mariveles would be taking on a more permanent aspect. If that happened, we might be sitting there for some time and the army would be sitting in Bataan, right above us. We might have to wait there until our fleet and transports came and took us out. That could be a stay at Mariveles of maybe as long as six or seven weeks.

We knew that Bataan, with Corregidor guarding the entrance to the bay, made up an impregnable fortress, well stocked with supplies and ammunition, ready for anything that the Japanese might throw against it. This was no Alamo. If the Japanese forced the army to retreat to Bataan, we felt that MacArthur knew what he was doing there. Our main concern was what we in the navy would be doing while at Mariveles. The submarines were now based in Manila, so we would not have much to do with them. We figured that we would be seeing the PT boats down there and probably some tugs and minesweepers. That was not much of a fleet. After a few weeks, we probably would be bored to death. The time had come to put the show on the road and say goodbye to our quarters in Canacao and to Ah Tong. We each gave him most of the money that we had and told him to lose himself in the Chinese quarter of Manila until things settled down. It was a rough moment for all of us as he had been like family. We stood there silently, and each of us shook his hand. Ah Tong looked over each of us carefully as we came up to him, saying to each in turn, "Take care of yourself, sir."

We got into Red's van and headed to Manila. Driving at night in a potential war zone can be a little spooky. Like every other vehicle in the area, we had modified our headlights with black electrician's tape covering all but a thin slit, from which light feebly emerged. The blackout was complete in Manila and every barrio. We crawled through the pitch-black streets of Manila and the barrios, guided only by the vague outlines of the buildings on each side of the road. We cautiously negotiated the highway and roads to the end of Bataan and our new home. We arrived at Mariveles at two in the morning. We unloaded our cots and mosquito nets and stretched them out on the dirt road that overlooked the rice paddy.

The next morning, I awoke with the sun shining blindingly in my eyes and a terrific racket coming from above me. My cot was beside the road and under some tall, leafy trees. I squeezed out from under my mosquito net and stood up to see what was causing all the noise. Chattering with an ungodly babble were dozens of monkeys climbing among the branches of the trees above my head. Occasionally, they tossed down twigs or anything else they could throw at me. Some male monkeys would scurry down a large branch to take a closer look, bare their teeth, and give me fierce looks. Mama monkeys clutching babies, and junior monkeys, in twos and threes, stayed higher in the trees and merely swore at me. The odor of zoo permeated the air.

Cots lined the side of the road in both directions. Vans, cars, jeeps, and small trucks sat on the other side. I recognized sailors from the Yard who were walking the road or sitting on cots, their clothing a hodgepodge of khaki, denims, and whites. I walked down the ridge to the paddy below. The mess was serving breakfast and a long, snaking chow line had formed by the side of the field. Two cooks were placing pancakes and Vienna sausages from large metal pans into each man's mess kit. I noticed lister bags of water hanging from tripods of cut poles.[16] I filled my canteen and took a tentative sip. Hanging in the breeze, the lister bags kept the water cool, but the taste was pure swimming pool chemical. The little purple tablets had been added to kill the amoebas and other creatures in the water and make it safe for human consumption. I found that our bathing and shaving facilities were the waters of the bay or the river emptying into it. I was told that the bay was reserved for laundry as well. I became used to shaving in cold water quite quickly.

When the navy first designed our base at Mariveles, it was with peacetime eyesight. All our little green buildings were set up neatly in rows along the shoreline, and on the flat rice paddy. The peacetime navy had not given much thought to high-level bombers, dive-bombers, or strafing fighter planes. We figured that all these neat little buildings would attract a lot of attention from Japanese spotter planes, soon to be followed by visits from the air of a more destructive nature. Our ordnance experts told us that when a five hundred pound bomb hits the soft dirt of a rice paddy, its weight and momentum makes it dig in a good ten feet before it explodes. While it would make a big hole and throw around a lot of dirt, unless something was directly under it, not much damage would occur. We had also heard that both the British and the Nazis had constructed fake depots and even bases to fool each other's bombers. We decided to use the same ruse. We took everything valuable out of the green buildings and filled them with garbage and junk.

We put the valuables and the people around the perimeter of the paddy, safely hidden under the trees, and let the Japs bomb the hell out of our green buildings. We hoped that this would eat into their expensive bomb supply and give them nothing in return. We also hoped, most fervently, that their accuracy would continue. It took us the better part of a week to shift things around to our satisfaction.

The Supply Corps accomplished another task during those few days before Christmas. Since the bombing, the Filipino Yard workers had not been paid. Not only was Christmas coming, but it might be a long time before they would see another paycheck from the navy. This might even be their retirement pay. Carl Faires, the Yard Disbursing Officer and my former swimming companion, volunteered to go back to Cavite with a small staff and boxes of cash to pay the entire force. Word was sent back a few days in advance of the place and the time for payday to ensure that there would be a full house, including the next of kin of the men who either had been killed or were hospitalized. Paying several hundred workers at the entrance to a bombed Navy Yard, with half the countryside, including Japanese spies, knowing where and when you are going to do it is a hairy job. Everyone figured that this would surely attract a lot of attention from those fighter planes and twin-engine Japanese Navy bombers that had been harassing the Manila port area. Faires and his assistants were as nervous as the Yard workers and their dependents, but they tried not to show it. For hours, they checked lists and counted out the cash from big strong boxes ensuring that each worker or his family got their pay.[17] Finally, it was over. No Japanese planes strafed the crowd, and no bombs fell even close.

At the end of our second day in Mariveles, I decided to look up our friends on the PT boats. I had learned that they had set up a base adjacent to Mariveles Bay in a small inlet called Sisiman Cove. As we sat and talked, I found out that they had run into a streak of bad luck since the bombing of the Yard on December 10. They had not been touched the day of the bombing. When the first Japanese dive bombers approached, they took off into the open bay where they would have maneuvering room. One group of dive-bombers attacked then but missed completely. The PTs were more accurate and knocked down three of them with their machine guns.[18] While they had lost most of their spare parts in the bombing of the Yard, they had managed to cache a couple of engines and some spare parts in Manila. However, what they salvaged from the Yard was discouraging. Their next bad luck came a few days later when one of the boats suffered an explosion in the engine compartment. Luckily, it did not blow up the boat and the crew, but it did do a lot of damage to the propulsion system. As they were trying to move it, Japanese fighter planes caught the limping boat and inflicted more damage. I was told that it would be several weeks before the boat could be put back into action.[19]

Three days before our supply group arrived in Mariveles, the PTs went through a mission that placed them in an entirely different category from the one for which they were designed. They told me about it as we sat on their little dock that afternoon drinking coffee. The night of December 17 seemed to be blacker than most as the moon remained hidden by clouds. While there were few ships to run into, there was something more lethal: the minefields that guarded the Bay entrance. Early that evening, an interisland steamer, the SS *Corregidor*, had loaded seven hundred of the residents of Manila to take them to Australia.

The *Corregidor* left the Manila pier after dark and slowly made her way to Corregidor. Arrangements had been made to escort her through the minefields, but something went wrong. Either her captain did not follow the correct route or a mine had broken loose and drifted into her path. It was nearing midnight when there was a tremendous explosion. She had hit a mine in the North Channel between Mariveles and Corregidor and sank in less than ten minutes. As she went down, people jumped into the water. The screams of the panic-stricken passengers attracted no attention from Corregidor; however, Sisiman Cove and the PT boats were opposite from the spot where the *Corregidor* sank. The crews heard the explosion, and after a few minutes of listening determined a vessel had hit one of the mines. Whether it was friend or foe, they did not know. They started up three of the PTs and headed for the general area where they estimated the explosion had taken place. Within a mile, they saw tiny pinpoints of yellow lights on the water. As the PTs slowly maneuvered closer, they heard cries for help and finally saw people thrashing in the oily swells, suspended by life preservers or clinging to floating pieces of wood. Barely moving among the floating mass of people and debris from the ship, they started pulling the half-drowned, oil covered victims aboard the decks of the boats. Over the next two hours, they managed to save almost three hundred men, women, and children.[20]

On December 22, we heard that the Japanese were landing in force in Lingayen Gulf, a couple of hundred miles from us on the west coast. We were told that the convoy contained over eighty transports, and that the Japanese had not used air cover. Their only protection consisted of two light cruisers and some destroyers. There was a rumor that one of our smaller "S" boats had sunk a transport in the gulf during the landings. However, aside from that, there was no word as to what our big submarines had done to hinder this invasion. Later in the day, we heard that the Japanese had landed at several different places, extending over an area that was thirty miles long. We heard later the transports put ashore over 35,000 troops and eighty tanks.

On Christmas Eve, another Japanese force landed on the east coast of Luzon far south of Manila at Lamon Bay. This force had roughly 7,000 troops in it. Again, the landing was unopposed. There was a rumor that one of our submarines had attacked the enemy convoy at sea, but there was no report of any sinkings.[21]

The more we talked about the landings, the more confused we became as to why our submarines had done so little to attack them. Presumably, our entire undersea fleet had been out patrolling the coasts of Luzon. The large Japanese fleet of closely bunched transports had come down in the open waters from Formosa at probably seven or eight knots with little protection and made landings without opposition. The other smaller fleet from the east had done the same thing on the other coast. In all this, we had word of only two small attacks by individual submarines. Despite the fact that this was one of the most powerful submarine forces that the U.S. Navy had assembled, the results of their patrolling had been negligible. It did not make sense.[22]

The more we talked about it the more we felt that the command and the skippers of these submarines had let us down badly. We knew something of the changes that had been made in the operation of our submarines during the previous two weeks. On the first day of the war, eighteen were sitting in Manila Bay alongside the three tenders. Five of the big fleet-type boats and four of the smaller "S" boats were on their way to take up stations off the Luzon coast. The remaining two fleet-type boats were in the Yard being repaired. After the Yard had been bombed, all the submarines became dependent on the tenders for most of the supplies and any of the repairs that they required and the tenders were so vulnerable to air attack that Admiral Hart felt that he could not risk their loss. Within ten hours after the bombing of the Yard, the tenders were on their way to Surabaja in Java.[23]

The *Canopus* was equipped primarily to handle the smaller "S" boats. She stayed in the bay and went to one of the piers in the port of Manila. Also remaining was the submarine rescue vessel, the *Pigeon*, the ship that had saved the trapped fleet boat from the inferno at the Machinist Wharf during the bombing of the Yard.

Despite these slim maintenance and repair facilities, Admiral Hart was determined to fight his undersea war from his headquarters in Manila for as long as he could. Navy personnel had moved the bulk of the spare parts for the "S" boats and torpedoes salvaged from the wrecked Yard into warehouses in the Manila port area. We also had been told that Hart wanted to personally run his submarine campaign. Then, as soon as war broke out, the admiral made a series of changes in the plans. Unfortunately, these changes did not appear to have helped the submarines become a more effective combat fleet. The army and its air corps had not been ready for war with the Japanese and now it looked as though the submarines as a fighting force had been as ill-prepared and as poorly managed.

∼

When you think about it, it is amazing how rapidly news and gossip travels in a "jungle telegraph" system. With people coming and going from one command post to another, you could sit in a place like Mariveles and hear all sorts of skeletons being rattled. The day that the Japanese landed at Lingayen, we learned that our admiral and our general did not see the defense of the Philippines in the same light. In fact, we were told that they were not even communicating with each other. Ever since the Japanese attacked the airfields on the first day of the war, MacArthur had been telling Washington that he could defend the islands. He told the War Department to send him huge reinforcements of men, planes and armor, and to bomb the Japanese mainland. With them, he promised he could hold the Philippines against anything the Japanese would throw at him.[24] Hart was more realistic. He had a pretty good idea of the losses that the navy had suffered at Pearl Harbor. He knew the distances in the Pacific that ships would have to travel and how long it would take them, and he felt that the Philippines were a lost cause as far as the navy was concerned. The Japanese were now in Luzon in force, and there was not much the navy could do about it anymore.[25] He believed it would be better to join up with allied forces to the south and fight the Japanese with a combined fleet. His submarines had not been effective in stopping the invasion and in fact, he seemed to have lost touch with them.

We next learned that MacArthur went his own way and did things without discussing them with Hart. By December 23, the Japanese were moving inland. From their position that evening, it was only a short march to the network of good roads and the two main highways that led to Manila. MacArthur and his staff were positive that Manila was the main objective for the Japanese. He did not want the city damaged, so he decided, without consulting in any way with Hart, to declare Manila an "open city." The admiral found out about this when he read a dispatch on December 23 that predicted it would be made an "open city" and that the army would be retiring to Bataan, rather than defending the town. The next morning he found out it was definite: MacArthur, President Quezon, and other top people in the Filipino government would be leaving for Corregidor that day, and by that midnight, Christmas Eve, Manila would be declared an "open city."[26]

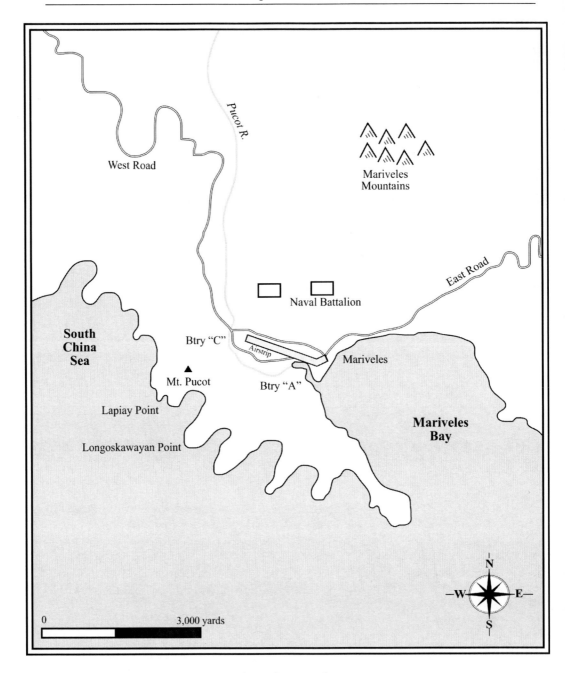

Mariveles and surrounding areas.

The admiral was told that an "open city" meant that all military personnel had to be out of the town. He had his headquarters still in the Marsman Building and his logistics staff had been conducting their submarine war from there. The submarine supplies, including the bulk of the salvaged Mark-14 torpedoes from the Yard, were still stored in Manila waterfront warehouses. The submarine tender, the *Canopus*, was still there. The major communications equipment for the fleet was firmly attached to the floors and walls of the Marsman Building. To put it mildly, our admiral was upset. MacArthur's directive left the navy less than fifteen hours to get everything out of Manila and over to Corregidor or Mariveles. The task was past being difficult—it was impossible.[27]

Such movement required transportation, both by land and by water, and the army grabbed everything that floated or ran on wheels to move their own items.[28] In an hour, the streets became a tangled jumble of every type of vehicle and traffic became impossible. To put the icing on the cake, the Japanese bombed the waterfront heavily on Christmas Eve.[29] The navy had to leave a lot of the things in Manila they needed, including most of those torpedoes that had been so carefully rescued from the yard, most of those "S" boat spare parts, and the headquarters communication equipment.[30]

One major item that was salvaged from the Japanese bombing of the Manila port area on Christmas Eve was the submarine tender, the *Canopus*. She had been tied up to a pier and was attacked that night by the Japanese bombers. A stick landed next to her, but she managed to get underway and out into the bay without damage. She pulled into Mariveles Bay during the small hours of Christmas morning.

The army rear echelon took a different definition of the term "open city" than the literal meaning forced on the navy. Despite MacArthur's directive to the navy, the army continued to move supplies out of the town until New Year's Eve and while they were conducting their troops through the streets of the "open city," they had a lot of men and vehicles to help in the movement.[31] On Christmas Day, MacArthur had his open city, at least for publicity purposes.

On Christmas Day, Admiral Hart not only left the "open city," but he also prepared to leave the Philippines. He turned over command of all naval activities on the islands to Admiral Rockwell in a tunnel in Corregidor. He stated that as each submarine finished its current patrol it was to head south and join the rest of the fleet. His parting gift to MacArthur was to turn over to the general all the naval and Marine personnel left in the Philippines.[32]

We spent our Christmas Eve sitting on the beach at Mariveles. We found out that McClure, as usual, could come through in a pinch. He supplied our old-fashioned Christmas cheer that night by producing two bottles of whiskey, the familiar shape gleaming in the moonlight. As we drank and talked and attempted to sing Christmas carols, we could see the glow of the fires around Manila. They were not just the result of the Japanese bombing the port area. Our demolition teams blew up and burned over a million gallons of navy petroleum that night.

6

Christmas and New Year's at Mariveles

Jack knew all about the traditions surrounding Christmas. On Christmas Day as we stood on the shore of Mariveles Bay in the bright tropical sunlight, he said, "Now we start the Twelve Days of Christmas. You know the old medieval celebration that lasts until January 6; the Partridge in the Pear Tree time. What are we supposed to be celebrating?" None of us had a reply for him. The twelve days of Christmas saw many things happen.

They saw the Fourth Marines leave Olongapo.[1] They saw us in and out of our rice paddy base with our west flank undefended, and apparently the army brass not giving a damn about it. They saw some supply officers play the role of pirates and escape with captured booty. They saw the heaviest bombing of the island of Corregidor to date and the start of an almost continuous bombing of our base and our belongings. They saw the army retire to Bataan and the Japanese occupy Manila. They saw permanence added to our stay in Mariveles.

For two days after Christmas, we continued to salvage anything that might be useful from Cavite and Manila.[2] The working conditions were not ideal. While the navy knew that Manila was an open city, and the Filipinos knew that it was an open city, MacArthur neglected to notify the Japanese military of the city's status. The night after Christmas the blackout was lifted and that night Radio Tokyo acknowledged that it thought Manila was an open city. Since MacArthur had neglected protocol on this open city announcement, the Japanese Air Force no doubt felt that they could still drop their bombs on Manila. On the December 27, their bombers came first along with some fighter planes. They bombed and strafed the port area. At midday, more Japanese planes continued this assignment. For three uninterrupted hours, they worked over the area, virtually destroying the port and the piers.[3]

The previous night and that day, our navy demolition teams added to destruction. After Cavite and the tank farms had been checked as well as possible for anything that might be of value to the enemy, our explosive experts went to work. They blew up anything that they could not move. While this was going on, the army was attempting to move anything they could from the open city to Bataan and Corregidor. What with all the bombers and a nervous labor force, they were not able to move as much as they would have liked. The net result of all this excitement was that the panic among the city's residents returned, heavier than ever. Everyone in town seemed to know that MacArthur and Filipino president Quezon had left for Corregidor. Everyone said that the general and the president would not be hiding in a tunnel with a lot of rock protecting them, unless they knew terrible things that the citizens did not know.

When the Japanese started to carry out their bombings two days after Christmas, the terror of the residents escalated. The Filipinos cursed MacArthur and the politicians with a ferocity that was unbelievable. They were angrier than we had ever seen before, not against the Japanese, but against Quezon and MacArthur. Family after family discussed the options for flight with one another and with their neighbors. The problem facing everyone was in which direction to flee. The Japanese were racing down from the north and from the southeast. There was nothing left floating that would take families by water and no one wanted any part of Bataan if they could avoid it. So, most of those terrified people just sat in Manila and waited for the worst to happen: rape, pillage, and death, just like it had in China.[4]

∼

The First Separate Marine Battalion from Cavite arrived just before Christmas and camped where the West Road crossed the Pucot River, on the west side of our rice paddy. They joined the battalion of Fourth Marines that had come down from Olongapo when hostilities began.[5] We began to feel a lot more comfortable about the defense of our base with these Marines around. Our navy training had not taught us how to handle infantry tactics should the Japanese try landings closer to us.

Our friend Lt. Bill Hogaboom, who had commanded an anti-aircraft battery at Sangley Point, was with them.[6] Unfortunately, the marines had not been able to bring their 3-inch anti-aircraft guns. They left them for the demolition crew to blow up. Their heavy machine guns were sent to Corregidor to bolster the air defenses of those tunnels, and the day after Christmas, their machine gunners were sent to the Rock to man them.[7]

That day after Christmas, more marines arrived. Trucks came rolling down the East road from Bataan, filled with Fourth Marine personnel. From the number of men and vehicles it was apparent that the rest of the marines were coming. During the next two nights, we towed the entire Fourth Marine regiment and all their supplies to Corregidor on some of the old lighters that we had. Most of the First Separate Marine Battalion from Cavite went with them. The defense of our west flank by experienced troops had not lasted very long.

It was the day before New Year's, well after the moving operation was finished, that we spotted a lieutenant who Hogaboom had introduced us to at the Army and Navy Club in Manila. "Why did the marines leave Olongapo and all of you go over to the Rock?" I asked him, and the lieutenant answered, "It seems as though we were in a beauty contest. Everyone wanted the marines to sit with them at the table. The navy was to get us, but we wound up working for the army. When the war started, Admiral Hart told our boss, Colonel Howard, that he had to transfer one of our battalions here to guard Mariveles. You fellows saw us up the road from here after the bombing of your Yard. The admiral retained the other battalion in Olongapo to guard Subic Bay. We found out that passage between here and Subic is difficult. From there the only way to Subic is by a trail so narrow that we could not get our machine gun carts through it and we had to walk single file. This did not make for a good connection between our two battalions.

"On Christmas Eve, our colonel learned that Admiral Hart was going down to Java. He also learned that the Cavite Marine battalion was going to be merged with us, and that all the marines were being placed under the army to use. The colonel got a little hot under the collar and went back to see Admiral Hart. The admiral told him that the army was boss now, and he would have to do what their generals told him. If they wanted to defend Corregidor instead of Bataan, that was their decision, and we were stuck with it. That was why we abandoned our northern bases. So now, we are beach defense for Corregidor, and our colonel is in charge of the combined Marine battalions. You know the marines always get the shitty jobs. We are bivouacked out in the open, not down in those nice bombproof tunnels with all the good food the brass is hoarding. We found out what it is like when they bombed the Rock. They dropped four right through our barracks and blew up one of our dumps of communication equipment. From now on, it's no more barracks. Looks like the Japs are going to be dropping a lot of stuff on top of the Rock from now on, and we are the only people up there for them to aim at, so it's going to get interesting. Believe me, we are going to be well-sandbagged. At least we'll be breathing fresh air and not getting tunnelitis like those army guys seem to have developed the past couple of weeks."

～

The day after Christmas and a few hours before the Olongapo marines arrived, we were standing on the shoreline in front of the ridge that divided the Mariveles plain into eastern and western halves. Behind us to the west were the thickly wooded ridges that separated us from the China Sea—all that stood between a Japanese landing force and us. Coming off the end was a skinny spike of land that protruded into the North Channel. It formed the southwest shoreline of Mariveles Bay, a long sweep of land that stuck way out into the entrance to Manila Bay and aimed like an arrow, pointing due south, toward the tip of the polliwog shaped island that was Corregidor. When we looked north and west from our position on the beach, we could make out the northern anchor of our western ridges. It was called Mount Pucot, but it was not really a mountain, merely a rounded hill about six hundred feet high. To the east of it towered the slopes of Mariveles Mountain, grim and forbidding, covered with a dense growth of tall trees, low brush, and thorn vines.[8]

When we looked to the east, we saw the shoreline of our bay curve in a completion of its half-moon. Due east was the escarpment that formed the other end of the Mariveles basin, and zigzagging down from the plateau above was the road that Red could negotiate so recklessly in daylight and at fifteen miles an hour in a blackout. At the end of the escarpment, jutting out into Manila Bay, were a series of jagged rocks that formed the eastern anchor of our bay and completed the curve. They protruded like a hand covered with a mitten, the outstretched palm aimed at Corregidor, to form a counterpoint to the arrow on the west.

On our side of this mitten, between the thumb and the palm, the almost vertical cliffs had formed another small bay, the bluffs a startling white, devoid of vegetation, exposing the limestone that had been quarried there in the past. The white cliff stood out in startling contrast to all the other cliffs and ridges that were jungle-covered. The *Canopus* was anchored in the little bay and in front of the exposed rock. Her crew had done a thorough job of camouflaging her from spotter planes that might be photographing our bay from on high. They had placed nets over her superstructure, tied tree branches to her masts, to the netting, and to anything else that might reveal her shape, and daubed her sides and decks liberally with green paint. From the sky, she should have photographed like a floating, green island. However, from where we stood, at ground level, her silhouette against the white cliffs identified her as a ship.[9]

As we stood there, the air raid sirens went off again. It seemed as if they had gone off so many times that they were tolling the hours. Up until then, they had been false alarms, and no bombs had dropped. This time they meant it. We looked up and saw the familiar silver dots, just a few of them, but headed straight for us. After all the false alarms, they caught us completely off guard. We ran as fast as we could up the side of the road on the ridge behind us. Red was in the lead; Swede was behind him; and I was in the rear.

There was a tremendous explosion and then a concussion wave slammed me down on the road and then lifted me up and hurled me down the side of the hill. Dirt showered over me. My head hit something, and I saw a bright flash of light. My ears rang to the sound of a shrill whistling that seemed to be coming from inside my head.[10] When I was running, I must have had my mouth open. They tell you that is the best way to be when you are hit by heavy concussion as it avoids rupturing the ear drums. What they do not tell is that when you are tumbled that hard, you will choke on all the dirt thrown into the air. I just lay there for a while. My head ached so badly that I thought I had been hit. I could not get my breath and a red haze clouded my vision. I finally sat up. Mechanically I checked myself; arms, legs, chest, neck, and stomach; except for the ringing in my ears and a mouthful of dirt, there did not seem to be any damage.

I slowly got up and climbed the bank to the road. On the ridge above me, there was a large pile of dirt scarring the foliage. The bomb had landed higher up on the side of the ridge, exploding well above me, covering me with dirt and blowing me off the road. I took a closer look. There was a wide, deep crater in the ridge. It looked just the way the ordnance experts had said it would. I walked slowly up the road looking for Swede and Red and about fifty yards further I saw Swede standing, looking around, with a blank expression on his face. He took a closer look at me. "What happened to you? The side of your face is bleeding." I rubbed my hand across my cheek and saw it was covered with blood. I had been sand papered either by the shower of dirt or when I tumbled down the bank. "It's nothing—just surface scratches. Where did Red go?" I asked. We looked at each other and Swede said, "He was ahead of me, I didn't see him after that stick landed, but I think something hit further up the hill."

We both started to run up the road. Up ahead, on the paddy side of the road, was a little wooden building; really just a shack. As we reached it, Red stumbled out onto the road, shaking his head and weaving on his feet, like a punch-drunk fighter. Like mine, his bomb had hit on the side of the ridge above him. It had exploded when his run had taken him directly opposite the little shed and the concussion had blown him through the door of the shack. He had wound up against the shack's back wall, out cold. We walked over to the shack and looked at the door. It had blown inwards and was intact: torn from the frame at the hinges. We checked Red over, carefully. There was not a mark on him. Like me, he was in one piece with no torn muscles or ligaments, and no broken bones. But, that night he was as stiff and sore as if, as he put it "the entire opposing line had dumped on him."

I said to both of them, "What happened to the Japanese bombing accuracy that we have been counting on? We have spent days giving them fake storage buildings to hit and the dumb bastards have to miss every one of them and land their damn bombs on a hill that has nothing but trees and us. Either they have changed bombardiers and sent the second team in, or up to now, they have been lucky as hell. Unless they improve we are in big trouble."

~

The navy junior officers did not always interpret army directives as literally as some navy staff did. Manila was now officially an open city, and military personnel were supposed to stay clear of it. The trouble was that we had a lead on some very precious supplies that still remained there. The afternoon of the 27th while the Manila port area was being bombed into rubble, our own private intelligence operative confirmed that this was not just a rumor, it was hard fact. This particular operative was a chief machinist mate of the old navy, one we relied upon completely. He had been making such intelligence trips back and forth to Manila since several days before Christmas. He informed us that neatly tied up to the bank in the Pasig River was a large lighter with its top tightly covered with canvas. As far as we were concerned, its cargo was an absolute necessity to our survival in Mariveles.

The lighter was big and held enough materials to last our base and its men for months. What we could not use ourselves, we could barter to the army. As the port was being bombed out of existence that very afternoon, it was imperative that we move without delay. If our lighter had not already been destroyed, it could be at any time. Well-armed, four of us boarded a small and very ancient tug and headed up the Bataan coast toward Manila. The Japs must have been really working the port over since noontime as we could see the smoke from the fires when we were half way up the peninsula.

"I wouldn't worry about that," said our leader. "The bombing will just create a lot of confusion to help us. Just let's hope the dumb bastards haven't completely blocked the entrance to the river. It will be dark when we get there and all that crap that has been sunk or is half floating around the port may make it tough to get in." I said, "Just pray that they haven't hit that lighter." Everyone said amen to that.

As it got dark, we cut across the bay. Even in the dark, we looked like pirates, our expressions grim and determined. We wanted that prize so badly we could taste it, and no one was going to stop us from seizing it. We knew that, after the long and heavy bombing that day, there would be a lot of nervous Filipinos. If any were left still guarding the port area, they would be the ones with enough guts to be sticking around, but they could be trigger-happy. Also, the army would be trying to make up for lost time in salvaging what they could, if anything was left we might be faced with all sorts of tactical decisions that would have to be made quickly.

At our top speed of five knots, we slid smoothly into the pier area.[11] The amount of damage the Japanese bombers had done that day made it almost unrecognizable. They had smashed every pier. Little ships and boats of every type were either sunk or burning in the water. The fires lit up the whole area. There was so much light that there was no concealment, but at least we could see well enough to avoid running into something. As we approached, the entrance to the Pasig River did seem to be blocked. Masts, pieces of wood, and steel were sticking up from the water. We slowly maneuvered our way into the river proper, easing our way past wrecked Fort San Diego, which had taken a terrific pasting. The appearance of the river was not encouraging. There was as much sunk in it as we had seen in the port area. We navigated cautiously around one broken or sunken boat after another and past several bodies of Filipinos who had been caught there earlier. Finally, we reached our objective. It was beautiful. As far as we could see, there was not a mark on it. From the looks of things, it was the only undamaged item in the area.

We fastened our towing lines. Slowly we opened our throttle, our lines tightened and the lighter inched away from the shore into the stream. We started to work our way back to the entrance of the river, our little tug straining to move the big lighter and all of us wondering how we would get a clumsy tow like that through the mess we had negotiated on the way in. We had moved about fifty feet when a spotlight suddenly hit on us from the shore. A Filipino yelled at us in what I guessed was Tagalog. The chief roared back, "Speak English and identify yourself. Immediately!" The chief had a way about him. When he gave an order, it made me think that he had missed his calling. He would have made a hell of a general. The light was turned slightly toward the lighter and the voice called back, "We are river security. Who are you? What are you doing here? What do you have there?" The chief bellowed, "Turn off that damn light and come over here." His tone was very firm. Four uniformed and armed Filipinos approached the river's edge. One moved forward to the bank. The other three stayed back with their rifles trained on us. We were not dealing with amateurs. "Identify yourself," thundered the chief. "I want to see real identification. Now!" When you are a pirate, you always fight fire with fire. The Filipino at the riverbank had not faced this one before. We could see that he was hesitating. The chief bellowed, "Oh hell. It's alright. I believe you men, but when we get back to Corregidor, I don't want to hear a word about this interference. We are on an important, confidential mission for the general personally. This lighter should never have been left here unattended. It must be in Corregidor before dawn. I want each of you men to forget you ever saw us. Is that clear?" The men on the bank were now definitely worried that they had stepped into something that was out of their league. The chief repeated, "Is that clear?" The four Filipinos saluted smartly and said, "Yes Sir!" They watched us as we slowly maneuvered our tug and its clumsy tow down the crowded river. It was dawn when we pulled into the little pier at Mariveles. We tied up the lighter and had breakfast.

Then we called the naval personnel and the marines to the pier to help unload our prize. Its contents were to be stored in the little tunnel at the top of our road. Everyone crowded around as we removed the canvas cover from the lighter. Exposed in the early morning light were the precious contents: case upon case of cigarettes, candy, pipe tobacco, soap, shaving cream, razors and blades, toilet paper, and on and on. Man does not live by rice and canned Vienna sausages alone. P-X supplies make life much more bearable, particularly when they are free.[12]

~

The following day we decided to visit the Supply Officer on the *Canopus*. As we neared the eastern end of Mariveles Bay, we heard the air raid sirens sounding on Corregidor. Our own sirens immediately followed. We moved our van off the road, got out, and stood on the shore. Within minutes, we saw the familiar "V" of silver dots, coming in from the northwest, heading straight for Corregidor flying at the usual high height. In less than a minute, a second formation followed and, then a third. Every gun in the area opened up on them. Our own 3-inch guns on the ridges behind us joined in the tremendous barrage from the Rock. The sky was filled with black and white puffs as shells exploded well below the formations of flying dots.

None of this seemed to affect the steady procession of the "V" formations. No planes broke ranks, and none fell smoking toward the water. It seemed to be a repetition of the Cavite Navy Yard bombing, only this time there were many more planes involved. Someone figured later that the Japanese used three hundred and fifty planes in the attack. Wave after wave dropped their bombs on Corregidor, while we sat on the beach watching for over three hours, hoping that the Fourth Marines this time had taken shelter and had not worried about the beach defenses that were so dear to the army brass.[13]

Finally, it seemed that the attack was finished. Ten minutes passed, and we could not see any more formations wheeling in from the west. Then suddenly we heard the sound of engines again. Coming out of the lowering sun and heading straight for us was a formation of nine twin-engine planes. They kept coming, and we saw the release of a stick of bombs, coming right at us. We hit the sand of the beach and heard the explosions. The Japanese were not aiming at us, but at the tender *Canopus* that was moored in front of the white limestone rock quarry. Their bombs bracketed the tender perfectly. Some hit the limestone above her, hurling down rocks on to her decks, others landed in the water beside her and ahead of her, throwing up fountains of water several feet high. One appeared to hit her stern, going through the decks and exploding below. The first explosion was followed by a series of muffled, smaller ones within the ship, and the tender shuddered in the water. Smoke started to rise from her deck and out from under her camouflage netting. Swede yelled, "That one bomb that went into her would have gone off damn close to her magazine. If the fires spread, they will get into her magazines and blow up the ship. They had better move fast."

We could not do much since we had no firefighting equipment and water lines. We only had people and a few buckets. The crew had to save the ship with what they already had. They fought the fires all the rest of the afternoon. As night was falling four hours later, they finally extinguished the fires. Luckily, shrapnel fragments from the bomb had severed water and steam pipes near the magazines and flooded the area enough to extinguish most of the flames and the magazines did not blow. The bomb had done some human damage. Six of the crew had been killed, and six more were badly wounded.[14]

The bombing did make a change in the operation of the *Canopus*. She was a sitting duck in that cove and the Japanese now knew it. From then on, only the gun crews stayed aboard during the daylight hours and most of the crew slept ashore with the rest of us during the day. They did most of the work in her shops during the nights. On January 5, seven heavy Japanese bombers tried once more to destroy the tender, and bombs again bracketed the ship. Fortunately, only one hit her, striking the side of her smokestack and spraying the upper decks with shrapnel. The gun crews had retreated behind the splinter shields before the bombs landed, but flying metal wounded fifteen men. Some of the near misses that landed in the water beside her had been contact bombs that exploded above the water, piercing both sides of the ship's hull above the water line. Others exploded deep under water and buckled in her hull several inches in places, shearing and cracking her plates and causing serious leakage with the loosened rivets. Small shrapnel peppered her upper decks and works to the point that she had a Swiss cheese appearance.[15]

While the tender still floated, we could not understand why the *Canopus* remained tied up in front of the rock quarry in Mariveles bay. We knew that the last submarine had gone south on the night of New Year's Eve to join the other boats and the other two tenders along the Malay Barrier. The *Canopus* had no pig boats left in her flock. For some reason the staff on Corregidor would not give her orders to go south and join the others, taking her chances in the open sea as her crew wanted. Instead, she remained tied to the shore with no submarines to service.[16]

～

New Year's Eve came and went like any other night on the shoreline of Mariveles Bay. We saw the glow in the dark sky of the lights in Manila. Things appeared to be quiet in the city; there certainly were no fireworks or other signs of wild gaiety. Shortly after nine that evening the glow began to fade. We assumed that the Filipinos were sitting down, awaiting the arrival of the Japanese troops. I did not think that the incoming year would be a happy one, and not worth staying up until midnight to usher it in. I wondered how Betty Lou was doing, and if she was celebrating the coming of the New Year. There would not be any of her "boys" to take her out celebrating that night. Everyone would be heading toward the ridges of Bataan, and I would be spending the evening in the company of other troops.

I had managed to telephone her a couple of times after the bombing of the yard and had seen her during one of my quick trips into Manila. During our brief visit, I had made certain that she drank straight Coca-Cola without the addition of rum. She was frightened and not sure that she could survive the violence or the change in her lifestyle that appeared to be coming. She told me that her boss knew people in Baguio and that they might go up there until they knew what was going to happen. I told her that I thought it would be a good idea. I did not see her again.[17]

By the end of the Twelve Days of Christmas, the army had accomplished its first objective. It had retreated to the Bataan peninsula to set up their first line of defense. U.S. and Filipino forces had slowed the Japanese troops advance long enough to get most of the infantry and much of the armor down to the peninsula.[18] Simultaneously they had pulled back their forces across the rough terrain and mountainous country of southeastern Luzon. We learned these facts on the last day of the twelve-day festive season from an army major who came over to Mariveles from Corregidor to see what was happening in southern Bataan.

Being on the operations staff, he was privy to all that the army had done with their retreat and told our assembled group what they had accomplished. He explained to us that MacArthur and his staff had pulled off an extremely difficult series of maneuvers, skirmishes, and holding of strategic points to achieve their successful retreat.[19] They had used a lot of untrained Filipino draftees supported by a few professionals from the Scouts and the Constabulary and a minority of Americans to stem the tide of the Japanese advance at critical junctures and avoid a rout. They had matched the Japanese time after time in handling artillery; they had clobbered the enemy in a couple of wild tank battles; and they had done all this without air support. Fortunately, the Japanese had not supported their own troops too well from the air, or things might have turned out differently. The Japanese did not fill the skies with strafing Zeros or blow up the bridges over some of the big rivers the retreating army had to cross; therefore, they had not trapped large pockets of the Filipino-American forces behind these river barriers where they could have annihilated them.[20]

He admitted that there was probably another reason for the success of the American withdrawal. The Japanese general had tunnel vision toward capturing Manila. It was his final objective. He did not give a damn about Bataan.[21] If MacArthur wanted to pull two entire armies into this malaria ridden, jungle covered, virtually uninhabited peninsula, the Japanese probably thought he was crazy. He could pull all his men down into these mountains and the Japanese, at least for now, were willing to let them rot there.

MacArthur's staff had apparently done a great job in getting his men and the arms that they carried down to the gateway to Bataan.[22] We wondered how he had done in getting his supplies to Bataan. His ammunition, clothing, food, and medical supplies would be needed to support all these troops. Our group knew a lot about the problems in moving large tonnages of supplies. We had shifted ours weeks before to Mariveles and Corregidor. We hoped that MacArthur's staff had done the same.

The Japanese marched into the Open City of Manila, unopposed, on New Year's Day.[23] Anything that had been left there by the army was now gone forever, as was anything outside the gateway to Bataan. The door was locked going both ways.

7

The Waiting Begins

The navy personnel who had gone to Mariveles and Corregidor were mainly specialists whose primary function was to support a fleet of seagoing fighting ships. These included those of us who were looking after the little green buildings on the shore of the bay, the *Canopus* with its machine shops and storerooms, the people on the Rock who handled such items as communications, and the inshore patrol that took care of the minefields and ran our little tugs, launches, and big lighters. We were the Shore Establishment of the Asiatic Fleet—the chop suey left over from Sangley Point, Cavite, and Manila.

In every other part of the world, Shore Establishments were busy. In every other part of the world, their members could look out at the water and see the reason for their being there. In every other part of the world, a Shore Establishment could gaze at a harbor and see the ships of different types and sizes, with small boats and tugs busily racing loading or unloading cargo on transports or warship. We sat in Mariveles or on Corregidor, looking at an empty bay. We were like castaways on a desert island. We would have to sit and wait until a vessel appeared on the horizon. The army personnel were in a different situation. They had a lot to occupy their minds. They had a Japanese army shooting at them. Realizing that we were sitting at the end of the line, we wondered how successful they would be in holding those ridges.

On January 10, we learned that MacArthur had come over to Bataan from Corregidor to examine the front. We knew it because one of our PT boats had provided the transportation. We had never heard of him visiting any of Luzon's battlefields before, and we wondered how often he would be coming over to our side of the water to inspect his troops in the future.[1] He did not seem to us like the sort of general who paced the front lines while he personally adjusted the disposition of his troops.

On the day of the visit from the headman, we had a visitor of our own, this time one of our Supply Corps peers who had been sent to the Rock. His name was Jim Bullock, and one of his main hobbies was to keep track of what the army was doing.[2] Jim was the sort of fellow that you would never find in a tunnel when an air raid siren sounded. He would be up on top, racing around, ducking bombs and estimating how well the army was shooting back. Jim knew the army pretty well. We figured he could tell us what we wanted to know about Bataan.

We sat on the beach not far from the Quarantine Station and started our questions with "Jim, exactly how big an area is the army covering?" He picked up a stick and started drawing a map of the peninsula, illustrating his points as he made them by sketching on the hard beach sand. "At the top of the peninsula from Olongapo on the west coast to the Bay on the east is about twenty miles across. From Route 7, or the gateway, is about twenty-five miles down to Mariveles. If the Nips did some fast driving with their armor, it might take them a couple of hours to make the trip down Highway 101."

Pointing with his stick, he said, "Here is Subic Bay, Olongapo, and here we are in Mariveles. You can see that Bataan is shaped sort of like a heavy mitten. Let's call the route across the top, the wrist. On the west coast, there is a bulge out into the China Sea, from Subic Bay about half way down, to just above Bagac, the thumb in the mitten. Then the other four fingers of the hand extend down below that and make the rounded end of the mitten that is formed by Mariveles and the area east of here.

"You know that the eastern part of Bataan is gently rolling country, facing on Manila Bay, and going inland for up to five miles. It is rice country with several swampy areas crossed by a lot of small rivers. Everything west of that is mountainous and extremely rugged, all the way to the west coast. If you ever walked down the center of the peninsula, you would know how rugged it is. The mountains start about a third of the way down with 3,000-foot high Mount Santa Rosa and right below Mount Natib, which is 4,200 feet high. South of that is Mount Silnganan at 3,600 feet high. Just below it is the saddle that crosses Bataan, the only place where they were ever able to build a road from the east coast to the west coast. Then below that are the Mariveles Mountains that you see behind you. The highest mountain in the peninsula is part of those, Mount Bataan, topping 4,700 feet."[3]

He added, "That is the good news: a string of mountains forming the backbone and running from north to south down the center of Bataan; mountains that are too high and too rugged for armies to climb in force and hold. The bad news is that in between these mountains is some of the worst country anyone would want to try and hold; deep valleys and ravines, swift flowing rivers, and large areas of swamps filled with malaria mosquitoes. Worse, there is only a single road from east to west going across the saddle. The only north to south roads are the two you know, one going all the way up the east coast along the bay and one going part way up the west coast, inland from the points and bays. If you want to take any other route through Bataan, you have to follow one of the jungle trails. Except for the saddle area that I mentioned, it is a hell of a country for moving around large groups of men and particularly difficult for moving heavy equipment."

Swede interrupted. "With mountains that high all the way down the middle of Bataan, what is the army's plan for holding the Japs?" Jim explained, "First, they have divided the army into two Corps. General Wainwright has I Corps holding the west side and General Parker has II Corps men holding the east side. They started out by forming an east to west line, but they found that they could not link up their flanks with Mount Natib in the way." "Wait a minute," I said. "Mount Natib is a third the way down Bataan, only about twenty miles above us. I thought they were holding a line across the top over to Olongapo." Jim answered, "They are a lot further down than that. The army has retired south all the way down to the saddle and formed a line with no breaks in it, from Orion on the east coast to Bagac on the west coast. That is the line they are going to try and hold for the duration of the campaign. The country across the saddle is not too bad as Bataan goes. Above them are those mountains and valleys the Japs have to go through to get to them, and at their backs are the Mariveles Mountains you see to the north of here."

McClure said, "Jim this line they are holding is almost on our door step." "That's right," said Jim. "The west anchor is only about twelve miles above us. On a quiet day, you guys may even hear the guns firing. A big advantage in moving this far down the peninsula is that they have cut the territory they are defending by fifty percent. It is down to two hundred square miles total. The Orion to Bagac line is the one they think they can hold until the relief comes. If they lose that line, they will have real problems. They have designed a final retreat line below but it is not a good line as it crosses Mount Bataan in the middle. They call anything below that line the Service Area, which includes all of you."[4]

∼

While Jim gave us our bird's eye view of Bataan, a few days later another authority gave us a detailed view of our backyard. He was Commander Frank Bridget.[5] He had been with the PBYs in Olongapo and when they were sunk, he was stranded in Mariveles with the rest of us. The morning we had our talk with him, Swede and I had walked up the West Road and were standing on the bridge that crossed the Pucot River, the little stream that bordered the west side of our paddy and emptied into Mariveles Bay. As we stood looking down at the riverbed, we saw Bridget coming down the road with two sailors trailing him. Swede said, "How are we doing, Commander?" and added, "We were wondering where the good trail starts that goes over the ridge to the points and how we can get up to Mount Pucot from over there."

Bridget said that he and the sailors had just come down from the summit of Mount Pucot and added, "That is the best view of the west coast that you will find around here. I am maintaining an observation post on the summit. One of these days, the Japs are going to try an end run around the west end of the army's line and somewhere along this lower coast is the best place for them to do it. If we hold the top of Mount Pucot, we should be able to see them coming and have a chance to assemble a force to drive them out." I asked, "What is the coast like on the other side of Pucot?" Bridget was as good a military lecturer as Bullock. He drew a map of the coast on the dirt of the road.

"Here is this bridge crossing the Pucot River, where we are standing. Here is the summit of Mount Pucot, about a half mile north and slightly west of us. Due west of the summit is the coast, maybe a half mile to the heights overlooking the nearest bay. The whole west coast of Bataan, from Subic Bay down to Mariveles Bay are points of land that stick well out into the China Sea and have long, narrow tidal bays in between them, with high cliffs forming most of the shoreline. In most places, the ridges border and overlook the points. Everything is covered with jungle, vines, and tall trees that grow on the ridges and on the points. It's rough country, all the way from Subic down to Mariveles."

He continued, "From a little bit above Mount Pucot to the most southernly point that juts out into Manila Bay and forms its north entrance is a distance of a little over two miles. That bit of coastline is the western flank of our base at Mariveles, and has five points on it. When I saw it from the air, it always reminded me of a hand, with the fingers sticking out into the ocean, with the thumb at the top and then the four fingers. The thumb is really made up of two points that are close together, the north one called Latain and the south one called Lapiay. Below Lapiay is a deep bay, and then we have the index finger of the hand called Longoskawayan Point. Then another deep bay followed by the middle finger called Maiklac Point; then another bay and there is Mahaba Point. What would be the little finger is called Talaga Point."

"It seems to me," I interjected, "that those points, jutting out into the sea, covered with heavy vegetation and tall trees, and those long bays in between them, offer an opportunity for the Japs to land a force and try and take Mariveles. If they got supported in strength, they could then move north and hit the army lines from the rear. The jungle along the ridges and out on to the points is thick enough to hide a small army. If I were the Jap general, I would probably take the top points first, the thumb, then move inland and take Mount Pucot and the ridges all the way down to where we are now. If it were done right, they could be in Mariveles within an hour after they landed."

Swede said, "The PTs patrol up and down the coast most nights. Wouldn't they see the Japs coming down?" Bridget replied, "On a dark night that is a lot of water and a ragged coastline out there. Given luck, several well-spaced barges could still sneak through and land a thousand men on the points, if they picked the right night. If they hugged the shoreline, the PTs might never see them." Thinking of the Fourth Marines and their west coast beach patrol experience and the army's disregard for defending the area from an amphibious invasion, I asked, "What does the army have now as a beach defense up the coast?" Bridget turned and looked up the road to the north. "There are not any trained infantry troops guarding this coast from here all the way up to Bagac, the west anchor for the army's front lines. So, that Fourth Marine lieutenant was right. Corregidor had grabbed them all. I said, "Isn't that sort of crazy, to leave a long stretch of the coast undefended?"

Bridget responded coolly, "I did not say it was undefended. I said there were no trained infantry troops posted along it. Just above Mount Pucot, they have placed two hundred of the pilots and the ground crews of the Third Pursuit Squadron. Then above them is a battalion of the Constabulary; and above them is another squadron of grounded pursuit pilots and ground crews covering Quinoa Point.[6] With the exception of the Constabulary, none of those are infantrymen." Swede said, "What about the coast below Mount Pucot; our immediate area? Since the army hauled all the Fourth Marines that were there over to the Rock, nobody is stationed guarding those five points."

"That is correct," said the commander. "Up to now it has been completely ignored. The army figures that stretch is the navy's problem. For the past couple of weeks I have been working on a plan to correct the situation. Starting immediately, we are forming a Naval Battalion. With the crew of the *Canopus* and you fellows on the base, we can easily put together a force of six hundred men.[7] We will use the Marine NCOs that are here now under Hogaboom to lead the platoons and teach you infantry tactics.[8] I figure we had better learn pretty quickly." Swede and I told the commander we would be glad to help in any way we could.

When you are sitting in a Service Area, you usually do not know what is happening to your defenders most of the time. You tend to forget about them, particularly when they are far enough away so that you don't hear the weapons being fired. After the confusion in retreating from Cavite and the way people had been spread around between Corregidor and the Mariveles shoreline, it was mid–January before we had a completely accurate head count of the number of men in our Shore Establishment and where they were located. One morning Swede had gone over to the Rock to do a final check on the figures so that we would know exactly the population that we were going to be feeding and supplying with the necessities of life.

Upon his return, he called the supply forces together and told us, "We now have accurate lists of the disposition of personnel from the Sixteenth Naval District in Mariveles and Corregidor. Except for the numbers being reduced by bombing attacks, they should stay the same until the relief column gets here. They sure aren't going to increase because they have accounted for everyone that is left." He took out a sheet of paper and read off the figures. "There are 98 officers and 453 enlisted personnel on Corregidor. They tell us that we do not have to worry about them as they have their own food and clothing supply. We may be called at times for a back-up, but as well fixed as they are, I doubt it." He looked around the curve of the bay and said, "Our main concern is the navy personnel in Mariveles. In total, we have 125 officers and 1,062 enlisted personnel. Twenty of the officers and 510 enlisted are on the *Canopus* so that makes up almost half of our total force.[9]

"In the expanded Fourth Marines, with our Cavite battalion, there are 77 officers and 1,275 enlisted men and NCOs on the Rock. Here in Mariveles, we have another four officers and 148 enlisted men and NCOs, and today they are sending over from Corregidor a contingent of two more officers and forty men to beef up our air defense. We are responsible for feeding the marines we have here. That means we have a total force as of today in Mariveles of just fewer than 1,400 to take care of.

"There should be no problem as far as food is concerned. We have enough in our stockpile to feed two thousand men for six months at a full ration of four thousand calories a day, and we are damn well going to see that we don't lose any of it to those Nip bastards who are trying to bomb us. We haven't lost any yet, but the base with all those buildings is going to look inviting to their planes, and so is the *Canopus*, so they probably will keep dropping on us. Let's hope they are accurate and keep hitting the buildings. Stay the hell away from those sheds when the alarm goes off. Hit the fox holes and stay there."

I asked what was to become the sixty-four million dollar question as the days dragged on during the ensuing weeks. "What do we do about those poor Filipino bastards in the army? The Scouts that came down the West Road yesterday said that their food is so slim that in a few weeks they will be starving." "I know it," said Swede, "and there is not one damn thing we can do about it. We cannot, I repeat not, let them have our food, or we will be in the same boat. What we have here is a drop in the bucket compared to the quantity the army needs. They screwed up completely when they retreated to Bataan. MacArthur and his staff were as responsible as the Quartermaster Corps. They got a hell of a lot of men and ammo here, but they forgot they had to feed and clothe them. It's a mess. They gave me the whole story when I was on the Rock this morning.

"It started with the way MacArthur planned to meet the invasions by the Japs. He thought that he could stop them at the beaches. The idea of falling back into Bataan was not taken too seriously until the Japanese landed and started to push toward Manila. By then MacArthur began to get a little more realistic concerning the ability of the Japs and the training of his Filipino draftees. Unfortunately, by then it was a little late to do the real planning he should have done before the invasion. Because he thought he would stop the Japs at the beaches, he made the tactical mistake of moving most of his supplies into the forward areas, as well as into stockpiles around Manila. Bataan was almost ignored in the advanced planning. It was not stocked with food, clothing, and medical supplies like Corregidor was or we were here.[10]

"When the Japanese started moving toward Manila within twenty-four hours after they hit the beaches, MacArthur's supply people were completely unprepared and poorly trained. In case after case, the Filipinos simply abandoned the supplies. The supply troops, with no combat training, and their civilian helpers, turned tail and ran. Railway workers deserted their trains and truck drivers didn't wait to get loaded.[11]

"A few of the big supply depots that were on the route of the Japanese advance were abandoned before there was any sign of the advancing enemy. A major depot was Fort Stotsenburg, a few miles above San Fernando. On Christmas Eve, MacArthur ordered it evacuated and the destruction of gasoline. A lieutenant colonel was smart enough to save some of it by sending some to Bataan and by filling the tank of every vehicle on the base before they took off in them. The troops at the fort took the order to abandon literally and headed south empty, days before there was a Jap in sight. They left behind 8,000 pounds of fresh beef, 30,000 units of dry rations, and a huge supply of clothing. Other depots were abandoned the same way.[12]

"The army Quartermaster is now claiming that they stocked canned meat and fish and some dry stores in advance on Bataan.[13] Maybe they did, but that major who came over here a few days ago said that he had done a survey and that they had moved only enough rice for twenty days; onions, cereals and canned fruits are in such small quantities as not to be worth counting. There are no fresh meats, vegetables, or fruits. They are trying to buy food from the locals and the Filipinos are down to a lot of scrounging. They are setting up a slaughterhouse to kill all the caribou they can round up, and they are using every native with a banca (a native boat) on the east coast to fish for them. If the Japs keep bombing the Bay, those fishermen will probably want to stay home.

"The Americans in the army will probably take the worst beating. The Filipinos are used to eating less. A week ago, they were down to half rations all over Bataan.[14] After a couple of months of that, they actually will be starving. Climbing those ridges and trying to stay alert on that kind of diet is going to be real tough. Corregidor is the one place the army has well stocked with food. They told me that they have enough food there to feed ten thousand Americans for six months on full rations; and on top of that, they have refrigeration over there that holds a hell of a lot of fresh meat and vegetables. To keep up the supply of fresh produce they have boats sneaking in at night from the south side of the Bay. It would be nice if some of them could come over this far.

"The clothing supplies for the Filipinos are as bad as the food situation. The Quartermaster brought down practically no clothing for the poor bastards. A lot of the Filipinos are shoeless and ragged already. They also goofed on their medical supplies. That big hospital just north of Mariveles and the one on Corregidor are it. They didn't bring enough of the kind of sulfa drugs they need for treating wounds, and they are without a lot of the medicines they need for treating dysentery. They will probably have a lot of dysentery because the Filipinos are drinking out of every stream and pond, and they don't have much in the way of water purification kits. They are already showing signs of malaria all over the front and there is damn little quinine to hold it in check or treat the bad cases.[15] It is obvious that Bataan is the area that is getting the short end of the stick. The Rock is a resort hotel by comparison. It pisses me off to see it."

Swede turned to me. "So to answer your question, yes, I think the Filipinos are going to be starving in the next few weeks, unless they can find enough lizards and snakes to eat, and no, we cannot do one damn thing from here. If their own leaders want to sit fat and happy on the Rock and let the poor bastards starve, we cannot do much about it. The navy planned our retreat well, and we did it properly. We brought down our supplies, and we brought the quantities we were supposed to have. The army could have done the same thing if MacArthur and his staff had had the brains to do so."

The next day Red said, "All this talk about food and starvation makes me hungry to try something different. How about we have an old fashioned barbecue?" Mac said, "I doubt if corned beef and Vienna sausages will taste any different if we barbecue them." "You are missing my point," said Red. "I mean a real old-fashioned barbecue with real fresh meat. Up the mountain, in those dry gulches and little streams, there are wild pigs. You know, boar, the kind with tusks. I say that we go up there and shoot some of them. Then, we bring them down here, dress and barbecue them, western style. Who wants to go with me?" The entire group of six of us volunteered. Just the thought of fresh pork, roasting on an open fire, made our mouths water. We were quite willing to do without the apples and the chestnuts if we had to.

Red planned the operation, saying the wild boar were difficult to see until you were right on top of them, and they could move fast, so we would use our .45s to do the work. We set off up the mountain and after about a two-mile hike we came to a draw that wound its way upwards through low growth so thick that at times it almost hid the bed of the draw. Every few hundred feet we came upon bamboo thickets that blocked our path and the only way to get through was to hack our way with our bolos. Vines hung down from even the smaller trees and interspersed with the large trees were clumps of thorn vines that all of us hated. Red was leading the party in single file when he suddenly signaled us to stop and listen. We could hear the pigs making a low grunting sound not too far above us. Red whispered, "I'll circle if I can and get above them; then I'll drive them down to you. They should follow the draw, so be ready."

I heard Red moving quietly along the side of the draw. Then all was quiet for about three minutes. Suddenly, I heard a loud screeching "Sooohoowheee" which we assumed to be Red's Iowa hog call. Then I heard a crashing in the bushes and a loud "Sonofabitch." I raced up the draw and found Red dusting himself off, his pants covered with mud. "What happened?" I asked him. Red glared at me. "These Filipino pigs don't know a hog call from a cat call. There were three of them and when I gave my call they charged me instead of running toward you guys."

We continued to trudge up the mountain. The higher we went the wetter the bottom of the draw became and within a half hour, our pants were covered with mud. Then we heard the grunting sound again, up ahead of us and still coming from the draw as far as we could tell. I said to Red, "This time forget the hog calling. Fire a shot in the air. That should drive them toward us." Red set off to do his part of the round up, and I took up the lead position of our troop. It was a deep, narrow section of the draw, and I found I could put a foot on each bank, allowing a good tunnel for the pigs to pass beneath me. I positioned myself and straddled the draw, one hand against a tree for support, the other holding my .45 aimed up the draw. A few minutes later, a shot rang out, echoing in the stillness of the growth on each side of me. Some birds flew out of a tree above me and at least a dozen monkeys started racing through the branches. Before I had time to figure out what was happening, my left foot started to slip on the bank and then I heard a loud snort. Right in front of me, tearing down the draw like an express train, was the biggest boar I had ever imagined. All I could see were two huge tusks, curving upward and outward toward my vital parts, two eyes that I swear were blazing fire and a hairy face. It was something straight out of a horror movie. I gave a hard push with my right foot and hurled myself away from the draw and into a thicket of low scrub at the side. As I flew through the air, I had the impression that more boar were tearing down the draw behind their huge leader. When I landed, I heard a succession of shots crashing out below me, the sound of a pig squealing, then two more shots. Then silence. I sat where I had landed and found myself shaking.

I was still sitting there when Red came running down the draw. "How many did you get?" he asked. "Not a goddamned one, but that big one almost got me. I hope the others down below got him." Red did not say anything, and I gathered that he was not too impressed with my pig hunting skills. We trudged down the draw and after rounding a bend, we found the others standing over three boar, the big monster and two females. They told us that there were six in the group, and three got past them. We wrestled those three pigs all the way down to the paddy, and it took us most of the afternoon. It was worth it. They were great eating, and our barbecue was a huge success with the whole base, even if the meat was a little strong and kind of tough.

~

We realized that if we wanted to hear tales of action on the high seas from the mouths of the men who were involved, we would have to hear them from the only attack fleet that was left on Luzon—the five remaining PT boats. We would send them off to attack the enemy and welcome them back when they returned from their missions. We would keep careful score of their results as we listened to the play-by-play description of their activities when they returned to their base in Sisiman Cove.

We had to wait until January 18 before the boats of Squadron 3 had engaged in a real attack against Japanese ships. On the afternoon that followed, Mac suggested we visit the PT boat crews and see how they made out the previous night since the army had claimed that there were four Jap ships near Subic. When we reached Sisiman Cove there was no sign of PT-31. We saw Ensign Chandler on the bridge of PT-34, and Mac called out. "Is Delong around?" Chandler came forward and looked at us. "Hi Mac. No he isn't. I hate to say it, but the 31 boat didn't make it back last night."[16]

He jumped down on the little pier and walked over to us. "What the hell happened?" asked Swede. He and Delong had been friends since the PT boats had come out to the islands. "We had a rough time last night," said Chandler. "We think that Delong and his crew may have bought the farm." "You mean you don't know? Weren't the two boats together up there?" Swede was getting a little impatient. Chandler took a deep breath and replied, "Yeah, we went up together, but when we got to Subic we separated. Bulkeley's plan was that he and I would take the 34 boat and check the western entrance of Subic and Delong and Ensign Plant would check the eastern side and then the two boats would meet later."[17]

Chandler continued, "We started along the western shore about midnight and it was dark as hell with no moon at all. We hadn't gone a quarter mile when we were challenged by a light from shore, about a mile off our port bow. Bulkeley cut speed to ten knots, and we sneaked in further. We heard firing on the far side of the bay, and we didn't know whether they were going after Delong or something else had spooked them, so we kept going and right away we were challenged by a patrol boat. It hit us dead on with its light, and we took off to the southeast. When we got to the bay entrance, two more Japanese lights focused on us, and they opened up with heavy machine guns." He added that later, "when we got to the rendezvous, the 31 boat with Delong and Plant wasn't there. After waiting for a half an hour, Bulkeley decided that our boat should go alone, so we cut down to eight knots and went down the bay. We hadn't gone more than five hundred yards when we saw a two-masted freighter dead ahead. As soon as we spotted her, she turned on her signal light to challenge us. Bulkeley ordered us to fire two fish at her. For the first time since we've had the boats, one of the fish hung up in the tube, and we had a 'hot run.'" Bulkeley ordered me to get the hell out of there and right after we turned there was an explosion and a flash behind us and then two more flashes, so we think that we got a hit on the freighter."

Chandler added, "While all this was going on and I was trying to barrel out of the bay, the damn torpedo was still sticking half way out of the tube, making noise and getting ready to detonate at any minute. Its propellers turned like crazy, and the rings around the fish's turbines got so hot you could see them glow in the dark. Our chief torpedo man saved our ass. He jumped on to the fish and shut off the air valve to the combustion chamber. He then stuffed toilet paper into the ring and jammed the blades so they wouldn't turn. He had to climb all the way out onto the fish while the boat was bouncing all over the swells. He is one hell of a sailor. We were still in deep trouble, because once a fish is armed it only takes an eight-pound punch to detonate it. We tried everything we knew to bounce that torpedo out of the tube. It took us four hours but we finally got it overboard. When we got back to the minefield, we waited until dawn, but the 31 boat never did show. We came back here, and we have waited all day, figuring they would come in. It doesn't look good."[18]

We waited the rest of the day and all the next for news of Delong and his crew, and Swede kept telling us that he was sure they would make it. As the hours dragged by, we got more and more pessimistic. We all knew it only took one hit from those shore batteries to finish off a plywood boat and its crew. At 5:30 that evening, we were walking on the West Road when a truck came down from the north. We could see that the back held a small group of Americans and that there were two men in front with a Filipino driver. As they got closer, we made out the familiar faces of Delong and men from the crew of the 31 boat. Delong looked beat, but he gave a big grin when Swede stopped the truck and called out, "Welcome aboard." We then piled into Red's van and followed the truck over to Sisiman Cove. As we sat on the bridge of one of the boats, drinking coffee and eating some of our supplies that Red always seemed to have stashed away for emergencies, Delong told us his story of the raid.

"After we left the 34 boat and had gone down the shore of Subic, our engines died on us. As soon as we got them restarted, our cooling system fritzed. We worked trying to fix it and of course, we were drifting. Then I felt the hull grinding, and the next thing I knew we were hung up on a reef. We tried rocking the boat off, but she wouldn't budge. We gave it hell in reverse with all engines and though she moved a little, we were still stuck. We tried reverse some more and wound up burning out our reverse gears. The Japs heard the engine sound and started searching for us with their 3-inch guns."

Delong sighed and continued. "There wasn't much we could do. We made a raft out of mattresses, and I ordered the crew and Plant to shove off and head for shore. I stayed long enough to wreck the boat. Then, I started swimming around looking for the raft. Unfortunately, it was too dark to see anything, so I swam to the beach. When it got light enough to see, I found a lot of footprints and followed them down the beach to a clump of trees and as I got near them one of the crew called out to me. They were all hidden there except for Plant and two of the men who had stayed with the raft because they didn't think they were good enough swimmers to make it to the beach. I figured we were going to have a tough time getting back to the base. By my reckoning the Filipino lines were about twelve miles south of there. We figured the best way would be to go by water.

We searched around and finally found two bancas with paddles. Near them, we found two shovels and a board. When it got dark, we shoved off. There were Nips all around us, and we could hear them talking about two hundred yards away. We had hardly made it through the surf when we hit a squall with a lot of wave and both bancas capsized. We lost the shovels and the board, but we managed to keep the two paddles. We finally got them righted and bailed out, and we tied them together and headed south. The waves and the currents were terrible. By three in the morning we were so beat I knew we would never make it to our base.

"We went into the beach figuring we would be about to our lines and right at the shore, we hit barb wire. We managed to crawl under it, and on the other side, we ran into a cliff face. In the dark there was no way we were going to climb that. We waited until it got light and then started walking south between the wire and the cliffs. Finally, we came to a beach and saw a Filipino sentry. He took us up to the field headquarters of his unit and they got us the ride back to Mariveles." Naturally we all wanted to know if there had been any sign of Plant and the two men with him since they last saw him heading south on the raft in the dark. There had not been. Ensign Plant and the two crewmen never did show up.[19]

When Delong finished his story, we all had the same unexpressed thought in our minds. How would it feel to drive a seventy-foot long PT boat into a place like Subic Bay, that the Japanese heavily patrolled and where the shoreline was loaded with heavy machine guns and artillery? Further, while you were roaming around the bay in the dark and looking for some ship to attack, you had to worry that at any moment your engine might fail and leave you drifting helplessly under the Japanese shore batteries. For the past month, the PTs had experienced so many mechanical problems, the chances were fifty-fifty they would have one on any patrol.

When we got back to Mariveles, Red said what had been on all our minds. "I wonder if their gas and oil really was sabotaged, or if when they picked up those drums and brought them to Sisiman Cove they had the bad luck to get lousy stuff that was full of crap. The skippers had told us what a rough time they had had with their fuel and their engine oil. They had towed over two lighter loads of gasoline and lube oil that had been stored at Sangley Point. They claimed that there was soluble wax of some kind in the gasoline and that it clogged the engines; and that they had found fine sand in the drums of lube oil. They felt that some Jap lover had sabotaged the drums when they were being stored. This meant that they had to filter all of it before they used it. When a boat's tanks hold two thousand gallons that is a long and tedious job. After all that filtering, you still had to clean the fuel strainers and carburetor jets almost hourly to keep the three big engines running smoothly. In addition, there were the maintenance problems inherent in the design and construction of the boats.[20] The amazing thing to us was that they kept the boats running as well as they did.

"Three nights later, Chandler took PT-34 back up to Subic. This time he had Bob Kelly and Bulkeley aboard. Kelly had been in the hospital on Corregidor because on an infection in his hand. This was his first outing since that attack, and he took over the running of the boat. The patrol was supposed to be routine; however, it happened to take place on the night that the Japanese came down the west coast to make a behind-the-lines landing. These landings ended up in what we later called the Battle of the Points. I did not hear the details of PT-34's exploit that night until a week later.

"PT-34 had gone up the coast into the vicinity of Quinauan Point, one of the two areas that the Japanese had targeted for landing their troops. The PT boat ran into one of the landing barges making its way to the beach and a fierce firefight developed. The PT charged the barge, firing its twin .50 caliber machine guns from the stern and .3-caliber from the bow. The men on the barge fired back with rifles and machine guns. Chandler was hit in both ankles as he stood on the unarmored bridge of the PT. By degrees, the heavier firepower and greater maneuverability of the PT turned the tide of the fight and the crew managed to put enough holes below the water line of the overloaded barge to sink it.

"Bulkeley and Kelly decided to high tail it back to Corregidor and report what they had seen. Then, they came upon another barge. This one was headed away from the beach. The PT sprayed it with .50 caliber rounds and got no response. They moved in close to it and Bulkeley tossed a hand grenade into its midsection. After it exploded, everything became quiet. They pulled alongside, and Bulkeley jumped into the landing craft. Lying in it were three Japanese: one dead, one private who was badly wounded, and one officer who was also wounded. They roped the prisoners and hauled them aboard the PT boat, while Bulkeley searched the barge. He found a dispatch case and brought it back to base. A couple of days later, when the contents of the dispatch case had been translated at Corregidor, they were found to contain the operational plans for the Quinauan Point landings along with a muster list.[21]

Little did we know what all of this would mean for us over the coming days."

8

The Battle of the Points

As we walked toward the Quarantine Station in Mariveles early in the morning, Swede said, "Do you fellows realize that it is only a month since the Japs landed in force? Today is January 23. When you look back, it's hard to believe how much has happened in the past month." Directly in front of us was a .50 caliber machine gun, pointing skyward inside a ring of sand bags and two marines were sitting nearby drinking coffee.[1] Other members of our Marine contingent were standing around in small groups. Before long the cooks would be bringing out their pans of food, and we would be eating our hot cakes and Vienna sausages. I looked at the marines and the sailors who were starting to assemble for breakfast. We had become used to our two meals a day routine. No one was starving in this sector of Bataan.[2]

The First Day

As we stood there, Hogaboom came running out of the Marine office toward the gathering men.[3] Red and Mac were watching him, and Red said, "Hogie is in a hell of a hurry this morning. I wonder what's up." Hogaboom started giving orders to the marines who were standing there, and three of them ran off toward the ridge behind us. We walked over to him and asked, "What's the excitement?" Before Hogaboom replied, he told another Marine to assemble all three platoons on the double with full gear and to be ready to move. Then, he turned to us. "We may see a little action this morning. Commander Bridget just phoned me and said a Jap force is trying to take Mount Pucot.[4] I had three of my men up there with some air corps people minding the lookout, and some Japs shot at them. Bridget said he heard the firing over the phone while they were reporting the attack to him. He told everyone to get off the hill and report down here to me. Right now, we don't know too much about the situation or how many Japs are involved, and as soon as my men get here I'm going up there. Bridget figures we can flush them out with the Naval Battalion."[5]

He had just finished speaking when a Marine private and an army corporal came pounding down the path from the ridge behind us. They stopped and bent over, breathing in heavy gasps. Between breaths the Marine managed to say, "Sir, the Nips are coming up Pucot!" another gasping breath, then, "Everyone got the hell off the summit after we reported to Commander Bridget." "Any casualties, McKechnie?" asked Hogaboom.[6] "No sir, but they were firing machine guns at us. I really don't know how many of them there are.[7] We figure the ones shooting at us were a small force, but well dispersed. The bush is so thick that we couldn't tell. I'm guessing no more than ten or twelve firing at us." Swede turned to me and said in a low voice, "The Naval Battalion may have a chance to show what they've learned since Bridget formed them a week ago."[8]

Men in field gear were running down the road toward us. Red turned and looked at them. "You mean the Naval Company, don't you? We only have one platoon of marines, the machine gun group. Then the two rifle platoons of sailors with their Marine NCOs, only sixty-five of them. Hell, that adds to just over a hundred men total, and don't forget Bridget only formed them a week ago, and the marines have had less than four days to teach them infantry tactics. The Nips probably have landed experienced troops up there. I don't think Bridget should fool around; I think he should call the Rock and get the Fourth Marines over here on the double and in strength."

We looked over the men who had come running toward us and were now forming into ranks, with Marine corporals directing them. Each man was wearing his flat steel helmet and carrying a .30 caliber army rifle. I had to admit that they were a rather distinguished looking group of infantrymen. They all were wearing their field gear: web belt with hanging canteen, canvas pouches and bayonet; and knapsacks on the back, tightly strapped. Some had bandoleers of ammunition crisscrossed over their chest and shoulders. The problem was the uniforms they wore. About half the men were wearing regulation khakis, long pants, and either short or long sleeved shirts. The remainder wore what looked like homemade camouflage uniforms, made from either navy denims or whites that had been soaked in strong navy coffee to dye them brown. Some of the whites ended up being a sickly yellow with brown blotches.[9]

A Marine sergeant yelled, "Second Platoon fall out. Get as much extra ammo as you can carry with you. Each man take six grenades." Lieutenant Pew from the Marine anti-aircraft battery stepped forward and said, "As soon as you have your ammo and grenades, climb up on those trucks."[10] He pointed to two trucks that had just pulled up with a navy driver sitting nervously behind the wheel of each. "We will drive up the West Road and then walk the trail to the ridge behind Pucot. When we get there we are going up to the summit." The men clambered up onto the truck beds and with a clashing of gears the trucks took off up the West Road, tires spinning and throwing up dust.

Hogaboom addressed the other sailors who were standing in the ranks and looking nervously at him. "You men in the third platoon; get your extra ammo and grenades, and fall back in. We will go west and up the ridge behind us. When we get to the top of the ridge, first squad under Corporal Paulson will take up position on the hill above us to watch for any Japs coming down to the base.[11] The rest of us will reconnoiter the ridge until we get to the trail leading up to Pucot. We want to be sure to flush out any Japs that may be on the ridge trail, so keep your eyes open and your mouths shut; no unnecessary noise as we move up. Machine gun platoon will stay in reserve here until I call for you, after we know more about the situation."

He turned to us and saw that we were still watching these preparations. "How about the Supply Corps meeting us on the top of Pucot later today and bringing up more water, food, and ammo? If we run into any problems and don't get to the summit, I'll send a runner back and give you the scoop, okay?" "Sure," we said, "we'll meet you up there."

We went back to the east side of the paddy and sat down to discuss our support tactics. I realized that my stomach was growling and that in the excitement we had not eaten breakfast yet. "Who wants to go up there?" asked Swede. We looked at one another, and I found myself saying, "We don't need an army to play water boy, Swede. Get me ten sailors and I'll take the stuff up." "How will you go?" I responded, "I'll take the West Road up to the trail and come into Pucot from the east. It's the easiest climb." "Be damned sure you're armed," said Mac. "Oh I'll be armed." I said, pointing to my holstered Colt .45, while realizing I had never fired it and had only pointed it realistically on our infamous pig-hunting expedition. Red motioned to me, and we walked over to his van. He lifted a seat, reached in and pulled out a Thompson submachine gun and a box of .45 caliber ammunition. Then he turned to me and said, "I'll lend you this for the trip." I looked it over, then lifted it and examined the round drum loaded with .45 caliber shells. It felt heavy and awkward. "How does it work?" I asked. He showed me. "See this. It can either be set for full automatic or single shot fire. Just aim and press the trigger. Pretend you are Al Capone. But be careful when you have it on automatic; hold tight because it has good recoil and wants to lift up on automatic fire, so keep pressing your aim down to compensate."

"Where did you get it?" I asked. "I swapped a carton of cigarettes to a Filipino colonel for it," he said quietly.[12] "And I want it back in good shape." I studied the Tommy Gun some more and heard Red saying, "You had better pick up a load of grenades also." "Grenades! You must be nuts. I have never thrown a grenade." Red looked sternly at me.[13] "This may be no tea party you got yourself into. Besides, it's simple. You just pull the pin, count to three, and throw the damn thing as far as you can at whoever is shooting at you. There is nothing to it."

By nine o'clock, we were in Bridget's office. He had turned it into a command post for the outing. A sailor was manning the telephone and another was sitting by a radio. We had told him what Hogaboom had asked for, and he had assigned a chief and nine sailors to gather up the supplies we wanted. A half hour later, the telephone rang and Bridget grabbed it. He listened and then said, "Drive the bastards into the sea," and hung up. Turning to us, he said that Lt. Pew and the Second Platoon had retaken Pucot. The Japs fired rifles and machine guns at them but when the platoon pressed the attack, the Japs retreated down the slope toward the points. Then he gave a broad grin. "For once we were ready for the little yellow bastards. If we hadn't acted fast and got back up to Pucot within three quarters of an hour after they first took it; things could have been rough around here."

Shortly after noon, a runner came in and reported that Hogaboom was at the foot of the trail leading up to Pucot from the west. He had heard automatic fire from the slopes and was proceeding to the top to join the squad Lt. Pew had left there. We sat there and waited. Nothing happened and the tension kept building. By two o'clock, I was thinking that the Japs had wiped out Hogaboom and all his people and were probably coming down the West Road with armor, heading for Mariveles. I could see that Bridget much preferred to be up above flying an airplane, from which he could see what was going on, rather than sitting in a CP blindly waiting for news from troops at the front. In fact, he was not sitting. He was pacing back and forth across his small office, then sitting down, getting up, and pacing again.

"Where in the hell are they?" He sounded frustrated. The phone rang, and he grabbed it from the sailor's hand. He listened for about three minutes, while the person at the other end did the talking. Finally, he said, "Keep looking. I'll send a truck up the road to the trail for them. Can they walk? Okay, have someone go down to the road with them and we'll get them back here." Bridget turned to us. "Hogaboom and his company were on the trail that leads to the summit, when they heard rifle fire and a call for back-up. Hogaboom figured that meant the Nips were down the slope, toward the water and coming up to the summit of Pucot again. He circled and went down to get behind the Nips so they couldn't get back down the ridge again to the point. He formed a skirmish line and started up the hill and part way up they came upon another unit firing into the woods up ahead. Two men had been wounded.[14]

"Hogaboom passed through the other group and swept the ravine at the foot of Pucot but didn't find any Nips. Then they went up to the top and joined the Second Platoon. Hogaboom and a squad are holding the summit of Pucot together with a squad from the other platoon. The rest of the battalion are all down on the slopes that lead to the water, trying to flush out the Nips. Every now and then, they establish contact and exchange fire, but whenever they close in the Nips have gone. Hogaboom thinks it is a small force that snuck down last night—not nearly strong enough to attack Mariveles. I'm inclined to agree with him. You had better round up your men and get up there so you can be back before dark."

I started up the West Road with my party of nine sailors and a chief, each carrying a pack of supplies, some with ammunition and grenades, and others with containers of water and food. I was the complete armament for the squad: .45 in side holster, Tommy Gun slung over my shoulder, bandolier of extra ammunition, bolo hanging from my belt, and a pack on my back strapped tightly so that it would not swing when moved as it held my six hand grenades. I felt as if I was a one-man army. Also, I was the only one in khakis. Six sailors were in denims, and four wore white. None had been camouflaged with navy coffee.

I looked back from my lead position and saw that my sailors were bunched together on the road, talking and laughing as if they were on their way to an afternoon ball game.[15] I stopped, knowing I would have to change this approach. "From here on you walk single file; and keep to the side of the road. If any Japs show up, hit the deck in the bushes beside the road. When we reach the trail up the mountain, stay spaced out at least six paces apart, and I mean stay that way. And walk quietly. No talking." The trail up to the top seemed to be narrower and much darker than the last time I had climbed it. You could not see three feet into the jungle on each side and the trees crowded together over it. It was like walking in a dark low tunnel.

Suddenly, one of the men yelled, "Japs! Hit the deck!" My entire work party fell flat on the ground. As I looked around, no bullets were flying past me. My Tommy Gun remained slung over my shoulder. I had heard nothing. Then a troop of small monkeys came swinging through the trees down the hill, right above my head. I guess we all were a little on edge. I said to the man behind me, "Get on your feet. Pass the word down the line. Those monkeys make a hell of a lot more noise than any Jap will. Get all that gear picked up and let's move. If we keep this up, it will be dark before we reach the top."

I think the idea of going back down that steep hill in the dark got through to them. I climbed quickly, and they kept pace behind me. They definitely had not had much practice in hill climbing; and I could hear the panting and grunting the whole way up. I made a mental note that if we were going to make a habit of this, some Marine boot training might be in order. We finally reached the clearing on the top. We got there without any stragglers. We had heard no firing, and we had seen no Japanese. Hogaboom was there talking to Lt. Pew, and about two dozen sailors and marines were sitting or standing in the clearing talking to one another in low tones. Hogaboom looked at me as I walked up, motioned to the Tommy Gun, and said, "Do you know how to use that thing?" With a laugh I responded, "I've had expert training. I come from a long line of bootleggers. Anyway, here are your supplies. If you have anyone going back down, can he lead my party? I would like to stay up and see what is happening."

He pointed to one of the marines. "The corporal is going to take my report down to Bridget, and he can lead your men back. If you want to stay up here all night, be my guest. The Japs seem to have disappeared down the slope and gone out on the points. At least we can't find any of them. It will be dusk soon, and I have positioned patrols all along the ridge, as far as a half-mile south of here. My squad will stay here on top tonight, and then as soon as it gets light in the morning we can sweep the slopes down to the water and out onto the points and see if we can find the little suckers. Have your men disperse the extra ammo and the other stuff you brought, and we'll pass it along to the patrols on the ridge. Then, your men had better shove off, and we'll button up for the night."

I learned that the night is much blacker on the summit of Mount Pucot than it is on the paddy at Mariveles. If you climbed one of the trees that the marines used for observation posts, you got a chance to see the stars and far off the occasional shimmer of water in the China Sea. On the ground, it was pitch black. The night noises were all around us; bird calls, rustlings, whisperings and the cry of some animal now and then. None of it sounded like the Japs might be signaling to one another Indian style.

I sat against a tree trunk and figured the Japanese were doing the same thing further down near the water. I must have fallen asleep, for the next thing I knew someone was shaking my shoulder and I heard a voice say, "We're moving out." Still groggy I looked up and saw a pale light filtering down through the trees above me.

The Second Day

In single file, we followed the trail down to Lapiay Point, the top of the thumb that Bridget had described to us a week before and the most northern of our five points. Along the way, the corporal in front of me kept picking up little pieces of paper that were stuck on to low bushes beside the path. "Nip trail sign," he said. "They must have scouted this area pretty good when they first came up the slope." The patrol suddenly stopped, and shots rang out. Something knocked down a twig from a tree beside me, and I felt it brush my face as it fell. Then I heard an entire volley from a BAR.[16] The corporal said, "Damn it, he missed them. Two of them got away down that ravine."[17]

The trail ended on a bluff and below was a point of land with the ocean at the end and a bay off to our right. "This here is Latain Point," said the corporal. "Mr. Hogaboom will probably go along the bluff to Lapiay Point, south of here." Hogaboom did just that and we all followed the bluffs until we stood on the top of a ridge that looked down on a second point, covered with clumps of trees in some areas and with low scrub in others. The underbrush looked dense all the way down the slope that led to the point, a drop of possibly two hundred feet. Hogaboom swept the point with his binoculars and said, "See the whole end of the point is wooded. I think I spotted something there, but the stuff is pretty dense and I can't really tell." He motioned to two of the marines. "Go down the slope and take a look in there. And watch yourselves." The two marines set off down the slope and disappeared in the growth below us. We sat there and waited. In about half an hour, we saw them emerge from some small trees below us to our right and come up the slope, climbing quickly.

One of them stumbled up the last few feet and puffed out to Hogaboom, "Sir, them woods at the end of the point is packed full of Japs, all sitting around under them trees." Hogaboom told us to stand by, and he scanned the point some more with his glasses. He called three of the corporals over to him. "If we go in force, there is no way we can get down on to that point and out along it without being seen. The center ridge and the north half of the point are too open. They could sit behind those trees and pick us off like flies, both coming and going. From here, you can't even see into those woods where you spotted the Japs. That is real thick growth. Now if we go down the southern half of the slope and out on to the point, I think we can make it. There is a lot of tree and scrub to give us cover, and we should be able to work our way through it without being seen. Joe you stay up here with your BAR, and you and Pete cover the open slope on our right, in case they try to flank us and come up.[18] The rest of you form a skirmish line and head down through that brush on the left. When everyone is in position, Corporal Collins, you take the left flank, and we'll all go down together on your signal."

We all proceeded to move down the slope. I was holding the Tommy Gun so tightly my hands were starting to go numb. We went through a small dip and toward a nose where the scrub faded out. I was starting to move out of the depression I was crawling through, when suddenly I heard a put-put-put sound and what sounded like an angry bee whizzed past my left ear. I dropped flat to the ground and so did the men on each side of me. We hugged the dirt and the Marine to my right whispered "Jap machine gun." I saw Hogaboom make a hand signal and Corporal Collins crawl rapidly on his stomach around the open nose and disappear into a draw that was on the other side of it.

Then Hogaboom crawled off on the other flank through a shallow wash. I figured that Collins would be positioned above the Japanese machine gun and Hogaboom below when suddenly there was the loud bang of a grenade exploding and then another, then two more close together, then two more. Then silence.[19] We started crawling toward the woods and upon our first movement, bullets buzzed over our heads. One threw up dirt about a foot to my left as the Japanese machine gun kept up its seemingly slow put-put-put. I cautiously raised my head to take a closer look at the woods in front of us. It seemed to be a dense wall of low growth, with tall trees rising above it and hanging vines filling in all the spaces between. It was perfect cover for the defenders. They could see out, but we could not see in. The jungle plants must have been thick enough to prevent the grenades from penetrating it before exploding. Hogaboom motioned to the man next to him and sent him crawling to the rear. I assume he was calling for reinforcements with heavier weapons.

As the day passed endlessly, more men joined us. They tried lobbing rifle grenades into the wall of scrub. I could not tell whether any had penetrated to where the Japs were sitting with their machine gun. The foliage seemed so thick it was like a green fortress. Every now and then, the Japanese would fire a few rounds from rifles, or there would be the sputtering of the machine gun. We would fire a few rounds back into the green wall. In late afternoon, Hogaboom brought down a BAR group with the intention of beefing up our left flank and possibly getting at the Japanese from the left side. However, before they got into position another machine gun opened up on them, and they had to wiggle their way back to find cover. It looked like the Japs had covered themselves from that side.

The sun was beginning to sink lower in front of us when suddenly the Japanese opened up with multiple volleys of rifle fire and the put-put-put of at least three machine guns. The next thing I knew there was a loud explosion and dirt flew up about two hundred feet in front of me. This was followed by a whole series of loud blasts and fountains of dirt exploding in a row across the scrub between us and the woods where the Japanese sat. I heard the corporal to my left say "shit." I looked over, and he was holding his left arm. "Those are mortar rounds and maybe they have a pack howitzer too. They are coming in from the left and from the angle I figure they are firing at us from across the bay." I saw his arm was bleeding. "Where were you hit?" I asked him. "Just a scratch. Something grazed me. I got it covered if you give me a hand with this dressing."

I crawled over to him and wrapped the bandage and dressing around his upper arm. It did not seem to be bleeding too heavily, and we both figured he had been lucky. We lay there for another half hour and then the man on my right called over, "We're pulling back. Pass the word. Pulling back to the ridge." In the twilight, we crawled back until we had the protection of the heavy trees and were able to make our way back up the slope to the top of the ridge. We stood in a group, and Hogaboom said, "There is no way we could have gone any closer with that mortar fire coming in on us. We're damn lucky they didn't spot accurately or we might have been in trouble. This is no small group of Japs. They are on both points now, and there must be at least a couple of hundred of them. We are going to need some help."[20]

A half hour later, we had climbed back up to the summit of Pucot, and while I ate my first real food of the day, I wondered just how many Japanese had established themselves on the two points. Holdredge, the commanding officer of Battery C, who came up the trail just as we were finishing eating, gave us part of the answer.[21] That morning he had taken his patrol down on to Longoskawayan Point. He told Hogaboom what had happened. "Hogie, we almost got our asses kicked today on Longoskawayan. Our point men came on a clearing in which the Japs were setting up a light howitzer. It happened so suddenly both my men and the Japs were caught by surprise. My point guys hit the deck and opened up with the BAR. They said they knocked down at least a dozen of the Japs. However, it then hit them that they were pretty exposed. My BAR man said to his buddy, "Come on. Let's get out of here as this has made them madder than hell." "We had to give my two point men cover fire with everything we had to get them out of there. We must have passed through Japs on the way down. On the way back up the slope, we had to take pretty good rear guard action for at least a hundred yards. One of my men felt a shot go right across in front of his face from his left side and figured it was one of the sailors who didn't know which way to shoot. He looked over and saw someone in the bushes and yelled at him, 'You idiot, quit firing at me!' He said the guy he saw turned out to be a Jap, who jumped up and went tearing away toward the trees further down the point."

Hogaboom got on the telephone to Bridget and told him that after today's experiences we were all of the opinion that there were at least two hundred Japanese involved and that he figured it would take an organized battalion with proper support weapons to eliminate them. He suggested that the commander call the Rock and get some help from the Fourth Marines, and that we needed heavy firepower such as the mortar group could supply.

I spent that second night sleeping against a tree trunk again.

The Third Day

In the morning a corporal told me, "During the night a couple of hundred of the Fourth Marines from the Rock came in. We got the mortar and machine gun sections, and they set up an 81-mm mortar northwest of Pucot.[22] From our post up here, Mr. Hogaboom can spot for Nips on both Lapiay and Longoskawayan Points. Those big trees and all that vine and bush is awful thick down on them points, but those mortars should stir 'em up. Our guys have one of the best mortar crews you're going to find."

By 10:00 a.m., the mortar section was ready, and Hogaboom climbed one of the tall trees to begin his spotting operation. I climbed another tree to watch. Hogaboom had a field telephone hooked up and started calling out targets to the mortar crew. He would call out a spot for them to hit, then a minute or so later, I would see a fountain of dirt fly up. He led the rounds systematically through each point, concentrating on clumps of high trees, where we all assumed the Japanese were hidden. I heard Hogaboom say to me, "Damn but that crew is accurate. They have put a round into every spot I've called, and I mean on the button."[23]

I noticed that he concentrated many of the rounds on the green fortress of tree and vine where the Japanese had pinned us down the day before. I hoped they were shaking up those machine gunners that had given us such a hard time. Another heavily hit target was the wooded area where the BAR man had been forced to retreat in a hurry. Further out on Longoskawayan was a large patch of dense forest that looked inviting, and Hogaboom directed several rounds into it. Suddenly, I saw a group of at least thirty Japanese running out of the right edge of these trees and head for a smaller clump about a hundred yards away. I heard Hogaboom say to the mortar crew, "Spot right one hundred yards and fire for effect." Round after round poured into the new position in which the Japanese had taken refuge. I could see the bursts as the rounds landed and trees and brush flew into the air. At least twenty rounds landed over an area of a couple of hundred feet. When the barrage was over, there was no further sign of life in that area.

Early in the afternoon, the marines lifted the mortar fire, and all the patrols started down the trail to the ridge to go out on the points. Hogaboom took his patrols out on Lapiay Point and Holdredge took a larger force and headed for Longoskawayan. I decided to go down with Holdredge. We followed the trail along the ridge, and then spread out a skirmish line and went down the slope to the Point. We moved through small scrub and trees on the way down and then out on to the Point itself, walking through clumps of much taller trees and thick brush, until I estimated we had gone about a quarter of the way out on the Point. A lot of trees were smashed from the mortar fire that had been poured in that morning, and I figured that any Japanese that had escaped would be well out at the end of the Point. I was with a group of about fifteen sailors and a few marines. We were moving carefully and slowly through a grove of trees, headed for a dense patch ahead of us, when suddenly all hell broke loose. Firing seemed to be coming at us from dead ahead and from both sides. A man to my left let out a cry and fell to the ground, and one to my right clutched his shoulder and spun around, landing on his side. I sensed another one of those bees fly past my head and threw myself down as fast as I could and rolled to my left as I landed. I heard the put-put-put of the machine gun, and it seemed as though it was only a few feet in front of me.

In a reflex action, I pressed the trigger of the Tommy Gun and felt the muzzle start to lift skyward. I pressed down and kept it firing. All around me, I heard shouts and curses, and a steady outpouring of shots, BAR automatic fire, and the put-put of machine guns. The Japanese had waited until we were practically on top of them and then had opened up with everything they had at close range. I heard grenades exploding in front of me and the noise became deafening as both sides kept up a continuous volley of firing.

I was hugging the ground and settling down to firing short bursts with the Thompson instead of using an entire drum on full automatic. From one side, I heard a voice yelling, "Fall back!," and out of the corner of my eye, I could see the entire line was pulling back toward the slope. No one was turning and running. Men would fire and then squirm back. I noticed to my left a sailor helping the man that I had seen shot in the shoulder. I did not see the one who had cried out and fallen. Behind us, I heard our own guns firing and figured our support was giving us cover fire as we retreated. While it probably only took a half hour or less, it seemed to last forever as we backed up toward the slope and the protection of the ridge that overlooked the Point. I was all the way to the top when I realized that the Japanese had not followed us and that the firing from their side had stopped.

We had not come out too well on our invasion of their stronghold on Longoskawayan Point. Five men had been killed and twelve were wounded, including Lt. Holdredge.[24] When I reached the top of the ridge, corpsmen were attending to the wounded, a couple of whom looked to be in pretty bad shape. I thought it was a miracle we had escaped with that few numbers of casualties considering the number of bullets that were flying around and the short distances that had existed between us and the Japanese. I counted my blessings and trudged back up the trail toward the summit of Pucot. A few hundred feet along the path, I noticed that a group of Filipinos were setting up a mountain howitzer on a rise that gave a clear view of Longoskawayan Point. Our firepower was being increased.[25]

When I got to the top of Mount Pucot, Hogaboom told me that when his patrols went down to Lapiay Point they covered it all the way to the very end with a skirmish line and found it deserted. The Japs had all pulled over to Longoskawayan during the night, and our barrage of mortar shells had been a waste of time as far as Lapiay was concerned. I told him it had a different effect on the ones that had assembled on Longoskawayan. As the BAR man had said, it had made them madder than hell, and they did their best to make us pay for it.

The night settled in, and we discussed our strategy for the next day and what we could do that we had not done to get these Japanese out of our backyard. If we went charging down at them gangbusters style, we were going to lose a lot of men and that was unacceptable. We all agreed that the least expensive way to solve things was to blast them off the points with artillery. Hogaboom said he was calling Bridget to see how the commander had made out on an idea they had been discussing earlier. I heard Hogaboom say over the phone, "Commander, what the hell do they think they have them for? Why are they hoarding them?" There was apparently a lot more conversation from the other end and Hogaboom said, "Yes sir. I hope so," and hung up.

He turned to me and said, "We have been asking the artillery officer on the Rock to use the big 12 mortars they have to soften up the Japs on Longoskawayan, and MacArthur's staff refuses to give him permission.[26] What the hell they are saving them for beats me. I doubt if they have been fired since they first tested them. The officer in charge of them is a Colonel Bunker. Bridget just told me that Bunker has asked the staff for permission to use them three times and the last time they threw him out."[27]

He continued talking as he looked out at the night closing in on the points below us. "It beats the hell out of me how that staff of generals thinks over there. They are sitting in those tunnels and asking us to go down on these points and knock out the Japs and doing damn little to back us up. Maybe the marines and the navy here really are expendable. Bridget is going to ask Colonel Clement to take another crack at breaking the mortars loose."[28] We sat and waited. About 11:00 p.m., the phone signaled and Hogaboom picked it up. I heard him say, "Great. We'll be ready for them." He turned and said, "Clement got permission for the army to start using the mortars. Lt. Fulmer is going to spot for them.[29] They'll open up on Longoskawayan at around 2400." About ten minutes past midnight, there was a flash of fire followed by a heavy explosion half way out on Longoskawayan Point. Hogaboom was watching with night glasses. "No good. It hit the shoreline." We watched as seven more rounds came into the point area. Three more hit along the shoreline and four missed the point completely and landed in the bay. Hogaboom said to Fulmer, "They might as well stop firing. We can't seem to give them the proper coordinates from here. Best wait until daylight and then spot from directly above the point, from the ridge." He turned to me. "Well it was a bust, but we'll make up for it tomorrow."

The Fourth Day

At dawn the next morning, Hogaboom and a small group of marines and sailors, me included, walked down the hill and back along the trail to the ridge overlooking Longoskawayan Point. The Naval Battalion had been busy. All along the ridge, they had erected a breastwork of cut logs, and the entire group was sitting behind it. They told us that during the night at least one Japanese machine gun had fired at the ridgeline. Hogaboom climbed up into the branches of a tree that stood in front of the breastwork and swept the slope and out on to the point with his glasses. He told us that he could see movement about half way out. We opened up with a breakfast attack that lasted for an hour, and during it, we fired everything that we had including the Filipino howitzer, the 75s, and the two 81-mm mortars that the marines were using.

After about a half hour of this, I heard the sound of a slow moving freight train passing over my head at a distance that I was positive was no more than ten feet. I hit the deck behind the log barrier in a reflex action and then looked up feeling a little foolish. I saw Hogaboom laughing at me. "Those twelve inch mortars do make a lot of sound and seem to be going real slow when they pass over, don't they." Then he added, "We are about the end of their range out here. It is around 14,000 yards and they are hitting a point about 12,000 yards from their firing position, so they have to clear the top of this ridge with not much to spare in order to land where we want them on the point. In case you don't know it, they are firing six hundred and seventy pound charges."[30] This time the spotting was accurate and so was the aiming. As each mortar hit the ground, it would cause an immense flash of flame and blow dirt, rocks, tree sections, and a huge cloud of dust into the air. The destruction of the trees and low foliage on the point was awesome.

The bombardment of the woods continued for slightly over an hour, and it was far noisier that anything I had ever experienced. The Japanese bombing raids had been nothing like it. There would be the almost continual crack of the artillery shells from the howitzer and the 75s, and the slightly duller bang of the Marine mortars, all interspersed with the slow freight train sound above my head and the enormous explosion of the big mortars as they chewed up the point. After witnessing the destruction that the shelling caused, I was convinced no group of men could have lived through it. If there were any Japanese left on the point, they were the ones who had retreated to the very end of the land and probably were too shell-shocked to resist us.[31]

In the mid-afternoon, we formed another skirmish line and slowly descended the ridge on to the point. We were about a quarter of the way down the point, when I saw the first Japanese bodies. Their troops in the advanced lines had been settled in small groups of two to five in what appeared to be well-camouflaged foxholes. The barrage had smashed large trees into splinters and torn the ground into a mass of craters, large and small. Where the Corregidor mortars had landed, they had torn up holes as big as the basement of a small house. The dead that we saw had either been caught where they lay before they had a chance to pull back further out on the point, or they had simply stayed in their foxholes and accepted the shelling we had poured in on them.

As we passed through these first torn bodies, word was passed along our line to the sailors, "Do not, repeat, not, touch anything. No souvenir hunting. The bodies may be booby trapped." We passed through this area of destruction and were headed further out through the craters and shell torn ground when once again we heard the put-put-put of the Japanese machine guns mingled with heavy volleys of their rifle fire. Our entire line sought refuge in the shell holes and started to fire back at the broken ground ahead of us. Every now and then a few of our people would make a dash forward and dive into a shell hole fifty feet or more toward the enemy. I saw at least two men receive hits from bullets as they tried this maneuver. The further we advanced the heavier was the fire from the Japanese. Finally, we received word to stay put and hold what we had taken. To advance further on out the point would mean losing more men.

Again, we were facing a stalemate. As the afternoon shadows lengthened, we cautiously and slowly started to pull back until we reached the shelter of the scrub and small trees behind us and climbed back up the ridge to behind our log barricades. Once more, I accompanied Hogaboom and a small patrol back up to the top of Mount Pucot, while the bulk of our forces held the line along the ridge behind the logs.

While I ate my daily meal and wondered just how long this flow and ebb on Longo-skawayan Point was going to continue, Hogaboom told me one of the weird things he had seen while spotting rounds that morning. "There was a small clearing about three quarters of the way out on the point. Standing in the middle of it, I saw a white robed figure, talking to about twenty Jap soldiers. At first, I couldn't figure it out, but then I was able to get a better look. I'll swear it was a Shinto priest they had brought with them. He was probably telling them to do or die for the Emperor. Then I thought it wasn't too weird. After all, we have our chaplains go in with the troops sometimes. I tried to get the 75s to aim in there to stir them up a bit."

The Fifth Day

This was a repetition of the day before. Shortly after dawn, we started our attack with an hour-long bombardment by our Marine mortars and the Filipino artillery, soon followed by the freight trains from Corregidor passing over our heads as we sat behind our log barricades. Hogaboom spotted the firing from his perch on a tree limb. At the end of this barrage, the ground was torn up and almost devoid of trees in large patches for at least two-thirds of the way to the end of the point.[32]

In the bright morning sunshine, we once more trudged down the slope and out on to the point itself. A Marine corporal who was walking with me said, "This should be a cake walk. Those Nips should be shook up pretty good by now and any that are left should be way out at the end of the point where we can round them up easy." We passed through the area where we had been stopped the previous day, and after this last shelling, the ground was so torn up it was difficult to see any remnants of their foxholes or any signs that they had once occupied this area. I saw no bodies or abandoned weapons. We were walking literally through No Man's Land. The destruction of the trees and the brush seemed to be complete, and the ground was pockmarked with shell holes. My Marine friend noticed the absence of signs that the Japanese had held this ground and said, "I wonder if they pulled back to the end of the point before the shelling started?" Suddenly heavy firing came out of a draw ahead of me to the left, followed by the crack of grenades exploding and the rapid pulsation of a BAR and our own rifles. We flopped on our stomachs and said, "With that much fire coming in on us, if they did retreat to the end of the point, they sure came back when the shelling stopped. It sounds like there are still a lot of them left."

The next few hours passed slowly. The entire skirmish line would move forward a few yards, and the men would take cover in shell holes or behind fallen and splintered trees. We would fire a volley, and the Japanese would return it. We repeated this advance until midafternoon, and it did not seem that we had advanced more than two or three hundred yards in our creeping movement toward the end of the point. We were approaching a deep draw that lay in front of a small forest of undamaged tall trees about two hundred yards in front of us, when suddenly a number of khaki uniformed Japanese came charging out of the draw, directly at us and behind them I could see others emerging from the trees to back them up. They all seemed to be yelling something at the top of their lungs and firing as fast as they could while they approached us. I heard my Marine yelling, "It's a banzai charge. Hold fast and unload on them."

Every man in our group stayed put in whatever shelter the ground had to offer and everyone fired at the oncoming Japanese as fast as they could. I realized that I had put the Tommy Gun on full automatic and was attempting to sweep across the group of advancing men. Our BAR men were doing the same. When it appeared that the line of Japanese were about a hundred and fifty yards away from us, explosions suddenly tore up the ground in front of them, among them, and behind them, and I realized that Hogaboom was directing our mortars and artillery on the ridge into the advancing troops with pinpoint accuracy. The results were devastating. We saw bodies hurl into the air, or be blown apart, literally before our eyes. The wave of Japanese sputtered, then broke and the few that were left turned and ran back into the shelter of the trees.[33]

"That was damn close," said my Marine. "If Mr. Hogaboom hadn't been able to spot them and if we hadn't had that support fire, you and I would have been trying to knock out Nips hand-to-hand." Then he said, "I doubt if the navy has had much practice using a bayonet." I had never given that one much thought and it chilled me. Besides, I did not possess a bayonet; just my Tommy Gun and .45.

In the late afternoon, we once more pulled back and climbed the ridge behind us up to our log barricades. We were all tired and on edge and wondering just how long this operation was going to last. As we sat along the ridgeline, tried to eat some food, and cleaned our weapons, I looked at the faces of the men around me, etched with fatigue and covered with whiskers, and I sensed that they were becoming as discouraged as I was.

That night the generals on Corregidor must have decided that the operation needed a new look; that we were either losing our aggressiveness, or we needed some sleep, or it simply would take a fresh group of troops to do the job.[34] Around ten that evening a company of five hundred Philippine Scouts showed up and took up position along the ridge behind us.[35] The captain in charge told Hogaboom that they were relieving us. Bridget soon called ordering the Naval Battalion to return to the base at Mariveles. I took the ridge trail down to our rice paddy and as I walked I realized that I was slightly punch drunk. Six nights with little sleep and five days of being shot at had worn me out. I decided that to be a good infantryman takes a special kind of training that the school at Harvard had definitely neglected. When Swede and the others asked me how it had gone, I remember saying to them we could discuss it in the morning. That night on my cot in Mariveles I slept for nine hours and only the loud monkeys in the trees above and the sun blistering my face finally awakened me.

The Sixth Day

I was determined to see the finish of this business of driving the Japanese off the point and back into the sea, though I had to admit that I was not too anxious to once more descend the slope to Longoskawayan Point and subject myself to being a target again. After telling my Supply Corps peers about the events of the previous few days and giving my word that I would not be a damn fool and join the attack unless ordered, I trudged back up the trail to the ridges and went back to the log barricades that overlooked the point. I positioned myself on the tree branch where Hogaboom had so accurately directed our artillery fire.

The Philippine Scouts now lined the barricades. They told me that over half their company had gone down the ridge and out on to the point at dawn and after a lot of firing and close encounters, they had driven the Japanese way out toward the end of the point. They now had the problem of not being covered by our artillery, as they were so far out our guns could not reach the area in front of them and the remaining Japs were all holed up in the trees that covered the end of the point. To give them covering fire as they advanced further, the Army had placed mortars and heavy machine guns at the ends of both Lapiay Point on the north and another point on the south.[36]

The Scouts formed a line a good three quarters of the way out on the point and held there. They stayed there all the rest of the day and all that night, firing everything they had at the Japanese, while their mortars and heavy weapons kept up the crossfire from the other two points. The Scouts wearily pulled back and came up the ridge to the barricades at dawn. From the sound of things, there were still a fair number of live and fighting Japanese at the end of the point.

The Seventh Day

Shortly after the sun rose, I heard the first of the freight trains coming in from Corregidor and saw the huge explosion as it landed, throwing up trees and brush far out on the point.[37] Then the artillery from the Filipino guns and the Marine mortars opened up, immediately followed by the mortars and heavy machine guns from the other two points. This barrage lasted for about half an hour and covered the last several hundred yards of the point, blowing up trees that until then had been standing and chewing up the ground to resemble the part we had earlier been attacking.

Five minutes after the firing stopped, I saw a ship coming up from the south. I recognized it as one of our minesweepers, the *Quail*. Suddenly, its deck gun started firing rounds into the end of the point and the shoreline below it. The naval bombardment lasted for over an hour and when it lifted, the main body of Scouts trudged down the slope and out onto the point.[38] The Scouts had gone far out on the point when we heard heavy firing again. Through my glasses, I could see that the advance had stopped. One of their spotters told me that as soon as the Scouts had retired back up the slopes at dawn, the Japanese had quickly advanced to the lines our forces had abandoned.

More of the Scouts went down the slopes and the intensity of the firing increased. Slowly, it moved further and further out toward the end of the point, out toward the high bluffs that overlooked the sea. As the Scouts slowly pushed the Japanese back, the covering fire from the other two points continued, staying just ahead of the moving Scouts. Around four that afternoon, I was looking at the end of the point and through a slight haze, I saw a flag raised and being waved. It was the signal that the Scouts had secured the point and pushed the Japanese out of our backyard.

Possibly, we had not disposed of the Japanese a hundred percent. There were probably a few shell-shocked remnants hiding in ravines and caves that the Naval Battalion would have to locate and take care of over the next few days. However, in military terms, this small war, that was called the Battle of the Points in the Mariveles sector, was finished.

I did not see the Scouts herding any Japanese prisoners as they slowly came up the slopes to the log barricades. When I asked one of the Scout sergeants how many of the enemy had surrendered at the end, he looked at me a little strangely and said, "Sir, we have taken no prisoners. The Japs are very brave or very, very crazy men. The ones we saw out at the end of the point jumped off the cliffs on to the rocks that are way below.[39] They are all dead, but then, we do not like to take prisoners. We have no place to put them." His expression hardened a bit.

Summation

When I returned to the safety and quiet of the paddy in Mariveles that night, and once more became part of the "Service Area," I sat on my cot and thought about the happenings of the past week. I suppose I had entered the Battle of the Points with preconceived notions about infantry warfare—notions obtained from seeing war movies or reading novels filled with feats of daring. Our battle was cast completely differently from anything I had ever seen or read. No writer had ever dreamed up a group of players such as we had used: several hundred sailors and airmen, all rank amateurs, myself included, with no training whatsoever for this type of combat, in fact even less training than the Filipino draftees had received, and many without uniforms that would blend with the foliage. Then scattered among us were the professionals, the Marine NCOs and the officers like Hogaboom who directed the attacks. They were complete professionals, who knew what they were doing, while the rest of us blindly pressed triggers at appropriate times, keeping up appearances. The rest of us might as well have been robots, and for my part, that was not a very satisfactory feeling.

In fictional battles, there were always heroes, cowards, and at least one leader who was a mean, tough son of a bitch who drove everyone to victory. When I look back over the previous days, I did not recall any such dramatic touches. The marines who stuck their necks out, flanking enemy positions and using their BARS and hand grenades, had not acted like heroes. They acted like men who were merely doing a job in an effective, workman-like manner. There had been no noble charges in the face of withering enemy fire (thank God). Instead, it had been a long, grinding effort to move in and hold a few yards of dirt, scrub and rock, pushing the Japs out of it. Each day we moved our line further out toward the end of the point and the China Sea. None of our people broke and ran when the enemy fired at them. They stolidly plodded down the slopes as ordered and when the Japs fired too closely at them, they sensibly hit the deck and stayed put. There were no stampedes. For a group of amateurs, the teamwork had been pretty good after the first day. I had seen that in a battle of this type, the true professionals played it conservatively and did not rush things. After all, time was on our side, as was the terrain and firepower. Hogaboom let all of this work for us.

No smart commander is going to send his men on a banzai charge against a well-entrenched enemy and get half of them killed. That is a Japanese desperation tactic, and we were not desperate. We knew that eventually the shelling would drive them back into the sea. All we had to do was hold a line that kept them pinned down. We foot sloggers were really just an armed fence that kept pushing forward behind the shelling, making sure that none of the bad guys got through it. When they tried to go over, under, or around it, the fence held its ground, and our friends shelled the hell out of them.

When bullets whizzed past me, it usually happened so suddenly and it was over so quickly that I did not remember too many details afterwards. However, there had been times when the bee buzzing got intense. I thought about that for a while and as I looked at the stars above Mariveles that night, I remembered a saying I had read somewhere, long ago. It went something like "War is made up of long periods of utter boredom, interrupted by brief moments of having the hell scared out of you." I think that summed up my reactions to the battle we had just experienced.

The Battle of the Points was a very small battle. Small as it was, it represented the first land battle in the Pacific War that we had won.[40] In every other battle up to then we had been in retreat, rather than advancing and defeating the enemy. I realized that what had happened on Longoskawayan Point might indicate what could take place in the future and what would be involved in recapturing the territory seized elsewhere by the Japanese. The Japanese soldiers did not quit even when they were unsupported and out-gunned. They kept fighting as long as they had ammunition. They literally fought to the death, and most preferred suicide to surrender.[41]

As I sat on my cot, it dawned on me that if this small group of infiltrators were representative of the Japanese infantry in the Philippines, when our relief forces from the States arrived it would not be a "cake walk" as the Marine corporal had described it. We would have to dig them out and kill them man by man. If we had to repeat our effort on Longoskawayan Point several hundred times, it would be a long war. I had only a vague sense of the future of the number of battles, large and small, yet to come, and the losses on both sides, before it was all over and the United States could once more walk tall in the Pacific.

A week later I learned the army brass were very big on statistics and body counts. Corregidor sent Bridget the final score on our ballgame:

Number of Japanese killed	Something around 300
Number of Americans killed	11
Number of Americans wounded	26
Number of Scouts killed	11
Number of Scouts wounded	40

Bridget told me that the generals on Corregidor had a whole staff keeping up with this sort of arithmetic.[42]

9

Alarms and Excursions

In the middle of February, as we looked back over the previous seven weeks, we all had the impression that the shrill call of the air raid siren followed by the explosions of bombs had been a daily occurrence. Jack McClure said that it had not been as bad as we thought, that while the air raid alarms had gone off almost daily—sometimes more than once—the air attacks had been sporadic as far as Mariveles was concerned, and it seemed as though the Japs were conducting a war of nerves rather than of destruction on our base. Mac agreed with him and said that he had been keeping a log on the subject. He showed it to us:

Dec. 27	Mariveles bombed; two of us bounced.
Dec. 29	Corregidor bombed heavily; Mariveles bombed; *Canopus* hit with casualties.
Jan. 5	Mariveles bombed; *Canopus* hit, casualties & damage.
Jan. 6	Corregidor bombed eight times, many fires; Mariveles missed.
Jan. 8	Several air raid alarms; no bombs on Mariveles.
Jan. 11	Several air raid alarms; bombs missed base.
Jan. 12	Strafing attack by two fighters; one man wounded.
Jan. 14	Corregidor bombed twice; heavy fires; Mariveles all hits in water.
Jan. 16	Mariveles bombed by high level planes and dive bombers; first real damage: four buildings destroyed in Section Base; three ammunition depots destroyed; two provision buildings damaged; one material building damaged.
Jan. 18	Several air raid alarms; all bombs missed base.
Jan. 19	Dive bombers hit Quarantine Station; Marine AA battery hit one Japanese plane, smoking into bay.
Jan. 20	Air raid alarms; no bombs dropped on us.
Jan. 21	Air raid alarms; no bombs dropped on us.
Jan. 23	Air raid alarms; no bombs dropped on us.
Jan. 25	Mariveles bombed; one provision building destroyed.
Jan. 27	Mariveles bombed; one provision building destroyed.
Jan. 29	Air raid alarms; all bombs missed base.
Jan. 31	Air raid alarms; bombs did no damage.
Feb. 3	Several air raid alarms; no bombs hit base.
Feb. 5	Several air raid alarms; no bombs dropped on base.
Feb. 6	Mariveles bombed; all misses, no damage; two planes hit.
Feb. 9	Mariveles bombed; no damage

Feb. 11   Mariveles bombed once by high-level planes, no damage; second attack by
dive bombers, three provision buildings destroyed, no casualties; AA guns
shot down one plane.

Feb. 14   Air raid alarms; no damage.

Feb. 17   Section Base bombed; slight damage.[1]

After we had all studied the log and the relatively limited damage we had suffered, Mac said, "We are just lucky that they did not use those big fleets with the good bomb sights that they started off with when they clobbered the air fields and the Yard. All that would be left of this place would be a pock marked valley of the Moon." Swede said, in response to our luck, "They have only so many horizontal bombers and good crews, and they have their job cut out for them along the Malay Barrier hitting the Dutch installations. I doubt if they want to waste gasoline, heavy bomb loads, and their good crews on guys like us sitting on a rice paddy or in a jungle."[2] Bud Snow said that for the limited damage they had done to us, we had cost them more than they had cost us. When you figured the cost of the bombs, gas, aircrew wages, and planes compared to the cost of erecting little wooden buildings and filling them with junk, and moving our valuables into safe spots under the trees, we were way ahead of them. Bud's two years in cost accounting put a happy perspective on what we had gone through the past seven weeks.

We tried to remember which of the attacks had been so intimidating as to leave a lasting impression. We agreed that three or four of them were pretty hairy. As I had learned from the time Red and I had been bounced, any bombing attack held the possibility that you could get hurt and had to be taken seriously. However, when being bombed became almost a daily occurrence, it can also develop into a sort of game between the people operating the AA guns and the planes in the air. We remembered how our gunners tried to use psychology on the pilots to see if they could sucker them down into range. There was one period when they held their fire for almost a whole week while the Japs were circling above us and tried to give the impression that they were out of ammunition. The pilots fell for it, and each day they came in lower. On the last day, the AA gunners took careful aim, and in a coordinated fire, they opened up with everything they could. That day, two of the planes went smoking toward the bay and hopefully, did not make it home.[3]

We remembered the attack during which the Japanese used a new type of anti-personnel bomb for the first time. We called it a "daisy cutter," and it scared the hell out of us when we saw what it could do. Up to then, when the usual Japanese bomb landed on our paddy, it dug in several feet, exploded and then threw dirt all over the place. However, unless you were directly under it, the only thing you suffered was a concussion. These daisy cutters were different. This bomb exploded before it had a chance to bury itself. The effect was not pleasant. We looked at one of our wooden buildings where the Japanese had dropped their bombs. Shrapnel peppered the siding from the ground level up to about seven feet.[4]

We all felt proud about our fake depot buildings. The bombs had destroyed nine of them and damaged several others, but we had not lost one can of our Vienna sausages in the process. We did admit that when they burned, they made a spectacular effect. The Japanese reconnaissance photographer, who we called "Photo Joe" and who used to fly over us after each attack, probably got some great pictures of the fire and destruction of the big U.S. Navy base of Mariveles, the kind the Tokyo newspapers would print.[5]

We unanimously agreed that the wildest attack was the time the two Jap fighters tried to strafe us on January 12. Things had been quiet for a few days previously and in the process, we had lost our respect for the Japanese bombing ability. We had started to eat in the mess hall instead of in a chow line out on the paddy. This was a long narrow structure with an equally long string of tables going down the center from one end to the other, leaving just enough room on each side for the cooks to get by between the chairs and the outside wall of the building. It could seat about seventy people at once, thirty-five on each side. That particular day I remembered that Swede, Red, Mac, and I had eaten at the first serving and that the four of us were outside waiting for Jack and Bud who were eating in the second shift.

As we were standing about a hundred feet away from the mess hall, a plane suddenly swept down on the base from over the ridge to the west and came straight at us. I heard someone yell, "Hit the deck!" and realized that the plane was firing at us from wing guns. In a reflex action, the four of us dove into a long ditch and looked back up at the plane. It headed straight for the mess hall and, in a matter of seconds, it had passed over it and swung out toward the bay. About the time the tail cleared the end of the building, the entire mess hall exploded, as about sixty people, thirty or so on a side, swarmed out of the building through the flimsy mosquito screening, hit the dirt, and in a single smooth motion, jumped into the nearest ditch.

About thirty seconds after the first plane had passed over, a second one followed using the same route. By then we had recovered from our initial shock and were more prepared. The second plane came in so low you could make out the helmeted pilot in the cockpit and again the guns were blazing. Every man in the base that carried a weapon returned the fire: rifles and .45s fired away. The whole attack seemed to take place in slow motion. As in an old world war movie, I could see the flash as the guns fired and the propeller turned. The bullets, or maybe they were small canon shells, made little puffs of dirt rise up as they hit the ground. I sat frozen to the spot and saw that down the ditch, about a hundred feet, was a sailor crouched as I was, facing the plane. The stick of bullets came straight at him. At the last moment he moved, maybe not more than six inches, in a sort of a twisting motion, and the line of dirt puffs passed harmlessly by him. He yelled back to me, and he was actually laughing, "Never take your eye off the ball."

In less than five minutes the planes returned, one behind the other. By now, everyone was ready for them and had reloaded. The planes did not seem to be moving that fast and I was convinced that when caught in murderous fire they would be blown apart into pieces of flying metal, sending them crashing into the bay just off shore. Instead, they kept firing as before and they kept going, seemingly untouched as they left us behind. We waited a good fifteen minutes to make certain that they would not return and then all of us went over to inspect the damage to our mess hall. Neatly stitched down the exact center of the tables, from end to end was a row of splintered holes. The pilot was a terrific shot. His only problem was that maybe he thought American navy people ate on cushions sitting on the table instead of in chairs placed at each side.

∼

That strafing attack was the beginning of several more on the Service Area of southern Bataan. The Japanese used to love to come down over the water from the north and then dive in over the ridges to shoot up anything they thought was worthwhile. Most of those ridges had our AA gunners on them, usually operating .50 calibers. After several days of these attacks, all of the gunners got a little trigger-happy. Early one evening in mid–February, our group was standing talking to Hogaboom outside his machine gun emplacement, when through the dusk we saw a lone figure come walking slowly toward us. When he was about twenty feet away he started shouting at us, "You trigger-happy, sons of bitches, you no good bastards." His face was red and his shirt soaked with perspiration. Dust caked his pants and boots. Clearly, he had been on a long hike. As he got nearer, he continued his tirade, "Do you know how many holes there are in my plane? Do you know there are only a few serviceable P-40s left in Bataan? Don't you stupid idiots know the difference between me and a Nip?" We repeatedly tried to tell him that the particular machine gun we were standing near had not fired at anything all day, but he was not listening. Finally, he seemed to run out of breath and sat down on the dirt, leaning back against the sand bags, his head bowed and his shoulders shaking.

After a while, he calmed down enough to answer our questions and tell us what had happened. His P-40 was based on the plateau above us to the east. That afternoon he had flown out to make a reconnaissance of the front lines across Bataan. On the way back, he had circled out to the west over the China Sea and headed down over the ridges above us to swing back to his strip. The sun was behind him and when he passed over the first ridge, the machine gunners opened up on him. The noise apparently alerted the gunners along the ridges all the way to his strip. Luckily, nothing hit him or any vital parts of the plane and he was able to land it. However, when his ground crew checked over the plane, they found twenty-six holes in the fuselage, wings, and tail. It was going to take some time to patch it up so that it could fly properly again.

We gave him coffee and from our hoard, candy and a carton of cigarettes. We felt he deserved the sympathy.

~

On another occasion, there was a captain in the Fourth Marines who had the responsibility of assembling intelligence information on the Japanese. His reports went into considerable detail. He described how the Japs built their foxholes; how they used camouflage; and how they placed booby traps under the bodies of their dead comrades. He described how some Japs who appeared dead were not really dead, and when the unsuspecting approached, the "dead man" would leap up and shoot them. He reported how Japanese snipers would tie themselves to limbs high up on trees, camouflaged with vines and branches, and stay motionless for hours until a patrol passed beneath them. Then, they would open up with their rifles and try to kill as many of us as possible.[6]

The captain described the dense jungles, the rugged mountains and ridges, the deep valleys, and numerous rivers that lay north of Mariveles and extended to within eight to ten miles from our base. He claimed that roaming through that inhospitable country were small groups of Japanese, well hidden from our eyes, sitting and waiting. He was positive that they had been infiltrating all through February. Some were remnants of the men who had escaped after previous enemy excursions north of us. Others were fresh troops who had sneaked through more recently. He held the theory that these small and isolated bands were waiting for the start of a new, big offensive, and when it began, they would play havoc behind our lines. After listening to the captain's lectures, I finally asked, "How many Japs do you think are hiding in the mountains above us by now?" He shrugged, "Oh, I don't think there are more than four or five hundred altogether, and each group probably doesn't have more than fifteen men in it."

He figured that the Japanese would be sticking close to jungle trails and that the best time to find them would be at night when they were camped near one of these paths. He said, "If we could locate just one of these groups and take prisoners, we could get enough information out of them to find out their general operational plans and then set about eliminating them." "What have you done so far?" I asked. "We have sent out a lot of patrols, but my problem is that the Americans, and even the Filipinos, that go out, end up getting lost in the jungle at night. So far, every patrol has come up empty-handed. They've claimed that they didn't see anything; that it's too dark to see anything; that the jungle is too thick and the trails too hard to follow. Now I think I have the problem solved." He said this in a tone that was quite impressive. "I think I have a sure way of finding at least one of their bands."

The captain elaborated, "The other day I ran into a group of Negritos camped above Mariveles on the mountain. They are native bush people; terrific trackers; very primitive; eyesight like a cat. They can find their way through any of that jungle, no matter how dense or how black the night. They have lived in these mountains for generations and know Bataan like the back of their hands.[7] If anyone can find out where the Japs are hiding, the Negritos can." The captain then produced a map of southern Bataan that included the outline of the West Road, starting in Mariveles, wiggling like a snake up to Bagac, inland about three miles from the west coast.

Pointing to one area on the map, he noted, "I have never been across there myself, but the patrols that have, say that the country is not too bad. Trouble is, I can't send a band of Negritos along that route without an American officer accompanying them to give an accurate report of what they find. Bush people get a little vague about distances and locations when they report on intelligence matters." He paused, studied the map some more and then looked up, straight at me and said, "Checking around I find that you've had a lot of experience in heavy bush, what with having been raised in Canada and all. How would you like to take my band of Negritos up into that country one of these nights and see if you can locate some Nips for me? No fireworks; just find them nice and quiet like. Then we could take a force back the next day and grab them for questioning."

Right then I should have told him to forget it. Instead, like a damn fool, I was intrigued. I pictured exploring the dense and tangled jungles of lower Bataan, leading primitive, native tribesmen with eyes like cats giving them acute vision on even the blackest nights. As a fool, I told the captain that I would be glad to go on such an exciting safari. All the others looked at me as if I was crazy. Red said, "Lots of luck. I think you're nuts. You are no Daniel Boone."

Two afternoons later, the captain showed up with his Negritos. They did not look like any Filipinos I had ever seen before. They were short, very dark skinned, and had kinky hair. All were barefooted except for the man who was their leader. He wore a badly scuffed pair of tennis shoes. He was dressed in what appeared to be cast-off Filipino Army fatigues: torn shirt and pants and a string around his waste from which hung a large bolo. The rest of the group wore a miscellaneous collection of clothing that ranged from torn shirts and pants to practically nothing. They looked like they had been outfitted in a skid row rummage sale.

The Marine captain waved expansively at the little band of Negritos and told me, "Here are your troops. Let me know what you find when we meet in the morning." I discovered that the leader spoke some English, and I said, "Let's get started." He looked at me and then at his men. "Can't go yet, boss. Men hungry. Men not eat for long time. Men got to eat first; so be strong." I realized that I could not take starving men into the jungle and have them operating at peak efficiency. I needed all those eyes that could see like cats to be at their best, so they would not miss anything. "Okay, I'll see that you all get fed. Then we go." "Sure boss. Men be good after eat."

Rice, Vienna sausage, corned beef, canned peas, and tomatoes, all disappeared as if by magic. For little people, they put away a tremendous amount of food. After they had licked all the plates and their fingers clean, they stretched out on the grass with contented looks and immediately most of them fell asleep. "Okay," I said, alarmed at the sudden relapse of my troops, "Get the men up and on to the truck. I want to hit the jungle before dark." The leader looked at me again, the same way as he had when he said his men were starving. "Can't go now, boss. Men eat too much. Got to rest little bit." I suppose this did make some sense in a way. An overfed Negrito might not have all his senses fully alert. Hunting animals, like lions, primitive jungle warriors, fierce predators of all types, always rested after a heavy meal; then they charged back into the fray. My Negritos were no different. "Okay, ten minutes. Then we start."

Ten minutes became twenty, then it dragged on to half an hour, and then to three-quarters. The leader was sleeping as soundly as his men were. I yelled, "That's it. Get the men up. We are moving out, now!" They all piled into the back of my waiting truck, and we drove up the winding West Road to the point where the map showed Trail 7. As the crow flies, we were about four miles due north of Mariveles, but with the twists and loops in the road we traveled, we probably had gone eight miles to get there. I could see Trail 7 cutting straight north, almost as wide as the West Road itself. We climbed down from the truck and started up the trail. When we had walked about a quarter of a mile, the leader said, "This is trail, boss. This is trail we walk to find Japon." In fading light, I made out a faint impression of a line through the thick brush and tall trees, so faint that I was not certain it was a trail, and so narrow with dense bush on either side that I had to walk by putting one foot in front of the other. There were no markings of any type, no blazes on trees, no little pieces of paper such as the Japanese had used around Mount Pucot. It was just a faint impression through the ferns and small growth, so faint it could have been made by nature rather than people or animals. I had not walked more than three hundred feet before I made a couple of missteps into the bush, missing the faint marking as the darkness continued to close in. I told the Negrito leader to take the head of the line after that and I would follow him.

Complete blackness settled in. I was left with the sensation that I was passing through thickets, small growth, circumventing large trees and big rock outcrops. I kept stumbling over roots, hitting low branches, and feeling thorn vines tearing at my pants and shirt. I stayed as close as I could to our lead guide, at times only sensing that he was in front of me. My only tie to civilization was the luminous dial of my watch, my pen light torch, my compass, and my map. I felt that if I lost any of these I would be doomed to a life of wandering in a jungle so hostile that finally only my bleached bones would mark my passage.

I tried to keep track of the valleys and the streams that we crossed, using my small torch to figure out where I was by glancing at my map. Every time I did so, I would find that my guide had moved on several paces ahead of me and I would have to hurry to catch up with him. It was apparent that he had no need for maps. It was also apparent that there were more creeks, streams, and rivers than were on the map. I stumbled over slippery rocks and heard rapids above and below me, the water gurgling noisily as it tumbled down the valley. We had to cross one river on a swaying rope bridge. I almost fell off halfway across. We were continually either climbing or descending steep slopes. I would struggle up a hill, or possibly a ridge, then suddenly we would descend into some sort of valley where I sensed that the growth closed in to be almost solid. Sometimes the ground would turn rocky; other times as we descended it would dampen and turn into swamp and then I would find myself sloshing through water up to my calves.

I kept shining my light on my compass. I figured that we were going in a generally easterly direction, but it was only a guess. The trail twisted and turned over every ridge and through every valley. One minute we would be going east, then suddenly, we would take an abrupt turn to the north, then east again, and then suddenly south. There was not a straight stretch of more than a hundred feet on the entire trail. We seemed to walk in one direction for a short way and then loop off in another direction, climbing another ridge or descending into another valley. I had to admit that after the first half hour I had no idea of where I was.

The Marine captain's statement that it was only three miles across to our eastern boundary was so far off as to be ridiculous. I kept glancing at my watch: nine, ten, and eleven. The Negrito leader was keeping up a steady pace, not fast, not slow. He was a good walker, and I knew that we had covered a hell of a lot more than three miles when it was getting close to midnight. By one in the morning, I was just plain tired. I was drenched with perspiration, scratched by thorn vines, and bitten by mosquitoes. My pants and boots were soaked from the water we had waded through. I admitted to myself that I had been a stupid fool to go on this expedition, and my nerves were beginning to act up. While I had given up trying to figure out where I was and had resigned myself to simply following the Negrito leader, I kept wondering whether he was keeping those cat's eyes wide open, looking for the Japanese we were supposed to find. As each minute passed, I expected them to be around the next bend.

As silently as we were traveling, and I had to admit that my troops were silent, as I had not heard a twig snap for the past two hours, a Jap sentry might still see us first and slaughter my guide. Then bullets would be flying at me. I was the only one who was armed with anything more lethal than a bolo, and I could rarely see more than three feet in front of me. My armament consisted of my .45. The .45 was in its holster, and I would have been very lucky to get it out before an entire band of hidden Japs had swarmed over me and my dead guide.

Aside from the thought of bumping smack into a group of well-armed Japanese, the night sounds were beginning to rasp on my frazzled nerves: small scurrying animals, buzzing insects, screeching night birds, and other things that seemed to either grunt or squeak. Any of these sounds could be the Japanese somewhere along the trail signaling one another. The one sound that I did not hear was the footsteps of all my Negritos who were walking behind me or any murmur of their voices. They really did move through the jungle like silent wraiths. It was spooky.

Finally, we walked into a small clearing. I looked at my watch: 2:00 a.m. I was dog-tired, soaking wet, and fed up with the entire operation. I told my guide, "Tell the men we are going to take a ten minute break." "Can't do that boss," he responded. "Why not?" I shrugged. "Men get tired boss. Go home long time ago." I started to feel the beginning of panic. "You mean there are just the two of us now?" "Yes, boss," came his reply. "But what about the Japon?" In the dim light of the clearing as I stood next to him, I could see him give another shrug of his shoulders. "No Japon in this part of Bataan, boss. We know." With that, I sat down on a fallen log and tried to think. All night long, I had been on a wild goose chase, and my Negritos had known from the beginning. They were being paid and they had eaten enough food to keep them stuffed for days. They were brilliant con artists. Then I thought of having to walk all those miles in the blackness back to the West Road. An even more somber thought hit me. What if my guide decided that he too was tired and wanted to go back to his home in the jungle and leave me?

I would have to wait until daylight and then try to find my way back through all those bamboo thickets and thorn vines by compass alone. It would be one hell of a trip. Carefully controlling my temper and trying to make my voice sound casual I said, "Do you know another way back, one that maybe is a little shorter?" "Sure boss. Much shorter. Much easier. We take big road." He crossed the clearing; we walked about a quarter of a mile, and there, in front of me, I saw a well-cut trail. He started down it at a fast pace. It descended steeply and then suddenly emerged on to an easier slope. We emerged from the trees on to a grassy plain and dead ahead of me, about a mile away, I saw a large body of water sparkling under a waning moon. Then I knew where I was. We had emerged from the side of Mount Mariveles that led down to the Section Base. I was home.

My report to the Marine captain the next morning was simply that we had not found any Japs; that his Negritos were great; that they did know Bataan like the back of their hands; and that we really covered miles of it. Finally, I suggested that he should keep up the good work and send out these fine jungle tribesmen again, with an American officer accompanying them to report the results. I concluded by saying how much I had enjoyed the experience and that it was unfortunate that I could not go out again myself, as my other pressing duties in Mariveles would keep me occupied. The captain was thrilled with my report. He assured me that I had made a great contribution to his intelligence efforts and that he was going to recommend that I be given a commendation of some sort for my fine work. From then on, I was careful to avoid the captain if I saw him on the base.

10

Desperation Before New Orders

I was standing on the shoreline looking out over the bay with Jack, Bud, Red, and Swede in early March. The water was a perfect turquoise, streaked with rows of sparkling light as breezes riffled the surface. The sky was a pale azure that lightened as it approached the water and was broken by a long row of white clouds. Bud said, "It is exactly three months to the day since Pearl Harbor was bombed." "Which means we have another five or six months to go before the relief fleet from the States comes in," replied Red. Mac was looking at the tip of Corregidor. "It sure has become quiet around here since the Japs last bombed the Section Base and the Inshore Patrol shifted to Corregidor." I had to agree. No vessel disturbed the water, not even a rowboat, and movement seemed to lessen as each day passed. Straight ahead, I could just see the western tip of Corregidor and to the west was the white and yellow rock of the quarry that formed the eastern end of our bay. The only familiar man-made mark on the water was sitting in front of it, the dark outline of the *Canopus* leaning in a sort of slant to give the impression that the Japanese had sunk her in their last attack.

Jack suddenly spoke up. "Do you think they have a snow ball's chance in hell of making it?" For a moment, he caught us all off guard and then we realized he was talking about the PT boats. They were down to their last torpedoes; the *Canopus*'s machine shops had kept them running by duplicating their parts; and the crews had to fuss with their propulsion systems day in and day out. A few days ago, we had heard that they were planning to make a run for it. Bulkeley and Kelly figured that if they loaded all their remaining drums of gasoline on the decks of the boats they would have enough fuel to make the China coast. They had set things up with a Chinese military attaché on Corregidor, so that if they did make the run successfully, they would meet Chiang Kai-shek's soldiers on the coast, burn the boats, and travel overland to Chungking. We all had our doubts about their ability to make the trip.

We talked about the trip Bulkeley had made with MacArthur on the first of the month.[1] They travelled out on the bay and along the lower part of the Bataan coast. Our general had presented Bulkeley with the Distinguished Service Cross during the ride. We figured MacArthur gave it to him so that it would be on Bulkeley's record before he drowned in the China Sea.

Jack suddenly changed the subject. "The Jap propaganda broadcasts are getting worse; even the music is getting lousy. And our own aren't much better." The military forces that faced one another on Bataan will not go down in history as masters in the subtle art of grinding out messages to encourage their own troops and discourage the enemy. The lowliest copy boy on Madison Avenue would have shuddered at their ineptitude. The Japanese dropped thousands of leaflets on the front lines to discourage the Filipinos, and during the past month, they had intensified their efforts. Most of these advised the Filipinos to either surrender or to go well behind the lines and hide until it was all over.[2] A lot of these leaflets became collector's items for the Americans. They showed sexy pictures of women that made *Esquire* look like a Sunday school text.[3] Others stated that the whole U.S. Fleet had been destroyed and that all convoys sent to the Philippines had been sunk. Vargas, the Filipino politician whom the Japanese controlled, signed a whole batch of them that said, "Lay down your arms since all is already lost."[4]

The main propaganda weapon on both sides was the radio. The Japanese controlled station KZRH in Manila and once a day, broadcast a special program to the Filipinos. It came on every night at 9:45 and because it carried music, people listened to it. The messages the Japanese composed were designed to hit the lowest basic emotions, such as "Surrender and enjoy the comforts of home" or "Did you know that your wife is fornicating with the guy next door?" These may have had some effect on the Filipinos who were feeling more miserable and hungry as each day passed, but all the Americans thought the Jap messages were hilarious.

Not to be outdone, Corregidor came up with the American answer and called it "The Voice of Freedom," broadcasting three times a day, covering the airways with music, which may have made some of the troops homesick; and basically informing everyone that they were not starving, despite the way they felt. They were going to win and help would be coming very shortly. MacArthur started this approach personally and what he said was such a blatant lie that it damaged his reputation for the rest of his life among many Americans.[5]

On January 15, MacArthur issued a message to all the troops and insisted that it be posted everywhere and read to every Filipino on Bataan. He told them help was on the way from the United States, including thousands of troops and hundreds of planes. He said no further retreat was possible, to hold, and that supplies were ample. MacArthur knew that none of this was true, as did the navy sitting in Mariveles; and it is hard to believe that even a desperate general would do this to his forces.[6] Admittedly, he aimed the message at the average Filipino soldier. That made it even worse. They worshipped their general. Many thought he was a genius who would show them how to defeat the Japanese, and he led them down the path with a positive statement that he knew to be a flagrant lie. For the following month, he pushed the lie so hard that most of the Filipinos believed it completely, even when they were slowly starving.[7] That declaration by their general may have helped to stiffen their backs during that month, but when they finally realized that it represented the Big Lie, it probably hastened the final collapse of Bataan.[8]

What it did for those of us in the navy was to start us seriously considering when help would arrive and how long we would have to hold out. We did not have all the facts on the Pearl Harbor disaster, but we had enough to know that the Japanese had seriously damaged the fleet. We also had learned the importance of an air force and that without fighter and bomber aircraft, we were not going to land troops successfully or drive the Japanese out of the Filipino countryside. We felt that the planes had to come first. The Japanese had knocked out our fighters and bombers before they attempted to land their troops. We would have to do the same. Moreover, once that was done, our naval guns could then clear the way for landings.

We knew that an invasion like this would not happen overnight. The planes, along with their crews, would have to come from all over the United States, probably out of factories and training schools. Somehow bases would have to be established and slowly pushed westward, around all those islands that the Japanese now controlled. The Malay Barrier and Australia would have to be held firmly, as they represented the only large forward bases that the planes and the Fleet could use to be able to help the Philippines.

Through the middle of February, when we talked about grand strategy, our estimates were that all this would take at least six months after Pearl Harbor, and that we would simply have to hold out until July or maybe even into September. Then Roosevelt gave one of his Fireside Talks on Washington's Birthday, February 23—a talk that was broadcast not only to the people at home, but to the armed forces, including us courtesy of the "Voice of Freedom." His talk on the world situation dampened any optimism that we may have been harboring. We learned that things were not going well anywhere in the world for the allies.

Many places needed help; and we had the impression that the Philippines were way down on the list.[9] Our estimates of a relief force successfully fighting their way to us in six or eight months suddenly dissipated. Instead, the navy personnel started using the slogan, "Golden Gate in Forty-eight." The more we heard about conditions in the front lines among the Filipinos and the air of pessimism that seemed to be coming from Corregidor, the more we were certain that the army on Bataan would fold before September and that when it did we would all be crowded onto the Rock. By the end of February, this prospect was looming plainer in our daily conversations, and it was not an appealing one.

$$\sim$$

Early in March, we had another one of the regular visits from Jim Bullock, our Corregidor expert, on what the army was doing. After we talked about the weather and the lack of activity on the bay, we got around to asking him what he knew of the activities among the troops. "They are still occupying the same positions that they were six weeks ago, and since the Battle of the Pockets, it has become a sort of stalemate. Our generals seemed to be content with that and are not trying to push them back. After all, the line goes across the best area in Bataan, so neither side seems to want to change it for something worse." "So they aren't doing much fighting; only sitting there and staring at one another?" I asked. "Oh there is plenty of action going on and people are getting killed every day, on both sides. Jap planes strafe and dive bomb. The Jap infantry keeps things interesting by getting through the lines, killing the Filipinos and in turn being killed. The main Japanese tactic has been infiltration, usually at night. The other thing that stands out is their use of snipers. They are experts at both infiltrating and sniping in heavy bush or jungle. These actions are small as far as the numbers of men are concerned, but they kill a lot of people in the course of a week."

I said, "In the Battle of the Points they didn't surrender when they were rounded up. Is this always the case?" Jim answered, "The army has learned a few things from the prisoners that they have taken. There have actually been cases where a Jap surrendered voluntarily, saying he was fed up, or that he thought the Filipinos would be on his side, not against him, but this is very rare. Most prisoners we capture are wounded and unable to resist. They usually say that they have been told that if Americans capture them, they will be killed. Their officers have warned them that if they are captured and not killed by the Americans, they will never be allowed to return to Japan, even when the war is over. That is why so many of them try to commit suicide when it looks like they are going to be captured."

"When the Japs infiltrate behind our lines, how do they keep eating?" I asked, thinking of my long hike with the Negritos. Jim responded, "They are usually supplied at night by parachute drops from low flying planes. Our guys have found some of these packages in the bush. They are dull brown in color and about three feet by eighteen inches by ten inches in size and contain food, cigarettes, medical equipment, and sometimes ammo. Finding these dropped cases gives us some indication of where they have infiltrated. By using the tactic of fighting in well-camouflaged small groups of infiltrators and snipers, the Japanese are tying up fewer troops in Bataan and still keeping the Filipinos and Americans occupied. I think they know we are not strong enough to pull off a counteroffensive and drive them out of Bataan. They couldn't help but know a lot about us, what with all the Filipinos that sneak in and out of Bataan from the bay.

"For our side, the past two months has been a period allowing the Americans and the experienced Filipinos to train all those draftees properly for the first time, so that even if the Japs do start a big offensive, our people will know what to do. This is the first real training that thousands of them have ever had. They are trying to teach them to think like the Japs: stay low and go slow; keep under cover at all times; be real jungle fighters and learn the buddy system the Japs use. Don't ever get careless; know about booby traps and that the only good Jap is a dead Jap and even then don't touch. It takes a long time to teach green troops all these things and still keep them aggressive."

"I guess the army has improved its defenses," said Red. "They have been working on that ever since the front line was first set up." Jim noted, "They have dug a lot of foxholes and trenches and camouflaged them; cleared away brush and trees to give clear fields of fire; strung as much barbed wire as they have in supply; set up tank barriers; and where they feel the most likely areas of attack will be, they have laid down minefields. They have made over a thousand mines." I asked, "Remember how we argued back in January as to how many troops the army has in Bataan? Have you got any more dope on that?" "I can guarantee it's crowded. When you figure it's only thirteen miles across the front from east to west and not much more than eleven miles from where we sit to the furthest northern bulge, it is a pretty small area." He responded, "There are close to 80,000 soldiers on Bataan and most are Filipino. No matter what anyone says, it's a Filipino Army. In addition to the Filipino soldiers there are around 6,000 more who are civilians working for the army as laborers."[10]

"So they have to feed at least 85,000 people working for the army on Bataan," said Swede. "It looks that way; and by now real starvation is occurring," said Bullock. "It's hard to believe how things have deteriorated in the past four weeks. The army troops up there are subsisting on eight to ten ounces of rice a day; and if they get the supplies distributed properly, they can add, on the average, an ounce and a quarter of meat or fish. When the slaughterhouses can round them up they get fresh caribou, but it is limited to no more than six ounces per man and doesn't happen very often. Those people are down to eating about a quarter of the food they should have just to stay healthy. They are eating what they can off the land, when they can find it, like snakes, lizards, iguanas, and dogs. Of course the cavalry killed off all the horses and mules a few weeks ago."[11]

There is more to the problem of slow starvation on Bataan than merely a lack of calories. These men are lacking a balanced diet; they are missing fats and protein, and most important, vitamins, and minerals. This means they are not just going through slow starvation and losing weight; they are going to develop a don't-give-a-damn attitude and get lethargic; lose their reflexes and their muscle tone. A skinny man can fight, but men who get into the shape these guys are in, make lousy combat troops.[12] To add to the morale problem, there are few comforts of home. Since the line was formed, Corregidor has sent over to them only four hundred cases of cigarettes to cover the whole of Bataan. I think that works out to one per day per man."

"What do you think is going to happen up there?" asked Mac. Bullock thought about it for a while and said slowly, "From what I have heard, General Homma is a capable general. He probably knows everything we do about our troops in Bataan. Homma doesn't want to lose a lot of men by fighting us on an equal basis. He is willing to wait and let the Filipinos sink deeper; wait until he can walk in over them. When he does decide to attack, I think he will come down on those poor Filipinos with everything the Japs can put together. Everything to soften things up before the infantry is even committed. We would do it that way. Then his infantry will simply sweep down the peninsula."

I said, "What about all those defenses and minefields the army has put down, and all the training they have given the Filipinos? Won't that stop Homma's drive?" Jim replied, "You haven't been listening. Sure, the defenses are impressive, and the Filipinos are being trained by actual combat. However, what will soon be missing will be the will to fight. Starvation does not just sap your strength. It brings on discouragement, and finally an attitude that it is no longer worth the effort. Homma knows this. That's why he isn't pushing."[13]

"How long do you think it will take him?" I asked. "Once he starts in earnest, I would guess that he could move from the front lines down into Mariveles in five or six days as things stand now." "How long do you think we have to try and improve things?" asked Swede. Jim responded, "If we started to feed these men properly tomorrow, it would probably take three or four weeks to get them back in shape. But, how are they going to do it? Where are the food and the vitamins going to come from? How is it going to get into Bataan in the quantities they need? I give Bataan six weeks or two months at the most. Then Homma is going to finish it off. I advise you to keep your bags packed and be ready to make a quick dash to the Rock. I have a feeling we are going to be roommates."

Three days later Jim was back in Mariveles, which was unusual, as we normally only saw him every ten days or so. He announced, "Well, today is Friday the thirteenth of March. Maybe it will bring us good luck for a change." He did not look as though he believed it. "And why are you here?" asked Red. "Did you see Schumacher pick up some people on PT-32 at the dock last night?" Mac answered. "I noticed one of the PT boats come in; but I don't recollect if they picked up anyone." Jim responded, "Well they did, and all four PT boats are on their way south; and they are carrying twenty-three passengers between them. MacArthur, his wife, his son and Chinese servant, along with General Sutherland are on the boat Bulkeley is running. He picked them up at Corregidor last night. Kelly and Akers loaded two more boats out of Sisiman Cove, and they have Admiral Rockwell and Captain Ray. When all the boats had loaded their passengers, they went out through the minefield separately and then took off together for Mindanao."

Red was incredulous. "You mean all the top brass has abandoned us?" Jim looked back out at Corregidor and said softly, "What would you call it?" "Why are they going to Mindanao? What do they have down there?" I asked. "Mindanao is only the first stop," said Jim. "Their destination is Australia. Bombers will pick them up at Del Monte and fly them the rest of the way." "Wait a minute, Jim," I said. "There is no way you can get the crews of the six PT's and twenty-three passengers on just four boats for a trip that long." Jim responded, "They didn't. MacArthur plays things very safe where his personal health is concerned. He made them leave Delong and two other officers on the Rock along with twenty of the enlisted men."

I could see that Swede was burning. "That's a long trip and one of the boats is in real bad shape. How are they fixed for gas?" Jim answered, "They should be all right. Each boat has extra drums stored on the deck, and they can always use the caches the PBYs laid down. Captain Ray has the complete chart of these."[14]

Mac had been sitting quietly listening to the conversation. He looked at Bullock and said, "Why would a general like MacArthur, who never sticks his neck out personally, go to Mindanao on a PT boat, instead of a nice safe submarine?" Bullock gave a cynical laugh. "The general thinks Bulkeley is lucky and will get him there in one piece. That is probably the reason he gave him the Distinguished Service Cross, sort of like a rabbit's foot. Besides, you guys have all heard that the general thinks a navy out here should be made up of PT boats. He doesn't trust anything bigger."

$\sim$

The week that followed was the worst that we had spent in Mariveles. Except for the minesweeper that we saw occasionally, the bay seemed devoid of vessels of any type. There were a few small launches and tugs at Corregidor, and the *Canopus* remained in front of the rock quarry, but movement on the water during the day seemed to have ceased completely. The craft that did cross between our shore and the Rock always sneaked back and forth at night. Air raid alarms were a daily occurrence and bomb dropping seemed to be increasing.

It was a week of frustration and suspense. The base was rife with rumors that the Japanese were preparing their big offensive to take Bataan. The constant air traffic overhead seemed to be watching every move we made, and these moves at our end of the peninsula were few. We had little to do except sit there. We kept in touch with our private naval intelligence group on Corregidor, scratching for every tidbit of news they could dig up for us. None of it was of the type that made us feel confident as to what the future might hold. We did hear that the PT boats with MacArthur, Rockwell, and party had made it safely to Mindanao and that they had all flown to Australia.

The bits of news that we picked up from Corregidor were almost universally discouraging. A lot of it concerned the continuing disintegration of the front line troops. There were stories of the spread of malaria, which was reaching the unbelievable size of hundreds of new active cases per day; stories of men and whole units literally starving; and stories that it was now difficult to find a monkey, iguana, or python alive below the front lines all across Bataan as the troops had eaten them all. Finally, nowhere in Bataan could you find a live dog. Equally discouraging was the news of the destruction of our Asiatic Fleet in the defense of Java and the Malay Barrier. After what our four old destroyers had done to the Japanese during the Battle of Balikpapan, we thought they would have a chance of holding their own.[15] We still had our two cruisers and the Dutch, British and Australians had some heavy ships down there. Then the bad news hit us, like hammer blows, one disaster after another. Some of it covered events that had taken place almost a month earlier and that we had not known about.[16]

~

At the end of the week, Swede took a launch over to Corregidor early in the morning. He did not tell us the reason for his trip, and this was unusual, as normally our entire group knew what everyone was doing, and why they were doing it. Swede returned in the early afternoon and spotted me. "Get Red and Mac and meet me here as quickly as you can," he said in a tone that implied something important had happened and it was urgent. Within five minutes, the four of us gathered by the pier.

"I want the three of you to get your gear packed and meet me here in fifteen minutes. Leave anything that you can't carry on your backs, like your cots and nets and any bulky loot that you've acquired."[17] He turned to Red. "Leave the keys in the ignition in the van." Then he added quietly to all of us, "Don't say anything to anybody. I mean not to anyone. We are taking a trip. It's confidential, so just get your gear packed and meet me here on the double." Under those ground rules, I did not have much to pack. I stuffed all my clothes and small items in my backpack. What did not go in the backpack, I hung on my belt. I was thankful that I no longer was loaded down with hand grenades and ammunition. I saw Jack and Bud walking across the flat and was going to say something to them but thought better of it. When Swede said not to talk to anyone, I assumed he meant it literally.[18]

The launch was waiting at the pier, and we climbed aboard. It took off immediately for Corregidor. As soon as we were out on the bay, Red turned to Swede and asked, "What is this all about; where are we going?" Swede addressed the three of us. "We are leaving Mariveles and going south—to Cebu.[19] We are part of a group of thirty that Captain John Dessez is taking down there.[20] Carl Faires and Willy Lipsitt are going; also Tommy Bowers and other people who were in the Yard." I asked, "Why Cebu?"[21] Swede answered, "We are going to start an organized blockade run from Cebu to the Rock. Our forces on Bataan are in even worse shape than we have been told. It is apparently running out of everything—not just food and medicines, but small arms ammo. It has been assembling supplies at Cebu, and we are going to run them up here in small inter island ships."[22] Red interjected, "You mean we are going to be blockade runners?"[23]

"As I understand it," replied Swede, "we will be in charge of seeing that the stuff is loaded properly on the ships. Army people will take them through the blockade with Filipino civilian crews." "Why have they waited so long to start this?" asked Mac. "It seems like a last minute move, with the barn door already locked." Swede replied, "It's a long story. Part of it is due to Wainwright taking over the command and getting things moving now that MacArthur is in Australia; but the other part is that the supplies are only now arriving in Cebu from the places where they rounded them up."

Then he told us the background of the operation and all the problems that the army had in setting it up and getting it moving. "This whole deal did not start until the end of January.[24] Originally, the army wanted to assemble three million rations in Australia, enough for fifty thousand men for at least sixty days, along with a big supply of ammo. They were going to send the supplies in freighters from the States to Australia and Java and then off load them into smaller, fast blockade-runners to take them up here. Then, they changed their minds and decided that to save time they could send freighters direct from both Australia and Java to the Philippines and collect the supplies they needed locally in both countries. They sent out a special team from the States to locate and purchase the supplies and the vessels to run the blockade.[25] They had a hell of a lot of money

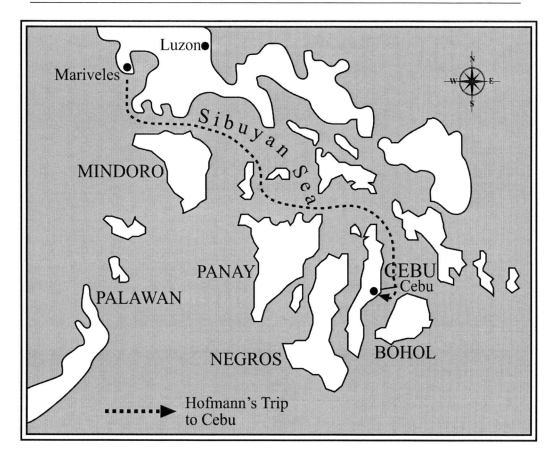

Hofmann's route from Mariveles to Cebu.

to spread around, but the problem was that when they explained the deal to ship owners and their crews, they had few takers."[26]

He added, "The Japs had started to bomb everything along the Malay Barrier and everyone got nervous. Also, it turned out that ships that could be used as fast blockade runners simply do not exist down there. Eventually, the army was willing to take anything, and pay almost any amount as a bonus to whoever would make the trip.[27] Its men offered the moon—bribes, cash bonuses, insurance policies, you name it. Everyone in the merchant fleets down there knew that any ship and crew that tried the run probably had an eighty to twenty percent chance of being blown up. Sometimes they would find a vessel and the owners would refuse to let them have it. Other times they would line up a ship and the crew would refuse to go.

"The army in Cebu claims that they have lined up twenty-five small inter-island vessels and their crews to run the blockade up here.[28] None of the navy people have seen them, but they are supposed to range in size from three hundred to a thousand tons. They will bring the stuff that came up from Australia and also a lot food, clothing, and medicines that they have had in Cebu warehouses. The plan is that they will travel only at night while hiding during the day. An American will go on each ship, and each ship will have its regular Filipino crew."

"Who are these Americans?" I asked. "I don't know," replied Swede. "Probably guys who live in the islands and now are wearing army uniforms. As I said, I haven't heard of any plan to have any of us go on them. They have made blockade runs in the past. One Filipino inter-island ship made two trips from Panay in January and February." Then he added, "The Japs didn't sink her until her third trip, when they got her off Mindoro the first of March. Another made it from Cebu to the Rock in February."[29]

Mac said, "It seems that your chances of being a successful blockade runner up here, even traveling all the time at night, are no better than fifty-fifty." Swede thought about it and stared out at the entrance to the bay and the minefield. He finally answered, "They may not be that good by now. The Japs have tightened up the screws all around the passages south of here and around the entrance to the bay.[30]

"They have doubled the number of patrol boats in the past two weeks, and the picket line off the minefield is solid now. It is going to be a lot tougher for any Filipino inter-island ship to get up here from Cebu and damn rough for them to get through the Jap patrols into the bay, no matter how dark it is." A thought had occurred to me as Swede was talking and I said, "Isn't it going to be pretty crowded on that submarine, with thirty of us aboard in addition to the crew?" Swede looked at me in amazement. "What submarine? Did you think you were going to Cebu in style? Mister, they reserve submarines for the brass. We are going out of here, through the Jap patrol boats, on a Filipino inter-island steamer, just like the ones that will be carrying the supplies up here. If we get through, they think the supplies have a chance of coming up."

I asked him. "What do you think the odds are of getting through the blockade and making it to Cebu?" "As Mac said, fifty-fifty, so brush up on your swimming. We leave the wharf at Corregidor at 2100 hours tonight. As soon as it gets dark, they are sneaking in the Filipino inter-island ship, loading us, and taking off before anyone knows we have left. Then we keep our fingers crossed that the ship can make her way back out and head south."

I asked another question. "How come Jack and Bud are not going with us?" This was the first time our supply group had been broken up. Swede shrugged and said, "I don't know. Their names were not on the list." I should have known. The navy always did things by lists.[31]

As Swede talked, this voyage out of Bataan and to the central Philippines was rapidly losing its appeal.[32] I had heard that the northern coast of Mindoro, the island immediately to our south, was firmly under the control of and loaded with Japanese. We would have to pass it to get to Cebu. The straits we would have to travel through for most of the way were not very wide and apparently crawling with Japanese warships, any of which could outrun us with most of their engines not working. For the first time in my short naval career, I was facing the very real prospect of either being drowned or taken prisoner by the enemy. I was not certain which I would hate more. From what the Filipino Scout had told me after the Battle of the Points, the Japanese seemed to like to use prisoners for bayonet practice. The whole idea of being in a position in which you were so helpless that escape was impossible and being captured was inevitable made my stomach churn. I started wondering what my reaction would be if I did face that situation: would I refuse to surrender like the Japanese, or would I throw in the towel and give up? I knew one thing. If there was the slightest chance of making it, I would keep running, or in this case, swimming, until my last breath.

For some strange reason I remembered a history I had read on the Boer War and what it said about my grandfather. The Boers had wounded and captured the colonel who led him and the other Canadian scouts. They then had tortured him to death. My grandfather made all the scouts swear an oath that after that, they would take no prisoners.[33] I wondered if the Japanese would apply the same vengeance on his grandson. It was not a pleasant thought.

On that night of March 20, we assembled on the North Wharf at Corregidor with our few possessions in our backpacks. We stood talking quietly in small groups, illuminated by a dim yellow glow from a building at the end of the wharf. Each of us was no doubt wondering how heavily the Japanese were patrolling the entrance of the bay, outside the minefield. From out on the water, I heard the vibration of engines that got louder as a ship slipped in out of the blackness beyond the wharf. I strained to see what it looked like as it slowly backed down and scraped the wood of the pilings. It was small, looked ancient, and the deck was painted a barn red. I felt that if this was what a blockade-runner looked like, the Japs did not have to worry about giving chase at high speed: eight to ten knots would probably overtake our vessel. I wondered whether the little ship had experienced any difficulty sneaking into the bay. Perhaps she looked so forlorn that the Japanese patrols had simply ignored her.

We boarded her in single file without talking. As each of us stepped on the deck, we headed for a place by the rail and dropped our packs. Slowly the engines vibrated, and the ship gradually inched away into the complete blackness of the bay. As we moved forward, the throbbing of the engines increased, the deck seemed to shake even more, and I was positive that any Japanese patrol within a mile of us would be listening to the uneven pulsations of our engines. As we slipped through the North Channel, past the lower bluffs of Bataan and our bay at Mariveles, I could just make out the hills against the night sky. There were no lights to be seen, and in the blackness, I thought about the first time I had entered Manila Bay, just five months before, headed in the opposite direction in the red glow of dawn, on a gleaming white cruise ship. A lot of things had changed in those five months, and I had changed with them. I thought about the thousands of Filipinos who were in the jungles or rice paddies of the peninsula who were slowly slipping away from our stern, and what Bullock had told us of their starvation and malaria as they stayed there waiting for the Japanese. I wondered how long they would hold out once the Japanese did start their drive.

I thought of the people in Mariveles and Corregidor that we were leaving behind, particularly Jack and Bud. It seemed senseless that some nameless navy strategist had left their names off the list. We had been together a long time. I hoped that when the push down the peninsula happened, that they would be able to get over to Corregidor in time. I resented the fact that I had not been able to say goodbye to them. The planners of these crazy secret operations did not seem to trust their own mother, yet with the jungle telegraph working the way it did, probably half the Filipinos on the Luzon shore and all the Jap patrols knew we were on our way and where we were going.[34]

I thought of Hogaboom, the intelligence captain, and all the other people I knew in the Fourth Marines, who were then on beach defense on Corregidor and the other islands guarding the bay. I thought about Jim Bullock and wondered what his reaction would be when he found that we were gone; then realized that he probably knew already, as he always seemed to know what was happening. I thought about DeLong and the other PT boat people that MacArthur had left on Corregidor so that he would not be crowded on his escape trip south, and I wondered if a submarine would be taking them out. I thought about the crew of the *Canopus* and Commander Bridget, and hoped that all these people would be able to make a safe retreat to Corregidor when the time came.

I wondered if Corregidor would suffer the same fate as Singapore. Corregidor, it seemed to me, was better situated to withstand a long siege; a rocky island, completely surrounded by water, a moat that was at least two miles wide at the narrowest point, with no soft underbelly attached to the land providing an invasion route as had been the case with Singapore. The artillery on Corregidor could fire at the enemy from every direction, not just out at sea. The tunnels were deep, and plenty of concrete protected the guns. Corregidor should be able to hold out until the relief forces arrived.

Red, who had been scanning the sea ahead of us with night glasses, interrupted my thoughts. Out of the blackness a ship appeared, one not much smaller than our own. I held my breath, waiting for a recognition signal to be flashed at us, and when we did not reply, to see the spiraling of tracers as they found us and swept our deck. Then I felt a little foolish as Red said, "The *Quail* is right on time to take us through the minefield."[35] We followed closely behind her and while we were doing it, I could not help but think back to the night when the *Corregidor* had tried to negotiate this same field without help. I could not take my eyes off our guide vessel as we moved through the bay entrance. Finally, the *Quail* veered off, and we left her behind, slowly, very slowly. We were like a cat burglar as we stole out into the open sea and felt the change in course as we turned to port and headed south. Soon I saw the first lights of the night, far off to port, from little villages along the shore of Luzon, faint pinprick glows at the bottom of the sky.

Suddenly the vibration of our engines reduced, and the ship slowed down almost to a drift with the sound of water along the side making a gentle slap. Red whispered, "It looks like a Jap picket boat, no more than half a mile off our port bow." "Is it moving?" asked Swede. Red kept staring. "It's moving, and it's gathering speed. It seems to be making a sweep toward the coast and pulling well away from our course." The vibration of the deck increased as we picked up speed and stopped rolling in the swells, and in a short time, we passed the spot where the patrol had been sitting.

"Shit!" said Red. "Here comes another one right across our course!" Again, the engine vibration cut down and finally seemed to stop altogether. The ship started to wallow in the eight-foot swells. "Where is it now?" I asked. "Damn, she kept right on going. I swear she crossed our bow not more than a half a mile ahead. No sign she saw us though." Red kept the glasses glued to his face as he tracked the patrol boat. After a few minutes, the engine vibration started up again and increased to the highest point I had heard so far. I had the impression the captain had opened up everything the engines could put out. We kept this up for hour after hour pounding down the passage at what I figured was our maximum speed. The seas slackened as we turned more to the east and the little ship was riding smoothly. Red kept looking through his night glasses. "I can see land dead ahead. It's probably the north coast of Mindoro." One of the men at the rail toward the bow moved back toward us and said to Red. "Did you see the ship we passed a couple of hours ago? It was a long way off. I could just make it out with my glasses. Looked like a Jap destroyer." Red admitted he had missed that one.

There was the faintest hint of light where the sky met the eastern end of the passage when I felt the engine sound change. Our little ship slowed and then the engines reversed as we backed very slowly. There was a slight bump and then we stopped completely. Three Filipino crewmen jumped off the bow near where I was standing. What they jumped onto I could not see. There was a black void all around us, whether water or land, there was no way of telling. We stood there silently, not a sound coming from anyone on deck. Slowly the blackness turned to dark grey and then began to lighten to a paler grey tinged with pink. I could see vegetation and a high, rocky cliff on our port side.

As the sky got lighter, I realized that we were hugging a bluff of rock, dirt, and scrub and that on top of it was heavy vegetation that hung like an awning over the topside of the ship. It was so complete that we were literally hiding under a roof of heavy foliage. The crew tied our bow and stern to trees that were growing on the bluff. On our starboard side, sticking out of the water about sixty feet away was an enormous jagged rock, much longer than the ship and twice as high, protecting us completely from any prying eyes that might be out at sea and cruising past our anchorage. We had to admit that our Filipino skipper was damn good to be able to know about a place like this and then to be able to find it in pitch blackness, as tight as the berth was. I resolved then that if I lived through all this and became a professional smuggler, the skipper would be my first employee. When everything settled down and we broke out some food, Captain Dessez informed us that we had traveled just under ninety miles during the night and were on the north coast of Mindoro. If all went well we should be able to cover the remaining roughly three hundred and thirty miles to Cebu in about twenty-four hours of running. We would probably hole up the next day on the coast of Panay and make Cebu by dawn of the following day.

We spent the day alternating watches and sleeping, and when darkness had once again set in, we moved away from our hiding place and continued on our eastern course. During the early part of the evening, I noticed a bright light behind us, not far above the horizon. I called to Red who was still scanning the sea with his glasses, "We may be spotted. That looks like a ship's light to the west." He swung his glasses to the stern, saying, "What light? Where?" I pointed to it. He looked at me and laughed. "You obviously need to brush up on your celestial navigation. That's Venus."

The night passed uneventfully as we continued eastward and then swung toward the south. At the first sign of dawn, we pulled into another hiding place for the coming day. This time we were among a group of small islands that Red said lay off the northeast end of Panay. The Filipino crew told him that this particular area was completely free of Japanese. Once more, we set up watches and tried to sleep. We were in a little cove and completely exposed, with no umbrella of foliage hanging over us. I hoped the crew knew what they were talking about concerning the absence of the Japanese.

Shortly after noon, a banca slid into our cove and tied up alongside the ship. Two Filipinos climbed aboard, and I saw them go into a huddle with our captain. After about half an hour, they went back over the side into their banca and paddled away. "I wonder what that was all about." I said to Red. An hour later, Red had obtained the story from the Filipino crewmembers. They told him that a Filipino guerrilla movement operated throughout the whole area and kept a constant watch among the islands to monitor the activities of the Japanese. The communication system was by banca, from one island to another. The men on the banca were the local telegraph system for this particular area. The system was efficient enough that news could pass in relays from Mindoro all the way down to the bottom of the central Philippines in less than two days. The two men had told the captain that during the previous night two Japanese destroyers had gone north headed towards the passage we used. Red said we must have been pretty close to them.

The third night of our cruise south was as uneventful as the previous one. When darkness settled in, we took off once more and headed south and slightly east, around small islands and finally around the northeast tip of the island of Cebu itself. The dawn broke and I saw a long coastline off our starboard side, with brown hills rising behind it. In the bright, early morning sunlight, we entered a channel between the mainland and another island to our port and within twenty minutes, we were tying up at a pier. Behind it, I saw the town. We had arrived at Cebu City, and everything looked peaceful.[36] The war with the Japanese could have been a million miles away.

11

Welcome to Cebu

As we walked around Cebu City that first day, we were both fascinated and amazed by what we saw. This part of the Philippines seemed to be completely unaffected by the war that we had left on Luzon only three days before. People had that happy-go-lucky air about them that we had seen in Manila before the war started. All sorts of merchandise filled shops. We entered a department store that was as modern as any in Manila, and we were like starry-eyed children as we looked over the array of goods they had for sale. There was plenty of food. Restaurants and bars appeared to be going full blast. Cars were driving around the streets burning up gasoline. The harbor front seemed normal. The whole atmosphere of the town was as if the war had never happened. It was hard to believe that the Japanese had completely ignored a town of this size and affluence, and that the residents were ignoring the war occurring all around them.

Though much smaller than Manila, Cebu was just as picturesque. From the Spanish, it had inherited the ancient Fort San Pedro, its Catholicism, and several old churches. From the Americans of the twentieth century, it had added commercial establishments, more warehouses, an oil tank farm, housing, better streets, and a number of small manufacturing plants, machine shops, shipyards, and processing plants for sugarcane and copra. All of these seemed to be operating on a peacetime "business as usual" basis.

An hour after our arrival, army personnel escorted our Supply Corps group to a white frame house on the western side of the city where the land rose toward the hills. We found it had comfortable beds and a staff of four Filipinos who would look after our needs. By afternoon, when we had finished our initial tour of the town, we discovered one more twentieth century addition—the American Club, complete with beer, liquor, and bartenders—all the things we had not seen for almost four months and had wondered if we would ever see again. We sipped our first cold drinks with ice in them and realized that the American Club was the hangout for the local American and European community. We had the impression that most of the Americans who had worked for the oil company were now wearing army uniforms. As we met them, we felt how remote from any war they seemed to be.

None of them, including a captain who we met and learned was one of the few regular army officers on the island, appeared to be greatly interested in what was happening in Bataan. He pointed out a brigadier general, named Chynoweth, at the bar and told us he ran the show in the central Philippines.[1] These people were in a completely different world from the one that we had just left. If they were planning any strategies to keep the Japanese from seizing Cebu, they were not discussing them with the navy contingent.

As the afternoon progressed, we began to feel that the American Club was the operational headquarters for the few American Army people who were on the island. We learned that most of the Filipino Army draftees and the members of the Constabulary, along with the few Philippine Scouts, had been sent to Mindanao to join General Sharp in its defense.[2] The captain told us that each island in the central Philippines had its separate, small garrison. The brigadier general who was holding court at the bar was technically in charge of all these garrisons, running the whole central Philippines' defense from Cebu. We found out that a Colonel Scudder was in charge of the Filipino armed forces on Cebu, and they were spread all over the island. Around 1,000 men, who formed the Cebu Military Police Regiment, protected the city itself.[3]

We were thankful that the Japanese were ignoring all this, for based on our Bataan experience; we did not think a spirited defense of Cebu City would last very long. By the end of that first day, we learned that General Chynoweth was of the same opinion and realized that he did not have the wherewithal to take on any sizable Japanese invasion force. His plan to meet an expected invasion of Cebu was to join his troops up in the hills as soon as the Japanese started to land. Our informant told us they would retire to hideouts that had been prepared and would be able to conduct a guerrilla campaign against the Japanese indefinitely.[4] One of the oil company men in describing these hideouts used words like "impregnable" and "completely hidden." He did not mention how they intended to eat and keep themselves supplied "indefinitely." We kept trying to bring the conversation around to the reason for our trip to Cebu. Finally, we learned that a captain who had come into the bar a short time before was heavily involved in blockade running. The regular army captain introduced us to him and told us he had just left his job as transport manager for the oil company to handle this project.

Swede started the conversation. "I understand that the army has lined up twenty-five inter-island vessels and their crews, and that they will leave as fast as they are loaded." The captain thought about it for a while and replied. "Well, we have not obtained quite that many as yet. However, we have requisitioned ten of them—great little ships and great crews. They are going to do a great job." Red asked, "How soon will you have the others?" "Well, we are working on it. We should be able to get them in a month or so."

The supply contingent looked at one another. It seemed that this had been a laid-back operation. "When do you start sending them up?" I asked. The captain looked at me with a shocked expression. Then he looked around the room before replying. "Don't you know that this operation is top secret?" "I'm aware of that," I replied, starting a slow burn. "And I assume that you are aware that we came down here to help you people, to say nothing of all the people on Bataan." Swede glared at me. He did not feel that this was the time or the place for an Army-Navy-civilian confrontation. Before the captain could say anything Swede stepped in quickly with "What he meant was, have any of the blockade runners left yet?" The captain ignored me and turned to Swede. "Well, as a matter of fact, one left three days ago." Red said, "I guess it will be getting there about now." The captain looked solemn. "Well, I am afraid not. We learned this morning that the Japanese had sunk it east of Mindoro."

Red said, "We came down that way. It was so black it's a wonder the Japs spotted it." "Well, this was not at night. It was in the afternoon. We had told the captain to keep going day and night to save time." We looked at one another again. This was turning into some kind of operation. The captain continued. "Maybe we rushed that one too fast. The trouble is General Wainwright's staff keeps pushing us to hurry up. I don't think he realizes how long it takes to load one of these ships and then plan its route up there." Swede said. "How do you mean, plan its route? Isn't that the skipper's job?" "Oh no, our general would not let one of the skippers figure the route to take. Those Filipinos are used to peacetime conditions. This is a military operation. We have to tell them how to do it and the route to follow."

Mac said, almost too quietly, "The one that brought us down here sure knew what course to follow. It seems to me that if a skipper has been traveling these waters for any length of time, and knows where and how to hide when he should, that he would know better than someone who has never made the trip before." The captain said. "I am afraid the general would not agree with that. He wants each vessel given a correct route and wants them to stick to it. That is why we put one of our men on each boat to see these orders are obeyed." None of us felt that we should tell this captain that they do not teach smuggling and blockade running in the trade schools. We dropped the subject and ended the conversation with the understanding that the captain would meet us in the morning and show us the nine vessels that he had left. We told him that we would be glad to help him with his loading plans.

We ate dinner at one of the cafés that evening. Halfway through the meal two civilians stopped by our table. One was an American and the other appeared to be Spanish. The American said, "We heard you fellows got in this morning. Made the run from Corregidor, eh?" We admitted that this was so. The grapevine in Cebu worked fast. The American continued, "We understand you navy people will be running the blockade up to Luzon. That makes sense. Navy people should run the ships. Guess you know we lost the first one a couple of days ago." So much for the army's top-secret operation. Apparently, the whole town knew about it—the Americans, Europeans, and Filipinos. I assumed that they had talked about this secret so much in the American Club and the cafés, that every detail was now available. I wondered why they did not publish it in the newspaper. The establishment on Cebu had obviously not experienced the stories of Fifth Columns and Japanese spies that had covered Luzon so well. By now, General Homma's staff were probably analyzing the details and tightening their blockade. As I said, we had entered a different and naive world.

We met the captain early the next morning. We had obtained the use of a green Ford sedan that evening as our official means of transportation. We divided our group between his station wagon and the Ford, and drove down to the waterfront at the south end of town. Spread among shipyards and two small coves were the nine inter-island vessels. We inspected them, one by one. Mac asked the captain when we had finished, "How come they're all empty? We understood you people had been loading them for several days now." The captain turned on his shocked look. "Oh no, the general has not given us the go ahead yet. We don't want to lose another one." We walked back to the cars realizing that the general and his assistants were running the show their way. Having made the trip, we wished them luck.

The next day a small freighter pulled into Cebu harbor. The captain turned out to be an Aussie, but his crew was definitely Chinese. The ship held a fair supply of provisional medicine and some ammunition. They must have loaded it in a big hurry, for the cargo was in sad shape after the trip, with broken crates and boxes and a lot of the canned goods had lost their labels. We got the ship unloaded and the material into warehouses where we tried to sort it out. By dusk, the ship and its crew headed back south. Three days later, the captain and men loaded and sent another inter-island vessel north. They were able to send another one three days after that. We learned that the Japanese captured both of them.[5]

After we had been in Cebu almost a week, we heard that Bulkeley, Kelly, Akers, and Richardson of the PT boats had come into town with the crews of two of the boats that had reached Mindanao with MacArthur. That night we met Richardson and Akers at the American Club, and over some drinks, we learned their adventures during the past two weeks. They had reached Cagayan, the nearest port in Mindanao to the Del Monte airfield, on March 13. MacArthur was so pleased with the way they had made the trip that he told them they were all going to be awarded the Silver Star and that after he reached Australia he would see that they too would be hauled out of the Philippines on bombers.[6] Mac-Arthur did not leave Del Monte until March 17.[7]

Kelly's boat faced the most difficulty. While he and his crew anchored off the beach at Cagayan, a fitting broke in the anchor on Kelly's boat, and the hull grounded fast on coral. It took almost two days to free the boat and when they did, they found the rudders, struts, and the propellers were damaged. Kelly took the boat down the coast to a little town where there was a machine shop and spent the next ten days trying to get it fixed.

President Quezon and his family had gone to their home in Negros after leaving Corregidor by submarine the third week in February, and MacArthur wanted them out of the Philippines. Bulkeley in the 41 boat and Akers in the 35 boat went to Negros to collect the president and his family, and take them back to Mindanao to fly to Australia. While Bulkeley made a twenty-seven mile drive to pick up the presidential party, Akers patrolled the Dumaguete harbor keeping watch in the 35 boat.[8] As he was doing this, the bow hit something and started to take on water, and Akers had to beach his boat. Bulkeley took a nervous President Quezon and his party across a rough Mindanao Sea in the remaining boat and turned them over to the army to fly them out of Del Monte. Bulkeley then returned to Dumaguete and took the damaged 35 boat in tow, bringing it to Cebu, where they put it in a small shipyard to have the hull patched up.

Kelly found that the repairs they had attempted in the machine shop in Mindanao had not been too successful. The top speed he could make without the boat vibrating apart was twelve knots. Kelly decided that he needed a decent repair facility, so he too headed for Cebu and a small shipyard. It was like we were back at Cavite. There were three PT boats in Cebu, but as usual, only Bulkeley's boat seemed to be working properly.[9] This meant, like us, their crews were getting an opportunity to enjoy civilized city life for the first time in months. It was about that point that the Supply Corps contingent decided to become salt-water sailors.

We felt that if the PT boats could survive all the running around that they had done, then we could do equally well, provided we had the right type of transportation and kept our noses clean. This all came about from a strategy meeting the navy contingent of blockade-runners had with Captain Dessez toward the end of our first week in Cebu. It was more like a bull session than formal meeting. We were sitting out in the sunlight after lunch and the captain said, by way of introduction, that he supposed all of us had heard of General Chynoweth's strategy if the Japs invade Cebu. He planned to set up this Camp "X" in the hills and wanted to fight the Japs in a guerrilla campaign.

He explained, "When we were up on Corregidor, we pretty much had to do what the army told us to do as we were under its command. Down here, we have a specific mission and no further orders until it is completed. However, I doubt if anything in our orders is ever going to tell us to be guerillas. Navy officers are not really trained in that department. So if the Japs do hit this place, and I certainly think they will before too long, I think the best thing is for the navy to be on its own and make tracks for somewhere that is a little better defended, and where we can do some good." Then he said something that started the Supply contingent thinking. "Probably the best place right now would be the Chinese coast. Bulkeley was going to take the PT boats over there at one point. There were a fair amount of sails going back and forth between the islands and China in normal times, and it is not a long trip from here, less than eight hundred miles. The Japs seem to be concentrating on the Malay Barrier to the south, so the right type of vessel might miss any interference from them once it was outside the islands."

We all kicked the idea around, analyzing such things as what the weather would be like, what navigation problems there might be through the Sulu Sea, around the long island of Palawan, and across the China Sea, what the coast would be like once we got there and what would be the safest spot to hit. I think the captain felt he was listening to boyish enthusiasm and curiosity, but he did his best to answer our questions. He really did not know his Supply Corps contingent very well. When someone put an idea in our heads, nine chances out of ten we would follow up, and between us, there was a fair amount of ingenuity.

By the following evening, Carl Faires and Willy Lippsit came striding into the house with Red and announced that our group was now the owner of a fifty-ton capacity rice banca and that the following morning we were going to try our hand at sailing it on a trial run.[10] Faires had done the government funding of our latest acquisition; Red was going to be the skipper in view of his Annapolis sailing record; and the rest of us would crew the vessel. Early the next morning, the six of us piled into the Ford and drove about four miles up the coast to a little bay.

Tied to a pier was our acquisition. The hull was fat and round, and about forty feet in length, with a good deck on both the bow and the stern and a large cabin amidships. Protruding several feet out from each side were the outriggers, cut from what appeared to be tree trunks that were at least a foot in diameter and extending the entire length of the hull. We all climbed aboard from the stern and inspected the interior. We could see how the hull could hold fifty tons of rice. It appeared cavernous when we went below. The interior of the cabin was large enough to hold six of us comfortably, and we figured those that were not on watch could sleep in hammocks or on mats. The more we studied our prize, the more we fantasized that we had our own personal yacht. Finally, we raised the sail in preparation for our trial run. It hung from the mast at the bow, was more or less square, very large, and controlled by two lines.

Red said as we shoved off from the pier, "She has no keel and the outriggers may handle a little differently. There will probably be some sideways slip and coming about may be quite different." We spent the entire day getting the hang of handling our new prize. Fortunately, we had a good wind behind us as we left the bay and ventured out into the channel. We then managed to hold things pretty well as we made our way out into the broader water between Cebu and Leyte. We quickly learned that when you do not have a deep keel digging into the water, a banca does not tack the same as other boats we had sailed. Coming about was a real experience the first few times we tried it. Bancas really do want to slip sideways, but they go great when the wind is behind you and pushing you dead ahead.

At one stage when we asked Red why he had not obtained the services of a Filipino experienced in handling large bancas to teach us how to maneuver, we unintentionally insulted him to the point where he did not speak to us for fifteen minutes. However, I felt that by the end of the day we were all doing pretty well. In fact, we came zooming in from the open sea into the channel and then into our bay, dropped the sail at the right time, and coasted into the pier without putting a scratch on the outriggers or ourselves. We all congratulated one another as having passed our first test. We not only tied our yacht to the pier, we used some chain and a couple of heavy padlocks we had acquired to make sure that if anyone tried to steal our boat they would have to leave part of it behind.

We decided that equipping our getaway vessel would be something of an art. We wanted to look as Filipino as possible. That meant we needed deck cargo that from the air made us look like natives and at the same time would be practical to use on our trip. We settled on a lot of large earthenware jars that would hold fresh water and some food. We had seen Filipinos travel with everything from goats to pigs on board bancas, but we decided that a few crates of live chickens would suffice for the animal life and provide a relief to catching fish to eat. We knew we had to have a decent radio and Swede found a battery operated set in town and, equally important, a generator that could be run by peddling a bicycle type apparatus, so that it would always have power. There were well-equipped Marine hardware stores in Cebu, and Red was able to pick up a good gimbal, compass, and a sextant. We figured our watches were good enough to serve as chronometers.

We picked up a map of the islands that at least showed all the coastlines and had a mileage scale on it. It could not be called a chart of the waters, but with some effort, it might suffice. We discussed at great length whether we should arm our vessel. In the end, we decided that this would be merely asking for trouble as any Japanese that came across us would have us outgunned from the start. It would be better to rely on guile and seamanship. Peaceful Filipinos in rice bancas did not carry cannons. In fact, about the only things we lacked when we got through outfitting the expedition were charts of the south China coast and a dictionary of the Chinese language, but as Mac said, you can't have everything.

$\sim$

During our first week in Cebu, while we caught up once more with civilization and urban living, we met a cross section of the local civilians. There were some interesting characters among them. One of the first friends we made was a mestizo Filipino whose family was big in the local sugar industry. He was native to the island and knew every hill and valley on it. He thought that the army was dreaming when they thought that they could hide from the Japanese and go guerrilla, particularly when half of Cebu seemed to know their plans in detail. He explained that Cebu was entirely different country from an island like Mindanao, or parts of Luzon, that had huge areas that were virtually unexplored. Cebu was mainly low hills and grassland, most of which was cultivated. The Japanese could easily examine it from the air, and there were few places to hide a large body of men, especially if you had to feed them and keep them supplied with ammunition.

He felt that the strategic reason behind a Japanese invasion of Cebu was that it was the cornerstone of the central Philippines and was the connecting link between Luzon and Mindanao. If the Japanese finally captured Bataan, Mindanao would remain a thorn in their side and have to be occupied. The Japanese already controlled some of Midanao's southern coast. With the central Philippines neutralized, they could concentrate on the western and northern coasts of the big island while their rear was protected. The army was defending only Mindanao's coastal areas. The interior was too big and had some of the worst jungles in the Philippines. Neither side would be able to do much about holding it.

He figured that the one thing the Japanese would want from Cebu was the petroleum stored in the tank farm, and he was determined to deny them this fuel. He told us that the army was so preoccupied with planning their excursion to the hills that they would probably forget to blow up the fuel tanks on their way out. He reminded us that most of the so-called army officers we had seen were former employees of the company that were not used to destroying their product, and he had things pretty well worked out as to how the tanks could be blown at the first sign of a Japanese invasion of the port.[11]

Two other military strategists in civilian clothes were Swiss nationals and were in charge of a copra plant for their European bosses. They were about as wild a pair as I had ever met. Nothing about the war or its future possible course seemed to bother them. They carefully explained that the Swiss were neutrals and were not about to become mixed up in the fighting with the Japanese. Like our sugar planter, they knew the terrain of Cebu and confirmed that any knowledgeable local thought the general was pipe dreaming if he thought he could carry out any sort of successful guerrilla campaign once the Japanese had landed a force on the island. One of them put it bluntly. "The general is like so many Americans. He is not realistic. With a small band of men, he might be able to survive for a few weeks until the Japs started to look for him seriously. Each man in his band would have to be fiercely loyal and anti–Japanese. He would have to be constantly on the move and always at night, to avoid discovery. There is no place in Cebu that is impregnable like they talk—not against experienced infantry and airplanes."

Another citizen whom we met was a pilot who owned a single-engine Beechcraft and flew it from a small strip not far from our house. He was an American and must have graduated from the barnstorming days. He could make that plane do just about anything. We dubbed him our air force. Almost every day he flew out over the waters off the coast to scout for Japanese ships and their movements. Each day he would report what he had seen, so that our island would not be subject to a surprise invasion. We figured that it took a lot of guts to make these flights. His Beechcraft was completely unarmed, and the enemy could surpass it in both speed and power. He liked to say that if the Americans out here had some decent planes and some of the pilots that he had known, there would not be a Jap plane flying anywhere in the Philippines.

We also met a pilot of another small plane. He was Dutch and had flown his little military spotting plane all the way from Java. Considering that our big bombers were having so much trouble making the trip to Del Monte from Australia, we thought it was a miracle that he had flown his Dutch scout as far as Cebu. Red had met the Dutchman in a local café and learned that he was making a tour of our islands to see how we were doing. We were not clear as to whether he was doing this to satisfy his own curiosity or whether it was part of some grand Dutch strategy. As the Malay Barrier was pretty much in the hands of the Japanese by then, it seemed as if he was really on a personal junket.

He wanted to know about our experiences in Bataan, and Red brought him back to the house so we could talk with him, as we wanted to know what had happened along the Malay Barrier. He had apparently seen it all and had been moving along ahead of the

Japanese ever since they first hit Borneo. He figured that as long as he could get fuel, he could fly his plane just about anywhere and, like our own local air force, did not seem to have any worry about the Japanese capturing him. He brought us two bottles of Dutch Bols gin as his contribution to our evening. None of us had it before and as I recall, tasting it was quite an experience. I believe we polished off his entire gift that night.

While our new friends and the diversions provided some relief, we never lost sight of our purpose as blockade-runners. However, from the day that we made our first visit with the captain of the blockade running vessels, we became more skeptical of the army's ability to successfully send supplies to Manila Bay. They apparently did not have enough confidence in the Filipino skippers to let them plan their own routes, hours of travel, and hiding places. The fact that we had let our own blockade-running skipper handle our escape vessel in his own way, and he had made a successful trip seemed to make no impression on the Army Quartermaster and other staff people in Cebu. They kept telling us that the Japanese had increased their air patrols and that they could spot anything that moved. We had no quarrel with that. Anything that moved during daylight hours deserved to be spotted. However, we also were positive that the Japanese did very little hunting over these seas with airplanes at night and so that was the time to travel. Only an idiot would be blockade running during the daytime. Yet, the army kept pushing their vessels to make time and lost most of them during daylight hours.

∽

During our short time in Cebu, while these discussions of tactics were happening, one of our fleet submarines, the *Seadragon*, suddenly appeared in the harbor.[12] After it tied up on the main pier, the navy contingent welcomed the skipper and crew to Cebu. The skipper let us know that this was not a social visit and that he was on a tight schedule. He had been on his way from Australia to start a patrol off when he had been diverted to Cebu to pick up provisions and diesel fuel and make a run for the Rock.[13] We had six hours maximum to load his post. Loading a submarine to its capacity with cartons of provisions is not an easy job since submarines do not have cargo holds like surface freighters do. The only decent storage space is the torpedoes storage area. In addition, you can fill the tiny wardroom or the skipper's bunk.

To make space, we removed all of the *Seadragon*'s torpedoes. We then selected cartons of the most nutritious food we could locate and hauled them to the pier and on to the boat. The crew then stored them below to the skipper's satisfaction. By the end of the day, our combined efforts had managed to squeeze aboard her 34 tons of provisions and about 12,000 gallons of diesel fuel. I think that the navy may have educated the army in Cebu that day on what might be termed "work ethic." The *Seadragon*'s crew had been on patrol for many days before they pulled into Cebu, and in all that time, few of the men had breathed fresh air. Yet, every man worked non-stop, most of them below the hull, while we maneuvered the provision cartons onboard.[14]

Soon, another one of our fleet submarines showed up at the pier. This time it was the *Snapper*.[15] We repeated the previous performance of high speed loading and we managed to do even better. We squeezed in 46 tons of provisions and 29,000 gallons of diesel fuel.[16] Once more, we demonstrated that the navy could work fast under these emergency conditions. Our opinion of our fleet submarines was pretty high after these two exercises: they may not have sunk many Japanese ships, but their crews sure worked like hell.

At the beginning of April, we tallied the results of our efforts to send relief to Luzon.

The only supplies that had reached Corregidor were the two submarine loads. The entire quantity that was on the *Snapper* had been unloaded satisfactorily, but for some reason the *Seadragon*'s unloading had been interrupted and she had left after only about a fifth of the items had been removed.[17] Mathematically that meant that all the effort that had been put into getting supplies and carriers to Cebu and from there to Manila Bay had resulted in only about 53 tons of food being unloaded at the Rock, along with maybe 35,000 gallons of diesel fuel. When you divided one hundred thousand men on Bataan and Corregidor among 53 tons of food, assuming it was distributed equally, each man could feast on a little over a pound of it.[18]

As we loaded the submarines, we were told that the Rock had developed a solution to the problem and had passed it on to MacArthur in Australia to work out the details. They proposed that he send a large fleet of heavy and medium bombers to Del Monte, each plane carrying a full bomb load. They would carry out a surprise attack against all the Japanese ships that were patrolling the waters of the central Philippines and around Subic Bay. They had the theory that a massive surprise attack of this type would completely disrupt the blockade, possibly even sinking most of the Japanese vessels that were patrolling Philippine waters, and that it would take the Japanese a long time to recover from the shock. During that period, we could move up to Manila Bay as much food, medicine, and war material as we had available.[19]

We loaded a 500-ton inter-island vessel with food on April 1 and heard that they had placed five hundred tons of fuel on one over in Iloilo, so it would be ready after the big attack. The rest of our seven inter-island blockade-runners were loaded with food and medical supplies during the first week in April and made ready to take off the minute our air armada had completed its attack and driven the Japanese out of our waters. By April 4, we heard that MacArthur's headquarters in Australia had advised that the planes were being assembled, and that they would be taking off for Del Monte in a week or less. However, that same day we heard that the Japanese had started the big offensive to take Bataan and were throwing everything that they had at the Filipinos, including fresh troops who had come over from other Japanese theaters. It seemed to us that time was running out, if the predictions that we had heard from Jim Bullock were accurate as to the length of time it would take for the Japanese to drive down Bataan.

That night, I came down with what they said was dengue fever, and I was sick for the first time since my arrival in the Philippines. They tell you that dengue is much better than malaria since it does not reoccur like malaria does. That may be true, but if that was what I had, it was the worst fever I have ever experienced. The high temperature lasted for about thirty hours and hit over 104 before it finally broke. At one time, they told me I went out of my head and started thrashing around and it took two of the Filipinos to hold me down. When it broke, it left me as weak as a kitten.[20] Unfortunately, Japan's plans for Cebu were going to rush my recovery.

12

Retreat Again

On April 7, the pilot of our "air force" flew over the western shore of Cebu and reported that he had sighted two Japanese destroyers, steaming between Cebu and Negros. The next day he flew the Cebu coastlines all day long but did not see any more Japanese activity. On the morning of the ninth, he flew due south out over the Mindanao Sea and came barreling back at noon. He reported sighting three warships, which from his description could have been either destroyers or light cruisers. They were shepherding a fleet of small transports and were headed north toward Cebu. When we heard this news we felt that time had run out. The invasion of Cebu was about to commence.

Early that evening we packed our belongings in our kits once more and checked our armament, consisting of our .45 side arms. Then we dozed and waited for the next move by the Japanese. An explosion awakened us around 4:30 a.m., and we all grabbed our packs and ran out into the street to see what was happening. There was another even louder explosion almost immediately, and we could see flames north of the harbor. Red scanned the area with his binoculars. "The army is blowing up the refinery. Looks like our friend really planted some dynamite." There was some wind blowing and as we watched the flames leaping higher into the air, I heard Red say, "That fire is spreading fast and reaching toward the buildings to the west of the tank farm. They are going to take out part of the town along with the refinery."[1] We stood there wondering what we should do, and as usual, Swede had control of the situation. "Right now, we don't do anything. We stay put. There is no sign of the Japs. We wait until daylight. If we go wandering around town in the dark, chances are good for getting shot by some trigger happy army guy."

We waited and finally the sky began to lighten. A half hour after dawn, one of the navy contingents pulled up in a truck in front of the house and called to us—"The Nips are landing near Toledo on the west coast and the army has spotted a destroyer and two small transports coming north toward Cebu City. They are about fifteen miles down the coast and seem to be headed for the channel—looks like their invasion fleet." He added, "Some of the fellows are talking about going to Camp 'X' with the army, but most of us figure it would be a lot smarter to head out for Leyte or Mindanao." With that, he drove off, and Red said, "I think it's time to go up and get on the banca. We can get out to sea while the Nips are busy landing in the port area."

It was then that I noticed that Faires and Lipsitt were not with us and realized that I had not seen them since the refinery had blown up. I found out that none of the others had seen them either. Swede said, "They may have gone off ahead to guard the banca until we get there. Remember, they didn't have to wait for us. Faires has his own car." The four of us piled into the Ford, and Red took the back road up the coast to the little bay that was our yacht harbor. We ran through the trees and down the dirt path to the dock. The banca was not there. We searched the shoreline; there was no sign of it. I said, "Maybe they moved it to a better hiding place. We should search further up and down the coast." Two of us covered every foot of the shore for over a mile north of our mooring point, while the others did the same to the south. After a half hour we returned to our starting point, all of us empty-handed. We stood there, not believing that our transportation to the Chinese mainland was gone.

Then Red yelled, "Look at this!" From the bushes, he extracted two open padlocks and some chain. "Son of a bitch. The bastards stole it." It was all I could say as I looked at the empty bay. Swede said slowly, "Not Carl or Willy; not on their own. Two men couldn't sail that banca. Someone else has taken it or someone else has made them show them where we had it hidden and a group of them have taken it." Mac added, "Maybe they thought we were with our buddy in the demolition of the refinery and got killed or blown up." No matter what the answer was, we were stuck.[2] Again, Swede put things into their proper perspective and spoke some common sense. "There is only one thing to do. We go back to the house. We gather up food and fresh water and see what the Japs are up to. Then we decide which way to go. No matter which way we head, I have a hunch we'll be doing some walking before the day is out."

We watched the Japanese landing from the fifty-yard line. We had such a clear view of the harbor that we hardly needed the binoculars. The two transports pulled up to the channel entrance and with them were two small inter-island steamers, each maybe a hundred feet in length. The escorting destroyer stayed behind them with its guns swiveled toward the port area. They all sat there while we watched them until after 9:00 a.m. Then the transports loaded the two smaller vessels with hundreds of men each. We did not see any armor or vehicles of any kind being put aboard the inter-island ships, and it appeared that they were planning a light infantry operation. The two little vessels with their troops proceeded up the channel in one column, and the lead one fired a few rounds from a small gun in the general direction of the port. They finally tied up at the pier where we had loaded the submarines. They had come in as if they were participating in a peacetime naval review. As soon as they berthed, the troops walked down the gang-planks and formed up into what appeared to be platoons on the wharf. Not a shot had been fired. I looked at my watch, and it read 10:27 a.m.[3]

The whole operation was insulting in the calm and deliberate way they had carried it out. After all the army had around 1,000 troops defending the town, to say nothing of the thirty officers who represented the U.S. Navy. While I was watching them march, I heard the sound of a plane's engines above us and through the trees. We could see that it was a seaplane. As it passed, it dropped some leaflets. On cheap paper, with poor printing, we read the English message printed on the face of each: SURRENDER. WE ARE YOUR FRIENDS. On the reverse side, the message was not as funny. It reminded me of a jail poster from a western movie. In essence, it offered substantial rewards for the capture of any American and handsome rewards for the capture of any American officer, in either case DEAD or ALIVE.[4]

As we were digesting this information, a barrage of small arms fire erupted from the downtown area, and we turned to see what had happened. Lt. Col. Edmunds and his men in the Cebu Military Police Regiment had played their cards well. They remained hidden and held their fire until the Japanese thought that they were going to march through town as conquering heroes. Then, the colonel's men opened up on the enemy with everything they had. We saw several of the Japanese fall from hits while the rest broke ranks and scrambled for the protection of any concrete or wood that they could find.

An explosion followed the first fusillade of rifle fire, and we saw one of the waterfront warehouses, full of all those carefully garnered supplies, go up in flames. It was immediately followed by another and then another until it seemed that the entire warehouse district was exploding behind the Japanese. Their troops did not seem to know what to do or which way to turn. We saw dozens of them retreat toward the pier area, while others formed a skirmish line and were firing wildly toward both the town and the exploding warehouses. The area was blowing up and burning around them from the pre-set demolition charges, and they were trapped in the middle of it, with no enemy to be seen or to attack. The colonel planned the whole operation perfectly. We might not have any confidence in the Camp "X" proposal, but this man Edmunds knew how to conduct a street fight.

The firing continued into the early afternoon as we watched. The Military Police pulled back slowly, block by block and corner by corner, in the process, sniping at every Japanese soldier who exposed himself. The enemy proceeded very cautiously. The troops we saw were in small groups scurrying from building to building, continually seeking cover. The Filipinos appeared to be following a well-rehearsed plan and had the advantage, as they knew the town intimately. The Japanese were in unfamiliar surroundings and proceeded from building to building slowly and warily. Swede said to us, "They're buying the rest of the army a lot of time with this delaying action. It will give the Filipinos a chance to blow the bridges and put up barriers across the road leading into the interior."

While Edmunds and his Filipino troops were containing the Japanese in the downtown area, our group was planning its next move. This was not the time to be blindly running around and risking capture, especially if the enemy was serious when they had printed those leaflets. The prospect of being a target for some bounty hunter was not appealing. We studied a map of the island, knowing that the Japanese would be following the roads in the initial stage of the invasion, rather than sending their troops into the open country. One road circled the island and covered most of the coastline. Another road crossed the island from east to west, connecting Cebu City to Toledo on the west coast. It started out curving southwest from the town into the hills behind us, then abruptly turning almost due west over the higher hills that formed the north to south spine down the center of the island, passing through the town of Cantabaco that was half way across to Toledo, and then swinging north to meet Toledo on the west coast. After we pondered this road network, Swede said, "The army will be pulling back from both Toledo on the west coast and from here, along the cross island road until they get to Cantabaco. Then, they will pull north from that point to Camp 'X.'" They should have plenty of time for both their western and eastern troops to fall back because they plan to blow all the bridges along the roads and put up barriers that will delay any vehicles." We agreed that this made sense. We knew that Camp "X" was basically their assembly point in the center of the island and that their supply caches were hidden in a long string north of there, up to the more rugged country in the northern tip of the island.

Swede continued, "As I see it, we have only a few choices if we want to avoid capture. We can't stay here. I figure that the Military Police will hold the town until maybe late afternoon or early evening and then retire over the road in those trucks they have stashed and head for Cantabaco and then Camp 'X.' So Cebu City will be given up and not be a healthy place. We should not follow the coasts because if I know the Japs, they will have infantry forces and eventually motorized ones covering coast roads. I don't think any of us feel like going to Camp 'X' and playing guerrilla. Just like Captain Dessez said, we are not trained for it, and it sounds like another Bataan situation. I think the best plan is to get off the island and go to a bigger one, and the two that look the best are Negros and Mindanao."

Red spoke up. "I think our best move is to walk across country to the west coast, then take a boat to Negros. The Japs may not have hit there. Once we get across we can plan our next move." We studied the island map some more and agreed that this was our best plan. We scaled the map. The direct line distance between Cebu City and Toledo was twenty miles. By going across the ranges of hills on foot and following what trails there might be, we figured we would have to travel about twice that to reach the west coast. We also figured that we had better stay well north of the cross-island highway and the central town of Cantabaco. It looked as though this would mean walking through barren country and over higher ridges, but it seemed to be a lot safer.

By three in the afternoon, we had filled our canteens and extra water flasks, and gathered up enough cans of meat to last each of us a week. We climbed into the Ford and drove up a dirt road to the top of the ridge behind the city. We left the car there and started down the other side of the ridge, walking toward the west. We had walked a little over a mile down the slope into our first valley, when we caught up with two civilians who were headed in the same westerly direction. We introduced ourselves and found that they were brothers who owned a sugar plantation on Negros. They told us that they had talked to their home early in the morning and that as far as anyone knew, the Japs had not landed on Negros, and they were in a hurry to get home and protect their property before any action might take place. We decided to join forces, though I must admit they had more to offer than we did. They spoke the local dialect, appeared to know the layout of Cebu, and said that they knew a good route across to the west coast that should avoid any contact with the invaders. They figured if we moved quickly that we could make the west coast by sometime early the following night.

After we had been walking for about an hour, we saw the solitary figure of a man approaching us at an angle from the southeast. As he got closer, we saw that he wore a naval officer's cap, and finally I made out the features of Bob Kelly of the PT boats. We waited until he caught up with us. Then Swede asked him, "What are you doing here? I thought you had your boat repaired and gone back to Mindanao." Kelly said in a voice that almost shook with anger, "The Japs wrecked my boat; killed two of my men and wounded two others. I think Richardson took off for Leyte from Mactan Island and Bulkeley and Akers took the 41 boat back to Mindanao, if they made it. Night before last the army sent our two boats out to take on a Jap destroyer. Only it turned out to be a cruiser. We hit it, but their planes bombed and strafed us, and I finally came ashore from the channel on to Mactan. I never saw Bulkeley after that, but I think he got away in the dark."[5]

Red said, "Sounds like you ran into a hornet's nest." Kelly looked at him. "You could say that. Did you hear that the army was supposed to be sending up bombers from

Mindanao to hit the Japs and help out the blockade runners?" It was a statement rather than a question. Kelly continued, "Well, they were supposed to be our cover. They never showed." Swede replied. "We heard it and chalked it up to one more rumor."

We started walking again and crossed two more of the ridges before the sun started to settle in the west. There was virtually no cover. The brown grasslands seemed to extend for miles on all sides of us. As the day wore on, I found that climbing the rises was becoming more and more difficult, and I began to realize how weak I was after my bout of dengue. As darkness approached, we saw a tiny collection of palm-roofed houses ahead of us, clustered in an oasis of flame trees, palms, and banana plants. Our Negros companions suggested that they go on ahead and talk to the Filipinos who lived there and find out if they had a place where we could sleep for the night. In a few minutes, they returned and said that everything was fine and that there had been no sign of Japanese activity in the area.

The Filipino residents were friendly. The older people cooked two chickens and boiled rice for us while some little kids and two skinny dogs watched us. The kids smiled and the dogs sniffed. We tried to pay for the food, but they refused to accept our pesos. Our guides from Negros explained that this was the way in the country districts. That night we put up no guard and slept the sleep of the dead. We felt that we were too remote from anything that might interest the Japanese. For my part, I knew that the fever had left me so weak that only a night's sleep was of any interest. The invasion of Cebu could keep until I felt better.

I was awakened shortly after dawn by the sound of airplane engines. We all rushed to the windows of our raised sleeping quarters and peered out cautiously. Three twin-engine bombers were crossing the valley in a V-formation, just in front of us, at an altitude of less than 2,000 feet. Suddenly Red yelled out, "They're ours. They're not Nips." There were stars on the wings instead of the familiar orange red sun discs. They kept going, climbing the ridge to the east. Within minutes, another three-plane formation passed by us, also flying low and heading toward the east. The Air Corp's long awaited attack from Mindanao had become a reality.[6] Unfortunately, MacArthur's operation was three days too late. The supplies that they were supposed to protect had been destroyed, and the Japanese warships had probably gone to other seas. To the east, we heard the dull crunch of bombs landing and guessed that they were hitting the Cebu waterfront. As we had been experiencing for months, it was too late and too little. Our operation to feed and supply Bataan had been finished the day before.

The supply group accepted this with some degree of resignation. It seemed that ever since the start of the war things had happened this way. All the great plans that had been talked about for the relief of the Philippines always turned out to be just that: plans, schemes, and ideas that were fanned by rumors, and operations that never came to fruition. Now that one finally had occurred, it had come too late to accomplish any results. Kelly was not as philosophical as we were concerning the army's lack of ability to produce positive results. However, he had just lost his PT boat and crew, and we felt that he had justification for his anger and disgust.

Shortly after the planes had passed, we set out once more on our trek to the west coast. The slopes of the hills became steeper and the walking more difficult as we crossed the higher ridges in the center of the island. Our Negros planters informed us that we were now several miles north of the cross-island highway and the barrio of Cantabaco. We guessed that we were north of the army's assembly point that they called Camp "X."

In the middle of the afternoon, we saw a small group of Filipinos on the down slope of the ridge. They were standing in a group and seemed lost.

As we approached we made out the fatigues of the Filipino draftees, but none seemed to have weapons. When we reached them, we learned what had happened to General Chynoweth's plans to defend the island out of his base at Camp "X." Our interpreters got the whole story. At 3:00 a.m. the previous night, one of the sentries on outpost duty on the road between Camp "X" and Cantabaco had heard the sound of vehicles coming up the road toward him. After calling out, he found he was facing a Japanese tank. It fired a round over his head. The men we were talking to had been on outpost duty in the same area and as soon as they heard the firing, the entire outpost line took off and ran back to the main camp base. The general was at Camp "X" with several hundred of his Filipino troops and when his terrified outpost guards descended upon him in utter confusion in the blackness of night, he moved further north. While the scared Filipinos did not know the details of the rapid Japanese advance through Cantabaco and up to Camp "X," it was obvious to us. Cantabaco was supposed to be the critical point to hold and it could no longer be defended. We learned that the majority of the troops had fled from Camp "X." The ones we were talking to were part of this exodus.[7]

We realized that the capture of the east-west road and Cantabaco spelled the finish of any heavy, organized resistance on Cebu. The general could probably escape to his defensive positions to the north with a couple of hundred men who would be "fiercely loyal and fiercely anti–Japanese" as the Swiss national had described them, but with the fall of Camp "X" he was reduced to a guerrilla band instead of an organized army. Our interpreters finished by telling us that the soldiers in this group were going to their homes as quickly as they could and putting on civilian clothes. For them, the twenty-hour war against the Japanese was over. After this briefing, we were pretty certain that the Japanese forces were to the south of us and that we were west of Cantabaco. The Negros planters told us that they knew a small village on the coast, about sixteen miles north of Toledo. They were friendly with its mayor who would put us up and probably find bancas for us. They said if we walked quickly, we should be there before dark.

We made the village by seven in the evening and while we lay hidden, in case the Japanese had come up the coast, the two brothers went to the mayor's house. They came back to us in about half an hour. The good news was that the mayor would hide us in his house until we were ready to go over to Negros and that there had been no sign of Japanese troops. The bad news was that there were no bancas in the village as the army had taken them all. The mayor suggested that we spend the night there, and on the following day, we could go out and search for bancas along the coast. There was another smaller village about five miles south on the road to Toledo, and we might find bancas there.

The mayor's house was fairly large, and we spent that night and most of the next day there. Like all the other houses in the town, it was on stilts with the main living quarters above and the cooking and toilet facilities on the ground. The mayor fed us chicken, boiled rice, vegetables, and bananas, and refused any offer of payment. The mayor told our interpreters how fortunate it was that his citizens had no use for the Japanese and liked the Americans. He told it like it was a huge joke, and he added that the Japanese were accusing the Americans of having blown up Cebu and that they were offering a fifty thousand peso reward for the capture of any one of us, dead or alive.[8] They did not seem to care in which condition. Fifty thousand pesos is more money than a country Filipino would see in several lifetimes. Despite the mayor's good humor, the idea did shake us a little.

We left the mayor's house at dusk and quickly walked the five miles down the coast road to the village he had mentioned. It was smaller, just a collection of palm-roofed little houses. One of the villagers directed us to one of these that was the military head-quarters in the village. A young Philippine Army lieutenant was in charge of a force of twenty men. Their only weapons were old rifles, and he told us they had little ammunition to go with them. When we asked about the Japanese, he told us that a Japanese tank had come up the coast road the day before. It had entered the village, poked around a bit, and then gone back south. He said that the soldiers had hid, as they knew they could not do any damage to the tank with their rifles. He added that if any Japanese tanks came up the road again, he and his men were going to leave and head for the hills. We did not blame him.[9]

The lieutenant may not have had anything to stop the Japanese, but he did know about bancas and went out to search for them. By nine o'clock, he took us to the beach and showed us three small sailing bancas lined along the sand. We thanked him for all his help, wished him luck, and shoved off immediately. On a straight course, the Negros shore was about twenty miles due west, and we figured that with the right wind condi-tions we could make it the next day. The two Negros brothers were in one boat, Kelly and Swede in the second, and Mac, Red, and I in the third. We kept our little fleet close together and had no problem maneuvering our sails under the light breeze.[10] There was a lot of moon that night, and the water under it sparkled. If we all had not been a little nervous about being discovered I think we would have admitted that it was a beautiful night and a relaxing trip. We arrived in bright sunlight an hour after dawn. Our landing spot was a sandy beach and behind it was a small rise with the coast road on top of it and dense foliage behind it.

Our Negros planters told us that their sugar cane fields were about twenty miles north, and their house was about a mile from the water; they took off at once to protect their property. They suggested that we head south to the town of Dumaguete. It was about a hundred and fifteen miles down the coast from where we had landed, and the town was almost as big as Cebu City. They believed that, because of its importance as a major port, there would still be American forces there, and since we wanted to go on to the big island of Mindanao, they felt that we might find transportation in the harbor.

While they were telling us this and we were thanking them for all their help and getting ready to say goodbye, a truck loaded with young Filipinos pulled up alongside us. We learned that these were "home guard" coast watching troops. One of them even had an old rifle. The sugar cane planters explained to them that we were trying to get to Dumaguete, and they gave us a ride most of the way down there. This was welcome news. After the hike across Cebu, another one hundred and fifteen mile walk seemed substantial and to use the bancas to sail down did not appear to be too wise.

On the way south, I found that one of the boys spoke a little English and asked him if any of the Japanese had come to Negros. He said no, and I figured that for the time being, for some reason, they were ignoring this island. From what he told me further, it seemed that Negros was as peaceful as Cebu had been four days before. We travelled most of the way to Dumaguete in the truck and then got a lift in a second one into the town itself. We arrived in the early afternoon and headed for a café. After eating, we found a couple of rooms that we could rent in a house nearby and sacked out for our first sleep in almost two days. I awoke after three hours and found that Kelly was gone and that Swede, Mac and Red were already up and talking quietly. "Where did Bob go?" I asked.

Swede said, "He is hot to find something that floats that will take him to Mindanao so he can find Bulkeley. He has the name of some Filipino here that Bulkeley met when he picked up Quezon, and he is checking with him to see what the transportation situation is like to go south." He kept looking at Red and Mac as he spoke. The three of them were acting a little strangely and I wondered what was going on. Red explained that we were going to meet him in the café where we ate lunch the day before.

An hour later, we were sitting in the café drinking a beer and Kelly strode in. He was looking grim and slumped down at the table beside Swede. He looked at each of us and said, "I have bad news. Bataan has fallen. They surrendered on the ninth, the day the Japs came up the coast to Cebu. They apparently were starving to death and just couldn't fight any longer." I was flabbergasted. We had been so close to sending up the food. "You mean everyone surrendered; Corregidor too?" Kelly responded, "No just the troops on Bataan. Some of them got over to the Rock at the last minute, at least most of the navy and a few of the airmen who were around Mariveles. Corregidor has not surrendered, and they say they can hold out for months. They are prepared for a long siege." Red asked, "Where did you get this dope?" "I looked up that Filipino that Bulkeley dealt with here, and he told me about Bataan surrendering. Then I saw a major who is stationed here for the army and he gave me more details he got on the radio."

We discussed this for a long time. We all knew that it would happen sooner or later, but when we received the news there was disbelief. It came as a complete shock, and initially we refused to accept it. Somehow, in the back of our minds, we had hoped that, even though they were starving, the army could pull off its defense until help arrived. As the realization that Bataan had actually fallen filtered in, shock gave way to outrage. We felt let down, and there was no use denying it. I kept wondering how things might have changed had we been able to get those supplies to Manila Bay. Then slowly I felt an emptiness creep over me and a sadness heavier than I remembered ever experiencing. After a while, we did not even discuss it any more. We just sat there, not talking, staring at the walls.

I finally asked Kelly, "How did you make out in finding transportation?" He answered, "So far nothing definite. However, I have been told that there is a smuggling trade going on between here and Mindanao. Believe it or not, each island has a tax on sugar alcohol and people with large bancas smuggle it from one island to another, even with the war on. They say we might get a lift over there with one of the smugglers." I noticed that Red, Swede, and Mac were looking at one another, and I had a hint of the feeling that I had at the house before we left. Finally, Red spoke up. "Bob, I don't think we want to go to Mindanao. It would mean being back under the army again and the same old crap we have been going through for all these past months and eventually watching the Japs come in and take over another island, while we retreat again and maybe finally get held up in some jungle being guerillas. We just want to get out of the Philippines, and we think the way to do it is to find another banca like we had in Cebu, outfit it, and head either for China or Australia, where we have a chance of doing some good."

Kelly nodded his head, but said, "I am going to Del Monte on Mindanao. I am damn sure that Bulkeley got back there, and by now is either in Australia or getting ready to go there on a bomber. General MacArthur said he would fly us out when a plane is available, and I believe he will keep his word. I have to be in Del Monte and damn soon if I am going to have that chance." Red said, "I can't blame you for that. However, your general sure as hell didn't promise to fly all of us out too. The only help we are going to get is if we dig up a banca on our own. I have a hell of a lot more confidence in us and the navy than anything the army has to offer."

Kelly was gone for most of the next two days, searching the harbor for transportation that would take him to Mindanao.[11] The rest of us walked the town. While we were walking, for the first time, I was thinking hard about our options. Up until then, I had simply gone along with the others or done what I was told to do. Now there appeared to be a fork in the road, and I had to make a choice. I could go along with Swede, Red, and Mac as part of the team we had been since the day I arrived in the islands. This meant finding and equipping a banca, with a chance of getting through the Malay Barrier to Australia, or across the China Sea to that mainland. However, I also could go with Kelly to Mindanao and probably get mixed up with the army again, which was not too attractive. On the other hand, Mindanao was a big island with a lot of places to fight from, and I had heard that the native populations down there were really hard-nosed and tough, and would not be taking anything from the Japanese. It was a toss-up. Was I a true saltwater sailor who would get out on the sea in a banca and take his chances in escaping that way, or was I still being influenced by all those summers spent in the bush in northern Canada and the feeling that I was pretty good at making my way in it? Frankly, I did not know which I was, or if I was either of the two.

Late in the second afternoon, Kelly returned to our rooms and told us he had found a boat that would carry us to Mindanao. There was room for any of us that wanted to go with him. This was the time for a decision. I chose to go with Kelly. It was the toughest decision I had to make since leaving New York the previous June. We had left Jack and Bud behind at Mariveles and that was the first break in our team. In a way, this was worse. The four of us had become close, and we had been through a lot, relying on one another, and working as a group. I felt that I was deserting the team and it was not a good feeling, and I knew they felt the same way—that I was running out on them. Yet something deep inside of me, something I could not explain, said I had to go to Mindanao. Looking back, it sounds crazy, but it was there, and it was stronger than anything else. It had nothing to do with Kelly or the army. I simply had to go to Mindanao.

When I left, it was like the time we had left Ah Tong on Sangley Point. We said the usual things, like look after yourself, be careful, and don't take any foolish chances. We shook hands, and I went out the door. Kelly and I walked down to the harbor about seven o'clock that night, and I met the skipper of the banca who would carry us approximately fifty miles across the Mindanao Sea to Dapitan, a little town on the north coast of Mindanao. It was hard to believe that I was not joining the cast of a Hollywood movie. This skipper was unreal. He was Long John Silver in the flesh and the only thing missing was the parrot. The first thing I noticed was that he was a very tall Chinese, as tall as Swede or Kelly.[12] He wore a bandana on his head, and he had a black eye patch. He had a gold earring in one ear and a big black leather belt around his trousers, holding a floppy and bright long sleeved shirt inside of what I swear were nineteenth century sailor's pantaloons. Hanging from the belt on one side was a short bolo, and from the other, what certainly looked like a horse pistol. He walked with a limp, and I decided that one of his legs was peg. I must have been staring at him as Kelly introduced us, for he gave me a fierce grin and slapped me on the shoulder.[13]

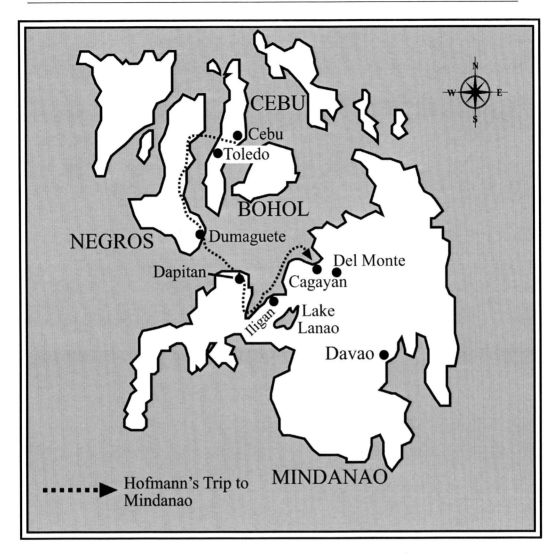

Hofmann's route from Cebu to Mindanao.

The crew was as unique as the captain. There were five of them, all short, even for Filipinos, and muscular. None of them wore shirts, and each wore a sort of breach cloth instead of pants. One had a bandana around his forehead, and another wore a peaked and very soiled fisherman's cap. I watched them walking around the outrigger supports, as sure footed as the monkeys that had climbed through the trees in Mariveles.

The banca was as large as the one we had purchased in Cebu. There was no cabin, but amidships it had a shelter made out of woven palm fibers that was shaped like a pup tent. There was decking on the bow and stern, and it had a large, square-shaped sail. The hull was quite large and the outriggers big in diameter and spread further out from the hull than most, to give support in crossing large bodies of water. The cargo was in drums that were stowed amidships and lashed securely. The captain told Kelly and I to sit toward the stern. Our deal was that we would pay the captain fifty pesos each for the trip. Kelly warned me to hide the rest of my cash in my socks as he had told the smuggler that was all the money we possessed. Kelly also told me to keep a tight grip on my .45 during the trip since you never knew what could happen.

I had heard that the Mindanao Sea between Negros and Mindanao could be one of the roughest bodies of waters in the archipelago. That night it lived up to its reputation. After we cleared the southern tip of Negros, the waves became enormous, with huge rollers sweeping from the Sulu Sea. They would tear at the banca, lifting it high and crashing it down into the troughs. We flew along, the sail taut, and everything straining and creaking against the howling wind. After midnight, the wind and the waves became even heavier, and we would rise several feet as we rode the crest of the huge rollers and then come pitching and roaring down into a churning trough. I held on as the outrigger on one side would slide down into a trough of madly swirling water and the one on the other side would be hanging in the sky. Then we would slam down again, and the position of the outriggers would be reversed as the boat crashed down on the water.

Around two in the morning, I heard a loud crack and immediately two of the crew leaped overboard into the foaming sea, and I saw them emerge clinging to the port outrigger. Through spray that lashed at my face, I could just make them out, grasping the outrigger and then straddling it. It was then that I realized it had been cracked or broken when it slammed down against a wave. The two men worked in a frenzy, wrapping rope around the cracked wood, often totally immersed in the sea as we continued to pitch and roll. At one point, the outrigger rose at least four feet above a wave and then crashed down again, and all the time the two men clung to it. The repair work seemed to last forever as I watched and probably said a prayer, but in a matter of minutes, the two men were back on board, and our wild race against the sea continued.

As the first light showed in the east, the waves began to lessen and by the full dawn, they had fallen off to a gentle slap. Ahead of me, I saw a green shoreline and then a jagged point of green trees. In the early morning sunrise, we rounded the point and sailed into a beautiful quiet bay of emerald green water. The wind had died to a few knots and I had survived my harrowing crossing of the Mindanao Sea. The banca ground its nose on the sand, and we jumped on to the beach. We shook hands with the captain and thanked him. He gave us a broad grin and said something in a Filipino dialect that we interpreted to mean either "good luck" or "give them hell." I felt a little foolish at the distrust I had harbored for our Chinese smuggler when we had started the trip. Our "cutthroat" pirate was a hell of a seaman.

We walked along the beach to a small barrio. Kelly told me this was Dapitan and that it contained an army post. We entered a little white building and found that a young Filipino first lieutenant was in charge of the local detachment. Kelly did the talking and gave the impression that we were on a mission of life and death, that no time could be lost. He explained that he had brought General MacArthur down from Corregidor the previous month and had to get to Del Monte as fast as possible. He gave the impression that the general himself was waiting for him to solve all the war's problems. After a brief wait, the lieutenant arranged transportation. He left the building and returned in about fifteen minutes with a car to take us east by road to the bottom of Iligan Bay. From there we would have to go by water along the coast to Cagayan as it would be the quickest way to make the trip.

Twenty minutes later, we were driving along a dirt road across the peninsula, and after a trip of about sixty miles, the lieutenant dropped us off on the waterfront of a small barrio. Apparently, the lieutenant was well organized. Our driver led us to a little shack by a rickety wharf and spoke to another Filipino in army fatigues, who led us out on the wharf and indicated a white launch with a small cabin and peeling paint on the hull. Neither he nor our driver spoke English, but with sign language and the repetition of Cagayan, we assumed that we were being offered the boat to complete our trip. We checked the engine and the gas supply. The man on the dock had a primitive chart of the coastline and we estimated that if we cut across Iligan Bay and then followed the coast line north and then east into Macajalar Bay, the trip would be about eighty miles. We did some arithmetic on gas consumption and the speed of our boat and figured that we could make Cagayan by nightfall, assuming a speed of eight knots for the old launch.

The trip proved uneventful. We followed the route we had selected, running past a bright green shoreline for most of the way. We must have averaged a little lower than the eight knots, and there were a couple of times when the engine let out disturbing sounds that made us doubt whether it would complete its journey, but by eight o'clock that evening we pulled into a pier at Cagayan. On the way in Kelly showed me where his PT boat had been anchored when the fitting broke and had run aground. I gathered that this bay was not one of his favorite anchorages.

Once more after landing, Kelly headed toward an army post and let the local captain know how urgent his mission was. After another short wait, we were shown a car and a corporal who would drive us. Less than an hour later, we were in Del Monte. We had covered an eight-mile stretch of road east along the bay front, made a turn to the south and climbed a series of hills on to a plateau. Within another few minutes, we were at the airfield. The army put us up in a house by the airfield, and Kelly tried to set up a meeting with General Sharp, the commander of the Mindanao Force. He was finally informed that the general would see him as soon as he was free. Going without sleep night after night while sailing the waters of the archipelago had me groggy by that point. I climbed into a cot and forgot everything about the war until eight o'clock the next morning.

I spent the next three days in Del Monte. There was nothing to do but sightsee, and there was not much to see. The airfield was empty most of the time. Two bombers came in while I was there, each carrying medical supplies for Corregidor. I still wondered how they were going to get this material up to where it was needed. Kelly showed me the pineapple plantation that gave the area its name. He told me how they had discovered it when they brought MacArthur down and how they had gorged themselves on ripe pineapples and then had the runs for two days afterwards.

It was not until the afternoon of the third day that Kelly was able to meet with General Sharp, and we learned what was planned for our future. Kelly came back from his meeting and sat down at a table in the mess hall where I was waiting. He explained that Bulkeley had gotten out on a bomber for Australia the day before we got there. They were making up lists of airmen and other people to evacuate to Australia and as the bombers came up with supplies, they were sending people back down with them. The general told him that his name would be on the list and that he would have a good chance of getting out within the next week. He added that Akers and Cox were up the coast and were coming down here to leave with him.

Kelly was pretty pleased with this turn of events, and I could not blame him. Australia was beginning to look a lot better than northern Mindanao. "Did they say anything about me? Has anyone got a job for me?" I asked. "That is the next thing I wanted to talk to you about," he replied. "The colonel in there questioned me about you and what you had done in Mariveles and Cebu. They want you to see them first thing in the morning. Something is cooking. They didn't tell me what, but I think it's important. They are going to send you over to General Fort's headquarters in Dansalan at Lake Lanao.[14] I understand that you are to report to the general personally for some kind of assignment. They didn't give me any details."

Here I go again, I thought. Just so long as it was not another trek through the jungle like the one I had made for the Marine intelligence captain. Mindanao was a lot bigger than crossing the mountain above Mariveles, and I had heard that down here they had real jungle. Early the next morning I said goodbye to Kelly. "I hope you get on that bomber and make it to Australia soon. Good luck. Eat some of that steak and eggs they talk about. And when you see General MacArthur tell him for me that his help for Bataan came in a little late."[15] I left him smiling and made my way to the Mindanao Force Headquarters and my transportation over to General Fort and the Lake Lanao area.

13

Mission Complete:
Lake Lanao and Australia

Mindanao Force Headquarters provided me with an old Ford sedan and a Filipino corporal from the Philippine Scouts to assist me in my duties at Lake Lanao. My assistant's name was Carlos Ramos, and he had come down from Cebu with the troops that General Sharp had transferred to help defend Mindanao.[1] Carlos was quiet, efficient, and smart— a true professional soldier. He knew weapons and tactics, and most important for me, he knew the local dialect. I found out that he was a devout Catholic, and he did not trust the Moros, who were the Muslims on Mindanao.

We drove the road west along the coastline for seventy-five miles to Iligan and then turned south. The first hills we passed had a high waterfall that Carlos said fell a hundred and seventy-five feet. The road kept climbing, and the vegetation changed. We left the sandy soil, dense jungle, and heat of the coast and emerged into a lush, green countryside, dotted with fields of low corn, and patches of grassland where I could see horses and caribou. Carlos told me that the Moros were not rice eaters to the extent other islanders were. Rather, they preferred bread and cakes made from corn meal. Also, they did not eat pork as it was against their religion.

When we were twelve miles from the coast, I saw my first Muslim mosque in a small barrio. We had entered the land of the crescent. The Christian and the Catholic cross had been left behind us, and the dress of the people had changed with the religion. The girls did not wear the flared skirts I had seen in the other islands. They had been replaced with a tubular sheath like a sarong, that Carlos called a "malong." The men wore round caps that he called a "kepiah," most of them black, some tan, and some trimmed with fur. A few of the men and women wore white turbans, and Carlos said that it signified they had made the "Haj," the pilgrimage to Mecca, and so were very devout Muslims.[2]

The road continued to climb, and finally we mounted a ridge and before me I saw a huge, shimmering body of water. We snaked downwards to a town at the northern head of the lake and I noted that we had driven twenty-four miles since leaving the coast. We had arrived at Dansalan, the main town for the Lanao region and General Fort's head-quarters.[3] The air was crisp and cool.

General Fort was thin, his face leathery and deeply tanned, and his white hair cropped closely. I had been told that he had been in the Philippines a long time and had come out with Pershing when the Americans defeated the Spanish and took title to the islands.[4]

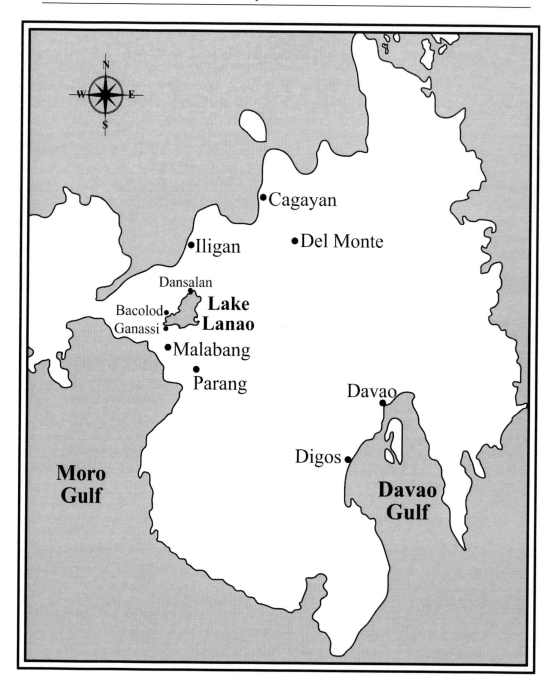

Mindanao and Lake Lanao.

He was supposed to know more about the Moros than any other living American. The general greeted me pleasantly and proceeded to ask me questions about what had happened at Cebu. I told him of the Japanese invasion of the city, the excellent delaying action by the Filipino troops, and of the army's disintegration and retreat to the north. His eyes wrinkled into a smile, and he said, "Chynoweth got his tail burned, eh?"

Then he changed the subject abruptly and asked me what I knew of the Moros. He went on to tell me about the local Moros. He explained, "They are fierce fighters and always have been. They never surrendered to the Americans or the Spanish." He added, "Of course, they are devout Muslims, so they are not fond of the Christian troops we have brought down here from the central Philippines. I have tried to explain to them that we have no choice if we are to defend their country against the Japs." He looked out the window and said disgustedly, "Of course, we had a choice. We could have armed the Moros and let them defend their own lands, and they would do it.[5] However, MacArthur absolutely rejected the idea."[6]

He made another change in the conversation. "We brought you over to Lake Lanao for a specific job. We want you to familiarize yourself with the shores of the lake, particularly the northern end. There are islands in the lake so check them out carefully as well as the lake itself. You should travel around by boat." I smiled and said, "It sounds like you are planning a naval operation on the lake." He did not laugh, but said, "Not exactly, but we want a naval view of the lake, and we want you to become very familiar with all aspects of it." All this sounded a little vague, but, as Kelly said, if they were planning some sort of hush-hush operation they were probably keeping it that way.

Fort's staff furnished me with a military map of Mindanao, and I spent the evening studying it, noticing that there were not many roads. The main highway started at the northeast tip at a place called Surigao and dropped straight south through a peninsula, turned abruptly west and followed the north coast to Cagayan and Iligan, dropped south and made a complete circle of Lake Lanao, and then took off to the south again joining the west coast at a place called Malabang. This map showed me one thing about Mindanao. With the Japanese already in control of the southern coast, holding the stretch from Davao to Digos, it would only take landings at the west coast ports to give them access to the north through Lake Lanao.[7] They also could cut up through the center to Del Monte, or if they wanted, they could land on the north coast and head south. The road network opened a lot of the island to them once they got started.

I obtained a room at a rambling white frame building in Dansalan that claimed to be a hotel, and Carlos and I spent the next four days exploring the northern part of the lake. I had not realized just how large it was. More or less triangular, it lay on an angle from northeast to southwest. Down the center, the overall length was twenty-two miles and it was sixteen miles across the bottom of the triangle. The entire shore of the lake appeared to be populated. There were tiny villages with small clusters of homes and garden patches. Some of the villages had names, but many did not. At the very bottom of the lake, one was called Ganassi, and up a few miles above that barrio was another called Bacolod. I never did get names for any of the other groups of houses that I figured were actual barrios.

Dansalan turned out to be the only real town on the lake and was the center of all the activity for the Maranao Moros. Sunday was market day in Dansalan, and a swarm of the local inhabitants came to town, most of them travelling up the lake by bancas. These long and slender boats were different from the ones I had seen in Luzon and the Viscayas. Most of them were decked in completely with a hatch at the stern, and the hulls must have been deep for the passengers rode below the deck. When the boats pulled into the shore at Dansalan, they exploded with color as the women stepped off wearing their bright, floral patterned malongs, and jangling, shiny, large bracelets on both arms.

I was never quite certain what financially supported the Maranao men. Most of the time they were turning hand operated grinding wheels and making intricately fashioned bolos and kris out of steel from abandoned automobiles. These were the sharpest knives and daggers I had ever seen. They often had beaten brass designs on the blades and fancy handles made from bone. Admittedly, some of the men worked in metal on other less lethal objects, while a lot of them had forges and made kitchen kettles, pots, gongs, and small drums. Another favorite item was to make a "lakob" out of bamboo pole that had been intricately painted. I found out that this was their version of a tobacco tin. The women seemed to do most of the work necessary to feed the family. They tilled the corn patches and the vegetable gardens in addition to handling all the domestic chores around the house.

We had been surveying the lake for two days before General Fort called me back in and told me about his plan. He said that on the night of April 28 two PBYs would fly to the lake from Australia.[8] They were to be hidden near an island in the lake during the daylight hours of the 29th, and that night, they would fly to Corregidor. They would then turn around and immediately fly back to Lake Lanao. They would remain hidden for the day and then that night would fly back to Australia.[9] Then he added the clincher. When they got to Corregidor and unloaded their cargoes, they were going to pick up army nurses and senior officers.[10]

The first priority was to find the right island where we could hide the planes. We had to stock it with drums of aviation gasoline and have sufficient boats available to handle the transportation to and from shore, but without attracting attention. Within a day, we had settled on the ideal island. It was not very large, possibly four acres. The shoreline had many small coves, and the whole island was covered with a heavy growth of large trees with limbs that hung out over the water. The coves had a virtual umbrella of foliage above them, enough to hide the wings and body of a PBY if it had its nose grounded to the shore. Also, there was plenty of room to cache our drums of gasoline. I felt that the location was perfect. The island was only about a mile south of Dansalan and less than a quarter of a mile from the western shore. I reported all this to General Fort, and he agreed with the assessment. The general concluded our meeting with, "We have not been bothered by Japanese planes around here, but there is always the possibility that some of their seaplanes might fly over the lake, and by luck, spot the PBYs while they are with us. If they do, they will try to strafe them. You need to set up an antiaircraft defense nearby." I looked at him. What was I supposed to use? It was at that point that I received help from the navy. I unexpectedly inherited the crews of Bulkeley's and Aker's PT boats.

On April 24, Carlos and I had driven from Dansalan to Iligan to chase down a rumor that there were some .30 caliber machine guns stored there. We did not find any, but we did find an operation in progress that I would have never believed. A team of horses was pulling a PT boat up a hill. It was nestled in a cradle made of timbers and the entire assembly was being rolled up the steep grade on logs. As it would move a few feet and clear the log at the stern, six Filipinos would shove that one to the lead in front of the bow. When we came upon the scene, they were about a quarter of the way up and had a long distance yet to go to reach the top and the coast road. Standing around the boat and lending direction to the Filipinos were a group of men who I recognized as coming from the PT boats.

I walked up to them and asked, "What are you trying to do?" Some of them recognized me, and a chief laughed. "Pretty wild, isn't it, sir? I'm glad we found you. We were

supposed to go up to Lake Lanao and report to you, once we got the boat up on the road."
I still could not understand what they were doing with a PT boat up on dry land. No one
in the army had told me about this operation. I must have looked puzzled, and the chief
continued. "Mr. Akers and Mr. Cox brought the 41 boat and all of us over here from
Cagayan. They beat it back to Del Monte yesterday. Cox, Akers, and Kelly all flew out
from there to Australia last night."[11] While they had made it as General MacArthur had
promised, that still did not answer why the boat was being pulled up the hill. "The army
told Mr. Akers that they wanted this boat hauled up to Lake Lanao to defend it from the
Japs. And that's what we are starting to do."

This was about as crazy an effort as I had seen yet and I said, "Do you have any idea
how long it will take to get this boat up the road to the lake? It's twenty-four miles from
here to the docks at Dansalan and there are hills to go up and down the whole way." The
chief looked at the Filipinos and the boat making its snail like progress up the hill. "Probably a month at the rate we are going." I knew that the PBYs would be long gone, back
to Australia, before the boat was anywhere near the lake, but as I looked at it, an idea
developed. The only reason for having a PT boat on the lake would be for anti-aircraft
defense and that would all come from its twin .50 caliber machine guns. I told the chief
what I had in mind. Within an hour, we had the PT boat guns on the way to Lake Lanao
in an old truck we had requisitioned from the army, with Carlos, the chief, and me in
our car and the rest of the two crews taking care of the guns in the truck.[12] I had my anti-
aircraft defense and experienced men to man it.[13]

We hauled the guns up to the top of a low hill that was opposite our island. It was
covered with trees, and at the edge nearest the lake, it dropped off on a bluff all the way
to the water. The field of fire appeared to be perfect, in an arc all around the shore extending out over our proposed flying boat base. By late afternoon, the crew had constructed
mounts and placed the guns on the top of the hill. There were houses behind the hill on
each side of it, but it did not seem that we would be bothering anyone on the top. To test
our installation and determine how well our field of fire covered the lake and the island,
the chief decided that we should test fire the guns. The burst was short and everything
seemed to work fine. While we stood there, expressing our satisfaction with our work, a
Moro came pounding up the hill.

He stopped short when he saw the mounted machine gun, then he slowly walked
over to and stared at it and then at us. "Sir," he said to me in halting English. "You cannot
shoot the gun here on the hill. It disturbs the women and children in church." We could
not blame him for being nervous about having noisy machine guns firing on a hill above
his house, but his spur of the moment explanation for wanting them out of there was as
unique as anything we could have imagined. We spent the next fifteen minutes calming
him down and convincing him that we would not fire the gun again, but that for appearance's sake they had to remain where they were just in case any Jap invaders might appear.
When he left, I decided that two men from the crews must stay on guard around the
clock until our planes had returned to Australia.

With the guns in place, the next step was to complete our gasoline storage on the
island. We used the truck once more to haul drums from Iligan where they had been
stored and then loaded them, one at a time, on our slender bancas and ferried them out
to the island.[14] It took time to get them there, and it was a painstaking business.[15]

I decided to make another survey of the lake around the island by banca and use
the experienced eyes of the PT crews to check for underwater obstructions and to plan

a landing path for the flying boats. We also laid out our plan for guiding them in by flash-light and who would man each banca for this job.

That evening Carlos came to me. He was very quiet and seemed upset. "Sir, I must leave the lake." Confused, I said, "Carlos, you are doing a fine job here. What is the problem?" He made a long face and said. "Sir, you know that the Moros hate us, because we are Catholics. They have told me that if I do not leave, they are going to cut out my heart and put it in my mouth." Having seen their daggers, I believed that the Moros could do it. I told Carlos to leave with my blessing.

I was called to General Fort's office on the morning of the 28th and told that the flying boats would be coming the 29th and to have everything ready for their landing, concealment, and protection by the evening. We spent most of the day checking on the island's foliage and adjusting the leafy umbrellas above the two coves we had selected as mooring locations. We did a further check on our gasoline supply, and the PT boat men assured me that it was good fuel. We once more looked over our supply of boats and bancas that we had hidden under brush. By noon there did not seem to be anything left to do, and I went in to Dansalan to report to General Fort once more.

After I made my report, I stopped for lunch at a café and saw Tommy Bowers and Captain Joe McGuigan, who I recognized as the ship repair officer from the Cavite Navy Yard. It came as a surprise to learn that there were other navy people in Dansalan. They asked me to join them and as we ate, they told me how they had reached the town. After the Japanese had landed at Cebu, Bowers had escaped as I had, by taking a banca to Negros, where he had met the captain who had come down from Panay. The two of them had travelled to Mindanao together and had reported to General Sharp at Del Monte to see what they could do to help the army. The general had told them that their services were more valuable to the navy and suggested that they go over to Dansalan right away where the PBYs were due. He had added that if there was room they should get on them and fly to Australia with the other escapees.

I explained what I had been doing on the lake the past week. They questioned me rather closely about the arrangements, obviously skeptical that a reserve ensign in the Supply Corps could play a significant role in a critical mission using the navy's valuable PBYs. That afternoon, I took them back to the island and they inspected our preparations carefully. Finally, the captain said, "It looks good to me. You seemed to have thought of everything."

We went back to Dansalan and tried to catch some sleep before starting my midnight to dawn vigil waiting for the two planes. I did not get much rest. Now that the operation was actually starting, the importance of it hit me. If anything went wrong at the lake, it would probably be my fault. I was back on the island shortly before dark and found myself checking things that had already been checked several times over the past few days. The hours dragged by slowly. At 3:00 a.m., we positioned the bancas out on the lake in case the planes arrived early. I went over to the shore for another check on the .50 cal-iber installation and then returned to the island.

Another hour and a half dragged by and shortly before 5:00 a.m., one of the men said, "They're coming in, sir. Those are our engines I hear. It's the PBYs." At first, I did not think I heard anything and then there it was, faintly, the sound of engines. They seemed to be low, the sound echoing from the hills along the shore. Then I saw the two planes. They were very close now, one behind the other, coming low over the water from the south, and heading toward the boats that were flashing the recognition signal of dots and dashes with their flashlights. We began flashing ours from the island as the planes landed and quickly turned toward us to taxi the few hundred yards to their mooring. As each plane reached us and edged toward its cove, we quickly attached a mooring line to a tree. The whole landing and mooring had taken only a few minutes, and I doubted if anyone on the main shore had seen it.[16]

I introduced myself to the pilots. Lieutenant Commander Neale captained the lead plane, and I remembered he had been with PAT Wing 10 at Sangley Point.[17] Lieutenant Pollock piloted the plane with Neale. Lieutenant LeRoy Deede piloted the second plane.[18] Neale was as surprised to see me as Bowers and the captain had been. It was definite that Supply Corps ensigns, particularly inexperienced, reserve Supply Corps ensigns, do not usually command two crews of veteran PT boat men and set up a base for a mission of this type. For my part, my nervousness had dissipated. We were over the first hurdle.

We arranged for Neale and Pollock and the co-pilots to go into Dansalan and get some sleep before their risky flight to Corregidor. I stayed on the island with the crews of the planes and the PT boats. We refueled the planes and then set up watches so that everyone could get some sleep before the night's operation commenced.[19]

At mid-afternoon, I went into Dansalan and got some bad news. I found out that today, April 29, was the Japanese emperor's birthday and his forces on Luzon were celebrating by giving Corregidor the worst pounding it had received since the start of the war. They had started at 7:30 in the morning with a savage air attack. A half hour later, they had opened up with a tremendous artillery bombardment from Bataan that hit all over the island and was doing an enormous amount of destruction.[20]

The other message that I received was that a Japanese amphibious force had landed early that morning at Parang on the Mindanao west coast.[21] By early afternoon, they had captured the town and appeared to be heading north toward Lake Lanao. My map told me that Parang was twenty-two miles south of Malabang, the next town up the west coast, and it was only an eighteen-mile drive from Malabang to the south end of the lake. They had also made another landing below Parang and were driving northward from Digos on the south coast. The Japanese invasion of Mindanao had commenced in force, and they were heading toward the lake.[22]

I hurried back to the island, and by 6:00 p.m., the pilots had joined us. At seven, one of the PT boat crewmen brought me a message from General Fort that the artillery attack on Corregidor was still going on and that the installations were wrecked. He reported that visibility was poor as dust and smoke covered the island, and fires raged uncontrolled. Despite this dire report, as darkness set, we towed the two planes out on the lake, and the pilots started the engines. They were grim faced. No one knew whether the shelling of Corregidor would continue through the night or what they would find remaining intact when they got there. In a matter of minutes, the PBYs had streaked down the lake and become airborne, banking quickly to the west as the sound of their engines faded.[23]

The vigil on our island started again. The hours dragged, one slow minute after another. I tried sitting on a round rock near the shore, but I found I was too keyed up to stay still. I would pace the little coves and check the foliage, the gasoline drums, and the boats, then look at my watch again, surprised to see how little time had passed. In my imagination, I kept hearing the sound of airplane engines, but in reality, the only sounds I heard were the night birds and the occasional fish leaping from the still lake. At midnight, we set out our guide bancas with their crews once more and continued to

PBY Catalina similar to the ones at Lake Lanao (courtesy George F. Fischer Collection, National Naval Aviation Museum).

wait. We had estimated that the entire flight up and back would take about nine hours, assuming everything went right. That meant they would be returning to the lake with the dawn and would be cutting things close to keep the landing hidden by the dark. I wondered where the Japanese were to the south of us and whether they too would have seaplanes over our air space by dawn.

As the hours wore on, my imagination started getting out of hand. What if the shelling continued throughout the night and the PBYs could not land? What if they did try to land while the Japanese were attacking Corregidor and were blown up or hit? What if the docks and all the boats at Corregidor had been destroyed and they could not land their cargo or pick up their passengers? What if the devastation had been so great that there were no passengers left? So many things could go wrong under the conditions that they were facing in landing and then taking off at Corregidor, that it seemed impossible to calculate the odds for success.

When you are sitting on a tiny island on a dark night having looked at your watch a hundred times, and your charges have not yet returned home, it is hard to keep thoughts of disasters from your mind. When I looked to the east and the hills beyond the lake, I saw that the sky was a shade lighter than it had been. I looked closer, straining my eyes, and knew that it was showing the slightest tint of red above the tree line. Then, I heard faintly the sound of a plane's engines coming from the north. The PT boat men heard it too. "It's them," said the chief. "They made it!" The engine sound became louder and a large winged shape swept down toward the surface of the lake. I saw the spray fly as the belly of the plane skimmed the water, settled in and then taxied back to our landing lights. However, there was only one plane. The nose approached the cove and our signal light, the engines stopped quickly, and once more, a PT boat crewman handled the mooring line.[24]

Commander Neale raised his thumb to me through the plexiglass window. When the crew opened the hatch, we saw the plane was filled with people. As they emerged, I counted seven nurses. I asked a crewmember who was helping the passengers disembark, "Where is the other plane?" He answered, "We separated on the way back, but don't worry. He's right behind us." While the last load was being ferried to the shore from Neale's plane, I heard the sound of engines again, and Pollock's plane came swooping down over the hills. It landed and then swung rapidly toward the island.[25] The dawn broke with blinding suddenness as we were tying the nose into its cove. The second stage of our operation was complete.

As the passengers stepped out of the hatch, each one looked around nervously and gingerly eased down into a waiting boat.[26] In contrast to the deeply tanned appearance of my crew on the island, the pale, tired faces of the escapees shocked me. The days of remaining buried in Corregidor's tunnels, under the stress of the continual bombing and shelling, showed in every feature. Their eyes flickered nervously; each face was etched with fatigue. I noticed that their hands shook when some of them reached out to steady themselves as they stepped into a boat. Everyone seemed exhausted. Two of the nurses were sobbing quietly as they sat down in their boat to be ferried to shore, and two others were laughing nervously.

An atmosphere of fright and weariness permeated the air around the group. Their movements were either slow or jerky with tension, and each of them kept looking around at the lake and at the shore, as if doubting they were really there, miles away from the terror they had left less than five hours earlier. I sensed that each was close to the breaking point yet refusing to admit it and that none of them was completely convinced that they had actually escaped. Their uniforms were wrinkled and soiled, showing that water conservation on the Rock had resulted in a low priority for laundry. I also sensed that bathing must have held an equally low priority as we lowered each person into the boats. I watched as the boats slowly and carefully took their loads of fatigued passengers to the shore, and I wondered how the rest of the people on Corregidor were holding up.

If these escapees were typical of the population, preventing the Japanese from capturing the Rock was going to be difficult. With the constant bombardment and bombing, eventually, the enemy would attempt landings on Corregidor's shores. The Japanese amphibious forces would be fresh, clean, and well fed. Further, they would be well armed with all the firepower that they could assemble. When they commenced their infantry attacks, I wondered if the marines and the army and navy forces on beach defense would be able to stop them or whether the island fortress would collapse. In our earlier estimates that they could hold out for months, we had not considered the destructive power of the Japanese artillery that ringed the island.

I tried to put these thoughts aside and spent the day keeping as busy as I could, commuting between the island, the lakeshore, and the .50 caliber gun that was mounted on the hill. I watched the crews on the island refuel the flying boats and the flight crews checking and rechecking the planes to ensure that everything was in perfect condition for the long night flight to Darwin. They did not talk much about the landing and take-off at Corregidor or the waiting time there while they unloaded all their cargo and the passengers boarded. They had not been shot at and the shelling had stopped shortly before they arrived.

By early afternoon, I received an update on the position of the Japanese invasion forces in Mindanao. The ones that were closest to us had not driven up the highway from Parang. Instead, they had returned to their transports and steamed up the coast to Malabang, a little over twenty miles closer to Lake Lanao. They had landed there at 3:00 a.m. and come ashore quickly. During the morning, the army had held them, but the Japanese forced them to retreat and by afternoon, the Japanese were pushing the Filipinos toward Ganassi, the town at the bottom of the lake. I was told that there was a flurry of activity at General Fort's headquarters in Dansalan, with officers and couriers dashing in and out, as they beefed up the defenses of our shore along the lake. As the afternoon wore on, I had another report that the Malabang line was still holding and that the enemy had not yet been able to push north as far as Ganassi. Our job was to get the two planes off safely in the evening. The army had its hands full defending the lakeshore and no time to worry about us.

As the sun was beginning to set, the entire group of passengers assembled on the shore opposite the island. It was amazing what a day away from the shelling and bombing of Corregidor had done for all of them. Everyone had taken hot showers, a luxury they had almost forgotten existed. They had rested, relaxed, and spruced themselves up. The faces that in the morning had been lined with nervousness and fatigue were now creased in smiles and laughter. The nurses were joking with the men and all of them looked positively feminine. Where a few hours ago the escapees had looked like refugees, now they looked like tourists about to embark on a holiday. In my whole life, I had never seen a group change so quickly. They all knew the Japanese were only about thirty miles to the south of them, but after spending the past few weeks within two miles of the largest concentration of heavy artillery the islands had ever seen, this new threat was remote, distant.

I saw that Tommy Bowers and Captain McGuigan had joined the group, and they told me that they were leaving on Commander Neale's plane.[27] The last thing I said to them was a repetition of what I had told Kelly. "Enjoy those steaks and eggs in Australia. I'll be thinking about you."

As darkness settled in, we ferried the passengers over to each plane and loaded them aboard. When there was no longer any sign of sunset and the sky above was completely black except for a few early stars, we pulled the planes out to face the lake. They started their engines, and Deede's plane took the lead, followed immediately by Neale's as they raced down the lake. I saw the first plane rise into the air, but Neale's plane stayed on the water. To my surprise, it made a turn and started back toward the head of the lake and the island. I yelled to the PT boat men, "Something has happened. Keep flashing the signal so they know where we are." I had no sooner said this than the other plane appeared over the hills to the west far down the lake heading back toward us, making a wide circle right above the island.

As Neale's plane came closer, I saw that it was riding too low to the water and was tearing at the island much faster than it should have been. As the PBY headed for the island, Deede's plane flew tight circles above us. Suddenly, it straightened out and headed west. The chief yelled out, "My God they hit something. That PBY's hull is ripped, and they are taking on water."[28] He paused and looked up at the second plane that was now disappearing into the night. "It looks like he told him to go ahead without them."[29]

I saw the nose of the plane coming at me and then the engines suddenly cut. The plane headed toward the mud bank in the curve of the cove. A PT boat crewman and I jumped onto the nose, and I was about to pass my line to one of the men on shore when the plane hit the bank with a hard thump, and I went hurtling through the air onto the island. Something hit me above my left eye, delivering a sharp blow. I got to my feet, dazed, and the next thing I remember was someone yelling out. "The stern is sinking under."

Through a haze, I saw that the tail of the plane was starting to dip lower and lower into the water, until it was almost touching the lake's surface.[30] Someone else was yelling, "Get empty gas drums and push them out to the tail to keep it floating."[31] I soon saw men swimming in the water and two of the boats pulling alongside the plane as they pushed and pulled four of the fifty-gallon drums rapidly toward the tail of the plane. The crews passed ropes around them and up over the tail structure and the sinking appeared to slow. While still groggy from my dive onto the island, I yelled, "Get the passengers out and into the boats."

Within two or three minutes the two boats were loaded and on their way to the shore and two more took their place and emptied the hull of its passengers. I got into another boat and moved along the side of the plane. When I looked up, I saw that the entire crew was forward, standing in the bow, which was now resting solidly on the sand and mud of the cove. Commander Neale stepped down into the boat and motioned me to take him back to the tail. He turned back, and he said to me. "We hit something just as we were getting up to speed. At the rate that water came in, it must have made a hell of a gash. Can you get a decent pump in town to get the water out so we can see what we have?" Then he looked at me again and said, "What happened to you? Your face is covered with blood."

I raised my hand to my left cheek, and after looking at it, saw that my palm was dripping blood. The eye would have to wait. Right now, pumps were the most important thing and unless we got them fast, the gas drums would not keep the plane's tail from sinking to the bottom. I told one of the island crew to get me to shore as fast as he could and told the chief to put everyone else to work bailing the water from the plane. "Use the gas pumps, use anything else you can, try to find some buckets, anything, but let's try and contain that water."

As soon as I got to town, I ran to the army headquarters to see if I could find anyone who might know where a pump could be located. All the passengers were there in a group and the smiles they had shown a half hour before had given way to the frightened looks they wore when they first arrived from Corregidor. Bowers was also there, standing a little apart from the rest of the group. He told me that General Fort had already arranged for a bus to take them to Del Monte and that when they got there the army would request a bomber to come up from Australia and take them out.[32]

I said, "I came in here to see if there are any decent pumps in town. We have to bail out the hull or the plane is going to sink for sure." I must have sounded a little too excited. Bowers looked at me and said, "Slow down. Before you do anything else get a bandage on that cut or you're going to lose an eye. The captain is already rounding up a pump. By now, he's probably on his way back to the plane. The captain and I are staying with you and the crew. We're going to patch that plane and get it off, don't worry." One of the Filipino soldiers got out a first aid kit and placed a dressing over my eye, and then wrapped a roll of gauze around my forehead to hold it in place. The bleeding seemed to have stopped.

Bowers and I headed back to the island. Captain McGuigan was already there when we arrived and water was pouring out of the plane in spurts from buckets, and in a steady stream from the fuel pumps and the additional pump the captain had located.[33] Slowly the tail of the plane began to rise. An hour later, the water was low enough for the captain to inspect the damage. McGuigan used a bright flashlight to examine the bottom of the hull closely. He turned to Neale and said, "It's a single rip in the skin, just like it's been cut with a knife. There is no structural damage. It's behind the step, and if you can get up enough speed to get up on the step, you will be able to get airborne.[34] What we have to do is stop water coming in long enough for you to get the hull in that raised position. We need something that will work as a temporary patch to stop the water for the time it will take to get there." He turned to me. "Have you any idea where you can locate some rubber sheeting, something that is waterproof and tough? Also, thin metal sheet and blankets?"

It sounded like a tall order. I went back into Dansalan and spent the rest of the night and the first two hours of daylight rounding up the supplies. They were probably the weirdest collection of items for a PBY hull repair kit that the navy will ever see. I had never seen naval mechanics repair a rip in the hull of PBY, but I assumed they would first haul the plane out of the water and then work on it in daylight, or with bright flood-lights, so that they could see what they were doing. I also assumed that they would have tools, rivets, and sheet aluminum they would need to perform the work. We had none of these items. We only had willing hands and Captain McGuigan's many years of expertise in hull repair.[35] As I worked along with the plane crew and the men onshore, I could not help but think of the expression "Chewing gum and baling wire."[36] The person that came up with that one had probably gone through a disaster of a similar type.

When the work was finished and the patching and bracing done to the captain's satisfaction, we pumped and swabbed out the last traces of moisture and the flying boat was floating once more as it was meant to be.[37] The captain looked it over for a final time and said, "It is one thing to make the hull watertight while it is sitting still here. The test will be when we are running over the lake trying to hit ninety knots or better to get into the air, with the water friction and vibration. One thing is in our favor; the lake is pretty calm today."

Shortly after this, we received another message from General Fort's headquarters. Early in the morning, the Japanese broke the defense positions at Ganassi and forced the Filipinos to retreat to a new line at Bacolod. They hoped to be able to hold this position for a while, but the Japanese were throwing artillery and tanks at them and were strafing them with a seaplane. They then gave us the bottom line. Unless we got off immediately, we might not get off at all. The Japs could be on the shore opposite us in a matter of two or three hours. As I looked inside the plane, I realized that it was now defenseless. There were two .50 caliber machine guns, but they had been totally immersed in the sinking and were now useless. We gathered around the captain, and Neale asked him what he thought of our chances. He said, looking at each one of us, "It may hold long enough; if you can get up enough speed soon enough and onto the step. I think you can get off the water. We don't have much choice. If we stay here, we are finished, and we will lose a good airplane." I glanced at my watch with my one good eye. It was now 4:00. The sun was still very bright in a cloudless sky.

The lake looked peaceful, and it was hard to believe that the Japanese were only a few minutes south of us. Neale turned and looked at me. "Get in the plane. You are flying to Australia."[38] The chief and three of the PT boat crew were in the boat with me beside the hatch, and I nodded toward them. Neale saw this and said, "I know. But if we try to take any more we will never get off the water."

The chief gave a grin. "Don't worry about us, sir. We have been figuring on taking to the hills anyway. We know the Filipinos can't hold the Japs much longer. We'll take our chances with those Moros we met with you, those friends of the general." I shook their hands and said, "Don't try to be heroes. There is not much you can do against those 4,000 Japs that are coming up the road. Get out as soon as we leave and stay with the Moros. Unless you are with them, don't go roaming around. And I promise you one thing. If we make it, I'll do my damnedest in Australia to get you out of Mindanao. I don't know how right now and it may take a long time, so stay free and stay healthy and keep away from the Japs." It was a long speech for me and at the time I did not know how or when it would be accomplished, but something inside of me said that it was one more reason for the feeling that I had earlier, that I was supposed to go to Mindanao.

I got in the plane, and the hatch was closed. Neale told us to crowd as closely as we could into the area immediately behind the pilots' seats, so we would place maximum weight on the bow and keep the tail up. This would reduce the water friction until we got on the step. The PT crew undid the mooring lines and pulled the PBY away from the island. Neale started the engines. He pointed the plane straight down the lake, and he pushed the throttle up to what I thought was full power.

Flying boats cannot perform fast take-offs. With the friction of the water over their big hulls, PBYs start slowly and gather speed slowly. They strain to break the bond between the water and the hull, striving to rise higher and higher from the surface, until they break the hold of the water on the hull completely and the lift of the wing lets them climb into the air. No matter how hard the engines work and the propellers pull, the laws of physics still apply.

As Neale pushed the throttle further, we started to move slowly down the lake. The engines were screaming louder, and I heard Bowers say, "He's red lining it." I could feel and hear the water rushing past, a rasping, drumming sound with the spray flying away from our sides in a huge fountain, curtains of it getting higher and higher as our speed increased. The hull was slapping hard now against the lake, but I could tell that the stern was still well down even though we were going much faster. All of us were straining as far forward as we could, pressing against the pilot seats, intent on forcing the stern up even with the bow.

I gave a quick look down at the deck and saw that I was standing in water that was slowly covering my boots. Even as I looked, it rose to my ankles and then started to climb higher. We were moving faster, and the water was flooding in at an increasing rate. I feared we were not going to be able to get the stern up and the front of the plane onto the step. Then, the sound changed in pitch to a higher one of water screaming past us and I heard the captain say, "we're on the step." The hull was now tearing over the surface of the lake and I felt that freedom you sense when you are going at high speed in a boat race, the feeling that you are skimming the surface with only a thin cushion of water under the hull. There is a sort of continuous rattling sound, like steady hail, inside the thin aluminum hull of a PBY. With no sound insulation, it becomes almost deafening, and it means you are breaking clear of that mass of water that has been holding you down. We were going faster and faster, but the water was still rising, now almost to my calves. Then with agonizing slowness, the bow began to tilt upwards and in seconds the slamming of the hull and the drumming, vibrating sound lessened, and finally, I could no longer hear the rasping of the water against the hull. We were airborne.[39] There was a smooth stillness all around me, with only the steady drone of the engines in my ear. Slowly the water around my legs began to recede. We had made it. We were free of the lake. A ridiculous thought struck me. I wondered how we would look to someone below us on the lake, with water streaming out of the hull.[40]

I heard a crewman call out from the tower above me, "There is that Nip seaplane straight ahead." The copilot said, "I see him." Neale put the plane into a bank to starboard and headed to the northwest. The observer said, "I don't think he has seen us. At least he's not following." Neale replied, "Let's hope he's too busy down there to bother with us." We kept climbing, up over the hills on a northerly course, then made a wide circle to port and headed almost due west. Within three quarters of an hour, we passed the coastline and were over the sea, changing course once more, with the sun lower in the sky on our starboard side as we headed south. Captain McGuigan said to me, "We are heading out over the Celebes Sea, taking the same route they used coming up here. We'll be over water the whole way to Darwin."

The engines droned on smoothly, hour after hour, as we flew over the seas of the Malay Barrier. I watched a beautiful sunset from 10,000 feet as we moved south. I looked out from the waist gun blister and wondered if Swede, Red and Mac were watching this same sunset as they sailed their banca below us. The sun sank quickly, and night set in with a pale moon and a sky filled with brilliant stars. There were no lights or any sign of activity below. Neale had the Catalina on automatic pilot, and the pilots were getting some rest as they spelled each other. I noticed that the captain and Bowers were wrapped in blankets and sound asleep. There was no conversation among the crew and everyone finally seemed to be relaxed. I wrapped a blanket over my shoulders and tried to sleep but it was no use. I was still too keyed up. I suppose I was approaching a state of exhaustion, beyond mere tiredness. My head throbbed where I had been cut and the blood-soaked bandage was firmly stuck to my left eye and the bridge of my nose. I tried several times to sleep, but would awaken after dozing for a few minutes and feel cramped and cold. Then, I would get up and walk back to the blister, and stare out at the night through the plastic bubble, drained of all energy and yet still filled with nervous tension. For the first time in days, I had nothing to do, yet I could not relax.

With the dawn, everyone came awake as we approached a flat coastline. We flew over land for about fifty miles and then passed over a narrow body of water and then another long flat coast. Captain McGuigan said that we had flown over Melville Island and were approaching Darwin. We started our descent in a wide arc out over a long bay. I saw a few houses. It did not look like much, and I remembered the town had been pretty well destroyed by the Japanese in February. Neale straightened out the nose and headed for some small wooden piers, landing gently on the water and taxing straight into them.

As we taxied into the little pier, the water started to flow in over the deck again, not as fast as it had on the lake, but fast enough to be worrisome. The Japanese had not destroyed everything in Darwin, and we were at a pier where the Australian army and navy were in charge. Within a few minutes, they had an electric pump installed in the hull and the flow of water was contained. Also, they had materials that made the patching of a ripped hull easier than it had been at Lanao. The captain worked with their people all morning and by early afternoon, the hull appeared to be watertight once more.[41]

There was not much to see in what was left of the town, so I stayed on the pier and watched the repair work. The Australian military people seemed bored, and I could not blame them. The heat was dry, and buzzing flies filled the air. We finally got back up into the air about three in the afternoon and after circling the bay, headed on a course for Fremantle.

During the daylight hours we flew over country that was as bad as anything in the southwestern deserts of the States—red rock as far as the eye could see, with no sign of any real vegetation. I asked Commander Neale what was down there, as there was no sign of human habitation. He responded, "Some aboriginals, kangaroos, and maybe some rabbits. Most of the country down there is still unexplored. To the west are the Kimberly mountain ranges, where they raise wild cattle. They are so scrawny they make Texas open range longhorns look like prize Iowa beef." Again, the engines droned on smoothly, and I began to finally relax. We hit the coast above Perth about three in the morning and I saw the moonlight on the Indian Ocean. We started flying in big circles and the crew chief said to me, "With our radio on the fritz from the dunking in the lake, we have to be pretty cautious coming in. A month ago a single Jap bomber dropped a couple of bombs down there and the Aussies have been nervous and trigger happy ever since, sitting behind their AA guns all night."

He kept signaling through the waist blister with a powerful lamp—dots and dashes, telling them that we really were one of their airplanes returning to its nest, and for God's sake, not to shoot us down. It was a good fifteen minutes before we saw small flickering dots and dashes coming back to us from the beach.[42] Our signaler said, "It's about time someone recognized us. They surely couldn't think that a Nip would be stupid enough to keep flying this low over them, at 0300." Neale made a smooth landing in the ocean and immediately headed into the beach, firmly grounding the nose on the sand. We were safe.

～

Someone awakened me from my first real sleep in five nights by shaking my shoulder. I sat up groggily and saw a grey light coming through a window above me. A sailor was saying something to me. I finally understood the words. "Sir, you have to be in the admiral's office in twenty minutes. He'll raise hell if you're late." I looked around the room. It was small, the walls and ceiling constructed of fiberboard and painted a light green. The floor was covered with brown linoleum, showing cracks and torn spots that exposed the concrete beneath it. My forehead hurt. In fact, my whole head was throbbing. I had slept on a narrow cot under a couple of army blankets, and when I got up, I started to shiver. It was either a lot colder down here than it had been in the islands or I was running another fever. I touched the dressing over my right eye and found it as hard as if it had been made of plaster. I looked at the sailor and said, "Okay. Show me where the head is. Then I'll go with you to see this admiral."

He led me down a hall to a large washroom with toilets and washbasins. There was a mirror above each basin, and I had a chance to see myself for the first time since we had set up the base in Dansalan. I did not look too good. My face was gaunt; I had a five-day growth of beard; my short-sleeved shirt and long pants were badly wrinkled and stained with dirt and oil; my cap looked as though it would not last out the day; and the dressing over my eye was stained a brown red from the dried blood. I did not even possess a toothbrush, much less shaving gear. I had left all my meager possessions in the hotel in Dansalan. My reaction was the hell with it. If the admiral had to see me for something so earth shattering that it could not wait long enough for me to get some rest, he would have to see me in my present shape. I splashed some water on my face and rinsed out my mouth. I turned to the sailor and said, "Let's go."

I arrived five minutes late for my appointment with the admiral, and a lieutenant ushered me into his office.[43] The admiral was sitting behind a government-issued desk with three government-issued chairs in front of it. He was reading some papers and did not look up when I entered the room. I noted that he was dressed immaculately in his blue uniform with the gold braid on the sleeves, his white shirt well starched at the collar, his black tie knotted perfectly, and his grey hair with every strand in place. He finally looked up at me standing there. He gave me a cold, fish eye stare and examined me from foot to head, taking in my scuffed boots, then my soiled and wrinkled pants and shirt, then my face with its stubbly beard and my eye patch. He examined me as if I was some specimen from outer space. I could see a look of disgust coming over his features. He did not ask me to sit down.

Finally he spoke. "Didn't they tell you that the uniform of the day in Fremantle, Western Australia, is dress blues?" I felt it rising inside of me, higher and higher, getting out of control completely. The sanctimonious son of a bitch. I could not hold it back. I blurted out, "I'm sorry admiral, but the Japs didn't allow me to pack my dress blues." Those were the last words I spoke during our meeting. He glared at me. Then he started in. "I suppose you have come down here, figuring you are a hero and we are going to send you back Stateside to help sell war bonds and tell the reporters all about your experiences. Well, you are mistaken. I understand you have spent the past few months running around the jungles on the islands playing cowboys and Indians with the Japanese, like some Marine. You are a naval officer in the Supply Corps, and we need Supply Officers in Australia. We are cutting you orders to send you to Melbourne by first available transportation to report to Commander Antrim, the Supply Officer, Southwest Pacific Fleet. You are going to start doing what the navy trained you for. Do I make myself clear?"[44]

Before I could reply, he said, "The first thing you are going to do is report to dispensary and get that mess cleaned up on your eye. After that, go to the Supply office and get some clothes. The Australian Navy will furnish you with dress blues and an overcoat. Winter is coming to Australia, and we don't want you getting pneumonia. Also get yourself shaving gear and other things and get yourself back looking like a naval officer." Then he added, still not smiling but in a better tone. "Maybe you can be of some use to Commander Antrim over in Melbourne." He did not say it as though he believed it. He nodded a curt dismissal and returned to the papers on his desk. I do not remember if I saluted. I turned on my heel and headed for the door. I was definitely back in the U.S. Navy.

The next day, as a navy surgeon was working on my eye and brow, another medic came into the room and said, "They just got a message. Corregidor is falling. It's all over for the Philippines."

Epilogue

After we had arrived in Darwin, an air corps bomber flew into Mindanao to land at Del Monte with a load of medical supplies and the intent of picking up the Corregidor evacuees we had sent over from Lake Lanao. When the pilot got over the field, he found it in the possession of the Japanese. When Mindanao surrendered, the nurses and officers who had come down with Neale were taken prisoner.[1] That same night of May 3, the submarine *Spearfish* snuck into Corregidor and took out ten more nurses, along with some navy officers. They had a rough trip on the way down, but they made it to Fremantle and safety.[2]

Swede Jensen, Red Carson and Mac McGibony did obtain a sea-going banca in Dumaguete and set sail for Australia. The Japanese captured them at sea and put them into a prison camp along with British and Australian captives on Java. Dysentery continually swept the camp during their internment and by the end of the war when the camp was liberated, only Red had survived.[3]

After I had been in Melbourne for a month, Carl Faires and Willy Lippsitt showed up, along with a line commander who had been at Cebu who had convinced the two of them that we had all been killed.[4] They had taken off in our banca and after a peaceful trip south had made it to New Guinea and then were ferried by the Dutch to Queensland.

A month after that trio showed up, we were joined in Melbourne by another group of escapees. Lieutenant Commander Morrill, the skipper of the *Quail*, had scuttled his minesweeper when Corregidor fell, and with seventeen members of his crew, had boarded a thirty-six foot motor launch. The commander had navigated the little boat, with about a fifteen-inch freeboard, all the way down through the Malay Barrier to Darwin, miraculously avoiding capture as they ducked Japanese patrols.

None of the others who were on Corregidor when the Japanese arrived managed to escape. Jack McClure and Bud Snow were wounded during the final fight.[5] They were sent to a prison camp in Japan and released after VJ Day in 1945.[6] Jim Bullock was taken prisoner on Corregidor, and we heard he was interned in the camp at Davao. He did not survive the captivity.[7] Bill Hogaboom was another victim of Japanese internment. Taken prisoner on Corregidor, he survived prison camps until we returned to take back the islands in 1944. The Japanese loaded him and several others of our personnel into the hold of an old freighter for transfer to Japan. The ship had no identifying marks on it, and our planes sank it. The survivors were transferred to another old transport and our planes sank it also. Hogaboom did not survive the second sinking.[8]

Bulkeley, Kelly, Akers, and Cox of the PT boats were sent back to the States after they arrived in Australia. We needed heroes in those days, and the press and then the movies extolled their exploits.[9]

We ran a fair intelligence operation from Australia up through the islands while the Japanese had them in their possession. It took almost a year to get it rolling, landing people and making contact with guerrilla groups and getting our people out. *Life* magazine made a big story out of one of these rescues.

A bigger story was never reported. Eleven months after I left them on Lake Lanao, the entire crews of the two PT boats were picked up on Mindanao by submarine and taken to Brisbane.[10] We gave them a big party in Sydney. They were in perfect health and had stayed with the Moros the entire time. We learned that the Japanese had developed a respect for the Moros and were cautious about wandering through their lands in the interior of the island.

As for myself, the navy kept me in Australia until the late fall of 1944, finally doing what the admiral had stated was the function of a U.S. Naval Supply Officer, complete with progress charts and a staff of expediters. They made me the navy member of the joint Army-Navy procurement office, in charge of all purchasing and manufacturing in Australia under what they termed "Reverse Lend Lease." Once more, I was technically under MacArthur and his staff of generals, who continued to try and ignore the fact that the navy is the senior service. I am afraid that after my experience in the Philippines, I developed the British outlook, and at times things got downright hostile when I was accused of putting the navy's interests ahead of the army's. But, those years are another story.

When the war was finally over and the losses were tallied, we realized just how enormous those losses had been among the navy and Marine Corps personnel who had gone to Bataan and Corregidor. In early February 1942, there were about 1,800 Naval and 1,500 Marine Corps personnel, a total of 3,400 officers and men, at Mariveles and Corregidor.[11] Only a small group of us saw the fighting all the way through, from Bataan to Cebu to Mindanao, and escaped to tell about it at the time Mindanao fell. During the months of fighting, sixty-three other Naval personnel had been taken out by airplane or submarine or had escaped on their own by small boat to Australia, and after the collapse I estimated that, including the crew of the *Quail*, the PT boat men and a few others, only thirty-nine others made it.

The military attempted a complete tally to determine how many Americans in all the forces were taken prisoner when Bataan and then Corregidor and then the other islands surrendered. At best, this turned out to be a series of estimates. In the confusion of conquest, even the Japanese did not seem to know how many men were in the prisoner count when Bataan and Corregidor each surrendered. Many were seriously ill or wounded, and many died along the way before they made the first prison camp, including thousands who did not last through the Bataan death march.

In our wars during the twentieth century, I cannot think of any other campaign in which we had such vague figures on how many of our men were either missing in action or killed, how many were captured, and how many did not survive internment. As you have learned from this account, one of MacArthur's problems was in not knowing how many people he had working for him once hostilities got under way. However, one thing is clear: the odds for success in "fighting and running away to live to fight another day" were not too satisfactory during the Philippine war.

Afterword
by Anne B. Craddock

I will begin this narrative with a few biographical highlights of my father, Ross E. Hofmann, the author of the memoir you have just read. He was born June 9, 1917, in Minneapolis, Minnesota, and moved with his parents to Toronto, Canada, about 1923. After attending Ridley Preparatory School, he entered the University of Toronto where he graduated with honors in political science and economics in May 1939. In June 1939, he went to work at McGraw Hill Publishing Company in New York City and stayed with them until December of 1940. He ventured out on his own in January 1941, starting a publishing company and successfully printing a variety of materials. This was cut short in June of 1941 when he was inducted into the U.S. Navy with the position of ensign by Reserve Officer's Commission. He left New York for Boston and attended the Supply Corps Training School at the Harvard Business School until September 1941 when he was sent to China and landed in the Philippines at the end of October.

For me, Ross Hofmann's life really begins here. Over the time that I spent trying to bring my father's book to print, I found out more about him than I could have ever imagined. I know that all he had experienced and seen plus the loss of so many good friends and companions must have affected him for the rest of his life; but even though he may have felt these losses deeply, on the outside, he always approached life with a very upbeat attitude and lived very much in the present. Yet, when he got the information about his friends being captured, it must have hit him hard. Swede, Red, Mac, Bud and Jack figured so prominently in this period of his life and they really had helped each other survive in many tight situations. The fate of these friends that were left behind probably weighed on his mind and heart so I am sure he did what he could from Australia to get people out of those islands and to safety.

Another person I was curious to know about was Dorothy, the young woman from New England that Dad met at Harvard. I found out from Louisa, Dad's second wife, that he tried to call Dorothy either when he was shipped back to the States or from Australia. She had meant a lot to him and he may have been wanting the consolation of reconnecting with someone who knew him before all of this horror, when the world still made sense. Unfortunately he found that this wonderful girl had died of TB sometime during the war. To be so young and faced with all this death plus the shock of everything that he had been through must have been a great weight to carry and sleep with at night. No wonder it took him so long to write these pages and that the images and details were still so vivid and specific.

I remember, when I was young, asking him to tell me about the war and his turning to me with a stunned look and just saying that children should never hear about these things. His face went white. It was a moment when I sliced into his world with my question and I saw in his eyes so much unspoken shock. I never brought up the subject again.

When Dad landed in Australia in mid May 1942, he went on to work for the Navy and found himself stationed in Melbourne. He first spent a short time in Perth and Fremantle, Western Australia, where he met my mother, Verna Cecilia Mansfield, who was an Australian citizen working for the U.S. Navy as a secretary and as a liaison for survivors of the Philippines. She was a beautiful young debutante from Perth, and fifth generation Australian. Mom always had so much light when she smiled, which she did often, that I'm sure she must have seemed like a safe harbor to this man who had survived so much darkness and death. My mother was cultivated, soft spoken and had been raised with the values of another age. Brought up in an upper-class family and isolated in Western Australia, she was a product of an earlier century full of elegance and grace.

However, her family's whole existence was about to be tossed upside-down. As it was in the States and all across the world, the war had thrown many of these very protected young women out of their former lives and into a new way of life. The Australians had sustained great losses to their male population during World War I, and now they faced a potentially even greater threat from the Japanese. The threat was on their doorstep and the women went to work in any capacity possible. My mother's younger sister, Lynette, became a nurse in the war and Mom went to work for the U.S. Navy, as a secretary.

Her family's peaceful way of life was soon changed when, at the beginning of the war, her older sister Roma, who had been living in Siam with her English husband and son, was captured by the Japanese and spent the course of the war in a prisoner of war camp. My aunt was forced to see her beloved horses gutted before her eyes and was separated from her two-year-old son. She and her husband were not reunited until after the war. The family returned to Perth, five long years later, barely surviving the ordeals they were made to endure. My grandmother, Cecilia, was very attached to her lovely oldest daughter and her health and spirit greatly deteriorated during this time.

This event and the bombing of Darwin gave my mother the push she needed to leave her safe nest and join the war effort. From that point on she went where the Navy sent her. I remember her telling me that she met Dad briefly in Fremantle before the Navy sent him to Melbourne. Her job in Fremantle was to find housing for these wartorn young men who were coming to Australia out of the horrors of the Philippines. Even though she must have seen hundreds of these men, she remembered my dad very well from her first meeting with him. I recall her saying, "He had this large bandage over his eye and forehead and dove under the desk at every loud noise in the building."

After being sent to Melbourne Dad was put in charge of Navy supply and manufacturing until January when he was sent to Sydney. Eventually he became the U.S. Navy member of the joint Army-Navy Procurement Office, in charge of all purchasing and manufacturing in Australia under what was called "Reverse Lend Lease."

I do not believe Dad remembered Mom from Fremantle. However eventually she must have made quite an impression on him because later, during June 1943 at Saint Mary's Catholic Cathedral in Sydney, they had a full Naval wedding—dress blues, drawn-sword-canopy ceremony and a four tiered wedding cake. I am not sure how they got the sugar and the flour but how Dad was able to acquire Mom's large, stunning diamond engagement ring is an interesting war anecdote in itself. He purchased it from a third party who had bought it when a young English couple needed funds for safe passage on a ship home to England from China just as the Japanese were about to invade. My mother always loved that ring!

So they were married and then honeymooned in the rugged mountains of Victoria, Australia. The early pictures of them show so much love, vitality and zest for life. They left Sydney by ship and arrived back in the States in October of 1944. My mother said this was quite a wild trip as they spent the entire journey from Sydney maneuvering and "zig-zagging," as she put it, to avoid Japanese submarines that were prowling in the Pacific waters with all the Australian war brides sleeping apart from their American husbands in cramped, blacked-out quarters below decks, ten to a cabin. The officers staying above decks, with better living conditions and food, would sneak down at night to visit with their sweethearts and slip them some good morsels from their linen-covered tables above. Finally, and to the relief of everyone aboard, they docked in San Francisco. They were met at the dock by Dad's uncle, who had settled in California.

Dad was then called to Washington, D.C., where he gave his speech at the Statler Hotel on November 13 concerning the lend-lease program with Australia. After a short time in D.C. the couple headed to Toronto, Canada, to meet my father's parents. It was late 1944, and my dad had not been back to the States since 1941.

Since my father was still in the naval reserves and later worked as a contractor with the government, first under the Roosevelt administration and later with Harry Truman and Dwight Eisenhower, Washington, D.C., was the best place for them to start their new life together. When Dad first came to Washington, he worked for the Bureau of Supplies and Accounts and then in January of 1945, with the Army/Navy Liquidation and Foreign Liquidation commissions. Then Dad returned to the Pacific in April, working on Army and Navy bases under Secretary of the Navy James Forrestal, and stayed there until returning to the States in September after Japan surrendered.

Dad was honorably discharged from the U.S. Navy on March 14, 1946, with the rank of lieutenant commander. He re-entered civilian life and formed Southern Cross Manufacturing Corporation, again returning to the Pacific in 1946 to identify and turn over surplus to the American Institution of the Far East. Dad also spent several months in the middle of 1947 in Mexico making attempts at mechanization and procurement of U.S. materials and products. Early in the 1950s he began more experimental work with Southern Cross Manufacturing on carbo sand.

Despite the constant travel, my parents were able to have five children in quick succession. The three oldest children were all in cloth diapers at the same time! Mom could have used her mother's help but never saw her mom again as Cecilia died in 1951 and her father followed a few years later. This was a great loss to my mother. Mom became a U.S. citizen in 1956. Dad always had many responsibilities as he was not only supporting us but also his parents and a grandmother in Toronto. I now realize this was a lot for a young man to carry but I always remember my dad in those early years surrounded by a light easy grace and open smile and my parents as being very loving with one another, happy and laughing. They had survived the war and were on top of the world. Everything

Ross and Verna Hofmann on their wedding day, June 25, 1943 (courtesy Hofmann family).

was fresh, new and exciting. Although their lives were very busy and they had very little money, they were ambitious and were working together.

Dad moved the family to Chambersburg, Pennsylvania, in 1954 and started a manufacturing plant in Shippensburg. This plant developed sterilization equipment for hospitals. An inheritance from my mother's father infused Southern Cross Manufacturing at the start.

Mom also helped him with her secretarial and bookkeeping skills. My mother's investment paid off as they were both hard working and willing to make sacrifices. Dad began to develop many other enterprises. He traveled extensively worldwide and eventually became a prominent businessman.

My parents were married for more than 32 years. After they divorced, they remained close friends their entire lives. In 1968, Mom attempted to go back home to Perth and re-establish a life there with her three youngest children, myself, Curt and Susan. The older girls, Gale and Carolyn, had already left home. Eventually, only Curt stayed in Australia.

Later in Miami, Florida, Dad met and married Louisa, a widow. Southern Cross was still operating but became more limited in production and, at some point, my father started Ross Hofmann Associates, an engineering consulting firm. He began taking government contracts for designing and building installations that burnt municipal waste to run cities. This was the "job site" that he was visiting at the beginning of his memoir. Also his father, Elwood, had owned vast tracts of forested land in northern Canada, where, as a young man, he staked out a claim. This property also had mines, including a gold mine. As a teenager Dad spent some summers there working in the logging camps, riding the logs down river to the timber mills and exploring the wilderness. When we visited as children, we found it still a raw, pristine, natural place full of huge moose, rattlesnakes, bear and black flies. In my father's later years he spent a lot of money, time and physical effort trying to develop some ventures in Canada.

Dad never stopped working and, with Louisa, assisted in founding the Miami Ballet Society. They brought many internationally known dancers to the Miami area. Their hospitality and philanthropic generosity made a vast cultural contribution to the city. Louisa had three children at the time she met Dad, so he had a hand in helping to raise and educate them. All of his children are well educated professionals who are scattered between the U.S. and Australia. Dad had many grandchildren and great grandchildren, who are also making their own impacts throughout the world.

We know we had an amazing father but didn't know any of his war experiences until he decided to write this memoir in 1987. In fact he wrote it from his desk at home in Coral Gables, Florida, looking out from his window at a huge banyan tree, in a tropical setting full of palms and fruit trees perhaps reminiscent of the same humid air and vegetation of the Philippines and the world he lived in all those years ago. There was even a jai alai stadium not far away. He was surrounded by Miami's easy-going Spanish culture and way of life that suited him so well, and I think he might have found a restaurant that served those gigantic spicy prawns he loved so much. My parents still cooperated well with each other and my mother was with Dad's mom in her Toronto apartment nursing her until her death. Dad and Louisa took loving care of Dad's father in their home in Coral Gables until he died peacefully in his sleep at the age of 100.

My father tried, while he was alive, to get his manuscript published with disappointing results. However, now is the time for the world to know the story of this very brave, compassionate man. His writing shows a sense of humanity and grace under pressure and gave me a chance to know him better. Ross Hofmann died suddenly of heart failure in October 1996.

Appendix—Hofmann's Address Before the Washington Board of Trade, November 13, 1944

Mr. President, members of the Board of Trade. This evening I would like to tell you something of the events that led up to the successful invasion of the Philippines by the American forces under General MacArthur and the smashing of the Japanese fleet units by the U.S. Naval forces of Admiral Halsey and Admiral Kinkaid.

Up until the fall of Corregidor, I was fortunate enough to serve with the American forces in the Philippines and to have participated in the defense of these islands, which, though short lived, taught us much about the Japanese and many valuable lessons in amphibious supply for the western Pacific. Being a supply officer my interests naturally lie in that direction, and it was in the Philippines that we of the Supply Corps received our baptism in advance base supply work under fire. The experience gained by the handful of us who managed to escape at the fall has proven most valuable to us in later operations. It is ironic that some of those lessons learned while defending the islands from the Japanese, have solved some of the problems that have arisen in our recent efforts to recapture them.

With the destruction of the Navy Yard at Cavite, our warehouses and handling equipment were bombed out of existence; we were forced to salvage what we could and fall back on Bataan; to the primitive conditions of a tropical jungle, where stores had to be dispersed on beaches and rice paddies and under clumps of thorn vines, to protect them from the daily bombings from the Japanese heavy horizontals where heat and dampness and insects could start the rapid process of deterioration common to the tropics; where our warehouses were native huts or palm lean-tos.

Our prime mission was to feed the Fourth Marines, who were protecting the western coastline, and to keep Bulkeley's PT boats running and the minesweepers and harbor craft that guarded the approaches to Manila Bay. I say that was our prime mission. Some of us had the additional job of leading navy and Marine troops in the front line fighting by day and moving and issuing our supplies by night. Acting as Marine infantry officers was probably the last function any of us could have imagined when we took our specialized training courses at Harvard Business School. I was fortunate to be Supply Officer for the Fourth Marines on Bataan and got into the action at Longoskawayan when the

Marines and the Philippine Scouts completely wiped out the entire force of shock troops the Japs had landed on the west coast of Bataan in an attempt to encircle the peninsula.

A few weeks before the fall of Bataan, a small group of us ran the blockade off Corregidor and in a tiny steamer made the trip south to Cebu. MacArthur had been able to obtain two transports from Australia, and we set up a supply base to unload them, transferring their supplies into native schooners. We were then to attempt to run the blockade in these native boats back into Bataan and Corregidor. I think that mission had more problems in it than any I have ever been on. The Japs had several destroyers roving off Manila Bay and an almost fool-proof blockade; all movement on our part had to be at night and with complete silence. Needless to say, the risks were fairly high, and it is a miracle that any vessel succeeded in making the Rock. These runs had just commenced when the Japs put an end to the project by landing on Cebu. It is estimated that their landing forces numbered over twelve thousand troops. To oppose them we had less than one hundred white men. The fight did not last long. But we did succeed in destroying all stores that were left at Cebu and managed to hold the city for twelve hours while we carried out this demolition.

During our short stay at Cebu I learned one lesson that has proven extremely valuable since. General MacArthur's forces were desperately in need of rifle parts, hand grenades, and clothing. Cebu, with its primitive Chinese foundries and a few Singer sewing machines, was his only hope of supplying these needs quickly. Three of us went to work with the local population and somehow we developed some production out of the town's resources. By the time the Japs struck the island, we had turned out thousands of hand grenades and suits of crude battle clothing; in fact we had even produced a substantial number of running shoes out of some salvaged canvas and sheet crude rubber. This was my first lesson in the procurement possibilities of a local area and how they must be utilized to the full when shipments of supplies cannot come from the United States and when men's lives depend on finding a local substitute.

I was one of the lucky few who managed to fight their way out of Cebu and escape the net of the Japs. Bob Kelly of the PT boats and I managed to get out of the town when the demolition was over and into the hills; traveling by foot, and at times in native bancas or canoes, we dodged the Jap patrols and made the three hundred mile journey to General Sharp's Mindanao headquarters.

Kelly went on down to Australia by bomber and I was ordered to remain in Mindanao and set up a seaplane base. Mindanao was a repetition of Cebu. No sooner had the base been built and gasoline collected, when the Japs moved in from all sides. About the time Corregidor surrendered, the few men I had under me and the crew of one of the seaplanes were cut off on the base. For a while, it looked as though the war was over as far as we were concerned. Our only hope of escape was a PBY that had crashed and sunk at the base and to get it into the air looked almost impossible. Somehow we did manage to get it floating and more or less watertight. And somehow the pilot managed to get it into the air. The next stop was Australia, and it certainly looked like heaven to us after the Philippines.

After a few days' rest in Perth, I was ordered to Melbourne for duty as a supply officer again. The job I was assigned to was setting up a local procurement for the Navy in Australia that would take full advantage of the system known as reciprocal aid or reverse lend lease. I remained in Australia administering that program up until a few weeks ago, when I returned to the Bureau of Supplies and Accounts here in Washington.

Lend-lease and its companion reverse lend-lease, are not too well understood by the American public, in spite of the many articles that have been written and the many speeches that have made on them. In my present duty, I have occasion to talk daily to businessmen and members of government agencies in Washington. And questions they frequently ask go something like this: "Just what is lend-lease about?" or "Aren't we *giving* everything we own to those foreigners and getting nothing in return? Do they ever give us anything?" or "Why does America fight all the other nations' battles; why do we support the rest of the world by giving them everything they ask for under lend-lease?"

These questions are typical and show that the American public still does not appreciate the job that lend-lease is doing in this war. Lend-lease was originally designed as a means of assisting nations whose *fighting efficiency* was deemed necessary to the defense of the United States. England could not hope to produce enough in her heavily bombed factories to stave off the German Army, and she had to have American equipment to continue fighting. And so did the Russians and the Free French in North Africa and the Australians and New Zealanders in the Middle East. When we were ready to land in North Africa and to push on up into Sicily and Italy, we had well equipped Allies and what is more important, we had bases close by that the Germans had not been able to capture and from which we were more able to operate. When we landed in France, we were able to take off from a strongly fortified England only a few hours away from the French coast; and all through the months preceding this invasion, we had been able to reduce German strength by bombing missions from bases that lend-lease had made safe for us.

I don't think that anyone [who] realizes [these] facts will argue that lend-lease was not worthwhile. The successful invasions of the past year have proven its worth. Admittedly it cost the American public money. By June 1944, we had rendered aid at a cost of more than twenty-eight billion dollars. But think what the expenditure would have been if the Allies had been allowed to go down in defeat because they did not have the money to pay cash for war materials; and if we had had to fight Germany and Japan alone, starting our invasions of their home territories from bases in America rather than from the enemy's backyard in England, Australia, and New Zealand.

Yet while most American businessmen will agree that lend-lease has been worthwhile, they still want to know, and rightly, what we are getting in tangible returns from foreign nations. The mere fact that we can start our invasions from the shores of an allied country is not enough. They want to know what we are getting as reverse lend-lease or reciprocal aid, to offset in a tangible way our expenditures on lend lease. The operations in Australia over the past two years offer one of the finest examples to be found anywhere of what we are getting under reverse lend-lease and how the whole system of reverse lend-lease functions. The Australian reciprocal aid program was started by the U.S. Navy when I arrived in the Commonwealth in May of 1942. Only when the present war is over will historians be able to evaluate the exact role this program played in the fighting in the Southwest Pacific over the past two years. One competent observer stated recently that the reverse lend-lease program was responsible for speeding up the timetable of our advance westward along the New Guinea coast and northward toward the Philippines by several weeks. This was due to the fact that ship bottoms from the United States were saved for critical materials not available in Australia; and that emergencies arising in the field were solved largely by reciprocal aid services furnished by Australian workers and reciprocal aid supplies furnished by Australian factories.

One fact is clear. That the Australian government has furnished us with thousands of tons of supplies and millions of man hours of labor over the past two and a half years, on a reciprocal aid basis. This has resulted in over four hundred million dollars' worth of supplies for the war effort in this one theater alone. In procuring under this reciprocal aid program, it was not the intention of the U.S. Navy to exploit unfairly Australian materials or manpower, but rather that shipping distances across the Pacific rendered impractical the shipment to Australia of any supplies or materials that could be obtained locally under reverse lend-lease. It was agreed that each government, Australian and American, would furnish to the war effort in the Southwest Pacific whatever it most efficiently was able, determined on the practical grounds of availability of materials, production facilities, manpower, and shipping, within the jurisdiction of each.

Australia is a long way from the United States, a minimum of twelve days by the fastest vessel or forty odd hours by air transport. Shipping supplies to the Southwest Pacific thus takes about three times as long as to the European theater. Or to put it another way, this has the effect of reducing a given fleet of ships by two-thirds. Coupled with this, in 1942 ships of any type were difficult to obtain. And, it was lack of ship bottoms that gave the first real impetus to the reciprocal aid program in Australia. The Japs in the second half of 1942 were pressing south through New Guinea or Port Moresby and we were throwing in everything we had of our meager resources to stem the tide of their advance. Our men had to be clothed and fed; attack bases had to be built; ships and equipment had to be maintained and repaired; and new equipment had to be designed and hurled into battles quickly.

Months before any formal agreement was signed, the Commonwealth government determined that the U.S. Navy could obtain whatever supplies and services we might need under reciprocal aid if Australia could possibly supply them from her existing facilities. The Commonwealth possessed fair stocks of raw materials and limited manufacturing plants; she was an exporter of foodstuffs; she had several good harbors; she had land both in the interior and in port areas, to allow for large base construction and expansion; her railway and communication system were not up to American standards of efficiency, but she was willing to spend the huge sums necessary to modernize them for peak war loadings; her manpower was extremely limited, only seven million standing against one hundred million Japanese and three hundred million Asiatics whom Japan controls, but she was willing to take drastic measures to regiment the whole nation and ensure that each man, woman, and teen-age child was engaged in actual fighting or war production. In brief, reverse lend-lease would always supply the answer when we could not get supplies fast enough from the United States. Local procurement in Australia could be used to full advantage no matter how it might use up valuable stock piles of raw materials or wear out plants and machinery. And no expenditure of American funds was necessary.

In the early days of 1942 and 1943, our meager fleet in the Southwest Pacific accomplished wonders in sharp, short battles against superior Japanese forces. But we did get hurt. Ships received torpedo, shell, and bomb hits. The ship repair facilities of Australia, being close at hand, meant that vessels could be patched up quickly and hurled back into new battles, saving combat vessels the necessity of limping the long voyage home to the west coast of the United States, to be out of commission for the extra weeks this would take.

Food supplies were even more important, for food was difficult to get in those early days from the United States and refrigeration vessels were extremely scarce. Australia has supplied over ninety percent of the food in combat areas. Australian reverse lend-lease saw that they had the balanced diet required to keep alert during the long hours of battle watches.

The tropical conditions of New Guinea are as bad as anywhere in the world. Equipment that lasts indefinitely in other areas, rots or rusts away in a few weeks under the extreme heat and dampness of New Guinea: white ants eat anything made of wood, cloth, or leather. I can recall a case of field shoes that were carefully stowed in a New Guinea warehouse. Somehow ants got into one of the cases. In less than a week there was nothing left of the shoes but the steel tips on the laces, and the eyelets and the nails in the soles. Hence, new equipment had to be designed that would resist this kind of attack. New Guinea became a sort of huge laboratory under the technical guidance of the advancing Australian and Americans. Food was placed with metal; metal was made corrosion-proof; cloth and canvas were rot-proofed; electrical and radio equipment was tropic-proofed; new methods of packaging and preserving were invented on the spot. And Australians provided the factories and the manpower under lend-lease to get production started and emergency quantities of new designs into action until mass production could be started in the United States for bulk shipment to the area.

Diseases of all types and kinds had to be combatted. The malaria mosquito can take a tremendous toll on fighting efficiency unless stamped out; scrub typhus, rot, dengue and dysentery, and other tropical diseases flourished during the early days in New Guinea, for it is a land of everything that crawls or flies, stings or bites, to spread contagion. We learned quickly how to control the insects carrying these plagues and gradually with the help of the Australian reverse lend-lease, we stamped them out. As we started a base in a new jungle area, our first move was to set up a drainage system and other methods of housekeeping that would rid the jungle of these pests. Our Seabees got from Australian factories the necessary pumps, piping, and sprayers to do the job.

For our first year of our operations in the Southwest Pacific, most of our procurement was of the type I have described to solve the emergencies arising from a lack of shipping from the United States. But gradually the complexion changed. The shipyards of the United States have done an unbelievable job in turning out transport and cargo carrying vessels. By degrees ships became available to send us huge quantities of supplies directly from the United States. As this American-produced equipment began to pour into the area, we changed the type of demand we were placing on Australian reverse land-lease and asked the Commonwealth to produce only the heavier and bulkier items, that have a low value per ton and that we preferred not to haul over eight thousand miles across the Pacific. This freed ships for the more complicated mechanical items, such as machinery, machine tools, electrical and radio equipment and precision instruments that can be produced more efficiently in the United States than in any other country in the world.

Our reverse lend-lease production in Australia was placed on a sound forward planning basis. We continued to obtain the bulk of our foodstuffs, both fresh and processed provisions. We continued to order a fair proportion of the special clothing required for the heat of the tropics, as it is bulky to ship and wears out quickly. One of the biggest tonnage savers on our American shipping has been our continued procurement of steel and other metals and of building materials under Australian reverse lend-lease, for these have low shipping priority usually and vast amounts of them must be consumed in island warfare and its accompanying base construction. Cement, gravel, wood, tar, and other products can be hauled the relatively short distances from the Australian mainland to battlefronts. Even with Australia's limited pool of manpower, services such as stevedoring, carting and hauling, and trans-shipments of supplies have been a big item, saving American resources for active front line fighting.

By June of this year our Australian lend-lease procurement program involved over two thousand major items, and deliveries of supplies, services, and construction from the Commonwealth were hitting a million dollars a week to the U.S. alone, with corresponding amounts to the U.S. Army. The Navy's portion of the Australian reverse lend-lease program was involving the major operation of the output of several hundred factories: with the consequent savings of millions of dollars to the American taxpayer and the savings of American manpower for the production of essential items that cannot be produced in the field. The Australian lend-lease program has proven to be one of the most comprehensive of its kind in the world. The spirit of the Australian people is wonderful; I feel confident that they are giving as much help to their Allies, in relation to national resources, as any country in the world. Their determination to assist to the limit in our joint war effort is reflected in every phase of their total regimentation for war. All production is controlled and rationed to an extreme degree. Production of consumer goods as we know them in this country is limited to the bare necessities of life. Every man, woman, and child over sixteen and under seventy has his every move controlled by the Directorate of Manpower and can be put into any job deemed necessary to the war effort. Out of seven million people only 300,000 are producing what might be termed consumer goods, or selling and distributing them to the public. Of the manpower available, over 92 percent were in the forces or in war production for Australia and her allies.

Possibly this severe regimentation is sparked by the knowledge that just outside her borders wait a hundred million Japanese controlling the efforts of three hundred million other Asiatics and the huge supplies they can draw upon to fight this war. One thing is certain, the Australians feel, and I feel certain they are right, that Japan is prepared to fight a hundred year war if necessary to win their objectives in the Pacific. They know that the war will not be over when Germany is defeated and there is a long fight ahead of the Allies to defeat Japan. We in this country should realize this and do everything we can to speed the conclusion of this Pacific War.

Address by R.E. Hofmann [SC] USNR
Statler Hotel, Washington, D.C.

Chapter Notes

Preface

1. For a biography of Charles Ross, see Neil G. Speed, *Born to Fight: Major Charles Joseph Ross DSO, a Definitive Study of His Life* (Melbourne: Caps & Flints Press, 2002). For a description of Major Ross in the Boer War, see Jim Wallace, *Knowing No Fear: The Canadian Scouts in South Africa, 1900–1902* (Victoria, BC: Trafford, 2008), 15–19, 47–49, 78–81, and 118–20.

2. Charles Ross married Eleanora Buchanan, and they had one daughter, Jessica, and a son. Jessica married Charles Elwood Hofmann, and they later had Ross in 1917. "Mrs. Charles Ross: Lived 101 Years, Husband Officer in Boer War," newspaper article in David L. Snead's possession.

3. Franklin D. Roosevelt, "Proclamation 2352—Proclaiming a National Emergency in Connection with the Observance, Safeguarding, and Enforcement of Neutrality and the Strengthening of the National Defense Within the Limits of Peace-Time Authorizations," September 8, 1939, The American Presidency Project [hereafter APP], http://www.presidency.ucsb.edu/ws/index.php?pid=15806&st=national+emergency&st1 (accessed December 16, 2014).

4. There is no source that focuses solely on the Supply Corps in World War II. The best sources of information are Frank J. Allston, *Ready for Sea: The Bicentennial History of the U.S. Navy Supply Corps* (Annapolis: Naval Institute Press, 1995), and Julius Augustus Furer, *Administration of the Navy Department in World War II* (Washington, D.C.: Department of the Navy, 1959), 433–36.

5. Gerald Linderman, *The World Within War: America's Combat Experience in World War II* (Cambridge: Harvard University Press, 1997), 1.

6. For a discussion of the limited military spending and manpower shortages in the interwar period, see Stephen Wentworth Roskill, *Naval Policy Between the Wars*, vol. 2—*The Period of Reluctant Rearmament, 1930–1939* (London: William Collins Sons, 1976), 468, 473, and 479.

7. Navy Supply Systems Command, "Logistics Quotes," Air University, http://www.au.af.mil/au/awc/awcgate/navy/log_quotes_navsup.pdf (accessed June 18, 2014).

8. Between the end of World War I and the mid–1930s, there were no formal Supply Corps Training Schools for active duty officers. The training of reserve

Supply Corps officers was even more haphazard. The training of reserve officers involved some correspondence courses. See Furer, *Administration of the Navy Department*, 477–78, and Joseph Lennox, "Training the Reserve Supply Corps," *Proceedings of the United States Naval Institute* 60:5 (May 1934): 647–50.

9. "Officer in Charge to the Chief of the Bureau of Supplies and Accounts, 30 September 1944, History of Supply Corps Schools in World War II," National Archives of the United States [hereafter NA], Record Group [hereafter RG] 143—Records of the Bureau of Supplies and Accounts (Navy), 1885–1967, Box 2—Quddy Village, Maine, to Naval Supply Corps School Harvard, Folder I-36, n.p.

10. "Officer in Charge to the Chief of the Bureau of Supplies and Accounts, 30 September 1944, History of Supply Corps Schools in World War II," n.p.

11. "Officer Qualifications Questionnaire for Ross Elwood Hofmann, Apr. 1, 1945," in David L. Snead's possession.

12. For photographs of the reserve supply officers as well as some of their training, see *The Class Book: Navy Supply Corps School, Harvard University* (Boston: Harvard Graduate School of Business Administration, 1941).

13. "Proclamation 2487—Proclaiming That an Unlimited National Emergency Confronts This Country, Which Requires That Its Military, Naval, Air and Civilian Defenses Be Put on the Basis of Readiness to Repel Any and All Acts or Threats of Aggression Directed Toward Any Part of the Western Hemisphere," May 27, 1941, APP, http://www.presidency.ucsb.edu/ws/index.php?pid=16121&st=national+emergency&st1= (accessed December 16, 2014).

14. "Radio Address Announcing an Unlimited National Emergency," May 27, 1941, ibid., http://www.presidency.ucsb.edu/ws/index.php?pid=16120&st=national+emergency&st1= (accessed December 16, 2014).

15. Waldo Heinrichs, *Threshold of War: Franklin D. Roosevelt and American Entry Into World War II* (New York: Oxford University Press, 1990), 84–84.

16. *The Statistical History of the United States: From Colonial Times to the Present* (New York: Basic Books, 1976), 1114.

17. Ibid.

18. See Allan R. Millett and Peter Maslowski, *For the Common Defense: A Military History of the United States of America* (New York: Free Press, 1994), 416–20, and William L. O'Neill, *A Democracy at War: America's Fight*

at Home & Abroad in World War II (Cambridge: Harvard University Press, 1993), 18–32.

19. Akira Iriye, *The Cambridge History of American Foreign Relations*, vol. 3—*The Globalizing of America, 1913–1945* (Cambridge: Cambridge University Press, 1993), 143.

20. Louis Morton, *The Fall of the Philippines* (Washington, D.C.: Center of Military History, United States Army, 1953), 4–13.

21. Akira Iriye, *The Origins of the Second World War in Asia and the Pacific* (New York: Longman, 1987), 126. See also Ronald H. Spector, *Eagle Against the Sun: The American War with Japan* (New York: Vintage, 1985), 82–83.

22. The attack in the Philippines was technically on December 8 since the islands lie west of the International Date Line.

23. Morton, *Fall of the Philippines*.

24. D. Clayton James, *The Years of MacArthur*, vol. II—*1941–1945* (Boston: Houghton Mifflin, 1975).

25. John W. Whitman, *Bataan: Our Last Ditch: The Bataan Campaign, 1942* (New York: Hippocrene, 1990), and Michael and Elizabeth M. Norman, *Tears in the Darkness: The Story of the Bataan Death March and Its Aftermath* (New York: Farrar, Straus, and Giroux, 2009).

26. William Bartsch, *December 8, 1941: MacArthur's Pearl Harbor* (College Station: Texas A&M University Press, 2003), and *Doomed at the Start: American Pursuit Pilots in the Philippines, 1941–1942* (College Station: Texas A&M University Press, 1992).

27. Elizabeth M. Norman, *We Band of Angels: The Untold Story of American Nurses Trapped on Bataan by the Japanese* (New York: Pocket Books, 1999).

28. Edwin Palmer Hoyt, *The Lonely Ships: The Life and Death of the U.S. Asiatic Fleet* (New York: David McKay, 1976), and W.G. Winslow, *The Fleet the Gods Forgot: The United States Asiatic Fleet in World War II* (Annapolis: Naval Institute Press, 1982).

29. James Leutze, *A Different Kind of Victory: A Biography of Admiral Thomas C. Hart* (Annapolis: Naval Institute Press, 1981).

30. Dwight R. Messimer, *In the Hands of Fate: The Story of Patrol Wing Ten, 8 December 1941–11 May 1942* (Annapolis: Naval Institute Press, 1985).

31. William L. White, *They Were Expendable: An American Torpedo Boat Squadron in the U.S. Retreat from the Philippines* (Annapolis: Naval Institute Press, 1998).

32. J. Michael Miller, *From Shanghai to Corregidor: Marines in the Defense of the Philippines* (Washington, D.C.: Marine Corps Historical Center, 1997).

33. John Gordon, *Fighting for MacArthur: The Navy and Marine Corps' Desperate Defense of the Philippines* (Annapolis: Naval Institute Press, 2011).

34. Ross to Dear Folks, November 18, 1942, 2, in David L. Snead's possession.

35. See the copy of the speech in Appendix I.

36. I would like to thank John Gordon and Jim Zobel for raising this possibility after they read a draft of Hofmann's memoirs.

37. W.L. White, "They Were Expendable," *Reader's Digest* (September 1942): 5–9, 147–76.

38. "Air Force Large in Philippines," *Washington Post*, October 27, 1941, 9.

39. Arthur Krock, "Philippines as a Fortress: New Air Power Gives Islands Offensive Strength, Changing Strategy in Pacific," *New York Times*, November 19, 1941, 10.

40. "Foe Rules the Air Over Philippines: United States Aviation Units Never Recovered From First Surprise Attacks," *New York Times*, December 29, 1941, 3.

Introduction

1. Louisa was Ross's second wife.

2. Hofmann had last been in the Philippines in 1946.

3. The Japanese conquered Singapore in February 1942. See Spector, *Eagle Against the Sun*, 132.

4. For the Japanese occupation of Singapore, see Yoji Akashi and Mako Yoshimura, eds., *New Perspectives on the Japanese Occupation of Malaya and Singapore 1941–1945* (Singapore: Singapore University Press, 2009).

5. For descriptions of the Spanish-American War and the Philippines Insurrection afterwards, see Brian Linn, *The Philippine War, 1899–1902* (Lawrence: University Press of Kansas, 2000). For an overview of U.S.–Filipino relations between 1900 and World War II, see H.W. Brands, *Bound To Empire: The United States and the Philippines* (New York: Oxford University Press, 1992), 60–158.

6. The Manila Hotel is the most luxurious hotel in the Philippines and is where General Douglas MacArthur and his wife lived from 1935 to December 1941.

7. Corregidor: A Memorial for the Courage, Sacrifice, and the Heroism of Its Defenders, "Libingan Ng Mga Bayani: Cemetery of Heroes," http://corregidorisland.com/bayani/libingan.html (accessed December 16, 2014).

8. In November 1941, there were 31,095 men in the U.S. Army in the Philippines, almost 19,000 American soldiers and 12,000 Philippine Scouts. There were another approximately 80,000 Filipinos in militia units. See Morton, *Fall of the Philippines*, 49.

9. Tagalog is the primary language of Luzon, and along with English, one of the two official languages of the Philippines.

10. Douglas MacArthur's performance in the Philippines will be addressed later in the memoir. For an excellent biography of MacArthur, see James, *The Years of MacArthur*, vol. II.

11. Americans treated MacArthur as a hero in large part because the situation in the Pacific was deteriorating and they needed some symbol of confidence. See Kenneth S. Davis, *FDR: The War President, 1940–1943* (New York: Random House, 2000), 409.

12. Hofmann is alluding to America's failure to be prepared for World War II. In the European theatre, the Germans used blitzkrieg tactics to conquer most of Europe by the end of 1941. Billy Mitchell was an outspoken critic of America's reluctance to embrace the full capabilities of airplanes. For more information on the military debates over tactics and strategy in the interwar period, see Williamson Murray and Allan R. Millett, *Military Innovation in the Interwar Period* (New York: Cambridge University Press, 1998).

13. Admiral William "Bull" Halsey was one of America's leading admirals in the Pacific theatre of World War II. For an excellent biography, see E.B. Potter, *Bull Halsey* (Annapolis: Naval Institute Press, 2003).

Chapter 1

1. It is unclear exactly when Hofmann enlisted in the Supply Corps. However, there is no evidence that he had any training prior to June 1941.

2. Immediately prior to being called to active duty, he owned a publishing company. "Officer Qualifications Questionnaire for Ross Elwood Hofmann, Apr. 1, 1945," in David L. Snead's possession. He graduated from the University of Toronto in 1939 and went immediately to work for McGraw-Hill. See "Naval Training and Experience," n.d., in David L. Snead's possession.

3. The average base pay for a U.S. ensign in 1943 was $150 per month, not including any possible housing allowance, hazardous duty pay, or other extra pay. "WWII U.S. Navy Officer Information," Valor at Sea, http://www.valoratsea.com/officer.htm (accessed May 30, 2014).

4. This is the U.S. Navy officer hierarchy—admiral, vice admiral, rear admiral (upper), rear admiral (lower), captain, commander, lieutenant commander, lieutenant, lieutenant junior grade, and ensign. See "Rank Insignia of Navy Commissioned and Warrant Officers," Official Website of the United States Navy, http://www.navy.mil/navydata/nav_legacy.asp?id=266 (accessed May 30, 2014).

5. In late June, around 425 students arrived for the three-month course. "Commandant, First Naval District," July 16, 1941, Baker Library Historical Collections [hereafter BLHC], Harvard Business School [hereafter HBS], U.S. Navy Supply Corps School (Harvard) Records [hereafter UNSCSR], C.1, F. 5—"Mobilization and Training Agreements, 1939–1941," 1.

6. For an overview of the Supply Corps in World War II, see Furer, *Administration of the Navy Department*, 429–79.

7. Hofmann's course of study was divided into three parts: June 16–28—Indoctrination and Orientation, June 30–August 9—Disbursing Afloat, and August 11–September 11—Supply Afloat. Navy Supply Corps School, Graduate School of Business, Harvard University, July 16, 1941, BLHC, HBS, UNSCSR, C.1, F. 5—"Mobilization and Training Agreements, 1939–1941," 1.

8. For descriptions of the U.S. Navy between World War I and World War II, see Thomas Hone, *Battle Line: The United States Navy, 1919–1939* (Annapolis: Naval Institute Press, 2006).

9. While the records for 1941 are not available, a Supply Corps' course description from Harvard in 1943 echoed this idea. It argued, "The fundamental objective of a Supply Officer must be *to get things done*; in many cases this involves the accomplishment of the mission first and the completing of the details later" [emphasis in original] "Ready for Sea—Introduction to Supply," November 1943, BLHC, HBS, UNSCSR, C.1, F. 6—"Introduction to Supply, 1943," 1.

10. As of 1943, the lowest ranked U.S. Navy sailor made around $50 a month, not including any housing, hazardous duty pay, or other allowances. "WORLD WAR II U.S. NAVY RATINGS & PAY GRADES," Valor at Sea, http://www.valoratsea.com/paygrade.htm (accessed May 30, 2014).

11. The U.S. Navy's main clothing factory was in Brooklyn, New York. See "Map of U.S. Naval Clothing Depot, Brooklyn, NY, June 30, 1933," Library of Congress, http://www.loc.gov/pictures/item/ny1697.photos.350385p/ (accessed May 30, 2014).

12. The battalion consisted of seven companies of approximately 60 students each. "Navy Supply Corps School, Graduate School of Business, Harvard University, July 6, 1941," BLHC, HBS, UNSCSR, C.1, F. 5—"Mobilization and Training Agreements, 1939–1941," 2.

13. They had physical drills every morning. They also practiced military drill three times a week. Ibid.

14. Hofmann had ash blond hair, was five feet, 9½ inches tall, and slender. Anne B. Craddock to David L. Snead, July 25, 2013, in Snead's possession.

15. The Statler Hotel was part of a chain of hotels owned by E. M. Statler. "The Boston Park Plaza Hotel History," Boston Park Plaza, http://www.bostonparkplaza.com/overview/history (accessed June 18, 2014).

16. Scollay Square was the main entertainment district in downtown Boston until it was torn down in the 1960s. See David Kruh, *Always Something Doing: Boston's Infamous Scollay Square* (Boston: Northeastern University Press, 1999).

17. While Hofmann was in the first graduating class, by the end of the war, 8,000 Supply Corps' ensigns had completed their training at the Harvard Business School. Lt. Cmdr. A.C. Lyles, Jr., "Harvard University—The Graduate School of Business Administration," BLHC, HBS, UNSCSR, C.1, F. 7—"Account of the School for Navy Supply Officers Attending It by A.C. Lyles, ca 1949," 1.

18. At the start of the war in December 1941, there were 638 active duty Supply Corps and 1,425 reserve Supply Corps officers. Furer, *Administration of the Navy Department*, 477.

19. Among the other graduates was John Roosevelt, the youngest son of President Roosevelt. "President's Son Becomes an Ensign," *New York Times*, September 13, 1941, 4.

20. It is unclear how much Hofmann and Dorothy communicated during the war, but the Hofmann family believes she died during the war from tuberculosis. Craddock to Snead, July 25, 2013.

21. San Francisco was the main port of embarkation for military personnel headed to the Pacific Theatre. Over the course of the war, almost 5,000 ships left there. James W. Hamilton and William J. Bolce, Jr., *Gateway to Victory: The Wartime Story of the San Francisco Army Port of Embarkation* (Stanford: Stanford University Press, 1946), viii.

22. "Navy Wives in Philippines Ordered Home: Will Be Evacuated Along with Civilians from Far East Areas," *Washington Post*, October 22, 1940, 8; Hallett Abend, "The Great American Exodus from the Orient," *New York Times*, December 8, 1940, 134; and "Hull Indicates That American Vessel May Go to Orient to Get U.S. Nationals," *New York Times*, August 5, 1941, 5.

23. Navy crews recognized crossing the equator for the first time as a momentous event. Sailors who had crossed the equator previously, called "shellbacks," would initiate those who had not, called "polliwogs." For a description of one of these ceremonies, see James J. Fahey, *Pacific War Diary, 1942–1945: The Secret Diary of an American Sailor* (Boston: Houghton Mifflin, 1963), 8.

24. Racial attitudes were prevalent from both the Japanese and the Americans in the Pacific War, see John W. Dower, *War Without Mercy: Race & Politics in the Pacific War: Race and Power in the Pacific War* (New York: Pantheon, 1986).

25. The Asiatic Fleet was America's main naval force in the western Pacific before the start of World War II. For its composition at the start of the war, see "Asiatic Fleet, 8 December 1941," HyperWar: U.S. Navy in World War II, http://www.ibiblio.org/hyperwar/USN/TF/Asiatic Flt-1.html (accessed June 18, 2014).

26. Sangley Point and Cavite Naval Yard were two naval installations located on the eastern shore of Manila Bay. See Paolo E. Coletta, ed., *United States Navy and Marine Corps Bases, Overseas* (Westport, CT: Greenwood Press, 1985), 297–98.

27. Admiral Thomas C. Hart was commander of the Asiatic Fleet. See Leutze, *A Different Kind of Victory*, 206.

28. For a history of the Cavite Naval Yard, see Coletta, *United States Navy and Marine Corps Bases, Overseas*, 67–68.

Chapter 2

1. John Douglas Carson, nicknamed "Red," became one of Hofmann's best friends in the Philippines. See "Roster of Officers and Seniority list, Sixteenth Naval District," November 1, 1941, Supply Department, NA, RG 38—Records of the Office of the Chief of Naval Operations [hereafter ROCNO], Records Relating to Naval Activity During World War II, World War II Diaries, Fifteenth Naval District to Seventeenth Naval District, World War II Command File, Shore Establishment, Naval Districts, 14th Naval District, Ser. Rosters 1944–17th Naval District, Box 399, Folder—16th Naval District—Series, Rosters, 1941–Mar 1942, n.p., and "John D Carson–World War 2 POW Record," World War 2 POW Archive, Crafted Knowledge, http://www.ww2pow.info/index.php?page=directory&rec=127279 (accessed June 20, 2014).

2. "Admiral Thomas C. Hart, Narrative of Events, Asiatic Fleet, Leading up to War and From 8 December 1941 to 15 February 1942," June 11, 1942, United States Army Heritage and Education Center [hereafter USAHEC], Louis Morton Research Materials [hereafter LMRM], Box 19, Folder—Admiral Hart's Narrative, 9. For more on the movement of the dependents, see "Narrative by Lt. Comdr. Denys W. Knoll, Philippine Campaign," July 9, 1943, RG 38—ROCNO, World War II Command File, World War II Oral Histories and Interviews, 1942–1946, Box 9, Folder—Knoll, D.W., LCDR, 4.

3. On limitations on having dependents, see "Memorandum to Commanding Officers of all Posts, Camps, Stations, and Depots (Philippines)," February 24, 1941, MacArthur Memorial Archives and Library [hereafter MacArthur Archives], Record Group 15—Materials Donated by the General Public, Box 37, Folder 4, 1.

4. For the status of the Asiatic Fleet on the eve of the war, see Hoyt, *The Lonely Ships*, 139–44; and Winslow, *The Fleet the Gods Forgot*, 299–304.

5. The United States had maintained a naval presence on the Cavite peninsula since the Spanish-American War. On the eve of the war, Cavite Naval Yard and Sangley Point dominated the peninsula.

6. For a description of the *Houston*, see "USS *Houston* (CA-30, originally CL-30), 1930–1942," NavSource Naval History, http://www.navsource.org/archives/04/030/04030.htm (accessed June 19, 2014).

7. The flagship is the ship where the overall fleet commander resided.

8. For a description of the *Marblehead*, see Winslow, *The Fleet the Gods Forgot*, 14.

9. When Hofmann uses the term, "four pipers," he is referring to a class of 273 destroyers with four smoke stacks that the Navy had built between 1917 and 1920. By World War II, they were obsolete but still were useful. See John D. Alden, *Flush Decks and Four Pipes* (Annapolis: Naval Institute Press, 1965), 1 and 63–89.

10. The *Langley* was America's first aircraft carrier. The navy converted it to a seaplane tender after it introduced more advanced carriers. See "USS *Langley* (CV-1, later AV-3), 1922–1942," NavSource Naval History, http://www.navsource.org/archives/02/01.htm (accessed June 20, 2014).

11. For a history of the Patrol Wing 10, see Messimer, *In the Hands of Fate*, 9.

12. Hart later explained, "My problem was for the fleet to be sufficiently alert and not to be surprised, but at the same time I had to be careful not to wear my people out by keeping them under constant alert." Thomas C. Hart, "War on the Horizon," in John T. Mason, ed., *The Pacific War Remembered: An Oral History* (Annapolis: Naval Institute Press, 1986), 19.

13. This was a common assessment of the Japanese capabilities prior to war. See Norman and Norman, *Tears in the Darkness*, 18.

14. This was an exaggeration of the numbers, but the United States was increasing its air capabilities in the fall of 1941. Bartsch, *December 8, 1941*, 143–45.

15. Clark Airfield was located about 40 miles northwest of Manila. See Richard B. Meixsel, *Clark Field and the U.S. Army Air Corps in the Philippines* (Quezon City: New Day, 2002).

16. The B-17 was a four-engine, long-range bomber. For a good overview of the B-17, see Martin W. Bowman, *Combat Legend: B-17 Fortress* (Shrewsbury: Airlife, 2002).

17. Hofmann probably lived at 12 Canacao Blvd. This was Red's address at the start of November. "Roster of Officers and Seniority list, Sixteenth Naval District," November 1, 1941.

18. American nurse Ethel Blaine Millett, who was serving in the Philippines in 1941, recalled, "We would be invited out to the Officer's Quarters, to their homes. Maybe four officers would live in the same house and they'd have a houseboy and cook and maybe two or three servants and they'd invite us to dinner." "Transcription of Interview with World War II Nurse Ethel Blaine Millett," April 9, 1983, MacArthur Archives, RG 135—Papers of Drs. Michael and Elizabeth Norman, Authors, Box 62, Folder 24.

19. See Speed, *Born to Fight*.

20. Jensen and McGibony's full names were Michael Howard Jensen and William N. McGibony. See "Roster of Officers and Seniority list, Sixteenth Naval District," n.p.; "William N McGibony—World War 2 POW Record," World War 2 POW Archive, Crafted Knowledge, http://www.ww2pow.info/index.php?page=directory&rec=31833 (accessed June 20, 2014), and "Milton Howard Jensen—World War 2 POW Record," ibid., http://www.ww2pow.info/index.php?page=directory&rec=30861 (accessed June 20, 2014).

21. See Messimer, *In the Hands of Fate*, 9 and 12–15.

22. According to Michael and Elizabeth Norman, "The officers lived liked aristocracy." See Norman and Norman, *Tears in the Darkness*, 15.

23. Prior to 1940, Japan imported many of its raw materials from the United States, including steel and oil. After the Japanese occupied the northern half of French Indochina in the summer of 1940, the United States initiated a limited embargo against Japan. Over the next year and culminating with cutting off of the export of oil to Japan in late July 1941, the United States expanded the embargo in hopes that it would pressure Japan to stop its expansion into China and Southeast Asia. See "Executive Order 8832–Freezing Japanese and Chinese Assets in the United States," July 26, 1941, *The American Presidency Project*, http://www.presidency.ucsb.edu/ws/?pid=16148 (accessed June 20, 2014). For more detailed discussion of the embargo, see Heindrichs, *Threshold of War*, 132–36, 145, and 159–60.

24. At the end of World War I, the Treaty of Versailles established the mandate system. Under this system, colonial holdings held by Germany and the Ottoman Em-

pire were divided between main allied powers. The Japanese received a mandate over parts of the Caroline, Mariana, and Marshall Islands. See Mark R. Peattie, *Nan'yō: The Rise and Fall of the Japanese in Micronesia, 1885–1945* (Honolulu: University of Hawaii Press, 1988).

25. For Hart's concerns about the fleet's safety and Japanese plans, see Leutze, *A Different Kind of Victory*, 219–21.

26. General Hideki Tojo became prime minister of Japan in October 1941 and served until July 1944. See Robert J.C. Butow, *Tojo and the Coming of the War* (Princeton: Princeton University Press, 1961).

27. The presence of the American bombers was widely known. See Arthur Krock, "Philippines as a Fortress: New Air Power Gives Islands Offensive Strength, Changing Strategy in Pacific," *New York Times*, November 19, 1941, 10.

28. The Sino-Japanese War began in July 1937. See Mingkai Chang, *History of the Sino-Japanese War (1937–1945)* (Taipei: Chung Wu, 1971).

29. The submarine fleet in Manila represented the largest concentration of submarines in the U.S. Navy prior to the war. See Glen M. Williford, *Racing the Sunrise: Reinforcing America's Pacific Outposts, 1941–1942* (Annapolis: Naval Institute Press, 2010), 65.

30. The basic objectives of Plan Orange were:
 (a) To prevent enemy landings at Subic Bay and elsewhere.
 (b) Failing in this to, to eject the enemy at the beaches.
 (c) Failing in this, to delay to the utmost the advance of the enemy.
 (d) To withdraw as a last resort the mobile forces to the Bataan Peninsula and defend the entrance of Manila Bay.
"Philippine Department Plan (1940 Revision) for Defense of the Philippines against attack by Orange (short title HPD WPO-3)," April 1, 1941, MacArthur Archives, RG 15—Materials Donated by the General Public, Box 49, Folder 4—Papers of John Gordon, 2. For the best study of War Plan Orange, see Edward S. Miller, *War Plan Orange: The U.S. Strategy to Defeat Japan, 1897–1945* (Annapolis: Naval Institute Press, 1991).

31. For a description of the basic defense plans of the Philippines under War Plan Orange, see *American Defenders of Bataan & Corregidor*, vol. 1 (Paducah: Turner, 1991), 28.

32. The Rock was the nickname for Corregidor.

33. Dunnage refers to material placed on the ground to protect supplies.

34. "History and Culture—Fort San Felipe," Global Cavite, http://cavite.info/historyandculture/fort-san-felipe.html (accessed June 20, 2014).

35. The PT stood for Patrol Torpedo. The best single source on the PT boats in World War II is Robert Bulkley, Jr., *At Close Quarters: PT Boats in the United States Navy* (Washington, D.C.: Naval History Division, 1962).

36. For a description of the Army-Navy Club, see Lewis E. Gleek, Jr., *Over Seventy-Five Years of Philippines-American History: The Army and Navy Club of Manila* (Manila: Carmelo & Bauermann, 1976).

37. Admiral Hart issued the orders for the 4th Marines to pull out of Shanghai on November 10, and most were out by the time the war started. See Miller, *From Shanghai to Corregidor*, 1–3.

38. Subic Bay is on the west coast of Luzon. Coletta, *United States Navy and Marine Corps Bases, Overseas*, 310.

39. For a brief description of the squadron, see "Destroyer Squadron 29," Destroyer History Foundation,

http://destroyerhistory.org/flushdeck/desron29/ (accessed June 20, 2014).

40. For these plans, see Winslow, *The Fleet the Gods Forgot*, 5.

41. The Jai Alai Building housed jai alai games and other entertainment.

42. The P-40 was a strong plane and could match the Japanese aircraft if the pilots used the correct tactics. However, the way the Americans used the plane in the Philippines gave the Japanese the advantage. Further, while the American pilots were generally well-trained, they lacked combat experience. Most of the Japanese army and navy pilots had obtained combat experience in China. See Christopher Shores, Brian Cull, and Yasuho Izawa, *Bloody Shambles*, vol. 1: *The Drift to War to the Fall of Singapore* (London: Grub Street, 1992), 64–66, and Richard R. Slater, "And Then There Were None! The American Army Air Corps' Last Stand in the Philippines," *Airpower* 17:6 (November 1987), 14.

43. One of the major problems was that many of the planes arrived in the Philippines in November and early December. The pilots had only a limited time to train with them, and there were often shortages of parts and especially ammunition. See Bartsch, *Doomed at the Start*, 28. Lt. John Burns, a pursuit pilot, recorded in his diary on December 7 before the Japanese attacked, "Would like to get some practice in tactics, shoot the guns." Burns had arrived in the Philippines about three weeks earlier, and still had not fired the guns on the plane because of a shortage of ammunition and some problems in the gun-charging mechanism. Bartsch, "'I Wonder at Times How We Keep Going Here,'" 35. Glen Williford discusses U.S. efforts to reinforce Pacific outposts in 1941 and 1942. See Williford, *Racing the Sunrise*.

44. At the time of the Japanese attack, the U.S. Far East Air Force possessed 92 P-40s, 26 P-35s, 35 B-17s, and miscellaneous other planes. See Bartsch, *December 8, 1941*, Appendix C, 427.

45. For a description of the 19th Bombardment Group and its squadrons, see "19th Bombardment Group," Army Air Corps Library and Museum, http://www.armyaircorpsmuseum.org/19th_Bombardment_Group.cfm, (accessed June 20, 2014).

46. All of these planes were obsolete before the start of World War II. For descriptions of them, see Douglas B-18 (http://www.nationalmuseum.af.mil/factsheets/factsheet.asp?id=2457), Martin B-10 (http://www.nationalmuseum.af.mil/factsheets/factsheet.asp?id=340), North American A-27 (http://www.nationalmuseum.af.mil/factsheets/factsheet.asp?id=3156), National Museum of the U.S. Air Force (accessed June 20, 2014).

47. Clark and Nichols Airfields were two of the principal Army Air Corps bases on Luzon. Del Monte was the main airfield on Mindanao further south in the Philippines. For a description of the status of the Army Air Corps in the Philippines on the eve of war, see Morton, *The Fall of the Philippines*, 37–43.

48. A "two striper" refers to a lieutenant.

49. This view of Japanese plans was common in the Philippines in late November, especially among MacArthur's officers. See Norman and Norman, *Tears in the Darkness*, 17.

Chapter 3

1. For a description of the Viscayans, see Celedonio A. Ancheta, ed., *The Wainwright Papers*, vol. 3 (Quezon City: New Day, 1982), 1.

2. Samuel Elliot Morison, *History of United States Naval Operations in World War II*, vol. III: *Rising Sun in the Pacific, 1931–April 1942* (Boston: Little, Brown, 1984), 154.

3. Williford, *Racing the Sunrise*, 65–66.

4. A wolfpack was a tactic used by a group of German submarines that worked together to find and attack enemy ships. See Philip Kaplan, *Wolfpack: U–Boats at War, 1939–1945* (Annapolis: Naval Institute Press, 1997).

5. There were several classes of U.S. fleet submarines. See Theodore Roscoe, *Pigboats: The True Story of the Fighting Submariners of World War II* (New York: Bantam, 1958), 14–15.

6. For descriptions of the S-boats, see ibid., 15–17.

7. Morison, *Rising Sun in the Pacific, 1931–April 1942*, 158.

8. For MacArthur's time as a military adviser, see Hiroshi Masuda, *MacArthur in Asia: The General and His Staff in the Philippines, Japan, and Korea* (Ithaca: Cornell University Press, 2012), 5–7.

9. See White, *They Were Expendable*.

10. Kelly provided much of the main narrative. See White, *They Were Expendable*, vi.

11. For common American stereotypes of Asians see Dower, *War Without Mercy*, 148–57.

12. Japanese popular literature in the 1930s supported similar images of the United States. See Shoichi Saeki, "Images of the United States as a Hypothetical Enemy," in Akira Iriye, ed., *Mutual Images: Essays in American-Japanese Relations* (Cambridge: Harvard University Press, 1975), 113.

13. For the lack of cooperation between the army and the navy in the Philippines, see Robert Lee Dennison, "The Philippines: Prelude to Departure," in Mason, *The Pacific War Remembered*, 35–36.

14. For discussion of Quezon and MacArthur's relationship, see Richard B. Meixsel, "Manuel L. Quezon, Douglas MacArthur, and the Significance of the Military Mission to the Philippine Commonwealth," *Pacific Historical Review* 70:2 (May 2001): 255–92.

15. On July 26, 1941, President Roosevelt announced that all Filipino forces would be brought under American command. Franklin D. Roosevelt, "Order Placing Armed Forces of the Philippines Under United States Command," July 26, 1941, *The American Presidency Project*, http://www.presidency.ucsb.edu/ws/?pid=16149 (accessed June 25, 2015). Throughout the fall of 1941, different Filipino units were officially brought under the control of the U.S. Army. For example, see General Orders No. 24, Nov. 7, 1941, NA, RG 407—Records of the Adjutant General's Office, Philippines Archives Collection, Pre-Surrender USAFFE Orders, Box 1368.

16. I have not been able to identify a Lt. Joe or Joseph Williams in the available records.

17. While the situation had improved after MacArthur's appointment, earlier assessments of the Philippine Army's capabilities support the lieutenant. An early report on the readiness of the army claimed, "The Philippine Army consists of one regular and ten reserve divisions of very questionable combat value." "Military Attaché Report—Philippine Army—Composition and Combat Estimate," March 26, 1941, NA, RG 165—Records of the War Department General and Special Staffs, Military Intelligence Division, "Regional File." 1922–44, Islands, Philippines, Box 1851, Folder—Islands (5940)—Philippines, 1. An assessment at the end of June 1941 was even more damning. It claimed, "As the matter now stands, we have not a single tank, few anti-tank weap-

ons, no anti-aircraft with which to defend our airfields or supply bases…. A continuation of the present policy will result in the sacrifice of American troops, loss of the Far East base, and a forced retirement to defensive positions in the eastern Pacific." "Memorandum to the Assistant Chief of Staff, G-2, War Department," June 25, 1941, ibid., 1–2.

18. See "Report of Operations, Quartermaster Corps, United States Army in the Philippine Campaign, 1941–1942" by Brig. Gen. Charles Drake, NA, RG 407—Records of the Adjutant General's Office, Philippines Archives Collection, Invasion and Surrender, Lists and Rosters, Box 9, 20.

19. See Gleek, *Over Seventy-Five Years of Philippines-American History*, 40–41.

20. For information on Navy's 14–6 victory, see Ted Meier, "Larson's Luck Over Army Still Prevails," *The Washington Post*, November 30, 1941, S3.

21. For a description of U.S. Navy anti-aircraft weapons and tactics, see "Antiaircraft Action Summary- World War II," October 8, 1945, Naval History and Heritage Command, http://www.history.navy.mil/research/library/online-reading-room/title-list-alphabetically/a/antiaircraft-action-summary.html (accessed June 20, 2014).

22. Morison, *Rising Sun in the Pacific, 1931–April 1942*, 193.

23. "Bird's Nest Soup," About.com Chinese food, http://chinesefood.about.com/library/bltrivia33.htm (accessed June 21, 2014).

24. Because the Philippines are west of the International Date Line, this was the day before the Japanese attacked Pearl Harbor.

Chapter 4

1. Dwight Messimer describes the dissemination of the news at 3:15 a.m. Messimer, *In the Hands of Fate*, 31. It is unclear who Tom was. It could potentially have been Lieutenant Tom Pollock. Hofmann knew him at the time and mentions him in later chapters.

2. The official diary of the 16th Naval District notes that word of the attack on Pearl Harbor came at 2:53 a.m. "December 8, 1941—War Diary," NA, RG 38—ROCNO, Records Relating to Naval Activity During World War II, World War II Diaries, Fifteenth Naval District to Seventeenth Naval District, Box 432, Folder—16 N.D.—Commandant, December '41–Feb. '42, 1.

3. See Gordon W. Prange, Donald M. Goldstein, and Katherine V. Dillon, *At Dawn We Slept: The Untold Story of Pearl Harbor* (New York: McGraw-Hill, 1981).

4. The figures were lower than this on Luzon. At the time of the Japanese attack, the U.S. Far East Air Force possessed 92 P-40s, 18 P-35s, 35 B-17s, and miscellaneous other planes. See Bartsch, *December 8, 1941*, Appendix C, 427.

5. For a brief description of the air war in December, see Shores et al., *Bloody Shambles*, 163–197.

6. There is a huge controversy as to why the B-17s were caught on the ground. General Lewis Brereton contends that he wanted to launch the B-17s against Formosa soon after getting word of the Japanese attack on Pearl Harbor, but that General Richard Sutherland, MacArthur's Chief of Staff, did not allow it. For a short timeline supporting Brereton's position, see "Memorandum Reference Activities in Philippine Islands," December 18, 1941, MacArthur Archives, RG 15—Materials Donated by the General Public, Box 55, Folder 7, 3.

7. For a description of the attack, see Bartsch, *Doomed at the Start*, 72–85.

8. Victor Mapes was in the 14th Squadron stationed at Clark Field and described the casualties: "Our first job [after the attack] was work we had never done before. We gathered truckloads of our comrades' bodies, many with mangled arms and legs and some without heads…. Blood was everywhere, and there was the odor of burnt human flesh…." Victor L. Mapes with Scott A. Mills, *The Butchers, Baker: The World War II Memoir of a United States Army Air Corps Soldier Captured by the Japanese in the Philippines* (Jefferson: McFarland, 2000), 17.

9. For a description of this attack, see Bartsch, *Doomed at the Start*, 86–97.

10. The Japanese did lose three planes in this attack, but most likely P-40s shot them down. Because of the low quality of the P-35, it is doubtful that one would have successfully shot down a Zero. See Bartsch, *December 8, 1941*, 358–62.

11. By the end of December 8, the Japanese had destroyed approximately half of America's B-17 and P-40 planes. See Bartsch, *Doomed at the Start*, 121.

12. For the most balanced description of the debate, see James, *The Years of MacArthur*, vol. II, 5–14. James argues that while the actual events of December 8, 1941, remain murky, "MacArthur still emerges as the officer who was in overall command in the Philippines that fateful day, and he must therefore bear a large measure of the blame." Ibid., 14.

13. There was only one fully operational radar site on Luzon at the time of the Japanese attack, and the Japanese destroyed it on December 8. Charles H. Bogart, "Radar in the Philippines, 1941–1942," *Journal of America's Military Past* (Fall 1999): 27–32. For other deficiencies in the early warning system, see Bartsch, *December 8, 1941*, 235–36 and 299; Williford, *Racing the Sunrise*, 10–12; and Slater, "And Then There Were None!" 16.

14. Brereton had started doing this, and some B-17s had left on December 5. Unfortunately, Del Monte airfield on Mindanao had limited facilities and could not handle the entire B-17 force. "Memorandum Reference Activities in Philippine Islands," 3.

15. Winslow, *The Fleet the Gods Forgot*, 10.

16. Bartsch, *Doomed at the Start*, 122.

17. One report has the Japanese planes over the Philippines at around 12:35 p.m. See *American Defenders of Bataan & Corregidor*, vol. 1, 32.

18. Unfortunately, the Marines' 3-inch anti-aircraft guns only had a range of 15,000 feet, and the Japanese bombers were attacking from 23,000 feet. See Miller, *From Shanghai to Corregidor*, 7.

19. William F. Hogaboom, "Action Report: Bataan," *Marine Corps Gazette* (April 1946), 25.

20. Admiral Hart's official report on the bombing explained, "The Naval Station, Cavite, was destroyed at noon, 10 December, by Japanese bombers which bombed with deliberation, from above the range of the nine 3-inch 50 guns…. The damage was mostly from fire." "Admiral Thomas C. Hart, Narrative of Events, Asiatic Fleet, Leading up to War and From 8 December 1941 to 15 February 1942," 38.

21. For a description of the attack, see Hoyt, *The Lonely Ships*, 158–161.

22. An assessment on December 12 noted, "The visible scattered dead were all in an advanced state of putrefaction, the stench horrible, and the whole area reeking with burnt and decaying flesh…. Large bomb holes were utilized, supplemented by dug trenches, and the bodies and parts of bodies were dumped into them from

dump trucks and covered." "Extract from Hayes Report on Medical Tactics 4th Regiment, USMC, Medical Personnel Manila Bay Area," 7 Dec 41 to 6 May 42, USA-HEC, Morton Research Materials, Box 18, Folder—Admiral Rockwell's Report Volume 2, 1.

23. The *Perry* and the *Pillsbury* were four piper destroyers. See Alden, *Flush Decks and Four Pipes*, 79.

24. For a description of the *Sealion*, see "*Sealion-I*," NavSource Naval History, http://www.navsource.org/archives/08/08195.htm (accessed June 24, 2014).

25. For a description of the *Seadragon*, see "*Seadragon-I*," NavSource Naval History, http://www.navsource.org/archives/08/08194.htm (accessed June 24, 2014).

26. For a description of the *Bittern*, see "*Bittern-I*," NavSource Naval History, http://www.navsource.org/archives/11/02036.htm (accessed June 24, 2014).

27. Lt. Comdr. Denys Knoll was the weather officer at Cavite at the time of the attack. He reported, "nothing could be discerned but fire and smoke." "Narrative by Lt. Comdr. Denys W. Knoll, Philippine Campaign," July 9, 1943, RG 38—ROCNO, World War II Command File, World War II Oral Histories and Interviews, 1942–1946, Box 9, Folder—Knoll, D.W., LCDR, 7.

28. For descriptions of the *Pigeon*, see Winslow, *The Fleet the Gods Forgot*, 25–26.

29. For an account of the attack and escape of the *Seadragon* from the its commander, see "Narrative by Lt. Comdr. William E. Ferrall, USN," Apr. 23, 1943, RG 38—ROCNO, World War II Oral Histories and Interviews, 1942–1946, Box 9, Folder—Ferrall, W.E., LCDR, 1–2.

30. The navy awarded Tommy Bowers the Navy Cross for his actions. See Works by McClelland Barclay in the Navy Art Collection, Naval History and Heritage Command, http://www.history.navy.mil/our-collections/art/artists/the-art-of-mcclelland-barclay/mcclellandbarclay-heroes-of-the-south-seas/ordnance-men-lcdr-t-k-bowers.html (accessed December 4, 2015).

31. Admiral Rockwell decided to let the fire on Cavite burn itself out. See "Thursday, December 11, 1941," NA, RG 38—ROCNO, Records Relating to Naval Activity During World War II, World War II Diaries, Fifteenth Naval District to Seventeenth Naval District, Box 432, Folder—16 N.D.—Commandant, Dec. '41–Feb. '42.

32. For a full description of the attack, see Gordon, *Fighting for MacArthur*, 43–64.

33. Lt. Dorothy Danner, a nurse at the Canacao hospital, recalled, "After the raid, we rushed to the hospital, and patients were all over the place…. Triage was impossible. You just tried to find out which were the worst ones to go to surgery and so on." "Oral Histories–U.S. Navy Nurse Prisoner of War in the Philippines, 1942–1945," Naval History and Heritage Command, http://www.history.navy.mil/research/library/oral-histories/wwii/navy-nurse-pow-philippines.html (accessed on June 24, 2014).

34. Lt. Bob Kelly explained, "There was half an inch of blood on the landing platform at Canacao—we could hardly keep on our feet, for blood is as slippery as crude oil." White, *They Were Expendable*, 19.

35. The navy recognized by Dec. 11 that Cavite was untenable as a base of significant operations. See "Daily Information Material Used by the Director of Naval Intelligence at the Navy Department Morning Conference held on December 11, 1941," RG 38—ROCNO, World War II Command File, CNO: Intelligence: Information Material, Dec. 10, 1941—Jan. 9, 1942, Box 133.

36. For a description of the PT boats on December 10, see White, *They Were Expendable*, 16–18.

37. The orders from Admiral Hart in the days after the attack on Cavite were "Save everything we can" and to build up Mariveles. "Notes from CinC (handwritten)," Dec. 13, 1941, NA, RG 38—ROCNO, Records Relating to Naval Activity During World War II, World War II Diaries, Fifteenth Naval District to Seventeenth Naval District, Box 432, Folder—16 N.D.—Commandant, Dec. '41–Feb. '42, 1.

38. For these suspicions and the activities of the Filipino government, see Teodoro A. Agoncillo, *The Fateful Years: Japan's Adventure in the Philippines, 1941–45,* vol. 1 (Quezon City: R.P. Garcia, 1965), 74–75, and Peter Elphick, *Far Eastern File: The Intelligence War in the Far East, 1930–1945* (London: Hodder & Stoughton, 1997), 285–87.

39. For similar claims, see Clark Lee, *They Call It Pacific,* 46. Morton argues that there are no reports of this incident or other Japanese espionage in the official records. See Morton, *The Fall of the Philippines,* 116–18.

40. The various American intelligence offices did try to track Japanese activities in the islands before the attack. For an example, see "Intelligence Report from Comdt. 16th Naval Dist., August 25, 1941," NA, RG 165—Records of the War Department General and Special Staffs, Military Intelligence Division, "Regional File." 1922–44, Islands, Philippines, Box 1851, Folder—Islands (5940)—Philippines, 1.

Chapter 5

1. Mariveles was on the southern tip of Bataan. See Messimer, *In the Hands of Fate,* 173.

2. On December 14, 1941, the following Supply Corps officers were in Mariveles: Ensigns McGibony, Lipsitt, Cotton, Hofmann, McClure, and Snow. "Memorandum for the Commandant (Chief of Staff H.J. Ray)," December 14, 1941, NA, RG 38—ROCNO, Records Relating to Naval Activity During World War II, World War II Diaries, Fifteenth Naval District to Seventeenth Naval District, Box 432, Folder—16 N.D.—Commandant, December '41–Feb. '42.

3. Lt. Cmdr. Knoll described all the gear left at the Army-Navy Club, "When I evacuated Manila, they [his personal items] remained at the Army-Navy Club together with hundreds of other trunks, suitcases, and other personal effects of the U.S. Army Air Forces, the U.S. Army troops and the Navy officers who had placed it there in rooms, in the basement or on the dance floor of the Army-Navy Club." See "Narrative by Lt. Comdr. Denys W. Knoll, Philippine Campaign," 12.

4. They never recovered their footlockers.

5. There were a few more fighters than Hofmann remembered, but the situation was deteriorating. General Brereton wrote General Henry "Hap" Arnold, the Army Air Corps Chief of Staff, "My Pursuit [fighter planes] is hopelessly outnumbered and is being conserved (about 21 P-40s, 7 P-35s) for reconnaissance." MacArthur Archives, Box 55, Folder 7, 1.

6. For a description of the attack, see Messimer, *In the Hands of Fate,* 59–62.

7. See ibid., 64–69.

8. See Spector, *Eagle Against the Sun,* 128.

9. This attack proved false, but MacArthur even passed along the report to Washington. "Telegram from MacArthur," December 10, 1941, MacArthur Archives, RG 2—Records of Headquarters, U.S. Army Forces in the Far East (USAFFE), 1941–1942, Box 2, Folder 1, 1.

10. For salvaging, the navy requested "any boat with extra space to carry ammunition, gas, fuel oil, diesel oil, lubricating oil, provisions, guns, tools, etc." "Suggested (from W.H. Harrington, Commander, U.S. Navy Reserve, Commanding, U.S. Navy Section Base, Mariveles, Bataan, Philippine islands)," December 14, 1941, NA, RG 38—ROCNO, Records Relating to Naval Activity During World War II, World War II Diaries, Fifteenth Naval District to Seventeenth Naval District, Box 432, Folder—16 N.D.—Commandant, Dec. '41–Feb. '42, 1.

11. The 16th Naval District Diary entry for December 13 explained, "Spent day in digging shelters, organizing, moving explosives from the Naval Ammunition Depot, salvaging material from the Navy Yard, controlling the fires, burying the dead." "Saturday, December 13, 1941," ibid., 1.

12. For a study of London during the war, see Philip Ziegler, *London at War, 1939–1945* (London: Mandarin Paperbacks, 1995).

13. For a description of the fear, see Morton, *The Fall of the Philippines,* 115–16.

14. When Hofmann uses the term "Fifth Column," he is referring to groups in the Philippines who helped the Japanese.

15. While there is little doubt that Hofmann believed this story, investigations afterwards have not confirmed it. Richard Sakakida, a Japanese-American serving in the Army's intelligence office in Manila, had infiltrated the Japanese community in the Philippines prior to the war. While the Japanese had excellent intelligence on American military positions, it did not come from Peggy. Richard Sakakida, and Wayne Kiyosaki, *A Spy in Their Midst: The World War II Struggle of a Japanese-American Hero* (Lanham, MD: Madison Books, 1995), 63 and 80–81.

16. Lister or lyster bags are military issued water containers.

17. The navy awarded Faires and several others Navy Crosses for their efforts. See "Full Text Citations For Award of The Navy Cross To U.S. Navy Personnel, World War II," Welcome to the Home of Heroes, http://www.homeofheroes.com/members/02_NX/citations/03_wwii-nc/nc_06wwii_navy.html (accessed June 27, 2014). See also George H. White, "The Incredible Story of Three World War II Supply Corps Heroes," in David L. Snead's possession.

18. This claim is unverified, but Robert Bulkley does mention it in his book on the PT boats. See Robert Bulkley, Jr., *At Close Quarters: PT Boats in the United States Navy* (Washington, D.C.: Naval History Division, 1962), 5.

19. Ibid., 6.

20. See White, *They Were Expendable,* 31–33.

21. For descriptions of these landings, see Morton, *The Fall of the Philippines,* 125–29.

22. Historian John Gordon argues, "It was the worst performance of U.S. Navy submarines in the Pacific War." Gordon, *Fighting for MacArthur,* 87.

23. See Hoyt, *The Lonely Ships,* 163.

24. Masuda, *MacArthur in Asia,* 30–32.

25. Hart's Chief of Staff's declared on December 10 that the United States was potentially "facing the loss of … the Philippines." "Chief of Staff, U.S. Asiatic Fleet, U.S.S. *Houston,*" December 10, 1941, MacArthur Archives, RG 2—Records of Headquarters, U.S. Army Forces in the Far East (USAFFE), 1941–1942, Box 3, Folder 1, 1.

26. For a brief description of MacArthur's decision to withdraw from Manila and declare it an open city, see Morton, *The Fall of the Philippines,* 232–34.

27. Because the navy had dispersed most of its munitions and supplies in the Manila area, MacArthur's

surprise declaration created a significant problem. Dennison, "The Philippines: Prelude to Departure," 32–33.

28. See C.C. Drake, "'No Uncle Sam': the Story of the Hopeless Effort to Supply the Starving Army of Bataan and Corregidor," MacArthur Archives, RG-43: Papers of Weldon B. Hester, Box 1, Folder 55—"No Uncle Sam: The Story of a Hopeless Effort to Supply the Starving Army of Bataan and Corregidor," Brigadier General Charles C. Drake, 3.

29. For a description of this bombing, see "Day of Terror," *New York Times*, December 26, 1941, 4.

30. A naval intelligence briefing indicated the navy had finished officially moving material by December 26. "Daily Information Material Used by the Director of Naval Intelligence at the Navy Department Morning Conference held on December 27, 1941," RG 38—ROCNO, World War II Command File, CNO: Intelligence: Information Material, Dec. 10, 1941—Jan. 9, 1942, Box 133.

31. James, *The Years of MacArthur*, vol. II, 30–1.

32. Discussions concerning placing extra marine and naval personnel under MacArthur's command began about a week before Christmas. Admiral Ernest King told Hart to reassure MacArthur that "upon your departure place all remaining naval and marine personnel under MacArthur's command." "NPO #28," December 17, 1941, 7 Dec. '41 to 6 May '42, USAHEC, Morton Research Materials, Box 18, Folder—Admiral Rockwell's Report Volume 1, 1. MacArthur requested the use of sailors for the defense of Bataan on December 20. He wrote Hart, "It is also requested that such sailors as may become … available … be used immediately for guard purposes on the southern part of Bataan." "Letter to Commander-in-Chief, U.S. Asiatic Fleet," December 20, 1941, MacArthur Archives, RG 2—Records of Headquarters, U.S. Army Forces in the Far East (USAFFE), 1941–1942, Box 2, Folder 2—Personal Files, December 16, 1941–December 24, 1941, 1. On December 25, Hart told Admiral Rockwell to use "excess naval personnel" in "infantry units." "The Commander in Chief, U.S. Asiatic Fleet to the Commandant, Sixteenth Naval District," December 24, 1941, USAHEC, Morton Research Materials, Box 18, Folder—Admiral Rockwell's Report Volume 1, 2.

Chapter 6

1. Olongapo Naval Yard was on Subic Bay on the west coast of Luzon. The marines withdrew from there on December 26 to southern Bataan and Corregidor. See Miller, *From Shanghai to Corregidor*, 14–5.

2. For a description of the movement of supplies, see Allston, *Ready for Sea*, 253–54.

3. See Morton, *The Fall of the Philippines*, 232–34.

4. Japanese military forces had gained notoriety in their earlier campaigns for their terrible mistreatment of Chinese civilians. See Iris Chang, *The Rape of Nanking: The Forgotten Holocaust of World War II* (New York: Basic Books, 1997).

5. See Gordon, *Fighting for MacArthur*, 90–92.

6. First Lieutenant William F. Hogaboom commanded Marine anti-aircraft Battery A at Mariveles. See Hogaboom, "Action Report: Bataan," 25, and Miller, *From Shanghai to Corregidor*, 20.

7. See Miller, *From Shanghai to Corregidor*, 18–19.

8. The Mariveles Mountains dominate the central part of southern Bataan with the highest peaks, including Mount Mariveles and Natib, around 4,000 feet.

9. See Walter Karig, "CANOPUS' Last Stand," *Sea Classics* 41:9 (September 2008), 20.

10. This attack is unconfirmed, but there is no reason to doubt that it occurred as Japanese planes bombed Manila and around the Bay that day.

11. Army and navy personnel scavenged for any boat that could make the trip from Bataan to Manila. The tug that Hofmann mentioned using represented a common boat at that time. Alvin P. Stauffer, *The Quartermaster Corps: Operations in the War Against Japan* (Washington, D.C.: Center of Military History, United States Army, 1956, 1990), 12.

12. At least one other group also maneuvered to the Pasig River to retrieve shipping. Handwritten Commendation from the U.S. Navy for "directing removal of ships from the Pasig River on Dec. 27th and Dec. 28th 1941," MacArthur Archives, RG 110—Papers of Lieutenant Commander Frederick Worcester, USN/10th Military District, USAFFE/American Guerrillas of Mindanao, Box 1, Folder 1.

13. The total casualties on Corregidor from the raid were 20 dead and 80 wounded. See Miller, *From Shanghai to Corregidor*, 19.

14. "Monday, December 29, 1941," War Diary, NA, RG 38—ROCNO, Records Relating to Naval Activity During World War II, World War II Diaries, Fifteenth Naval District to Seventeenth Naval District, Box 432, Folder—16 N.D.—Commandant, Dec. '41–Feb. '42, 1. For a description of the attack on the *Canopus*, see Walter Karig and Welbourn Kelly, *Battle Report: Pearl Harbor to Coral Sea* (New York: Farrar & Rinehart, 1944), 307.

15. For a description of this attack, see Karig and Kelly, *Battle Report*, 308.

16. For the Japanese attacks on the *Canopus* and the navy's decision to turn it into a repair ship, see Morison, *Rising Sun in the Pacific, 1931–April 1942*, 198–99.

17. Baguio is a city 200 miles north of Manila. It is unclear what happened to Betty Lou, but most likely, the Japanese captured and put her in an internment camp. The Japanese interned roughly 5,000 American civilians during the war. See Frances B. Cogan, *Captured: The Japanese Internment of Americans in the Philippines, 1941–1945* (Athens: University of Georgia Press, 2000).

18. For a thorough description of the retreat, see Morton, *The Fall of the Philippines*, 161–230.

19. James, *The Years of MacArthur*, Vol. II, 37–45.

20. Morton, *The Fall of the Philippines*, 57 and 237–38.

21. The Japanese did not expect the Americans would defend Bataan and placed the priority on capturing Manila. Masuda, *MacArthur in Asia*, 57.

22. See Morton, *The Fall of the Philippines*, 230.

23. Japanese forces entered Manila late on January 1, 1942. See ibid., 235–36.

Chapter 7

1. For MacArthur's visit to Bataan on January 10, see Morton, *The Fall of the Philippines*, 268.

2. Bullock was a lieutenant in the Supply Corps. "Roster of Officers and Seniority list, Sixteenth Naval District," November 1, 1941, NA, RG 38—ROCNO, World War II Command File, Shore Establishment, Naval Districts, 14th Naval District, Ser. Rosters 1944–17th Naval District, Box 399, Folder—16th Naval District—Series, Rosters, 1941–Mar. 1942.

3. For a description of Bataan's physical features, see Agoncillo, *The Fateful Years*, 124–5.

4. See Morton, *The Fall of the Philippines*, 296–97.

5. Commander Frank Bridget was a naval aviator who was in command of the naval forces that retreated to Mariveles. See William F. Prickett, "Naval Battalion at Mariveles,"*Marine Corps Gazette* 34:6 (June 1950), 40.

6. Bartsch describes the role of the aircrews as infantry. See Bartsch, *Doomed at the Start*, 247–50.

7. The best short account of the naval battalion is Prickett, "Naval Battalion at Mariveles," 40–43.

8. NCO is an abbreviation for non-commissioned officer.

9. The totals match numbers in the official records. See "Disposition and Employment of Naval Forces, Manila Bay Area," January 14, 1942, USAHEC, LMRM, Box 19, Folder—Naval Administrative Matters, 3.

10. Drake later explained the difficulties caused by MacArthur's decision to defend the beaches concluded that "the withdrawal was much too fast for us." Drake, "'No Uncle Sam,'" 7.

11. For the Quartermaster's difficulties, see Morton, *The Fall of the Philippines*, 254–59.

12. James, *The Years of MacArthur*, Vol. 2, 31–32.

13. For the best account of the Army Quartermaster's role in the Philippines, see Stauffer, *The Quartermaster Corps*, 1–35.

14. The army and Filipino forces went on half rations on January 6, but, even then, normally received less than this. Through January and February, soldiers received less than 30 ounces of food daily. A full ration for American soldiers was 71 ounces. See "Report of Operations, Quartermaster Corps, United States Army in the Philippine Campaign, 1941–1942," 32–33.

15. For a description of the medical situation, see Morton, *The Fall of the Philippines*, 256 and 376–84.

16. The two officers were Lieutenant Edward DeLong and Ensign Barron Chandler.

17. Chandler was referring to Lieutenant John Bulkeley and Ensign William Plant.

18. For a description of this mission, see White, *They Were Expendable*, 66–71.

19. The other two crew members were Rudolph Ballough and William Dean. "Lieut (jg) E.G. Delong, U.S. Navy, Commanding Officer, U.S.S. PT-31 to The Commander, MOTOR TORPEDO BOAT SQUADRON THREE," January 23, 1942, found at http://skulljam0.tripod.com/id14.html (accessed July 7, 2014).

20. On the issues of mechanical problems and sabotage, see White, *They Were Expendable*, 13, and Bulkley, *At Close Quarters*, 11–13.

21. See Gordon, *Fighting for MacArthur*, 138.

Chapter 8

1. The 4th Marine Regiment had been stationed in Shanghai until late November when Admiral Hart ordered it to withdraw to the Philippines. The 1st Separate Marine Battalion was based at Cavite and ultimately absorbed into the 4th. Most of the marines ended up on Corregidor with a small number on Mariveles manning anti-aircraft batteries. See Gordon, *Fighting for MacArthur*, 14–18 and 89–90.

2. The navy started to conserve food in mid–December by placing its men on a ration of two meals per day. "Tuesday, December 16, 1941," War Diary, NA, RG 38—ROCNO, Records Relating to Naval Activity During World War II, World War II Diaries, Fifteenth

Naval District to Seventeenth Naval District, Box 432, Folder—16 N.D.—Commandant, Dec. '41–Feb. '42, 1. It estimated it had enough food for 3,000 men for 90 days. "Wednesday, December 17, 1941," ibid.

3. Lieutenant William Hogaboom commanded an anti-aircraft battery on Cavite when the Japanese attacked on December 10. See Hogaboom, "Action Report: Bataan," 25–26.

4. The Japanese objective was to cut the communication and supply lines between Mariveles and allied forces further north on Bataan. Mount Pucot overlooked Mariveles and the southwest coast of Bataan. See Clyde Selleeck, *The War Diary of Gen. Clyde Selleck, Commanding General, 71st Division, USAFFE: The Battle for Northern Luzon, The Initial Phase of the Battle of Bataan* (Quezon City: R.P. Garcia, 1985), 27.

5. The Naval Battalion consisted of about 600 men, including men from Patrol Wing 10, the *Canopus*, and the Cavite Naval Yard, as well as about 100 marines. It was the brainchild of Lieutenant Commander Bridget who realized the vulnerability of the Service Sector. He proposed creating a battalion of reserve infantry from the remnants of navy and air corps troops who had withdrawn to the Mariveles area. "Thursday, January 8, 1942," War Diary, NA,RG 38—ROCNO, Records Relating to Naval Activity During World War II, World War II Diaries, Fifteenth Naval District to Seventeenth Naval District, Box 432, Folder—16 N.D.—Commandant, Dec. '41–Feb. '42, 1. Rockwell issued orders the next day asserting that the battalion would provide security, help with defense, and support the army. Memo for Captain Dessez from F.W. Rockwell, USN," January 9, 1942, US-AHEC, Morton Research Materials, Box 19, Folder—Naval Maintenance Matters, 1. For a discussion of the creation of the Naval Battalion, see Gordon, *Fighting for MacArthur*, 127–28.

6. The Marine was Private Robert McKechnie. See Hogaboom, "Action Report: Bataan," 27.

7. There was widespread confusion as to how many Japanese had landed. MacArthur's headquarters initially estimated 100–150. "G-3 Information Bulletin," January 23, 1942, MacArthur Archives, RG 2—USAFFE, G-2 Journals, December 30, 1941–March 21, 1942, Box 4, Folder 1, 1.

8. At the time of the attack, the men in the Naval Battalion had at most three days of infantry training. Hogaboom, "Action Report: Bataan," 27. See also Donald J. Young, *The Battle of Bataan: A Complete History*, 2d ed. (Jefferson: McFarland, 2009), 87.

9. Since most of their uniforms were white, many men dyed them in coffee to make them less distinctive. However, it left the uniforms looking various shades of yellow, or as one soldier described them, "sickly mustard-colored." Quoted in Gordon, *Fighting for MacArthur*, 138.

10. Lieutenant J.G. Leslie Pew had been a PBY pilot and transferred to Mariveles after the destruction of most of the PBY planes. For the movement of the PBY crews, see Messimer, *The Fall of the Philippines*, 89–112 and 173–85.

11. The Marine was Corporal Fred Paulson.

12. The trade of a carton of cigarettes, generally ten packs of twenty cigarettes, for a Thompson submachine gun may seem improbable, but that fails to take into account the scarcity of cigarettes on Bataan. While cigarettes were plentiful on Corregidor, soldiers generally received only one cigarette per day on Bataan. See Stauffer, *The Quartermaster Corps*, 29. Morton describes how the scarcity of cigarettes on Bataan caused significant

morale problems and led to a thriving black market for them in early 1942. Morton, *The Fall of the Philippines*, 372–73.

13. Several Marines later remembered just how ignorant the sailors were. In an initial engagement with the Japanese, "a Marine shouted, 'Grenade,' and dove for cover. The sailors stood looking around asking, 'Where?'" Miller, *From Shanghai to Corregidor*, 21.

14. Commander Bridget reported the wounding of the two men to Rockwell late on January 23. "Friday, January 23, 1942," War Diary, RG 38—ROCNO, Records Relating to Naval Activity During World War II, World War II Diaries, Fifteenth Naval District to Seventeenth Naval District, Box 432, Folder—16 N.D.—Commandant, December '41–Feb. '42, 1.

15. A sailor from the *Canopus* remembered the activities of the naval battalion—"Five days of what was probably the weirdest jungle fighting in the annals of warfare ensued, with all accepted principles violated." "Unpublished Manuscript—'Courage Personified,'" MacArthur Archives, RG 15—Materials Donated by the General Public, Box 40, Folder 16, C-11-C-12.

16. BAR stands for Browning Automatic Rifle, and it was a light machine gun used by U.S. forces in the war.

17. See Hogaboom, "Action Report: Bataan," 28–29.

18. See ibid., 29.

19. Corporal Raymond Collins led the advance and earned the Silver Star for his gallantry. Ibid.

20. See also Prickett, "Naval Battalion at Mariveles," 42.

21. 1st Lt. Willard B. Holdredge was awarded the Navy Cross for his actions on Bataan. See Military Times Hall of Valor, "Willard Barrett Holdredge," *Military Times* http://projects.militarytimes.com/citations-medals-awards/recipient.php?recipientid=8138 (accessed December 11, 2013).

22. For discussion of the deployment of the 81-mm mortars, see Morton, *The Fall of the Philippines*, 306.

23. See also Prickett, "Naval Battalion at Mariveles," 43.

24. Gordon reports that five men were killed and another 24 were wounded. Gordon, *Fighting for MacArthur*, 146.

25. General Sellleck had sent a Philippine Army pack howitzer to provide some support. See "The Battalion Commander to the Commandant, SIXTEENTH NAVAL DISTRICT."

26. The "big 12 mortars" were 12-in. mortars that could fire shells ranging from 670 to 1,100 lbs. up to 14,000 yards. Gordon, *Fighting for MacArthur*, 144.

27. Colonel Paul Bunker commanded the 12-in. mortars on Corregidor and was "inwardly raving with disappointment" when he was initially denied permission to use them. Quoted in Morton, *The Fall of the Philippines*, 306.

28. Lieutenant Colonel William Clement was on Corregidor and supported the use of the mortars.

29. Lieutenant Richard Fulmer was the forward observer who provided firing solutions for the mortar battery. Whitman, *Bataan: Our Last Ditch*, 262.

30. See Miller, *From Shanghai to Corregidor*, 22.

31. While Hofmann underestimated the number of Japanese survivors, a Japanese prisoner later recalled, "We were terrified…. Before I was wounded, my head was going round and round, and I did not know what to do. Some of my companions jumped off the cliff to escape the terrible fire." Quoted in Morton, *The Fall of the Philippines*, 306.

32. For a description of the attack, see Gordon, *Fighting for MacArthur*, 148.

33. Hofmann was actually part of a unit that had advanced further than any other group. He did not know it, but there was a real danger of the unit being cut off. Gordon, *Fighting for MacArthur*, 149.

34. By this point, MacArthur's headquarters realized that this was not a full-scale invasion of the Service Sector, but the Japanese attack was still a serious threat. A G-2 report concluded, "It is believed that small landings on the southwest coast of Bataan are primarily to divert our reserves and thus weaken our front, but if not promptly and successfully ejected these landings will be the beachheads in force which would jeopardize our forces in the Reserve Battle Position." "G-2 Report," January 28, 1942, MacArthur Archives, RG 2—USAFFE, G-2 Journals, December 30, 1941–March 21, 1942, Box 4—Folder 3, 1.

35. The Filipino Scouts were from the 57th Infantry. Morton, *The Fall of the Philippines*, 307.

36. For the fighting of the Filipinos, see Gordon, *Fighting for MacArthur*, 151.

37. The 12-in. mortar fire was scheduled to last from 7:00–7:30 a.m. "Tel Msg from Lt. Comdr McGervan," January 28, 1942, MacArthur Archives, RG 2—USAFFE, G-2 Journals, December 30, 1941–March 21, 1942, Box 4, Folder 1, 1.

38. For a description of the naval attack, see Gordon, *Fighting for MacArthur*, 152–55.

39. MacArthur headquarters received a report on January 29, 1942, that "Japanese are jumping off the end of the cliff and committing suicide." "G-2, Journal USAFFE)," January 29, 1942, MacArthur Archives, RG 2—USAFFE, G-2 Journals, December 30, 1941–March 21, 1942, Box 4—Folder 1, 1.

40. Hofmann actually underestimated the importance of the battle. Admiral Rockwell later wrote, "The importance of the combat service rendered by this organization [Naval Battalion] of non-military personnel cannot be overstated. There remains no doubt that had the Japanese been successful in their landing attack at Longoskawayan Point their siege of Bataan would have ended then and there." "F.W. Rockwell to George C. Groce," June 2, 1948, USAHEC, Morton Research Materials, Box 18, Folder—Admiral Rockwell's Report Volume 1, 2.

41. One Japanese soldier who fought in the Battle of the Points, Private Kiyoshi Kinoshita, is a perfect example. He fought until he was severely wounded and fell unconscious. When he awoke, he realized he was a prisoner of war in an American hospital and felt humiliated. Even when he escaped to his own forces, his comrades treated him as an outcast. See Norman and Norman, *Tears in the Darkness*, 105–07.

42. "The Battalion Commander to the Commandant, SIXTEENTH NAVAL DISTRICT."

Chapter 9

1. There are records verifying most of these attacks. Admiral Rockwell's War Diary contains entries confirming attacks on December 29, January 5, January 8, January 16, February 6, and February. 11. See entries for those dates in NA, RG 38—ROCNO, Records Relating to Naval Activity During World War II, World War II Diaries, Fifteenth Naval District to Seventeenth Naval District, Box 432, Folder—16 N.D.—Commandant, Dec. '41–Feb. '42. For the January 6 attack, see Gordon, *Fighting*

for MacArthur, 114. For the January 14 attack, see "Daily Information Material Used by the Director of Naval Intelligence at the Navy Department Morning Conference held on Jan. 15, 1942," NA, RG 38—ROCNO, World War II Command File, CNO: Intelligence: Information Material, Dec. 10, 1941—Jan. 9, 1942, Box 134. For bombings on January 25 and 27, see Naval Message from COM 16 to OPNAV, Jan. 25, 1942, USAHEC, LMRM, Box 18, Folder—Admiral Rockwell's Report Volume 3 and Rockwell Diary, January 27, 1942, ibid., Box 19, Folder—Naval Operations.

2. When Hofmann discusses the Malay Barrier, he is primarily referring to the Dutch East Indies as well as Malaya. Admiral Hart took command of the ABDA-COM (American, British, Dutch, and Australian Command) naval forces after he left the Philippines. See Spector, *Eagle Against the Sun*, 127–34.

3. Since Hofman did not provide a date for this attack, I cannot confirm it. However, an intelligence briefing on January 15 reported one plane shot down by the Marine battery the day before. See "Daily Information Material Used by the Director of Naval Intelligence at the Navy Department Morning Conference held on Jan. 15, 1942."

4. Bryan Wilburn, "Japanese Bombs of World War II," HyperScale, http://www.clubhyper.com/reference/japanesebombsdw_1.htm (accesssed July 29, 2014).

5. The Japanese reported at least the January 6 attack on Mariveles. See "Japan Tells of Bombings," *New York Times*, January 7, 1942, 2.

6. It is unclear who the captain was. I have identified 19 captains serving with the 4th Marine Regiment who were taken prisoner by the Japanese either on Bataan or Corregidor. For the complete roster, see "Roster of the 4th Marine Regiment," http://www.west-point.org/family/japanese-pow/Marines/4thMarineRegt.htm (accessed July 29, 2014).

7. For information on the Negritos and their history, see John M. Garvan, *The Negritos of the Philippines*, ed. Hermann Hochegger (Vienna: Verlag Ferdinand Berger Horn, 1964).

Chapter 10

1. Smith, *MacArthur's Escape*, 167–8.

2. For examples of some Japanese propaganda and overall racial attitudes, see Dower, *War Without Mercy*, 191–200 and 262–90. For Japanese propaganda in the Philippines, see Morton, *The Fall of the Philippines*, 384–86.

3. See "War Propaganda," Outsider Japan, http://outsiderjapan.pbworks.com/w/page/9758560/War%20Propaganda (accessed July 24, 2014).

4. Jorge B. Vargas was a Filipino politician who worked with the Japanese. For some of his propaganda, see "Christmas message to the people of the Philippines of Jorge B. Vargas, Chairman of the Philippine Executive Commission," December 25, 1942, Republic of the Philippines Presidential Library and Museum, http://malacanang.gov.ph/7413-christmas-message-to-the-people-of-the-philippines-of-jorge-b-vargas-chairman-of-the-philippine-executive-commission-december-25-1942/ (accessed July 23, 2014).

5. For the impact of MacArthur's lies, see Matthew S. Klimow, "Lying to the Troops: American Leaders and the Defense of Bataan" *Parameters* 20:4 (Dec. 1990): 52–54.

6. For MacArthur's order that every unit commander

ensure that the message was distributed to the troops, see Morton, *The Fall of the Philippines*, 387.

7. MacArthur clearly knew in January that his troops faced dire prospects. In his notes on January 23, he wrote, "Heavy and Mounting" casualties "will soon force me to a shortened line on which I shall make my final stand." "Notes of General Douglas MacArthur," January 23, 1942, Topic—Recognition of Dire Situation, MacArthur Archives, RG 2—Records of Headquarters, U.S. Army Forces in the Far East (USAFFE), 1941–1942, Box 2, Folder 4—Personal Files, January 23, 1942–April 11, 1942, 1.

8. For support of this assessment, see Klimow, "Lying to the Troops," 59.

9. In his address, President Roosevelt explained, Immediately after this war started, the Japanese forces moved down on either side of the Philippines to numerous points south of them—thereby completely encircling the Philippines from north, south, east, and west.

It is that complete encirclement, with control of the air by Japanese land-based aircraft, which has prevented us from sending substantial reinforcements of men and material to the gallant defenders of the Philippines....

It has been said that Japanese gains in the Philippines were made possible only by the success of their surprise attack on Pearl Harbor. I tell you that this is not so.

Even if the attack had not been made your map will show that it would have been a hopeless operation for us to send the fleet to the Philippines through thousands of miles of ocean, while all those island bases were under the sole control of the Japanese. Franklin D. Roosevelt, "Fireside Chat," February 23, 1942, The American Presidency Project, http://www.presidency.ucsb.edu/ws/?pid=16224 (accessed July 23, 2014).

10. Morton reports similar numbers. See Morton, *The Fall of the Philippines*, 405.

11. Drake reported that by mid–March, the soldiers were on quarter rations. "Report of Operations, Quartermaster Corps, United States Army in the Philippine Campaign, 1941–1942," 33.

12. Lt. John Burns, a pilot who was serving in the infantry on Bataan, wrote in his diary on February 18, "Climate is getting me or improper diet is doing it. Getting awful lazy and tired out quickly. Everyone seems to be that way." On March 20, he wrote, "One day's food for 250 men—14 loaves of bread, 15 cans of milk, 17 cans salmon." Bartsch, "I Wonder at Times How We Keep Going Here," 42 and 45.

13. For the impact of the limited rations and disease on Bataan, see Morton, *The Fall of the Philippines*, 376–80.

14. For the best description of MacArthur's escape, see White, *They Were Expendable*, 118–43.

15. Balikpapan is a port city in Borneo that at the time was part of the Dutch East Indies. In January 1942, the Japanese captured the port as part of their conquest of the Dutch East Indies. During the landing, a group of U.S. destroyers attacked the Japanese transports sinking four of them and one patrol boat. Despite this success, the Japanese were still able to seize the port. For a description of the battle, see Winslow, *The Fleet the Gods Forgot*, 151–58.

16. Throughout February, the Japanese fought a series of naval battles with the combined Allied fleet (American, British, Dutch, and Australian) around the

Java Sea and achieved overwhelming success sinking over ten allied ships with few losses of their own. For an overview of these actions, see *The Java Sea Campaign: Combat Narratives* (Washington, D.C.: Office of Naval Intelligence, 1943).

17. In a similar situation in January, approximately a dozen officers who were being evacuated from Corregidor were instructed, "Only one change of clothing and toilet articles may be taken aboard by each passenger." "To the Commanding General, U.S. Army Forces in the Far East (from Adm. F. W. Rockwell)," January 22, 1942, MacArthur Archives, RG 30—Papers of Lieutenant General Richard K. Sutherland, USA, Chief of Staff, SWPA, 1941–1945, Box 1, Folder 9—Correspondence with Military Commands, 1941–1945, U.S. Army Forces in the Far East, 1941–1942, 2.

18. This was the last time that Hofmann saw either Jack or Bud during the war. The Japanese took them prisoner with the fall of Corregidor.

19. General Richard Sutherland reported the creation of an Army Transportation Service in Cebu on February 18 and the initial sending of naval personnel to help in the process. He wrote, "We are sending material, also a few Quartermasters to assist him down there in procurement, and a considerable group of Navy personnel from the Navy Yard at Cavite who serve no useful purpose here but who may be of considerable value down there." "Sutherland to Brig. Gen. B. G. Chynoweth," February 18, 1942, MacArthur Archives, RG 30—Papers of Lieutenant General Richard K. Sutherland, USA, Chief of Staff, SWPA, 1941–1945, Box 1, Folder 9—Correspondence with Military Commands, 1941–1945, U.S. Army Forces in the Far East, 1941–1942, 1. Sutherland sent a separate letter to the commandant of 16th Naval District about the movement of some naval personnel. He wrote, "certain specialist personnel have become surplus in the force on Bataan and Corregidor. A number of these men can perform service of great value in the unoccupied islands of the Archipelago.... It is suggested that Naval personnel who fall in this category be evacuated." "Major General R. R. Sutherland to Commandant, 16th Naval District," February 20, 1942, USAHEC, LMRM, Box 18, Folder—Admiral Rockwell's Report Volume 1, 1. Brigadier General Bradford Chynoweth, who was the commander of U.S. and Filipino forces on Panay from January to March, reported that a group of naval officers arrived in Panay for him to use during this time. Bradford Grethen Chynoweth, *Bellamy Park* (Hicksville, N.Y.: Exposition Press, 1975), 219.

20. Captain John H.D. Dessez was the commander of the Mariveles naval base. See Miller, *From Shanghai to Corregidor* at http://corregidor.org/USMC/chs_41-42/from_shanghai_to_corregidor.htm (accessed on July 23, 2014). Dessez received his orders to begin transferring some naval officers to help with the blockade on February 20. "Carlisle, Commandant, Sixteenth Naval District to Captain J.H.S. Dessez, U.S. Navy," February 20, 1942, USAHEC, LMRM, Box 18, Folder—Admiral Rockwell's Report Volume 1, 1.

21. Cebu was the base depot to get supplies to Bataan/Corregidor. "Report of Operations, Quartermaster Corps, United States Army in the Philippine Campaign, 1941–1942," 39. Lt. Cmdr. Knoll reported that "the majority of the officers went to Cebu and assisted with the collection of supplies, mainly of food in the Cebu area for eventual transfer to Corregidor and Bataan." "Narrative by Lt. Comdr. Denys W. Knoll, Philippine Campaign," 21.

22. Even in December, MacArthur and other allied leaders began looking at ways to get supplies through the tightening Japanese blockade of the Philippines. The Headquarters of the Far East Air Force concluded on December 22, 1941, "The limitations of ferrying facilities, and possible interdiction of the ferry route from Australia make it impossible to effect deliveries into the Philippine Islands except in comparatively small increments." "Air Estimate of the Situation," December 22, 1941, Headquarters Far East Air Force, MacArthur Archives, RG 2—USAFFE, G-2 Journals, December 30, 1941–March 21, 1942, Box 12, Folder 2—September–December 1941, 4.

23. For the best description of the blockade-running efforts, see Robert L. Underbrink, *Destination Corregidor* (Annapolis: U.S. Naval Institute Press, 1971).

24. In January, pressure mounted to get more supplies to Bataan and Corregidor. A report in January noted, "Authorities in Australia being pressed to exert every effort to get food to MacArthur by whatever means that are available or be improvised including use of local shipping and native boats." "Copy Com16," January 17, 1942, USAHEC, LMRM, Box 18, Folder—Admiral Rockwell's Report Volume 3, 1.

25. The navy issued the following directive: "A joint Army and Navy General Purchasing Board will be established in Australia under chairmanship General Roop US Army to coordinate contacting and purchasing for American forces. Request one of five Supply Corps Officers now enroute Australia be designated to serve as member." "OBNAV to CINCAF," January 24, 1942, USAHEC, LMRM, Box 18, Folder –Admiral Rockwell's Report Volume 3, 1.

26. For an excellent overview of the efforts to break the blockade, see Williford, *Racing the Sunrise*, 228–47.

27. For an example of the military's willingness to pay up to four times the normal amount, see Underbrink, *Destination Corregidor*, 93 and 122.

28. According to overview of the blockade running activities, "there were approximately twenty-five interisland boats ready that could be used to run the blockade" by mid–January. "Historical Report—Visayan-Mindanao Force, Defense of the Philippines, 1 Sept. 1941–10 May 1942," no date, MacArthur Archives, RG 2–USAFFE, G-2 Journals, December 30, 1941–March 21, 1942, Box 13, no folder, 38.

29. Underbrink, *Destination Corregidor*, 140–51.

30. There was not much optimism in MacArthur's headquarters that blockade-runners could reach Bataan or Corregidor safely. A March 17 memo reported, "Under present warship activity and hostile air capabilities, doubt if even destroyers could get through with 50% chance of return." "To: G2 and G-3 (Re: Memo—Plans for Running Blockade)," March 17, 1942, MacArthur, RG 2–USAFFE, G-2 Journals, December 30, 1941–March 21, 1942, Box 8, Folder 4—G-3 Journal, March 1, 1942–April 10, 1942, 1.

31. I have not been able to find the list. The impetus for the move of the naval officers could have been a conference on Corregidor on March 18. After the conference, Brig. General Drake requested "air and naval units to be sent to our help in convoying ships between CEBU [sic] and Corregidor." "Report of Operations, Quartermaster Corps, United States Army in the Philippine Campaign, 1941–1942," 44.

32. The navy recognized that by this point, "the Visayan Islands [where Cebu was located] appear to be under close enemy blockade." "Daily Information Material Used by the Director of Naval Intelligence at the Navy Department Morning Conference held on Mar.

23, 1942," NA, RG 38—ROCNO, World War II Command File, CNO: Intelligence: Information Material, Dec. 10, 1941–Jan. 9, 1942, Box 136.

33. Charles Ross had been second in command when his commanding officer, Major A. L. Howard, had been killed. There are various accounts as to how Howard died, but several witnesses claimed the Boers captured and then executed him. Believing this account, Ross made his men swear that they would take no more Boer prisoners. See Miller, *Painting the Map Red*, 448.

34. While the specific orders sending Hofmann and the other naval personnel to Cebu are not available, the navy did later report that they had moved south while Jack and Snow were left at Mariveles. See "Appendix "A"—List of Officer Personnel as of March 10, 1942," NA, RG 38—ROCNO, World War II Command File, Shore Establishment, Naval Districts, 14th Naval District, Ser. Rosters 1944–17th Naval District, Box 399, Folder—16th Naval District—Series, Rosters, 1941–Mar 1942, 5–9. While the roster is dated March 10, it was put together later as there are asterisks on it pointing to later dates. For example, there is an asterisk by Hofmann's name indicating that he had reached Australia sometime between March 11 and August 1, 1942.

35. The USS *Quail* was a minesweeper. See "*Quail*," NavSource Naval History, http://www.navsource.org/archives/11/02015.htm (accessed July 23, 2014).

36. According to a later intelligence report, "General MacArthur had transferred about 60 Naval officers and a group of Army personnel to Iloilo, Cebu and points in the Southern Islands to organize natives, collect food for the troops on Luzon." "Memorandum From Lt. Commander Denys W. Knoll, U.S. Navy, District Intelligence Officer, Sixteenth Naval District to Vice Chief of Naval Operations (Director of Naval Intelligence)," no date, USAHEC, LMRM, Box 19, Folder—Knoll, Intell Rept, 16th Nav Dist., 8–9.

Chapter 11

1. Brigadier General Bradford Chynoweth had recently been given command American and Filipino forces in the central Philippines. He arrived in Cebu City in mid–March. B. G. Chynoweth, "Lessons from the Fall of the Philippines," *The Military Engineer* 46:313 (September/October 1954): 370.

2. Brigadier General William Sharp was overall commander of the defense of Mindanao. See Morton, *The Fall of the Philippines*, 499 and 501.

3. Colonel Irving Scudder commanded the Filipino troops on Cebu. Ibid., 502.

4. For Chynoweth's plans, see Chynoweth, *Bellamy Park*, 239–43.

5. I have found no records of the loss of these ships. However, Stauffer reports that the U.S. Army Transport Service acquired 49 ships between 300 and 1,000 tons, and "a large majority were eventually lost, destroyed, or captured while engaged in blockade-running." Stauffer, *The Quartermaster Corps*, 19.

6. Richardson recounted MacArthur's response in an unpublished memoir. Iliff D. Richardson Manuscript, National Museum of the Pacific War, Fredericksburg, TX, accessed on May 14, 2015, http://digitalarchive.pacificwarmuseum.org/cdm/singleitem/collection/p16769coll3/id/2, 100.

7. See Bulkley, *At Close Quarters*, 18.

8. White, *They Were Expendable*, 148–53.

9. Ibid., 156.

10. Hofmann had first met Faires at Cavite when they would swim together. See Chapter 3.

11. Chynoweth gave field promotions to several civilians on Cebu who had worked for Standard Oil. See "Appointment and promotion of officers, Visayan Force, P.I.," Oct. 22, 1945, Nam RG 407—Records of the Adjutant General's Office, Philippines Archives Collection, Invasion and Surrender, War Support Services Bataan and Corregidor, Box 10, 6.

12. The *Seadragon* arrived on April 4. "Historical Report—Visayan-Mindanao Force, Defense of the Philippines, 1 Sept. 1941–10 May 1942," "Historical Report—Visayan-Mindanao Force, Defense of the Philippines, 1 Sept. 1941–10 May 1942," no date, MacArthur Archives, RG 2–USAFFE, G-2 Journals, December 30, 1941–March 21, 1942, Box 13, no folder, 8.

13. For the orders to divert to Cebu, see Underbrink, *Destination Corregidor*, 162–63.

14. Ibid., 163–64.

15. "Historical Report—Visayan-Mindanao Force, Defense of the Philippines, 1 Sept. 1941–10 May 1942."

16. Underbrink, *Destination Corregidor*, 164.

17. "Blockade Running to the Philippines," n.d. US-AHEC, LMRM, Box 19, Folder—Philippines Relief—Summary Rpt., 12–13.

18. Underbrink, *Destination Corregidor*, 168. Morton reports that in late March neither the American nor Filipino soldiers were receiving even 20 ounces of food per day, or less than one-fourth a full ration. See Morton, *The Fall of the Philippines*, 368.

19. See Underbrink, *Destination Corregidor*, 179.

20. For a description of dengue fever, see Julia O. Flikke, *Nurses in Action* (Philadelphia: J. B. Lippincott, 1943), 175.

Chapter 12

1. For other descriptions of the burning of Cebu City, see Chynoweth, *Bellamy Park*, 249.

2. Hofmann later found out that Faires and Lipsitt thought the rest of the men had been killed. According to Commander Walter Bicknell, he left on a sloop or banca very similar to the one Hofmann described. He later wrote, "When, on 10 April, news of an approaching Japanese convoy was received and it was certain that a landing soon would be made, it was decided to evacuate aboard the sloop. A party consisting of Captain Dessez (now a litter patient), Lt. Cohen (MC), Lt. Faires (SC), Chief Pay Clerk Bruun, Pharmacist's Mate J.H. Luther and myself boarded the sloop" and escaped to Mindanao. See "32 Months as a Japanese Prisoner: Experience of a Supply Officer," Oryoku Maru Online, http://www.oryokumaruonline.org/32months.html (accessed June 25, 2014).

3. For a description of the Japanese conquest of Cebu, see Morton, *The Fall of the Philippines*, 503–06.

4. In *They Were Expendable*, William White quotes Kelly, "the three seaplanes … were flying over the city, dropping leaflets telling the Philippines to surrender, 'We are your friend,' and offering *substantial* reward for any American, dead or alive, and *handsome* reward for any American officer or his body." White, *They Were Expendable*, 183–84. It is unclear whether Hofmann borrowed this description from Kelly or not, so this has to be considered a possibility. However, Hofmann does describe the leaflet in more detail. Unfortunately, I have not been able to find a copy of this leaflet. The closest leaflet I have found is one that claimed, "A HANDSOME

REWARD WILL BE YOURS" for the capture of or information on American military personnel. See Herbert A. Friedman, "Japanese Psyop During WWII," accessed May 30, 2015, http://www.psywarrior.com/JapanPSYOP WW2.html. The Japanese did use leaflets widely through the war. For some examples of the Japanese propaganda leaflets in the Philippines, see "World War II—Japanese Propaganda in the Philippines," U.S. Naval Academy Digital Collection, accessed May 14, 2015, http://cdm 16099.contentdm.oclc.org/cdm/landingpage/collection/p16099coll3.

5. For a fuller description, see White, *They Were Expendable*, 162–76. While White's account of Kelly's escape from Cebu never mentions the Supply Corps officers, they were with him. After receiving news of Kelly's arrival in Mindanao, General Wainwright sent Gen. MacArthur a telegram explaining how Kelly arrived: "With Navy QM Corps Lieut. R.B. Kelly reached Mindanao on foot and native boats to avoid invasion." "Telegram from Wainwright to MacArthur," Apr. 22, 1942, RG 38—ROCNO, Records Relating to Naval Activity During World War II, Box 1336, Folder—PT 34. The QM means Quartermaster and is the army's equivalent of the Supply Corps.

In a later interview, Kelly described crossing Cebu with some sailors and civilians. "John Wayne Played Him in a Movie," *The Evening Sun Accent*, Baltimore, May 5, 1978, B1. I owe a special thanks to Alyce N. Gutherie from PT Boats, Inc., for bringing this article to my attention.

6. Hofmann probably saw a flight of B-25s that attacked Cebu City. See Underbrink, *Destination Corregidor*, 180.

7. For more on the collapse of Cebu's defenses, see Chynoweth, *Bellamy Park*, 250–52.

8. In his memoir, Chynoweth explained that after he surrendered, the Japanese commander in Cebu City blamed him and the Americans for burning the city. Ibid., 284.

9. White, *They Were Expendable*, 189.

10. There is a hint in White's *They Were Expendable* that the group was larger than he recorded. White quotes Kelly as saying, "we finally located enough bancas to carry us." The need for multiple bancas indicates more than three or four people. See ibid.

11. In his account, Kelly explained, "It took me days to get to Mindanao around and through the islands begging rides in cars, hiring small boats to cross little island channels." Ibid., 191.

12. Ibid., 192.

13. "Mr. Kelly and a young ensign made contact with a sugar smuggler and persuaded him to ship them to Mindanao." "John Wayne Played Him In A Movie," B1.

14. Brigadier General Guy O. Fort commanded the 81st Philippine Division at the start of World War II and forces around Lake Lanao on Mindanao in 1942. See Morton, *The Fall of the Philippines*, 514. Since all Filipino units were brought under U.S. command in the second half of 1941, Fort and the 81st Division would have been under MacArthur's command. "Pursuant to provisions of the Proclamation of the President of the United States, dated July 26, 1941, the units of the Philippine Army ... are hereby called into service of the armed forces of the United States in the Philippines." This order specifically included the 81st Division. General Orders No. 24, Nov. 7, 1941, RG 407—Records of the Adjutant General's Office, Philippines Archives Collection, Pre-Surrender USAFFE Orders, Box 1368.

15. MacArthur did keep his promise, and Kelly made it to Australia on a B-17. Bulkley, *At Close Quarters*, 26.

Chapter 13

1. MacArthur ordered General Sharp to send one of his two divisions to Mindanao on December 30. "Daily Information Material Used by the Director of Naval Intelligence at the Navy Department Morning Conference held on Jan. 8, 1942," RG 38—ROCNO, World War II Command File, CNO: Intelligence: Information Material, Dec. 10, 1941–Jan. 9, 1942, Box 133. See also Morton, *The Fall of the Philippines*, 500–501.

2. For a description of the Moros on Mindanao and their Islamic faith, see John Hugh McGee, *Rice and Salt: A History of the Defense and Occupation of Mindanao During World War II* (San Antonio: Naylor, 1962), 2 and 4–5.

3. Dansalan is now called Marawi City.

4. There is little information on General Fort. He served much of his pre-war military career in the Philippines, was captured by the Japanese when Mindanao fell, and was executed in November 1942. See "Guy O. Fort," American Battlefield and Monuments Commission, http://www.abmc.gov/search-abmc-burials-and-memorializations/detail/World War II_107682#.U9ug TVP5fa8 (accessed August 1, 2014).

5. In early March 1942, Senior Sultan Sal Ramain-Alonto from Lanao, Mindanao sent a message to MacArthur and President Roosevelt offering the Moros as allies. He wrote, "we will fight with all of our strength against the Japanese and other enemies of the United States and Philippine government.... We will attack or defend as ordered." "War Department Communique No. 131," March 2, 1942, NARA, RG 165—Records of the War Department General and Special Staffs Military Intelligence Division, "Regional File." 1922–44, Islands, Philippines, Box 1851, Folder—Islands (5940)—Philippines, 1.

6. There is no record of MacArthur's refusal to provide arms to the Moros. As McGee points out, there was one company of Moros, approximately 85 men, in the Philippine Scouts on Mindanao and they were armed basically like the Christian company, but both suffered from antiquated weapons and limited supplies of ammunition. McGee, *Rice and Salt*, 4.

7. For the Japanese occupation of Davao and Digos, see Morton, *The Fall of the Philippines*, 112–13.

8. The initiative for this mission evidently came from General Wainwright on Corregidor who was particularly worried about evacuating the nurses on the island. Lt. Commander Denys Knoll later wrote, "General Wainwright repeatedly reminded me that the American people would never forgive him if he did not make an effort to evacuate some of the American Army Nurses from Corregidor." "Memorandum From Lt. Commander Denys W. Knoll, U.S. Navy, District Intelligence Officer, Sixteenth Naval District to Vice Chief of Naval Operations (Director of Naval Intelligence)," no date, USAHEC, Morton Research Materials, Box 19, Folder—Knoll, Intell Rept, 16th Nav Dist., 24. After discussions with naval officers on Corregidor, Wainwright sent a message on April 16 to MacArthur suggesting that he "assign a Navy seaplane to the mission of ferrying personnel between here and Lake Lanao." "Wainwright to MacArthur," MacArthur Archives, RG 30—Papers of Lieutenant General Richard K. Sutherland, USA, Chief of Staff, SWPA, 1941–1945, Box 1, Folder 10—Correspondence with Military Commands, 1941–1945, U.S. Army Forces in the Far East, 1941–1942, 4 April–10 May 1942, 1. MacArthur responded a few days later that "plans being perfected to send 2 Navy Patrol bombers to Corregidor at earliest date that phase of moon will

permit night landing." "MacArthur to Wainwright,"
April 19, 1942, ibid., 1.

9. For details on planning the mission, see Underbrink, *Destination Corregidor*, 191–93; and Messier, *In
the Hands of Fate*, 286–287. The flight from Darwin in
Australia to Corregidor was approximately 2,100 miles.

10. For a first-hand account of the nurses who left
Corregidor on the PBYs, see Juanita Redmond, *I Served
on Bataan* (Philadelphia: J.B. Lippincott, 1943), 149–60.

11. White, *They Were Expendable*, 202.

12. The PT crews included some ground crew members from the 30th Squadron of the 19th Bomber Group
who had been stationed at Clark Field in December
1941. They had been evacuated from Bataan to Mindanao in late December 1941 and early January 1942. In
late April, they were assigned to the PT boat going to
Lake Lanao. Tom Mitsos, "Guerrilla Radio, 30th Sqd,
19th BG," MacArthur Archives, Norfolk, VA, Ch. 2, 1–
6.

13. The PT-boat itself was destroyed soon after this
so that it would not fall into Japanese hands. See "John
D. Bulkeley to L. H. Hammand, Jr.," May 11, 1982, Mac-
Arthur Archives, RG 15—Materials Donated by the
General Public, Box 32—Bulkeley, John D., Vice Admi-
ral, USN (Ret.), Folder 2, 2.

14. Illigan is a coastal city ten miles north of Dansalan.

15. For some of the efforts finding fuel, see Mapes,
The Butchers, Baker, 95, 98–99.

16. Underbrink reports that "Ensign R. E. Hoffman
[sic] used a flashlight to lead" the first PBY. See Underbrink, *Destination Corregidor*, 196. For further detail,
see Thomas F. Pollock, "OPERATION–FLIGHT GRID-
IRON, 27 April–3 May 1942," http://lanbob.com/lanbob/
H-42Auth/PT-PBY.htm (accessed August 1, 2014); and
Messimer, *In the Hands of Fate*, 288–89.

17. For a description of Neale, see Messimer, *In the
Hands of Fate*, 26.

18. Pollock, "OPERATION—FLIGHT GRIDIRON."

19. Underbrink notes that "some of Hoffman's [sic]
men began refueling from 55-gallon drums." See Underbrink, *Destination Corregidor*, 197.

20. For a description of the attack, see Morton, *The
Fall of the Philippines*, 539–40.

21. For the landing at Parang, see "Historical Report—Visayan-Mindanao Force, Defense of the Philippines, 1 Sept. 1941–10 May 1942," "Historical Report—
Visayan-Mindanao Force, Defense of the Philippines, 1
Sept. 1941–10 May 1942," no date, MacArthur Archives,
RG 2–USAFFE, G-2 Journals, December 30, 1941–March
21, 1942, Box 13, no folder, 52.

22. For the Japanese advance in Mindanao, see Morton, *The Fall of the Philippines*, 510–11.

23. See Underbrink, *Destination Corregidor*, 198.

24. See Mitsos, 30th Squadron, 19th BG, Ch. 2, 7.

25. The second plane initially landed off the coast
because of fog, but arrived at the lake soon after the
first. Messimer, *In the Hands of Fate*, 293

26. There is some disagreement as to how many passengers were on the planes. Messimer reports that the
PBYs carried 56 passengers, including 20 nurses, plus
their crews. See Messimer, *In the Hands of Fate*, 291–92.
Underbrink explains that there were 49. See Underbrink, *Destination Corregidor*, 200. The fact there were
three stowaways on Neale's plane may help explain some
of the discrepancy. Pollock, "OPERATION–FLIGHT
GRIDIRON."

27. MacArthur specifically told Wainwright that if
there was room to evacuate McGuigan, he should.

"MacArthur to Wainwright," April 29, 1942, MacArthur
Archives, RG 30, Box 1, Folder 10, 1.

28. One of the nurses onboard, Rosemary Hogan,
took off her jacket and tried to plug the hole. One of
her colleagues later noted that Hogan, "tried futilely to
staunch the water's flow.... The water reached over
Rosemary's shoulders before she capitulated." Sally
Blaine Miller, "Escape from Corregidor," MacArthur
Archives, Record Group 135—RG-135 Papers of Drs.
Michael and Elizabeth Norman, Authors, Box 6—Johson-Nestor, Folder 8—Millett, Sally Blaine.

29. The plane hit an underwater reef and could not
take off because of the flooding. See Pollock, "OPERA-
TION–FLIGHT GRIDIRON."

30. For a description of the plane sinking in the
water, see Underbrink, *Destination Corregidor*, 203.

31. Messimer, *In the Hands of Fate*, 295.

32. Ibid., 296.

33. McGuigan had indeed acquired a pump and
other materials to fix the plane. See Underbrink, *Destination Corregidor*, 204.

34. The step is the position a plane taking off from
water must reach before it can successfully break from
the surface of the water. Air Force Brigadier General
(ret.) Dave Young explains the takeoff as follows: "The
pilot maneuvers the seaplane into the wind and retracts
the water rudders to start the take-off. Open the throttle
to take-off power and pull the stick all the way back....
The aircraft will 'climb-up' onto the step as the center
of pressure (of the water) moves back along the floats....
The step attitude should be maintained as steadily as
possible until take-off speed is reached, at which time
the aircraft will typically fly off the water." Dave Young
to David L. Snead, July 29, 2014, in David L. Snead's
possession.

35. Pollock later wrote, "It was certainly an act of Di-
vine Providence that sent Capt. McGuigan along to keep
us afloat. He worked naked in the bottom of a greasy,
slimy hull half covered with marine glue for six long
disappointing hours." Pollock, "OPERATION–FLIGHT
GRIDIRON."

36. See Messimer, *In the Hands of Fate*, 19–20 and
Mapes, *The Butchers, Baker*, 100–1.

37. For a description of the efforts to patch the hole,
see Mitsos, 30th Squadron, 19th BG, Ch. 2, 7.

38. According to Messimer, "In addition to Captain
McGuigan and another officer, five sailors who had
worked on the plane were told they could go too." Messimer, *In the Hands of Fate*, 297. Hofmann would have
been the other officer. Pollock listed the following passengers, not including the three stowaways: Capt. J. L.
McGuigan, Ens. R.E. Hofmann, and five PT boat crewmen, M. W. Hancock, C. C. Richardson, J. X. Balog, J.
Lawless, and C. C. Beckner.

39. Pollock and Neale thought it was the longest
take-off that they ever had. See Underbrink, *Destination
Corregidor*, 206.

40. Messimer, *In the Hands of Fate*, 298.

41. See Pollock, "OPERATION—FLIGHT GRID-
IRON."

42. According to Underbrink, the message that the
PBY would be reaching Perth around midnight did not
arrive and the plane's arrival actually triggered an air-
raid alarm. Underbrink, *Destination Corregidor*, 207.

43. It is unclear who the admiral was. It was possibly
Vice Admiral Herbert Leary, commander of allied naval
forces in the Southwest Pacific. "Leary, U.S. Admiral,
Will Head Fleets Of United Nations In Anzac Waters,"
Washington Post, February 8, 1942, 1.

44. Commander Archie A. Antrim, a Supply Corps officer, had recently been appointed to Vice Admiral Leary's staff in Melbourne, Australia. "Premiers Hear MacArthur," *New York Times*, Apr. 24, 1942, 3.

Epilogue

1. Hofmann and the PBY crew had left ten nurses and the other passengers from Corregidor on Mindanao, believing they would be able to catch a flight from Del Monte. One of the nurses, Sally Blaine Miller, recalled, "There was never any criticism because the nurses were left in Mindanao." Sally Blaine Miller, "Escape from Corregidor," MacArthur Archives, Record Group 135—RG-135 Papers of Drs. Michael and Elizabeth Norman, Authors, Box 6—Johson-Nestor, Folder 8—Millett, Sally Blaine.

2. For the rescue by the *Spearfish*, see Underbrink, *Destination Corregidor*, 222–3.

3. Little is known about what happened to Swede, Red, and Mac. The Japanese held them as prisoners on Java, and both Swede and Mac died at some point. All three are listed in a prisoner of war database. See "John D Carson—World War 2 POW Record," World War 2 POW Archive, Crafted Knowledge, http://www.ww2 pow.info/index.php?page=directory&rec=127279 (accessed June 20, 2014); "William N McGibony–World War 2 POW Record," ibid., http://www.ww2pow.info/ index.php?page=directory&rec=31833 (accessed on June 20, 2014); and "Milton Howard Jensen–World War 2 POW Record," ibid., http://www.ww2pow.info/index.php?page =directory&rec=30861 (accessed June 20, 2014).

4. For a recounting of what happened, see note 2, Chapter 12.

5. Based on the last roster I have from the veterans' association, American Defenders of Bataan & Corregidor, in 1998, both Snow and McClure were still alive. See *American Defenders of Bataan & Corregidor*, Volume 2, 247 and 251.

6. Snow and McClure spent much of their imprisonment at the Zentsuji prisoner of war camp. For their picture when American forces liberated them, see Joseph Rust Brown, *We Stole to Live* (Cape Girardeau: Missourian Litho and Printing Company, 1982), 183.

7. Jim Bullock was evidently executed after being captured by the Japanese. "Bullock," World War II Multimedia Database, http://worldwar2database.com/ mansell/index.php?-table=mansell&-action=browse&-cursor=5871&-mode=list&-limit=300&-skip=5700&-recordid=mansell%3FKey%3D5872 (accessed August 1, 2014).

8. See "Hogaboom, William Frederick," STIWOT, http://en.ww2awards.com/person/31853 (accessed August 1, 2014).

9. See White, *We Were Expendable*.

10. For a description of the PT boat crews as guerrillas on Mindanao, see Tom Mitsos, http://lanbob.com/ lanbob/FP-AGOM/FP-AGOM-TM.htm (accessed August 1, 2014).

11. John Gordon argues that "the data on Navy and Marine casualties during the [Philippines] campaign contains some inconsistencies." However, his numbers match Hofmann's pretty closely. He contends that the Japanese took almost 1,500 marines and 2,000 sailors as prisoner when Corregidor fell. Approximately 1,200 of these prisoners died in captivity. Gordon, *Fighting for MacArthur*, 317.

Bibliography

Primary Sources

ARCHIVES

Harvard University Archives (Pusey Library), Cambridge, MA
    Records, 1941–1945 (inclusive), Navy Supply Corps School
Harvard Business School Archives (Baker Library), Boston, MA
    United States Navy Supply Corps School (Harvard University) records, 1939–1949
MacArthur Memorial Archives and Library, Norfolk, VA
    Record Group 2—Records of Headquarters, U.S. Army Forces in the Far East (USAFFE), 1941–1942
    Record Group 15—Materials Donated by the General Public
    Record Group 30—Papers of Lieutenant General Richard K. Sutherland, USA, Chief of Staff, SWPA, 1941–1945
    Record Group 43—Papers of Weldon B. Hester, Box 1, Folder 55—"No Uncle Sam: The Story of a Hopeless Effort to Supply the Starving Army of Bataan and Corregidor," Brigadier General Charles C. Drake
    Record Group 110—Papers of Lt. Commander Frederick L. Worcester, USNR
    Record Group 135—Papers of Drs. Michael and Elizabeth Norman, Authors
    Tom Mistsos, "Guerrilla Radio," 30th Squadron, 19th Bomb Group
National Archives of the United States, College Park, MD
    Record Group 38—Records of the Office of the Chief of Naval Operations
    Record Group 143—Records of Bureau of Supplies and Accounts
    Record Group 165—Records of the War Department General and Special Staffs
    Record Group 407—Records of the Adjutant General's Office
National Museum of the Pacific, Fredericksburg, TX
    Iliff D. Richardson Manuscript
United States Army Heritage and Education Center, Carlisle, PA
United States Army in World War II, Fall of the Philippines, Louis Morton Papers

BOOKS, DIARIES AND MEMOIRS

Ancheta, Celedonío A., ed. *The Wainwright Papers*, vol. 3. Quezon City: New Day, 1982.
Bartsch, William H. "'I Wonder at Times How We Keep Going Here': The 1941–42 Philippines Diary of Lt. John P. Burns, 21st Pursuit Squadron." *Air Power History* 53:4 (Winter 2006): 30–47.
Brown, Joseph Rust. *We Stole to Live.* Cape Girardeau: Missourian Litho and Printing Company, 1982.
Chynoweth, B.G. "Lessons from the Fall of the Philippines." *The Military Engineer* 46:313 (September-October 1954): 369–72.
The Class Book: Navy Supply Corps School, Harvard University. Boston: Harvard Graduate School of Business Administration, 1941.
Evans, David C., trans. and ed. *The Japanese Navy in World War II: In the Words of Former Japanese Naval Officers*, 2d ed. Annapolis: Naval Institute Press, 1986.
Fahey, James J. *Pacific War Diary, 1942–1945: The Secret Diary of an American Sailor.* Boston: Houghton Mifflin, 1963.

Ferrell, Robert H., ed. *The Eisenhower Diaries*. New York: W.W. Norton, 1981.

Flikke, Julia O. *Nurses in Action*. Philadelphia: J. B. Lippincott, 1943.

Furer, Julius Augustus. *Administration of the Navy Department in World War II*. Washington, D.C.: Department of the Navy, 1959.

Giles, Donald T. *Captive of the Rising Sun: The POW Memoirs of Rear Admiral Donald T. Giles, USN*. Ed. Donald T. Giles, Jr. Annapolis: Naval Institute Press, 1994.

Gugliotta, Bobette. *Pigboat 39: An American Sub Goes To War*. Lexington: University of Kentucky Press, 1984.

Hogaboom, William F. "Action Report: Bataan." *Marine Corps Gazette* (April 1946): 25–33.

The Java Sea Campaign: Combat Narratives. Washington, D.C.: Office of Naval Intelligence, 1943.

Karig, Walter. "CANOPUS' Last Stand." *Sea Classics* 41:9 (September 2008): 18–25.

Karig, Walter, and Welbourn Kelly. *Battle Report: Pearl Harbor to Coral Sea*. New York: Farrar & Rinehart, 1944.

Kelley, Wellbourn. "The Battle of Longoskawan Point—*Canopus*' Last Stand: Bataan's Naval Defense Battalion." *Sea Classics* 32:6 (June 1999): 12–19, 27, and 42–43.

Labrador, J. *A Diary of the Japanese Occupation, December 7, 1941–May 7, 1945*. Manila: Santo Tomas University Press, 1989.

Lee, Clark. *They Call It Pacific: An Eye-Witness Story of Our War Against Japan From Bataan to the Solomons*. New York: Viking, 1943.

Lennox, Joseph. "Training the Reserve Supply Corps." *Proceedings of the United States Naval Institute* 60:5 (May 1934): 647–50.

Mapes, Victor L., with Scott A. Mills. *The Butchers, Baker: The World War II Memoir of a United States Army Air Corps Soldier Captured by the Japanese in the Philippines*. Jefferson, NC: McFarland, 2000.

Mason, John T., Jr., ed. *The Pacific War Remembered: An Oral History*. Annapolis: Naval Institute Press, 1986.

McGee, John Hugh. *Rice and Salt: A History of the Defense and Occupation of Mindanao During World War II*. San Antonio: Naylor, 1962.

Potter, David. "The Naval Finance and Supply School." *Proceedings of the United States Naval Institute* 62 (August 1936): 1138–40.

Redmond, Juanita. *I Served on Bataan*. Philadelphia: J.B. Lippincott, 1943.

Sakakida, Richard, and Wayne Kiyosaki. *A Spy in Their Midst: The World War II Struggle of a Japanese-American Hero*. Lanham, MD: Madison Books, 1995.

Selleck, Clyde. *The War Diary of Gen. Clyde Selleck, Commanding General, 71st Division, USAFFE: The Battle for Northern Luzon, The Initial Phase of the Battle of Bataan*. Philippines: R.P. Garcia, 1985.

The Statistical History of the United States: From Colonial Times to the Present. New York: Basic Books, 1976.

Newspapers

Chicago Tribune
New York Times
Washington Post

Secondary Sources

Agoncillo, Teodoro A. *The Fateful Years: Japan's Adventure in the Philippines, 1941–45*, vol. 1. Quezon City: R.P. Garcia, 1965.

Akashi, Yoji, and Mako Yoshimura, eds. *New Perspectives on the Japanese Occupation of Malaya and Singapore 1941–1945*. Singapore: Singapore University Press, 2009.

Alden, John D. *Flush Decks and Four Pipes*. Annapolis: Naval Institute Press, 1965.

Allston, Frank J. *Ready for Sea: The Bicentennial History of the U.S. Navy Supply Corps*. Annapolis: Naval Institute Press, 1995.

American Defenders of Bataan & Corregidor. Volumes 1–2. Paducah: Turner, 1991 and 1998.

Bartsch, William. *December 8, 1941: MacArthur's Pearl Harbor*. College Station: Texas A&M University Press, 2003.

_____. *Doomed at the Start: American Pursuit Pilots in the Philippines, 1941–1942*. College Station: Texas A&M University Press, 1992.

Beck, John Jacob. *MacArthur and Wainwright: Sacrifice of the Philippines*. Albuquerque: University of New Mexico Press, 1974.

Bell, W. F. *The Philippines in World War II: 1941–1945: A Chronology and Select Annotated Bibliography of Books and Articles in English*. Westport, CT: Greenwood Press, 1999.

Blair, Clay, Jr. *Silent Victory: The U.S. Submarine War Against Japan*. Philadelphia: J. B. Lippincott, 1975.

Bogart, Charles H. "Radar in the Philippines, 1941–1942." *Journal of America's Military Past* (Fall 1999): 27–35.

Bonner, Kit. "That Grand Old Lady: USS *Canopus* (AS-9)." *Sea Classics* 44:12 (December 2011): 10–13 and 48–49.

Bowman, Martin W. *Combat Legend: B-17 Fortress*. Shrewsbury: Airlife, 2002.

Brands, H.W. *Bound to Empire: The United States and the Philippines*. New York: Oxford University Press, 1992.

Breuer, William B. *Devil Boats: The PT War Against Japan*. Novato, CA: Presidio Press, 1987.

Bulkley, Robert, Jr. *At Close Quarters: PT Boats in the United States Navy*. Washington, D.C.: Naval History Division, 1962.

Burns, James MacGregor. *Roosevelt: The Soldier of Freedom*. New York: Harcourt Brace Jovanovich, 1970.

Butow, Robert J.C. *Tojo and the Coming of the War*. Princeton: Princeton University Press, 1961.

Chang, Iris. *The Rape of Nanking: The Forgotten Holocaust of World War II*. New York: Basic Books, 1997.

Chang, Mingkai. *History of the Sino-Japanese War (1937–1945)*. Taipei: Chung Wu, 1971.

Chun, Clayton. *The Fall of the Philippines, 1941–1942*. Oxford: Osprey Press, 2012.

Clodfelter, Mark. "Pinpointing Devastation: American Air Campaign Planning before Pearl Harbor," *Journal of Military History* 58:1 (January 1994): 75–101.

Cogan, Frances B. *Captured: The Japanese Internment of Americans in the Philippines, 1941–1945*. Athens: University of Georgia Press, 2000.

Coletta, Paolo E., ed. *United States Navy and Marine Corps Bases, Overseas*. Westport, CT: Greenwood Press, 1985.

Connaughton, R. *MacArthur and Defeat in the Philippines*. Woodstock: Overlook Press, 2001.

Davis, Kenneth S. *FDR: The War President, 1940–1943*. New York: Random House, 2000.

Dower, John W. *War Without Mercy: Race & Politics in the Pacific War: Race and Power in the Pacific War*. New York: Pantheon, 1986.

Edmonds, Walter D. *They Fought with What They Had: The Story of the Army Air Forces in the Southwest Pacific, 1941–1942*. Boston: Little, Brown, 1951.

Elphick, Peter. *Far Eastern File: The Intelligence War in the Far East, 1930–1945*. London: Hodder & Stoughton, 1997.

Evans, David C., and Mark R. Peattie. *Kaigun: Strategy, Technology, and Tactics in the Imperial Japanese Navy, 1887–1941*. Annapolis: Naval Institute Press, 1997.

Felker, Craig C. *Testing American Sea Power: U.S. Navy Strategic Exercises, 1923–1940*. College Station: Texas A&M University Press, 2006.

Feuer, A.B. "The *Pigeon* Valiant." *Sea Classics* 36:8 (August 2003): 42–45 and 60–61.

Futrell, Robert F. "Air Hostilities in the Philippines, 8 December 1941." *Air University Review* 16:2 (January-February 1965): 32–45.

Gannon, Robert. *Hellions of the Deep: The Development of American Torpedoes in World War II*. University Park: Pennsylvania State University Press, 1996.

Garvan, John M. *The Negritos of the Philippines*. Ed. Hermann Hochegger. Vienna: Verlag Ferdinand Berger Horn, 1964.

Gleek, Lewis E., Jr. *Over Seventy-Five Years of Philippines-American History: The Army and Navy Club of Manila*. Manila: Carmelo & Bauermann, 1976.

Gordon, John. *Fighting for MacArthur: The Navy and Marine Corps' Desperate Defense of the Philippines*. Annapolis: Naval Institute Press, 2011.

_____. "The Navy Infantry at Bataan." *Proceedings of the United States Naval Institute* (Supplement 1985): 64–69.

Gould, Lewis. *The Spanish American War and President McKinley*. Lawrence: University Press of Kansas, 1982.

Hamilton, James W., and William J. Bolce, Jr. *Gateway to Victory: The Wartime Story of the San Francisco Army Port of Embarkation*. Stanford: Stanford University Press, 1946.

Hamm, Diane L., compiler. *Military Intelligence: Its Heroes and Legends*. Arlington Hall Station, VA: U.S. Army Intelligence and Security Command, 1987.

Harrington, Joseph D. *Yankee Samurai: The Secret Role of the Nisei in America's Pacific Victory*. Detroit: Pettigrew Enterprises, 1979.

Harvey, A.D. "Army Air Force and Navy Air Force: Japanese Aviation and the Opening Phase of the War in the Far East." *War in History* 6:2 (1999): 174–204.

Heindrichs, Waldo. *Threshold of War: Franklin D. Roosevelt and American Entry into World War II*. New York: Oxford University Press, 1990.

Hendrie, Andrew. *Flying Cats: The Catalina Aircraft in World War II*. Annapolis: Naval Institute Press, 1988.

Hone, Thomas. *Battle Line: The United States Navy, 1919–1939*. Annapolis: Naval Institute Press, 2006.

Hoyt, Edwin Palmer. *The Lonely Ships: The Life and Death of the U.S. Asiatic Fleet*. New York: David McKay, 1976.

Iriye, Akira, ed. *Mutual Images: Essays in American-Japanese Relations*. Cambridge: Harvard University Press, 1975.

_____. *The Cambridge History of American Foreign Relations*, vol. 3—*The Globalizing of America, 1913–1945*. Cambridge: Cambridge University Press, 1993.

_____. *The Origins of the Second World War in Asia and the Pacific*. New York: Longman, 1987.

James, D. Clayton. "The Other Pearl Harbor." *World War II* (2001): 74–80.

_____. *The Years of MacArthur*, vol. II—*1941–1945*. Boston: Houghton Mifflin, 1975.

Jose, Ricardo T. *The Philippine Army, 1935–1942*. Manila: Ateneo de Manila University Press, 1992.

Kaplan, Philip. *Wolfpack: U-Boats at War, 1939–1945*. Annapolis: Naval Institute Press, 1997.

Karig, Walter. "CANOPUS' Last Stand." *Sea Classics* 41:9 (September 2008): 18–25.

Kennedy, David M. *Freedom from Fear: The American People in Depression and War, 1929–1945*. New York: Oxford University Press, 2005.

Klimow, Matthew S. "Lying to the Troops: American Leaders and the Defense of Bataan." *Parameters* 20:4 (Dec. 1990): 48–60.

Kruh, David. *Always Something Doing: Boston's Infamous Scollay Square*. Boston: Northeastern University Press, 1999.

_____. *Scollay Square*. Charleston, S.C.: Arcadia Press, 2004.

Kuehn, John T. *Agents of Innovation: The General Board and the Design of the Fleet That Defeated the Japanese Navy*. Annapolis: Naval Institute Press, 2008.

Larrabee, Eric. *Commander in Chief: Franklin Delano Roosevelt, His Lieutenants, and Their War*. New York: Harper & Row, 1987.

Lebra, Joyce. *Japan's Greater East Asia Co-Prosperity Sphere in World War II: Selected Readings and Documents*. New York: Oxford University Press, 1975.

Leighton, Richard M., and Robert W. Coakley. *The War Department: Global Logistics and Strategy, 1940–1943*. Washington, D.C.: United States Army Center of Military History, 1995.

Leutze, James. *A Different Kind of Victory: A Biography of Admiral Thomas C. Hart*. Annapolis: Naval Institute Press, 1981.

Linderman, Gerald. *The World Within War: America's Combat Experience in World War II*. Cambridge: Harvard University Press, 1997.

Linn, Brian. *Guardians of Empire the U.S. Army and the Pacific, 1902–1940*. Chapel Hill: University of North Carolina Press, 1997.

_____. *The Philippine War, 1899–1902*. Lawrence: University Press of Kansas, 2000.

MacArthur, Brian. *Surviving the Sword: Prisoners of the Japanese in the Far East, 1942–1945*. New York: Random House, 2005.

Manchester, William. *American Caesar: Douglas MacArthur, 1880–1964*. Boston: Little, Brown, 1978.

Mansoor, Peter R. *The GI Offensive in Europe: The Triumph of American Infantry Divisions, 1941–1945*. Lawrence: University Press of Kansas, 1999.

Masuda, Hiroshi. *MacArthur in Asia: The General and His Staff in the Philippines, Japan, and Korea*. Ithaca: Cornell University Press, 2012.

Meixsel, Richard B. "Manuel L. Quezon, Douglas MacArthur, and the Significance of the Military Mission to the Philippine Commonwealth." *Pacific Historical Review* 70:2 (May 2001): 255–92.

_____. *Philippine-American Military History, 1902–1942: An Annotated Bibliography*. Jefferson: McFarland, 2003.

Messimer, Dwight R. *In the Hands of Fate: The Story of Patrol Wing Ten, 8 December 1941–11 May 1942*. Annapolis: Naval Institute Press, 1985.

Miller, Carmen. *Painting the Map Red: Canada and the South African War, 1899–1902*. Montreal: Canadian War Museum and McGill-Queen's University Press, 1993.

Miller, Edward S. *War Plan Orange: The U.S. Strategy to Defeat Japan, 1897–1945*. Annapolis: Naval Institute Press, 1991.

Miller, J. Michael. *From Shanghai to Corregidor: Marines in the Defense of the Philippines*. Washington, D.C.: Marine Corps Historical Center, 1997.

Miller, Roger G. "A 'Pretty Damn Able Commander' Lewis Brereton: Part II." *Air Power History* (Spring 2001): 23–45.

Morison, Samuel Elliot. *History of United States Naval Operations in World War II*, Volume III: *Rising Sun in the Pacific, 1931-April 1942*. Boston: Little, Brown, , 1984.

Morton, Louis. *The Fall of the Philippines*. Washington, D.C.: Center of Military History, United States Army, 1953.

_____. "War Plan Orange: Evolution of a Strategy." *World Politics* 11:2 (Jan. 1959): 221–50.

Murray, Williamson, and Allan R. Millett, eds. *Military Innovation in the Interwar Period*. New York: Cambridge University Press, 1998.

_____. *Military Effectiveness*, vol. 2, 2d ed. New York: Cambridge University Press, 1998.

Netzorg, Morton J., and Resil B. Mojares. "Cebu in World War II and to Independence (December 8, 1941–July 4, 1946): A Bibliography." *Philippine Quarterly of Culture and Society* 9:3 (September 1981): 225–255.

Norman, Elizabeth M. *We Band of Angels: The Untold Story of American Nurses Trapped on Bataan by the Japanese*. New York: Pocket Books, 1999.

Norman, Michael, and Elizabeth M. Norman. *Tears in the Darkness: The Story of the Bataan Death March and its Aftermath*. New York: Farrar, Straus and Giroux, 2009.

O'Neill, William L. *A Democracy at War: America's Fight at Home & Abroad in World War II*. Cambridge: Harvard University Press, 1993.

Perret, Geoffrey. *Old Soldiers Never Die: The Life of Douglas MacArthur*. Adams Media Corporation, 1997.

Petillo, Carol Morris. *Douglas MacArthur: The Philippine Years*. Bloomington: Indiana University Press, 1981.

Potter, E.B. *Bull Halsey*. Annapolis: Naval Institute Press, 2003.

Prange, Gordon W., Donald M. Goldstein, and Katherine V. Dillon. *At Dawn We Slept: The Untold Story of Pearl Harbor*. New York: McGraw-Hill, 1981.

Prickett, William F. "Naval Battalion at Mariveles." *Marine Corps Gazette* 34:6 (June 1950): 40–43.

Rogers, Paul P. *The Good Years: MacArthur and Sutherland*. New York: Praeger, 1990.

Roscoe, Theodore. *Pigboats: The True Story of the Fighting Submariners of World War II*. New York: Bantam Books, 1958.

Roskill, Stephen Wentworth. *Naval Policy Between the Wars*, vol. 2—*The Period of Reluctant Rearmament, 1930-1939*. London: William Collins Sons, 1976.

Schaller, Michael. "General Douglas MacArthur and the Politics of the Pacific War." In *The Pacific War Revisited*. Ed. Gunter Bischoff and Robert L. DuPont, 17–40. Baton Rouge: Louisiana State University Press, 1997.

Shores, Christopher, Brian Cull, and Yasuho Izawa. *Bloody Shambles*, vol. 1: *The Drift to War to the Fall of Singapore*. London: Grub Street, 1992.

Slater, Richard R. "And Then There Were None! The American Army Air Corps' Last Stand in the Philippines." *Airpower* 17:6 (November 1987): 10–29 and 47–51.

Smith, George W. *MacArthur's Escape: Wild Man Bulkeley and the Rescue of an American Hero*. St. Paul: Zenith Press, 2005.

Spector, Ronald H. *Eagle Against the Sun: The American War with Japan*. New York: Vintage, 1985.

Speed, Neil G. *Born to Fight: Major Charles Joseph Ross DSO, A Definitive Study of His Life*. Melbourne: Caps & Flints Press, 2002.

Stauffer, Alvin P. *The Quartermaster Corps: Operations in the War Against Japan*. Washington, D.C.: Center of Military History, United States Army, 1956, 1990.

Underbrink, Robert L. *Destination Corregidor*. Annapolis: U.S. Naval Institute Press, 1971.

Wallace, Jim. *Knowing No Fear: The Canadian Scouts in South Africa, 1900–1902*. Victoria, BC: Trafford, 2008.

Weinberg, Gerhard L. *A World at Arms: A Global History of World War II*. New York: Cambridge University Press, 1994.

White, George H. "The Incredible Story of Three World War II Supply Corps Heroes." In editor's possession.

White, William L. *They Were Expendable: An American Torpedo Boat Squadron in the U.S. Retreat from the Philippines*. Annapolis,: Naval Institute Press, 1998.

_____. "They Were Expendable." *Reader's Digest* (September 1942): 5–9, 147–76.

Whitman, John W. *Bataan: Our Last Ditch: The Bataan Campaign, 1942*. New York: Hippocrene Books, 1990.

_____. "Decision That Starved an Army." *Army Logistician* (March/April 1995): 36–39.

Williford, Glen M. *Racing the Sunrise: Reinforcing America's Pacific Outposts, 1941-1942*. Annapolis: Naval Institute Press, 2010.

Winslow, W.G. *The Fleet the Gods Forgot: The United States Asiatic Fleet in World War II*. Annapolis: Naval Institute Press, 1982.

Wukovits, John. *Admiral "Bull" Halsey: The Life and Wars of the Navy's Most Controversial Commander*. New York: Palgrave MacMillan, 2010.

Young, Donald J. *The Battle of Bataan: A Complete History*, 2d ed. Jefferson, NC: McFarland, 2009.

Ziegler, Philip. *London at War, 1939-1945*. London: Mandarin Paperbacks, 1995.

Index